THE LIVING CITY

How America's cities
are being revitalized by
THINKING SMALL IN A BIG WAY

ROBERTA BRANDES GRATZ

The Preservation Press
National Trust for Historic Preservation
1785 Massachusetts Avenue, N.W.
Washington, D.C. 20036

The National Trust for Historic Preservation is the only private, nonprofit organization chartered by Congress to encourage public participation in the preservation of sites, buildings, and objects significant in American history and culture. In carrying out this mission, the National Trust fosters an appreciation of the diverse character and meaning of our American cultural heritage and preserves and revitalizes the livability of our communities by leading the nation in saving America's historic environments.

Support for the National Trust is provided by membership dues, contributions, and a matching grant from the National Park Service, U.S. Department of the Interior, under provisions of the National Historic Preservation Act of 1966. The opinions expressed here do not necessarily reflect the views or policies of the Interior Department.

Originally published 1989 by Simon and Schuster.

97 96 95 94   4 3 2 1

Library of Congress Cataloging in Publication Data
Gratz, Roberta Brandes.
The living city: how America's cities are being revitalized by thinking small in a big way/Roberta Brandes Gratz.
        p.   cm.
Originally published: New York: Simon and Schuster, 1989.
Includes bibliographical references and index.
ISBN 0-89133-246-4: $16.95
1. Urban renewal—United States —Case studies. 2. Urban renewal—New York (NY)—Case studies. 3. Urban policy—United States—Case studies. I. Title.
HT175.G69 1994
307.76'0973—dc20   94-21414
                                                                                          CIP

Printed by BookCrafters, Fredericksburg, VA
Designed by Lynne Kopcik, Barbara Marks Graphic Design
Cover and additional composition by Rosita Sandoval-Parker, Mac Access Group

Foreword To The New Edition

I
PRESERVATION, TRANSPORTATION, ECONOMICS, AND PLACE

This was never meant to be a book about historic preservation. In fact, it is not. This is a book about conserving, preserving, renewing, rebuilding, and rejuvenating cities. This is also a book about renewing neighborhoods and small towns and downtown business districts. And, this is a book about change—appropriate, beneficial and enduring.

Coincidentally, this book is about historic preservation. Historic preservation is increasingly gaining recognition as one of the most vital and successful tools of economic rebirth. The examples in this book are the forerunners of a new urban vision. They are the cornerstones of a growing redevelopment movement that goes to the core of the pressing problems challenging communities and urban centers. As awareness of this New Urbanism grows, historic preservation is being redefined. Its relevance is unmistakable.

Not coincidentally, this book is about people who like cities, who don't try to reshape or rebuild cities into sterile look-alikes, about people who don't show contempt for cities with plans to transform them into something they are not already, erasing the local character that defines a real place. This is a book about people who appreciate the differences between one place and another—cities, towns, neighborhoods—and who understand the energy and spirit that animates them.

Many people proclaim the goal of wanting to save our cities. Few really mean it. Many intend instead to reformulate them into auto-dependent quasi-suburbs, not by any measure a solution to urban difficulties. People who really mean to "save" and "preserve" a city must start with what it is, strengthen it, build on it incrementally so as not to overwhelm it, add what's missing, encourage innovation and new inventions, and in the process let the city grow. People who understand cities recognize the primary importance of spontaneity, diversity, and novelty. People who have the best interests of a city at heart understand that big and new are not synonymous with constructive change. Healthy cities contain a rich mix of old and new buildings and uses, high style and ordinary, large and modest, all in place due to historical economic and social forces involving the actions of many different people and institutions over a period of decades, even centuries. And healthy cities recognize the crucial need to maintain or rebuild a mass transit infrastructure. Cities become suburban and cannot function as cities if auto-dependency overtakes mass transit options. They become office parks on top of shopping malls and parking garages instead.

Historic preservation respects the tradition and evolutionary growth of a place, establishes an area's identity, and provides a framework for managing change and new growth. This precludes demolishing functional and architecturally appealing buildings to make way for big, faddish but questionable redevelopment schemes. It includes building new to serve a real use and purpose. Mere new construction is an illusory economic stimulus at best. In fact, it may do harm. This constructive approach to change is what I define as "Urban Husbandry" and is illustrated throughout this book.

Urbanism: Redefining Terms

Today's nomenclature about renewing and rebuilding cities fails us. Favorite terms—economic development, master plan, urban renewal, community revitalization, contextual development, even community development—are too often misused. Such terms are used to advance top-down projects devised by a combination of government planners, economic development administrators, big developers and mayors or mayoral staff. Historic preservation, however, is a term not easily co-opted. Historic preservation recognizes that the form may be old, but the utility is not. In city after city that I have observed during the research for this book, when historic preservation is used as a starting point for creating a framework for change, broad citizen involvement and progressive change follows.   Thus, it is not such a coincidence that historic preservation figures so prominently in this book. But "preservation" is a limiting term that could easily be replaced by the broader term of urbanism of which preservation is only a part. Urbanism is the art of understanding cities. It is not a science. Urbanists understand and practice that art. Preservationists are one form of urbanist. True practitioners of community economic development are also urbanists because, in part, they are historic preservationists.

Urbanists learn how a city works through intimate contact with it. Experience, observation, common sense, and human values are fundamental to an urbanist's view of city issues. Urbanists focus on the micro before wrestling with the macro and understand that, in reality, the macro only changes for the better in micro steps. When an area is preserved and restored, the functional and economic uses are revived and new ones are born. Innovation and ingenuity are the prevailing characteristics. Perseverance in the face of naysayers and determination in the face of obstacles are requisites. Step by step, essential and natural growth follows and spreads until larger areas prosper over time. Any look, therefore, at the rebirth of cities inevitably spotlights areas rebuilt from the bottom up by citizen activists, urbanists whether residents, business people, design professionals, or small developers who understand what makes a real place work, who are the ones actively involved and getting things done. Only a few urbanists define themselves as preservationists or even recognize themselves as preservationists. Fewer preservationists define themselves as urbanists and are often too focused on singular buildings or on architecture.

Preservationists are not the only practitioners of the process of city rebuilding or necessarily the best practitioners. Their achievements, however, are probably the most visibly obvious and aesthetically appealing. But urbanists come in many guises. Community housing advocates, environmentalists, highway and mall opponents, urban gardeners, defenders of city streets against traffic engineers, school reformers, and others practice similar grass-roots activism. Thus, this book is very much a celebration of bottom-up activism. "Thinking Small in a Big Way" is the unifying message throughout these pages and is also the one common characteristic of almost every successful urban revitalization effort I found in my research. Over time, many successful efforts grew to large scale proportions—as many of the stories in this book attest—but the starting point, the kernel idea, the first step was most often a small one. Preservationists understand this notion well. This book does not offer easy solutions, but the lessons from the variety of successful efforts described offer proven and manageable approaches to constructive renewal.

One of the best explanations of why historic preservation is so fundamental to the strength of cities and small towns of any size has been offered by Donovan D. Rypkema, a real estate and economic consultant. Rypkema cites an interdisciplinary group of thinkers, observers, and theorists including a sociologist, a psychologist, a novelist, a law professor, and a journalist, not one claiming to be a historic preservationist who independently of each other have rediscovered the significance of place and proclaimed the critical importance of community in their writing or speaking.

"What virtually none of them has recognized," says Rypkema, "is that the two concepts community and place are inseparable. 'Place' is the vessel within which the 'spirit' of community is stored; 'Community' is the catalyst that imbues a location with a 'sense' of place. The two are not divisible. You cannot have community without place; and a place without community is a location. A group of people with a shared concern but not a shared place is an interest group, not a community."

"...in their search for meaning in place and community," this diverse group found "that our historic built environment is central to both community and place.

"I would further argue that the built environment in general, but historic preservation in particular, is the nexus at which the concept of community and the concept of place intersect."[1]

Ron Shiffman, the advocacy planner who figures prominently in this book, adds another dimension to this line of thinking. What Rypkema calls "an interest group, not a community," Shiffman identifies as a community of interest. "A community of interest in a city defines itself by ideas not place, but a community of interests that share a place is a neighborhood."

Thus can one explain why the alliances in battles to save "places" are frequently so broad based. Preservationists now are frequently found in citizen efforts to stop highways or regional malls; to create public transit links or build compact, walkable communities; to oppose plans to vacate and blow up deteriorated but rebuildable public housing projects; to reduce the scale of over-reaching new development proposals; or to avert the relocation of a post office from a rural downtown to the countryside. Since the first publication of this book five years ago, the historic preservation movement has become even more broad based. While preservationists once were mostly known to narrowly focus on buildings, they now represent a much broader array of related grass-roots issues. This is one of the most interesting changes that has really mushroomed in recent years.

Creative Change And Economic Growth

The rediscovered and restored older districts around the country are the genuinely lively and busy places, in fact, the liveliest and busiest quarters in many cities. They also happen to be the largest areas of creative change and economic growth. Often, moreover, the reuse of these districts was the catalyst for broad rebirth of the larger city. As Don Rypkema notes: "Today, for lots of reasons, economic growth will only take place on a sustainable basis where there is a high quality of life; and securing quality of life is at the heart of what historic preservation is all about."

San Antonio's River Walk; New Orleans's Vieux Carré and nearby Warehouse District; New York's Soho and numerous landmark row house neighborhoods; Old Town District in Portland, Oregon, and downtown Foreside District, in Portland, Maine; Seattle's Pioneer Square and Pike Place Market; Pittsburgh's Station Square and Northside neighborhoods; Minneapolis's

---

[1] "Place, Community and Economic Development", a talk delivered at the Annual Conference of the National Trust for Historic Preservation in St. Louis, September 29, 1993.

Warehouse District; San Diego's Gaslight District; San Francisco's Victorian and historic downtown districts; Miami's South Beach; Chicago's Printing District; Boston's North End, historic waterfront, Back Bay, and Quincy Market; Denver's Larimer Square and nearby Lower Downtown; most of downtown Charleston, Savannah, and Annapolis, and more. Undoubtedly, these districts will endure longer and exhibit more innovation than any Tyson's Corner, Virginia, or its smaller or larger clone.[2]

The list of such places is truly endless and can be found in communities of every size that have employed historic preservation as a tool for rebirth. These places exhibit enduring change and rational growth, attracting more new capital and investment. They have become popular destinations because they are interesting places. Excessive development pressure and overcongestion ensues, unless tight controls are in place. There has to be room for preservation to spread or it gets strangled. In fact, many of these places now suffer from being too lively, too busy, too crowded, and even too successful, not because of the preservation effort but because they are overwhelmed by tourists, beset by the big, new "economic development" projects with dubious economic claims and are overused, most likely, because the larger city does not have enough similarly appealing vibrant places for the inventive new uses to take root and grow.[3] Mistakenly, their overuse and gentrification are blamed on their preservation, not on the more complex failures of the larger city to be equally successful at nurturing and strengthening similarly diverse, often chaotic, areas. Neither the successes nor the urban fundamentals that go way beyond the historic preservation characteristics are broadly understood.

Economic Self-Crippling

Routinely, older sections of cities are demolished because no vision of reuse and regeneration is allowed to emerge and flourish. Officials too often use current disuse and disrepair as ammunition for a final death sentence. In 1989, for example, Omaha senselessly demolished the seven-block Jobbers' Canyon Historic District to make way for the corporate headquarters of ConAgra, the agribusiness giant. ConAgra insisted on a campus setting and demanded more buildings be demolished than space required.

The Jobbers' Canyon district, filled with great turn-of-the-century red brick warehouses, was completely leveled, the largest historic district in the National Register of Historic Places to be so. The area is adjacent to the city's Old Market

---

[2] At least one highly spotlighted edge city, Rockville, Maryland, is already beginning to crumble in less time than any traditional downtown ever began a slide downward. And Forrestal Village near Princeton, New Jersey, failed because it tried to formularize the urban fabric, not recognizing its essential evolutionary and innovative nature, and plop it down as a shopping center and residential development in the middle of massive sprawl.

[3] "The Remnant Complex" explores this issue on p. 258.

Historic District, one of Nebraska's leading tourist attractions. At the time of demolition, there were 500 jobs in a variety of functional businesses which were to be replaced by 430 ConAgra jobs. More than 1,700,000 square feet of space was demolished for less than 200,000 square feet of ConAgra's Phase I building project. This active commercial area would have been the natural site of rebirth spreading from the downtown core.

A more subtle version of what Jane Jacobs calls "economic self-crippling" is currently occurring in New York City. The Department of Planning has promulgated a new citywide policy that would encourage the conversion of many former manufacturing sites to big residential development. The department's assumption is that large loft buildings are obsolete, of no use to modern manufacturers, inaccessible to transportation, and thus unable to establish a national distribution of goods.

Isabel Hill, a staff planner during the study's development, found the opposite to be true. One Brooklyn waterfront site the department wants developed with expensive high-rise housing now is home to a water-dependent lumber distributor. Another site she found had 3,000 jobs and no unused buildings. More interesting, she found that many of these buildings are being innovatively retooled for both large and small manufacturers, some long-standing ones and others recent start-ups, making everything from furniture to sugar to plaster gargoyles. One such building has 50 tenants, including an assortment of woodworking businesses that gain strength from being able to network among themselves. The owners report these buildings are not only perfectly suitable for their use but that no other type of building is equally suitable. For more than 20 years, the city has owned and neglected many of these buildings. The city, moreover, thwarted private efforts to clean up and rerent some of them. "Manufacturing is not dead," said one of the business owners. "One just must be creative."

Hill discovered all this "data" by "tromping around the neighborhoods" and when she informed her planning department superiors, she was totally rebuffed, told that her information—call it "empirical data"—"conflicted with the department's statistical data" and that it was not real, just a "philosophical argument." She quit the department, is now a private planning consultant and produced a remarkable hour-long documentary called *Made in Brooklyn* that captures Brooklyn's vibrant manufacturing world and contradicts in living color the common perception that manufacturing is dead and loft buildings are obsolete.

In fact, one could argue that the loss of the country's industrial base is in part attributable to the loss of so many districts rich in the kind of industrial buildings that give birth to new industry. Few New Yorkers remember that Soho was scheduled for demolition to build an expressway until preservationists, artists, and highway opponents took on

■ ■ ■

Robert Moses.[4] One cannot imagine what New York City's economy would be like today without the intense economic resurgence of that area and the several lower Manhattan districts to which the rebirth spread.

In 1977 Pulitzer Prize-winning architectural critic Ada Louise Huxtable of the New York Times wrote: "What's good about preservation now is that it is part of a sense of the living city. It involves a deeper understanding of the continuity and contrasts of urban art and life. It is an index of a greater awareness of the relationships of the past, the present and the future. The definition of preservation has grown from a limited preoccupation with the individual landmark to concern with the nature of the neighborhood and the community."[5] Her words are truer than ever.

Fixing What 'Ain't' Broke

Too often, government leaders don't know how to leave well enough alone, especially when a famous historic district is at stake. Unfortunately, New Orleans is the best example of this[6]. One of the most celebrated historic district success stories, the rescue of the Vieux Carré from the wreckers ball was one of the country's earliest preservation battles, one of the many started by women, and one of the largest in an urban area—85 square blocks of city[7]. The size of this district fosters resilience and nurtures its qualities as a real place, despite its popularity as a tourist site. The rejuvenation long ago spilled over into the Garden District, one of the few remaining urban neighborhoods served by this country's once-great trolley system. More recently, the rejuvenation spread to an increasingly popular adjacent Warehouse District. But the city found the promises of the big ticket project of the moment irresistible. An unnecessary aquarium project and an oversized hotel and shopping mall complex—Canal Place—with the look of Anywhere, U.S.A., (both scaled down after stiff popular resistance) were built in the 1980s, adding crowds to the large numbers who already visit New Orleans to soak up its history, architecture, and ambiance. Tourist pressures have thus taken their toll on this popular 18th-century city. The tacky and quick-profit ventures are replacing the lasting values of the artful and genuine.

Now, a gambling casino to replace a former convention center appears likely to speed the homogenization of that unique city in the most negative

---

[4] See p. 261 for the whole story.

[5] Vogue magazine, March 1977.

[6] See "Bigness Has a Place,"p. 260.

[7] San Antonio's River Walk; New York's Soho; Miami's South Beach; Denver's Larimer Square; Providence, Rhode Island; Alexandria, Virginia;Charleston, Savannah, and Annapolis, Maryland, are just a few of the areas rescued through the initial effort of women.

of ways, increasing the cost of city services, undermining elements of the local economy serving permanent residents and employees, and destabilizing the delicate balance between visitors and local users necessary for a healthy city. As a consequence, New Orleans was placed on the 1993 "America's 11 Most Endangered Historic Places" list issued by the National Trust for Historic Preservation.[8]

In many cities, too much has been lost that is genuine and urban. In addition, too many places have milked the tourism dollar to the point of diminishing returns for the local population.[9] When any place turns overwhelmingly tourist-oriented, it rapidly loses the uses that appeal to local residents. When tourists overwhelm and replace local residents, the quality of an authentic place disappears. Soon the tourists disappear too. Only shreds of a real place remain, along with the need for enormous new public investment. Too much success, not failure, marks many restored areas, but it is difficult to find a preserved section of any city initiated by preservationists that has failed as a preservation effort.

Urbanists start with what exists and rebuild piece by piece. Practicing inventive problem solving, taking risks, avoiding formulas, and embracing the untested are shared characteristics—the antithesis of the characteristics of big developers who apply financial formulas, eschew creative risk, and avoid the untested like the plague. Understanding how a building functions, how a street works, how a neighborhood works, and by extension, how a city works is at the core of the preservation ethic. Urbanists know the place. They live, work, shop, or visit the place. Most important, preservationists *experience* a place. The mission to preserve is clear and specific. Nothing hypothetical intrudes on firsthand knowledge. Optimism, not doom-and-gloom defeatism, marks preservationists, an important key to their success. Urbanists' practicality leaves little room for the top-down vision that mercilessly leads to master plans that are out of date before they are published, either because they are based on out-of-date ideas or out-of-date data. Planning studies and many master plans are based on existing but constantly changing conditions that don't envision the steps of change or their impacts. Sound urban thinking should factor in steps of change,

---

[8] Noted the National Trust announcement: "Having survived wars, hurricanes, and a boom-or-bust economy, New Orleans now faces the potentially detrimental impact of the world's largest land-based gambling casino, currently slated for construction at the foot of historic Canal Street. Two landmark residential neighborhoods flank the proposed site of the casino, which is likely to generate massive traffic congestion, an increased demand for parking, and undesirable spin-off development. In the historic Warehouse District, now undergoing rebirth as a vibrant area of apartments, restaurants, and shops, residents believe the huge gaming facility will be an incompatible neighbor. And the famed French Quarter will be doubly hard-hit: on one side, the new casino; on another, a temporary gambling hall and proposed 'entertainment zone.' Without careful planning and renewed commitment to preserving and protecting the historic buildings and the quality of life in New Orleans's inner-city residential neighborhoods, the flashy new casino could be a disaster for one of the world's unique cities."

[9] The issue of "The Ice Cream Economy" is explored on p. 42.

much of which is unpredictable and thus unmeasurable ahead of time. The first increment of change alters most conditions and assumptions on which these plans are often based.

Many communities today suffer common problems, feel that most change has been for the worse and of no help to them, and are frustrated by the lack of obvious solutions. A common refrain heard in cites is the need for "planning," a term that means something different to almost everyone who uses it. Too often, however, earlier mistaken planning policies have caused the problems people now seek new plans to correct. Too often, as well, mindless planning is still occurring—formal, drawn out, burdensome, generated from the top down, removed from the users and advocates of a place, rarely respectful of historic preservation, and often contrary to the instincts of local residents, and overly dependent on the kind of "empirical verifiability" that reduces life to stultifying statistics and tries to turn the art of urban rebirth into a science—not the kind of planning for which citizens plead. Some planners are creative and can be found in this book. But many in the profession are too data bound and unwilling to let the first observation turn their statistical head, as was exhibited in the *Made in Brooklyn* story mentioned earlier.

Don't look for the "grand plan." Don't commission expensive market studies that can only project the past and predict the failure of anything innovative, are meant to delay action, and lead to government half measures.[10] Don't get hung up assuming tenants won't come without infinite parking capacity. Don't look to big name tenants, when new and small local businesses might be more of a draw. Understand that big retailers, like the big developers with whom they form partnerships, want the formula, big fix, pre-tested idea.[11] Don't become over-dependent on government assistance. Appreciate both the ordinary and the artful design. These traits mark the preservationist ethic knowingly or unknowingly embraced by those who simply set out to restore buildings and wind up saving whole sections of cities. Their vision, or their plan, is the vision of how to fix and reuse, to redesign and reshape. Invariably, the mission is accomplished either without the notice of or contrary to the will and approval of the political and development establishment and with minimum government and professional planning encouragement.

In all the successfully rebuilt areas listed earlier and discussed throughout this book, from Soho to Station Square to Vieux Carré, the regeneration process was well on its way before officially acknowledged or legally protected by government policies. Once under way, government recognition and conventional development investment frequently followed, sometimes trying to assume credit

---

[10] Market studies predicted failure for Quincy Market and Station Square. See pp. 285 and 287.

[11] See the Flatbush Kings/Toys 'R' Us story in "Formula Thinking Can Be Devastating," p.282.

for the momentum begun before their entrance on the scene. Risk-averse developers follow preservationists simply because the preservationists have taken the big risk out of the locale. Government is actually supposed to follow the creative public lead, and the quicker it does so, the more creative it is being. Acknowledging the primary initiator of change is important, as well. The whole Soho loft rebirth process actually started because of a creative response of government to the leadership of artists. Artists were illegally residing in, and converting to studios, empty manufacturing lofts. Residential use was illegal. Living and working in the same place was illegal. So the city changed the law, legalizing occupancy by artists. The letters AIR on building entrance doors signaled to the outside world that one or more artists-in-residence could be found here.

Redefining Success

Different standards can be used to measure the rebirth of cities tax base, retail sales dollars, square footage of new office space, size of middle-income population. But if reborn sections of cities are to be tallied in terms of human use and innovation along with other conventional standards, preserved districts win hands down. "Even on an economic basis, the cost benefit of public dollars invested and public return is better in reborn districts," notes Rypkema. "There is a higher return in property taxes, sales taxes, number and variety of jobs and businesses created." Successful new commercial building "projects" may exist, for example, filled with office workers and companies that allegedly might have left town without the new building or who have moved to town because of it. But these same buildings are narrow in their use, successful only in the limited sense, and of little help in animating or populating the environs.

Gateway Center in Pittsburgh is a prime example of this. One of the first downtown urban renewal clearance projects in the country and one that many cities chose to emulate, Pittsburgh's industrial heart was totally erased for one of the biggest downtown lawns in America. Neatly placed on the grass are look-alike buildings whose use is indistinguishable from outward appearances and which stand in stark isolation from the waterfront on one side and a living, breathing city on the other. Apparently those office buildings are successful as isolated and isolating office buildings. But other than for nine-to-five office users, lunchtime strollers, and special event goers, Gateway Center is as unpopulated and lifeless a section of center city as you can find, although many cities now have its equivalent.

A short distance across the Monongahela River, however, with miles of urban mindset in between, sits Station Square, one the country's most commercially successful historic preservation projects, accomplished despite market predictions of failure, lack of interest by conventional lenders, disbelief by planners and elected officials, and disdain by almost everyone but historic preservationists and untrained citizens.[12] All the animation and signs of real life missing at Gateway Plaza are present in Station Square, including continued growth and incremental change. And this almost 20 years after the effort began with the restoration of five mostly vacant and forgotten buildings.

Preservationists think in terms of places and of wonderful old buildings that warrant continued lives, not in terms of development projects. They think as human beings who use the space and the place and leave plenty of room for what's unique and unexpected. This helps explain their projects' popular appeal. (The more successful preservationists are getting more sophisticated at functioning on the established playing field of development and finance and community advocacy.)

If there are such things as "preservation principles," these are probably what they are. Take a building as it is. Recognize that minimum physical change is frequently enough to bring about maximum social and economic change. View limitations as creative challenges, not insurmountable obstacles. Where possible, respect the social personality of a place, rather than seek to create one. Assume that a building or neighborhood that once was productive could be so again. Don't rely on and, perhaps, even ignore extensive academic and professional consultations and reports. They typically predict failure or recommend inappropriate formulas. Learn the economics of development in order to enter the playing field of institutional finance. But don't ignore personal instinct. Rely on aesthetic, historical, and functional values.

Understanding these offers clues to rejuvenation successes initiated by preservationists. Understanding these also offers clues to why the pattern is not more mainstream and why it is so difficult to put together the financing to make preservation projects work. This is not the officially recognized way to rebuild areas of cities. Unfortunately, it is not an approach that financial institutions or mainstream investors seek or even want to understand. It cannot be reduced to a recognizable formula. Innovation is its fundamental characteristic.

People learn how to stretch the system, but that is why such projects take so long. Preservationists and community-based development groups have to put 100 pieces together versus the institutional financing a mainstream developer might enjoy. (All the more reason preservation successes are so remarkable.) The multiple pieces of a preservation project come together one piece at a time, slowly, and sometimes painfully. Each piece is held to a higher standard than conventional development, even if it is questionable as to what standard conventional development is held, if at all. A great number of projects would not have happened without the 1981 historic preservation tax credits that recognized

---

[12] Station Square is examined on p. 286.

the enormous importance historic preservation has to public policy. During the 16 years since the first version of the tax credits went into effect, $16.5 billion has been invested in 25,000 preservation projects. Of the residential projects, 130,419 units of housing have been rehabilitated and 62,895 new housing units created. But before the 1981 tax credits and now after the crippling changes of 1986, preservationists are forced to find other means to finance.

Social and economic disruptions that followed big physical changes like highways and suburban infrastructure development, even those that perhaps were well intentioned and planned in great engineering detail, caused most of the decline of historic neighborhoods, not the diminished usefulness of their assortment of old buildings. Architectural solutions alone or artificial economic schemes cannot stimulate the rebirth process. Preservationists are often accused of being interested only in buildings when, instead, they recognize that building reuse is just a starting point for a neighborhood or district rebirth process.

Misinterpreting The Preservation Success

Preservation schemes must reflect economic reality at least as much as other projects. Development projects using old buildings can fail easily if they are either antithetical to the fundamental nature of urban economies or reflect a failure to understand the incremental nature of the rebirth process. Only incidentally are they "preservation" projects. Two New York projects illustrate different aspects of this, both of which were not initiated by preservationists but by real estate investors and investment bankers.

The 1886 Puck Building, a handsome red brick New York landmark on the edge of Soho, is the former home of the humor magazine. In 1987, after the transformation of Soho was a national success story, a developer beautifully renovated the New York landmark with an investment of $14 million. But then, in a total misunderstanding of the Soho rebirth process the investor was trying to cash in on, the developer determined that all Puck spaces would be rented only to architects and artists. Architects and artists had snapped up the deteriorated Soho lofts for little money years earlier when those buildings were shunned by mainstream developers. Those architects and artists bought inexpensive raw space, transformed it themselves, exhibiting their own creative design talent. But did the developer really think that artistic and budget-sensitive space seekers would pay big prices for someone else's conversion? Apparently. Soho was reborn due to creative people moving into cheap empty lofts. Big spaces. Low costs. That was at the core of the Soho momentum. They could never have afforded what they got if a developer had done it for them. Eventually, the first Puck investors failed. The building was taken over by others and space rental proceeded normally based on the market.

■ ■ ■

A similar misreading of the way cities naturally function was exhibited in another New York City project, the International Design Center of New York. A sizable and high profile development because of the stature of the architects (I. M. Pei & Partners and Charles Gwathmey of Gwathmey Siegel & Associates) and of the organizing real estate investment firm (a division of Lazard Frères), this project represents an enormous wasted public investment. IDCNY, as it was popularly known, was created out of two (more were originally planned) extra-large but typical American factory buildings (Adams Chewing Gum and American Eveready), both built in Long Island City, the section of the borough of Queens closest to Manhattan that remains the industrial heart of New York.

In a total misinterpretation of the successful creation of design centers in other cities such as Atlanta, Dallas, and Los Angeles, and a San Francisco version in an old warehouse district, promoters of the IDCNY argued that New York City should have a design center too. But none of those cities had an existing and thriving design district. A design center in those cities filled a vacuum that did not exist in New York. Such natural agglomerations cannot be created. They have to evolve naturally. New York City has one of the best examples of the organically developed design district on the upper East Side of Manhattan. Here, amidst the chic department stores, expensive restaurants, and high-rent residential towers, design professionals of all kinds find a showroom displaying their every need. Why would showrooms abandon such a desirable location for a close but declassé section of city, for which van service, a car ride, or a subway ride is necessary? Who could risk losing those customers for whom the upper East Side Manhattan location had great appeal?

This was one of those bad ideas that required so much financial government assistance—a $23 million federal Urban Development Action Grant (UDAG) plus tax abatement and less obvious additional assistance—that anyone who understood the organic nature of cities would recognize ahead of time would fail. Perhaps there should be a rule of thumb that anything requiring that much government assistance has no inherent sustainability.

An awful lot happens without any real understanding of or sensitivity to the essential nature of cities. The goal of official plans is often a project or series of projects, not a genuine and organic regenerative process. Considerable urban development activity begins with the establishment of planning and zoning principles, more often disrespectful of the actual place than officials admit. Zoning policies then encourage that disrespectful style of change and institutionalize that change if it is already under way.

Houston is an interesting example. When I was in Houston several years ago, citizen activists were excited by the prospect of winning the long-fought battle to bring zoning to the city. Houstonians always expected it to control development or shape good development. Development of any place reflects a community's image and vision of itself, with or without zoning. Zoning won't change that. The vision itself or alone, as reflected in the zoning or nonzoning policies, will change things.

If the absence of zoning has caused Houston to develop the way it has, if the absence of zoning is responsible for either the mistakes identified by critics or the successes identified by anti-zoners, why does Houston and its prime residential subdivisions look so much like Atlanta, Los Angeles, Denver, and other cities predominantly built or rebuilt after World War II with zoning in place? Houston developed as it did because of its over-reverence for the automobile, not for lack of zoning. If Houston continues its vision of an auto-dependent, suburban-style, sprawling place, where the pedestrian is a misunderstood alien, then the introduction of zoning will only formalize that vision, not change it.

The Hollywood Syndrome of Development

Developers secure financial backing because the project is a formula and the developer has a good track record, not because it is innovative and creative. (We could call this the Hollywood Syndrome. Producers would rather do a "Son of..." or "Two" or "Three" than something not done before.) The investment or financing appeal is to something similar to what has just sold, not for anything innovative that might be different but equally, if not more, marketable.[13] The plan appears economically sound because it is based on the last successful project and is why the basic formula never changes, except for elements of design and packaging, until it fails.

The savings and loan scandal of the 1980s involved many development projects financed only because they replicated last year's successful formula. The market was oversaturated, but everyone was jumping on the same bandwagon. Whatever is missing to "make the numbers work" in these projects is what government can be counted on to help obtain, through zoning bonuses, tax incentives, or other of the myriad "economic development" tools created over the years to make projects work regardless of the real market. All of a sudden, the project takes on a life of its own, whether or not it has any inherent economic logic. No one person or conspiracy of people is responsible. The predictions may have been wrong, but if failure comes, or less than the predicted success, an amazing assortment of creative excuses are offered as the cause rather than the underlying thinking.

Mainstream lenders, planners, and developers are simply afraid of old buildings, small new construction projects that fit into existing

---

[13] For the kind of creative proposals that have the most difficult time securing financing, see the stories of Quincy Market (p.285), Oviatt Building in downtown Los Angeles (p.289), Station Square in Pittsburgh (p. 288).

neighborhoods, and small developers. But these are what go into the rebirth of cities and towns. That rebirth cannot be "formulized," "replicated" on a big scale, or reduced to "planning principles." Markets cannot be created by government where they don't already exist, but they can be enhanced and nurtured. There will always be developers to build if the incentives are generous enough. If there is a UDAG, or its next generation clone, to build a hotel, an oversized "mixed-use" project, parking garage, or downtown mall, developers will follow, as happened too frequently in the 1970s and 1980s to the detriment of the real place in many downtowns.[14]

Sometimes bad ideas, promoted by lenders and developers, are embraced by government, become public policy, and are subsidized in limitless ways still resulting in failure (as illustrated in the example of New York's International Design Center). But the system stands as ready to finance the next bad idea of the well-connected, as it resists learning from small, grass roots successes. Preservationists, however, often are as unable to approach lenders and real estate experts with the skills of a practiced business executive as bankers are unable to understand the rationale of preservation efforts. This communication deficiency on both sides results in continued lost opportunities for partnerships. Preservationists don't cultivate the financial establishment, and it rarely enters the minds of bankers that preservation advocates are potential developers worth investing in. Bankers don't understand preservationists, and preservationists don't understand bankers. Sometimes, perhaps, bankers don't want to understand preservationists because there is more short-term profit in new speculative construction.

Banks Profit From Preservation

Great achievements in Pittsburgh have been accomplished under the skillful leadership of Stanley Lowe, community activist now assistant to Mayor Tom Murphy for neighborhoods and housing policy planning. Lowe was for 10 years preservation loan fund director of the Pittsburgh History and Landmarks Foundation and remains board chairman of a coalition he founded of 30 neighborhood association groups. In those 30 neighborhoods, $600 million in bank commitments have been secured for historic restoration loans, mortgages, small business start-ups, and the myriad of critical bank investments long absent from so many urban neighborhoods. Lowe not only learned the intricacies of banking practices but researched in excruciating detail the lending history of each bank with which he sought to negotiate, using the Community Reinvestment Act (CRA) as a persuasive tool to get bankers' attention. When Lowe approaches a banker, he speaks the language,

---

[14] See "Urban Destruction with a Federal Subsidy," p. 244, for a discussion of th UDAG program.

understands institutional needs of the bank, and offers the investment possibilities funders cannot dismiss lightly. "We never ask them to make a bad deal," says Lowe. Banks are not only loaning in the Pittsburgh landmark neighborhoods they once redlined, they are lending to low-income property owners and business people with a lower default rate than most comparable loans among their wealthier customers, the bankers report. Moreover, by keeping the house price and income level guidelines broad, they are financing $200,000 homes on the same block as $20,000 homes with subsidized purchases, successfully reintegrating neighborhoods economically.

Preservation proposals, however, are still often passed over even if they are on sound financial footing and even if they offer a downtown an opportunity to have an attraction other cities can't offer.

Arthur Ziegler, Jr., president of the Pittsburgh History and Landmarks Foundation and developer of the great preservation success at Pittsburgh's 52-acre Station Square, had a financially advantageous proposal to restore and redevelop the former Oppenheim Department Store in downtown Scranton, Pennsylvania, a majestic 1897 neoclassical building, the kind so many enlightened downtowns are currently turning into renewed showpieces.[15] Not too many downtowns have this kind of Old World department store left, and not too many have the good fortune of having a preservation developer with a track record willing to take on a project like this one that is as well founded, analyzed, and studied as any responsible government official could want. The then-mayor of Scranton accepted Ziegler's proposal, which had emerged from a vigorous downtown historic preservation battle involving local citizen activists. An election intervened, however. The new mayor rejected the scheme and favored instead a most ordinary and inappropriate enclosed suburban-style shopping mall requiring the putting-out-of-business of many locally owned stores and the demolition of three blocks of historic 19th-century buildings. This city not only lost the opportunity to build on earlier incremental preservation successes that could have earned Scranton national attention, but also embraced instead a tired and banal formula as a downtown rebuilding scheme, backed by the politically well-connected whose own interests prevailed at the expense of the city.

A vicious circle often occurs. Preservationists are ignored in the beginning of revitalization planning. Scranton is a classic example. By promoting the retention of buildings that stand in the way of a large-scale rebuilding scheme already envisioned by planners and developers, the preservation voice has little chance. If, however, a preservation opportunity actually exists rarely with official backing and rarely without a fight then success or failure may depend on the ability of preservation forces to put together an alternative developer, lender, and

---

[15] See "Pittsburgh Does It, Too" on p. 286.

government team. Without doing this, and many times even with this, preservationists are accused of being naysayers.[16]

Traditional downtowns and historic neighborhoods frequently are used or lived in only by minorities and immigrants. In most government, financial, and development circles, this is usually interpreted as "urban decay." Conventional thinking makes it difficult to recognize the value of a place when the dominant user or resident is not white and middle class. Most people are unaware, for example, that there is a genuine downtown Los Angeles that preservationists have been defending and striving to rejuvenate for decades.[17] If one defines a real place as exhibiting diversity, animation, spontaneity, innovation, and plentiful pedestrians, then old downtown Los Angeles is a real place. Because the user population is predominantly low- and middle-income Hispanic and African American, this economically viable downtown retail and entertainment center is not valued by city leaders as highly as a white enclave might be. In Savannah, Pittsburgh, and Cincinnati, historic preservation served as an extremely effective tool for the regeneration of low-income neighborhoods with advantages way beyond just the production of renovated housing units.[18] And in scores of downtowns across the country, historic preservation is the starting point for commercial renewal as exhibited in the ongoing remarkable success of the National Main Street Center of the National Trust for Historic Preservation.[19]

More Than Bricks And Mortar

Beyond the proven value of historic buildings as a valuable resource for the increase in affordable housing and stimulation of commercial rebirth in a business district are less obvious issues that interfere with the rejuvenation process whether in a historic neighborhood or not. Herein lies one of preservationists' greatest challenges: recognizing the non-building issues of low-income communities. For instance, neighborhood bars when they become a center of drugs and other illegal activity instead of a potentially valuable social gathering place impede any kind of positive growth. Preservationists should help fight these types of negative forces, of which neighborhood bars are only one manifestation.

---

[16] See Chapter 15, "The Past Over and Over Again," and Chapter 16, "The Question Is Why: Concrete Bunker or Else," for the sorry tale of the demolition of the historic Morosco and Helen Hayes theaters to make way for architect/developer John Portman's Marriott Marquis Hotel. Vigorous and well-organized opponents—I among them— put forth a perfectly doable alternative proposal that would have *retained* the theaters *and* built the hotel. City and state officials stubbornly refused to entertain any creative alternatives and New York got one of the ugliest, anti-urban hotels imaginable. Whatever financial success the hotel enjoys, it could have had it without the negatives in a better designed, more creative combination of new hotel and old theaters. After all, the appeal of the site to begin with was the *theater* district.

[17] See "A Conventional Developer Learns Serendipitously," p. 288.

[18] See Chapters 2 and 3 for a treatment of gentrification and displacement.

[19] See "Process as Program," p. 264.

An active and articulate proponent of this view is Pittsburgh's Stanley Lowe. The rejuvenation of predominantly low- and moderate-income historic neighborhoods in Pittsburgh is one of the country's most impressive preservation success stories.[20] "Preservation, per se, is not our first order of business," Lowe explains. "It is, however, the best tool for neighborhood growth. But preservationists tend to be too pure and too interested only in buildings. These are not solely matters of architecture and bricks and mortar. Preservationists should help neighborhoods buy bars." Actually, they don't all have to be closed. If they are a positive social gathering place to congregate, the way many bars function well in many countries, they should be cherished. Instead, however, many have become a source of drug selling, gambling, and other illegal activities. Some could be transformed into positive neighborhood forces, locally owned and managed eating establishments, or other businesses, a source of local jobs and increased street security. This is but one non-preservation issue that must be confronted for the full potential of preservation to be realized.

II

TRANSPORTATION IS AT THE CORE OF EVERYTHING

An equally critical issue demanding the full attention of preservationists, as well as everyone else, is transportation. While I dealt in these pages with the origins of this challenge and the destructive impact on American cities of the interstate highway program, the issue is even more urgent and deserves additional attention.[21]

Some in the preservation community already recognize transportation as a critical issue.[22] In fact, for decades preservationists have been in the vanguard of anti-highway fights. Since World War II, the massive highway building program has been the driving force behind the redevelopment and/or destruction of small towns and big cities.[23] Preservationists have been getting involved in highway fights, street widening battles, bus depot closings, train and transit service

---

[20] See p. 73, "Instinctivists Change City Policy," for the earliest chapter of this great success story.

[21] Research for this section on transportation was made possible by the Surdna Foundation and the National Endowment for the Arts. The issues surrounding transportation arise throughout the book but are particularly highlighted in Chapter 8, "Urban Dispersal," p. 193.

[22] The National Trust for Historic Preservation in Washington, for example, has several staff people spending some time assisting highway-fighting communities and bringing the issue into focus for local preservation groups across the country.

[23] For an excellent and revealing look back on how the 1956 Highway Act was never meant to drive highways through towns and cities but only between them, see Bernard Frieden and Lynne B. Sagalyn, Downtown, Inc. How America Rebuilds Cities (MIT Press, 1989). This unplanned shift in the program explains a lot about how responsible our highway program has been in the decimation of urban and rural America. No one was more dismayed by the turn of events than then-President Dwight D. Eisenhower.

cutbacks, and parking garage construction fights, initially motivated by a threat of demolition of historic buildings.

Alert preservationists can quickly recognize the broader negative impacts of highway and road enlargement proposals. In recent years, preservationists have done well either sounding the alarm, leading the battle, or joining other activists fighting such ill-conceived projects as the Carter Library Highway in Atlanta,[24] the South Pasadena Freeway Extension in California,[25] new road proposals cutting through Pennsylvania's exquisite Amish farm land[26] or Kentucky's Blue Grass Country, and road widening proposals threatening historic homes and downtown main streets in small towns like Bay View, Michigan; Hickory, North Carolina; DePere, Wisconsin; and Russellville, Arkansas. In each case, while threatened historic resources were the obvious reason for preservationists' involvement, preservationists also understood the multilayered problems involved in continued auto-dependent development.

Erosion By Nibbles Continues

Every new road, every new highway, every widened road or highway, every shut down passenger rail line or discontinued transit route, every new tax advantage and hidden subsidy for truck traffic and disadvantage for rail freight, every continued favoring of the automobile over mass transportation options makes it more difficult to reinforce the already built areas of our country that represent billions of dollars of infrastructure investment, not to even mention the social, economic, historical, architectural, and energy resource values.

The "Malling of America" continues at a feverish pace. In fact, we've gone beyond malling to "sprawlmarting" where, to add insult to injury, one has to drive between the megastores, rather than driving to a mall and walking within. The forms continue to change with only two constants, auto-dependency and larger and larger scale. Large retailers and supermarket chains have rediscovered cities as well. They have targeted urban neighborhoods for much-needed stores, but they are trying to bring along their cornfield scale and excessive blacktop parking, a suburban form that tears asunder a fragile urban fabric and encourages even more autodependency. On the horizon, on yet more farm and wetlands, are monster malls packaged in theme parks adjacent to historic sites and promoted as history. Even the Disney company got on the bandwagon last year when it unveiled a proposal for a theme park in close proximity to Manassas, the Civil

---

24 Some 750 homes were demolished in historic neighborhoods to make way for the Presidential Highway before lawsuits forced a total scaling back and redesign of the road. The original larger road plan, with its increased vehicular capacity, has not been missed.

25 This plan is still alive and threatens 1,500 homes, five historic districts, and 7,000 trees—something like the kind of destruction caused by a California earthquake.

26 Lancaster farm land may be damaged instead by the proliferation of discount malls and the vehicular congestion they bring.

War battlefield. What all these megamalls have in common are acres of asphalt for parking, auto-dependent access, and enormous public investment in new infrastructure.

Not all megastores are by definition destructive. Those being fitted into existing downtown streetscapes whether in converted old buildings or new ones that front on and don't destroy the continuity of a shopping street are often functioning as a useful retail anchor much the way an earlier generation of department stores did.

After enactment of the 1956 Interstate Highway Act, Lewis Mumford wrote in a farsighted essay appearing in a 1958 Architectural Forum: "When the American people, through their Congress, voted a little while ago for a $26 billion highway program, the most charitable thing to assume about this action is that they hadn't the faintest notion of what they were doing...they will doubtless find out; but by that time it will be too late to correct all the damage to our cities and our countryside, not least to the efficient organization of industry and transportation, that this ill-conceived and preposterously unbalanced program will have wrought."

Jane Jacobs wrote in her seminal 1962 book, *The Life and Death of Great American Cities:* "Erosion of cities by automobiles...proceeds as a kind of nibbling, small nibbles at first but eventually hefty bites...A street is widened here, another is straightened there, a wide avenue is converted to a one-way flow...and more land goes into parking...No one step in this process is, in itself, crucial. But...it not only adds its own bit to the total change but accelerates the process."

Everything Mumford, Jacobs, and others predicted has come to pass. The erosion of cities by the automobile continues. Today, the manner is often more subtle. Perhaps neighborhoods are no longer being bulldozed wholesale, displacing whole populations for a road out of town, although this was true of an earlier generation of highways. But additional automotive capacity is being added to this road here and to that highway there, just as Jacobs described above. Poorly conceived, low-density housing in both cities and suburbs that encourages auto-dependency continues. Parking spaces proliferate daily, encouraging increased car use in, out, and around cities. Transit systems are expected to be self-supporting. Automotive travel remains highly subsidized beyond the known subsidized costs. Free parking, for example, is an issue gaining a lot of attention lately, since the change in the federal tax law that treats a free parking space as taxable income if it is worth more than $155 per month. Few stop to think of the multiple costs that go into free parking including the cost of parking lot or garage land and the cost of construction (garage space averages $15,000 a space to construct), maintenance, and security.

■ ■ ■

Many forces today converge to put transportation issues on the nation's front burner, including the effective educational work of the environmental movement, the aggressive resistance to auto-dependent proposals by historic preservationists, the greater advocacy of the architectural community, and the increasing numbers of elderly, handicapped, and poor residents, who are joining the coalition because they either physically or economically cannot function productively in an auto-dependant society.

Technical Gains

The strongest force driving this issue is one Mumford identified in his 1958 essay: "Perhaps the only thing that could bring Americans to their senses would be a clear demonstration of the fact that their highway program will, eventually, wipe out the very area of freedom that the private motorcar promised to retain for them." For millions of Americans, that ominous consequence has come to pass and it promises to get worse, regardless of all the technological gimmicks Smart Cars, HOV (High Occupancy Vehicle) lanes, electric vehicles, IVHS (Intelligent Vehicle Highway System) that promise to alleviate pollution and congestion but do nothing to reduce auto-demand.

Americans presently spend almost 1.5 billion hours each year stuck in traffic. The U.S. General Accounting Office estimates that figure will increase to over 4 billion early in the 21st century. Cleaner cars are not enough. *More people driving environmentally improved cars on more and longer trips are cancelling gains from vast technical improvements.* The object must be to use cars less. But four-wheel dependency will only decrease with good alternatives and strong incentives to alter habits. The federal government has taken a small but significant step in that direction by allowing employers to cover $60 per month in mass transit travel without being subject to tax and making some free parking taxable as income.

One of the most challenging national issues for the remainder of the 1990s and well into the 21st century will be transportation and the land use planning that is essential to make mass transit work. This assertion actually plays out quite unevenly across the country. Portland, Oregon, has been for several years the preeminent model of transit-oriented redevelopment, resulting in remarkable growth and economic resurgence accompanied by decreased traffic congestion, cleaner air, new transit-oriented development, and a well-used and expanding new light rail system.

Opened in the late 1980s, Portland's light rail line combined with an exemplary bus system carries the equivalent of two lanes on every road entering downtown. A city of 300,000 on the Columbia River and surrounded by mountains, Portland derives a unique compactness, comfortable scale and walkability from its short blocks of 200 feet square. But equally significant, Portland restricted two 12-

block-long streets to no-fare buses, pedestrians, and emergency vehicles, put a cap on the number of allowed parking spaces (most cities don't even know how many parking spaces they have), and traded in highway funds for the light rail system that has become a national model. A height limit was set for new buildings with the tallest kept inland away from the river, and preservation and restoration of the city's varied stock of old buildings was encouraged. Both new office towers and retail space have been built, and downtown has gained 30,000 jobs without any significant increase in auto traffic. Estimates indicate that 110,000 cars left the roads and 42 percent of downtown workers commute by transit. The number of days in which air quality does not meet health standards has dropped from about 100 per year to none.

Places where new or rebuilt transit links suffer disappointing usage are marked by the lack of essential transit-oriented land use planning, a difficult nut to crack where the transportation and planning professionals are still dominated by the entrenched highway mindset focused on moving vehicles not people. Notes traffic engineer Walter Kulash, who has been doing a good job spotlighting the ill-conceived premises of highway engineers and producing studies to challenge accepted notions: "We need to understand that the industry that we look to for moving people, the traffic engineering industry, has no constituency for doing so...The traffic engineering profession, which has perhaps the greatest influence of any group on how our new growth looks, is interested in one thing only— moving the maximum number of cars. The profession is fixated on this goal. It does not see its charge as moving people in an attractive setting; it does not even see its goal as moving people."[27] Fortunately, a new generation of transportation and land use planners is emerging who came of professional age and political consciousness on an Earth Day in the 1970s or 1980s or at least under the influence of the environmental movement. Some of them probably understand better than their predecessors the interconnectedness of transportation, land development issues and everything else.

Urbanists must be on alert to anti-urban forms of transit. Sometimes this is more difficult than just recognizing ill-conceived road projects. An elevated transit system, like Miami's, that takes all pedestrians off the streets and into the second floor entrances of new buildings is a guaranteed death sentence for urbanism. It is no better than the skywalk systems of Minneapolis and St. Paul that create two classes of buildings: the connected and the nonconnected. The nonconnected that rely on the street-level users lured away to newer upper-level buildings and their interior retail spaces will surely suffer with the disappearance of street-level urbanism.

---

[27] Walter Kulash, "Traditional Neighborhood Development: Will the Traffic Work?", a 1990 traffic study.

"Car as Culprit" is the heart of the story of so much that is wrong with America. There is no getting around it. No other country in the world has so transformed itself to accommodate the car. While others have accommodated cars, none has actively dismantled a fine railroad and trolley network like the United States. After four decades of aggressive highway construction and disinvestment in a once fine railroad network, car dependency is eroding *everybody*'s quality of life. Studies show, for example, that Americans spend more money on auto transportation than on groceries or on health.[28] We have done everything possible to make the automobile central to everyone's lifestyle and psyche. Neither countryside nor city center, neither urban neighborhoods nor rural communities can be appropriately developed when the car dominates. If the goal is to protect the vast public investment already made in the water, transportation, and energy infrastructure, if the goal is to make affordable housing and work places accessible to people who need them, if the goal is to reduce air and water pollution, if the goal is to preserve existing and stable communities, if the goal is to seriously tackle traffic congestion by reducing the ever-increasing vehicle-miles traveled, then the place to start is with the car and the development patterns it stimulates.

I am *not* suggesting that car owners junk the ultimate status machine. Nor am I suggesting that people who can afford to and are so inclined should cease buying multiple cars. Automobile manufacturers can relax. The goal should be to make everyone less car dependent. Those who don't want to depend on autos, perhaps, are a minority, but the majority, including those who own multiple cars, must be convinced of the necessity to use cars less and to support transportation networks that provide the opportunity to do so. Focusing on providing alternative options just to a minority doesn't solve the problem. If we do not set this goal, the growing environmental and development dilemmas will overwhelm us.

David Burwell, president of the Rails-to-Trails Conservancy, a founding member of the Surface Transportation Policy Project[29] and one of the savviest mass transit/land use advocates, has written: "Thanks in large part to our extensive highway system, the United States is the world's most powerful economy. But also thanks to this system, the country faces increasing traffic congestion, declining productivity, accelerating environmental damage, and few options other than a bulldozer approach of building our way out. Yet, with a heavy federal deficit and a big backlog of maintenance on our existing highways,

---

[28] The December 1993 Bureau of Labor Statistics report for 1992 expenses shows Americans' average expenditure for food was $4,273 and for transportation, of which most is automotive, was $5,228.

[29] STPP is a broad coalition of environmentalists, historic preservationists, transit and railroad transportation advocates, city officials, architects, and planners that mobilized to speak with one voice during the 1991-92 congressional debate over the renewal of highway and transit programs. This youthful, formidable, and determined coalition added a new dimension to broad transportation policy and land use planning debate.

■ ■ ■

Transit projects are not by definition automatically good. If you build them, riders will not automatically come, certainly not without requisite transit-oriented development or redevelopment. This alert extends to talk of suburb-to-suburb transit planning that continues and institutionalizes the bypassing and undermining of existing cities, the neglecting of already built urban transportation infrastructure, and the ignoring of its renewal potential. Because work and home destinations are so dispersed, suburb-to-suburb travel is impossible to serve by mass transit in the way that suburban-city patterns traditionally did and still do. Noted Jane Jacobs in a 1993 New York City public radio interview: "There is a kind of mass transit cities used to be very rich in and Toronto still is, the kind that is part of the fabric of the city itself, doesn't just go overhead and take people whoosh, but links all kinds of places within the city and that's the kind of mass transit we need to begin to reconstitute... It's a necessity for people to go to work. It's a necessity for people to get to hospitals, to schools. It isn't just a frill. In a really healthy city, it's something that knits the whole thing together and has a great deal to do with the economy.

It took the United States almost a whole century to get to this auto-dependent state, starting with small steps and growing in leaps and bounds. Now it may take as long to achieve a balance between the car and public transportation, but small steps can lead the way.

Transportation Shapes Everything

Transportation's crucial relevance may be hardest to comprehend in cities and towns not yet paralyzed by traffic congestion. Yet, cities and small towns alike will rise or fall on how transportation dilemmas are resolved. All development and redevelopment is shaped by transportation. How a city evolves is similarly shaped. Too many cities across America today have more parking lots and garages than they do buildings occupied by economically productive uses. Like urban cemeteries, each parking space in an open downtown lot is a memorial to the viable economic uses that once stood on that spot. Every downtown parking lot that interrupts the continuity of the streetscape makes the encouragement of pedestrian traffic between buildings and between blocks more difficult.

A well-functioning downtown is simply impossible with interrupted nodes of activity connected by parking. The intricate flow of urban functions are too disconnected when massive parking lots interrupt and each space represents missing activity. Density and intensity are what mark viable cities, not the thinness and sprawl of a suburb. Post-war suburbs, which have borne the brunt of new development, are as badly off, transformed from tranquil bedroom communities to frustrating traffic jams and increasingly besieged by so-called "urban problems" residents thought they were avoiding.

■ ■ ■

it will be hard to maintain what we already have, let alone expand it. We are stuck in a traffic jam of our own making."[30]

Undeniably, a difficult task confronts this country. To postpone the task or to approach it as less than an emergency is clearly dangerous. None of these problems can be mitigated as long as sprawl development is not reversed.

Overcoming The Culture Of Isolation

One of the more hopeful developments in recent years is the emergence of a group of planners and designers focused on re-creating the pedestrian community whose defining principle is again mass transit instead of the car. Central to this approach is the bringing together of work, school, day care, and government services. This is how traditional downtowns sometimes identified as historic functioned before the highway system led public and private investment to the countryside, now identified as sprawl. And, of course, this has always been the advantage of urban centers, where a dense network of highly connected streets adds up to a continuous fabric of intimately blended land uses reachable by multiple travel methods and routes. Sidewalks;[31] corner stores; neighborhood playgrounds; pocket parks; schools within walking distance; medical, sports, entertainment, and religious facilities; local businesses on pedestrian shopping streets; housing of assorted size, shape, and occupancy single, two-family, multiple; transit links to downtown centers; and long-distance transportation hubs. These are the uncomplicated strokes and colors of the urban art.

A great national street and transit infrastructure—a valuable national resource of a kind—still exists in urban centers. Appreciation of this functionally economic and socially integrating community form has always been an urbanist's trademark. The neo-traditional designers who now brilliantly and artfully advocate this compact, transit-oriented planning are still primarily focused on restructuring or designing new suburbs rather than first reinforcing cities where this proven form is already in place. This does not diminish the need to restructure suburbs as well. But, first, what exists everywhere—center city and rural town—needs to be reinforced and strengthened before one more inch of undeveloped farm land or open space is taken up for new communities. This is in keeping with the approach I referred to earlier: Urban Husbandry.

The efficacy of this traditional development is reflected in a myriad of ways, but none is so telling as the diminishment of time wasting, polluting, and economically draining automotive traffic. The 1990 study by Walter Kulash found that traditional neighborhoods where residents can walk to services generate 12 percent fewer car miles traveled overall by those residents, and 25 percent fewer on the big, wide arterial

---

[30] "Moving in the Future," The Environmental Forum, July/August 1991.

[31] Many suburbanites clamor for sidewalks these days, but it is not clear where they plan to walk to.

streets that these pedestrians would otherwise have used by car to get to services. Walking replaces driving in pedestrian neighborhoods. "The operation of these principles still can be seen in many historic districts and traditional downtowns," writes Constance Beaumont, director of state and local policy for the National Trust for Historic Preservation and one of the key people within that organization advocating a transportation focus. "By limiting the distances one must travel to get from one place to another, the mixed land use and compact development patterns make it feasible to conduct business and carry out essential functions on foot."

The traditional urban form now recognized with increasing value is what facilitated our cities' original great economic and social strengths and could again.[32] Even the trolley-car suburbs of the 1920s, now often considered inner-city neighborhoods, their mass transit oriented growth history long forgotten, provided transportation choices—trolley, bus, car, or foot. Garages, if there were any, were behind houses, often in sensible alleys. Extra space above the garage provided room for an office or small apartment if needed, adding residential and economic variety to the community. Driveways paralleled the house and didn't replace or overwhelm the front walk. Today, garage doors, often three of them, have replaced the front door as the face to the street. Frequently, the only ornamentation a passerby sees is the gas and water meters. Everything that once went in the back of the house is now on the front, as hostile and alienating a message as one could send.[33] Yet, now some of these same hostile suburban forms are being built in our inner cities. Vacant land in old urban neighborhoods is being covered with suburban housing of the worst kind. Developers both private and nonprofit blame consumer demand. Yet, the strong market for historic neighborhoods with garageless row housing belies that claim. The car pad, at best, and garage, at worst, are replacing the socially integrating value of front stoop and street-side activity. And then we wonder about the deterioration of neighborliness and the disappearance of community stability. But this is only symptomatic of the isolated lives we lead shaped by the car. The car has separated, segregated, alienated, and isolated us and helped to transform us into a highly divided society.

Highways in many places have been the most destructive dividing and undermining device. It is no coincidence that it is mostly through poor or working-class neighborhoods that highways were plowed; that the destruction in their path has never been fully, if at all, repaired; and that the separateness and

---

[32] See epilogue.

[33] In a now-famous 1971 study, "Environmental Quality of City Streets: The Residents' Viewpoint," Don Appleyard and M. Lintell graphically illustrated the impact of traffic on communities. People in low traffic streets know and are friendly with more of their neighbors than on high traffic streets. "High volume, speeding traffic causes people to retreat from street based community and both the public and private face of the environment deteriorates," notes Peter Newman, the increasingly well-known and effective Australian advocate of "traffic-calming."

isolation those highways created have not been overcome. Robert A. Peck, at the time a lawyer in Washington and now the vice president of external affairs at the American Institute of Architects, testified at congressional transportation hearings in 1991: "Highway planning has become a surrogate for land use planning in many communities...it has destroyed certain communities, walled communities off from each other, and in some places taken racially and economically well-integrated communities and then separated them."

Downtowns across America today are being rebuilt to institutionalize and formalize, rather than overcome, this culture of isolation, separation, and segregation. Skywalks that take people off the streets; interior shopping malls that kill street-level, locally owned retail; huge office towers and apartment complexes entered and exited through the parking garage; regional shopping centers that drain the center city of people and dollars all these factors expand the isolation. The mixing and mingling of people that is essential to a democratic society doesn't have a chance on the interstate.

III

PRESERVED PLACES DON'T STOP GROWING AND CHANGING

This book is about significant change constructive, meaningful, rational change, appropriate in scale and enhancing the character of its place. The initial change described in all the stories herein is never large. But its impact grows in modest steps until big differences and broader positive changes occur. The first edition of this book was completed in 1988. I continue to follow the developments in many of the places used to illustrate the central issues of change. And since each place, project, or person highlighted in these pages reflected a particular aspect of the process of change, it is useful to consider how that process continued after 1988.

New Haven remains a classic case of a city still struggling to come out from under decades of heavily subsidized, wrongheaded redevelopment, what architecture critic Vincent Scully aptly described as "cataclysmic, automotive and suburban."[34] Public and private committee after committee have been formed to come up with a new "plan" for city rebuilding, and Yale University has committed $50 million to renewal efforts. Little has happened, but whatever is possible at this point will certainly require an enormous public investment.

Some of the renewed historic areas covered in these pages Seattle's Pioneer Square and Pike Place Market, New York's Soho, Boston's Quincy Market are so successful, few people remember that they were once scheduled for demolition and fought for and rescued by determined urbanists. Those urbanists, like other

---

[34] See "Urbanism Repeatedly Destroyed in the Name of Renewal," p. 19.

successful city rebuilders in this book, were derided at the time of their battle as non-experts, impeders of progress and opponents of change, who should follow, not lead, the experts. They were, instead, the real innovators, the catalysts for meaningful and progressive change, the citizens who changed the course of the community in which they lived. None of them started out thinking of themselves as urbanists or preservationists, but they clearly are the preservers, conservers, and true rebuilders of cities.

All of the success stories illustrated herein have experienced continued change, most of it successful. In fact, some of them have suffered from the kind of excessive success described earlier. Savannah's waterfront and downtown historic district[35] has become a favorite tourist destination and, like Charleston and other overtouristed sites before it, has had to rein in tourist buses. The negative impacts that go with the cash register benefits of tourism are still little understood or widely ignored, and a growing number of small and large communities are looking to it as a new form of quick-fix economic rejuvenator. Without careful protection against the excesses, tourism can lead to troubling dilemmas that diminish long-fought-for improvements. In preparation for the sailing segment of the 1996 Olympics scheduled for Atlanta, Savannah is now focused on building a World Trade Center and Convention Center with enormous new parking capacity, away from the kind of local concerns that, first, make a city a desirable place to live in, and, second, a place tourists want to visit. Time will only tell what the impacts of such large-scale projects will have.

The best news is that small things are happening along Savannah's Broughton Street, the mile-long main retail street with a wonderful mix of historic buildings intact. Plans are moving ahead to restore a 1921 movie theater, the Lucas, and put it back into entertainment use and make it a center of community activity. A restaurant opened on the ground floor of a former Art Deco department store with banquet rooms upstairs. It was an immediate success. City government offices wisely moved into an empty J. C. Penney's, the best kind of anchor for any downtown main street. The Savannah College of Art and Design bought and restored 40 unused historic buildings scattered around the city, generating creative new uses including art galleries and art services. The dispersed nature of this development protects against an overwhelming impact in one place. Historically, downtown educational facilities always added to city life until many moved out of town to suburban campuses. This return is a major advantage for any downtown.

Savannah's racially and economically mixed Victorian District, however, is not experiencing the same slow and steady improvements. The district continues to illustrate the racial and economic integration potential of the genuine

---

[35] Chapters 1 to 3.

upgrading of existing but highly deteriorated inner-city neighborhoods. Private developers, however, have not been as scrupulous as was the locally based, now disbanded, catalyst, Savannah Landmark, which practiced rigorous tenant screening and high maintenance standards. And the original crucial tenant involvement in management was unfortunately allowed to slide. Here again, only time will tell if the Victorian District can sustain the process that led to its great success. If it does not, it will provide a new kind of lesson, a negative one exhibiting what must be avoided. Already, it underscores the value of active tenant management.

Cincinnati's Mount Auburn neighborhood turnaround, under the leadership of Carl Westmoreland, has become a model for grass-roots change in a low-income neighborhood with local residents and business people taking the lead in upgrading their community. In fact, Cincinnati was a key model for Stanley Lowe's neighborhood success in Pittsburgh mentioned earlier. Lowe also built on the trail-blazing work of Gail Cincotta in Chicago, who led the national campaign against inner-city redlining by banks and other financial institutions that resulted in the Community Reinvestment Act passed by Congress in 1977.[36] Lowe is now the country's foremost and most articulate advocate of neighborhood revitalization through historic preservation in low-income communities.

Banana Kelly in the South Bronx remains a favorite story of mine because it is in the one place in America that everyone declared hopeless.[37] Once a mostly burned out and abandoned area of a few stubborn holdouts, Kelly Street is now an anchor to a reborn community of more than 40,000. Banana Kelly, the grass-roots organization that started by cleaning out and rehabilitating three abandoned buildings, is now a multimillion dollar operation with rehabilitation, weatherization, homeless and social service programs, and several offices scattered around the neighborhood. Banana Kelly owns and manages 40 buildings with 1,000 housing units and has expanded into cosponsorship of new home construction on sites laid waste by earlier misguided government policies.

Urbanists Resist Suburban Planning And Design

Most of the new housing not built by Banana Kelly in this community has been inappropriately suburban. Poor communities desperate for new housing and new population cannot easily refuse the take-it-or-leave-it opportunities offered by nonprofit builders, foundations, or corporate sponsors. Even by official planners' standards, a density of 18 to 60 people per acre is a suburban measurement. For a neighborhood as well served by nearby mass transit, shopping, and employment opportunities and only minutes from an interstate

---

[36] See pp. 73 and 286.

[37] See Chapter 4, "Winning Skirmishes, Losing Wars," p. 82.

highway connection, nothing less than 60 to 100 people per acre should be the goal. Classic low-rise apartment houses should be interspersed with urban row houses. Either curbside or backyard parking should be the norm. Banana Kelly leaders in recent years joined with grass- roots groups elsewhere in the Bronx to force construction of higher density housing. The first new housing built in the South Bronx following the Charlotte Street fiasco recalled in these pages was single family homes with fences, a bizarre suburban site in the middle of a city, and much publicized and celebrated, even with a density per acre of only 3.2. Density was subsequently increased slightly with two- and three-story two-family homes. Currently, denser, more reasonable projects are under way. Through bottom-up pressure on government agencies and large nonprofit builders, increased density and less car-friendly design is just now beginning to emerge on the house market in New York City, Pittsburgh, and a few other cities.[38] The new housing may still not meet a fully appropriate urban standard, but it is clearly an improvement.

Under its third director, Yolanda Rivera, Banana Kelly is exhibiting another form of the best kind of grass-roots innovation by developing a major local recycling business that is at the cutting edge of 21st-century entrepreneurship. A $200,000 revolving loan fund has been established to help local businesses. The first recipient of assistance was a computerized bookkeeping firm.

There is a new spirit of optimism. People talk of the New Bronx. The old image of burned-out buildings and vacant lots is outdated. Banana Kelly is preparing to renovate an abandoned four-story synagogue for its social service office, day care center, health unit, and literacy program. The organization is but one of the "drops in the bucket" that is reversing the decline of the Bronx and putting it on the upswing. The grass-roots momentum took many different forms during the 1970s and 1980s and, in fact, laid a foundation for current initiatives coming from Bronx political leadership for a genuine community-based planning process leading to the redevelopment of the Bronx Civic Center, the borough's downtown.

Critics who claim that locally based community development corporations across the country only focus on housing have not been to Banana Kelly. There are Banana Kellys all over the country. They are rebuilding the inner cities in multiple and innovative ways.

The early infill precedent of West Village Houses[39] in Greenwich Village and the innovative and sizable new Saint Lawrence Neighborhood[40] in Toronto both remain workable and popular extensions of the existing city

---

[38] In Pittsburgh, new urban instead of suburban housing to fill in the empty sites is one of the earliest lessons Stanley Lowe absorbed.

39 See "An Early Infill Housing Precedent," p. 168.

40 See "New and Large but Not Overwhelming," p. 163.

■ ■ ■

fabric, genuine repairs rather than overwhelming replacements. Both developments continue to add strength to the city around them, rather than separating and segregating their occupants.

The lessons in downtown survival in Part Two of this book remain on a steady course with economic variations that parallel the national economy. The stories of four communities in particular continue to be useful illustrations of the ongoing variations of the battle between downtowns and malls still unfolding in communities across the country. Of these four—Ithaca and Corning, New York; Pittsfield, Massachusetts; and Burlington, Vermont—Pittsfield is probably the weakest because of the draining influence of a mall that did get built, although not in as bad a location as was first proposed. Ithaca saw expansion of the mall it fiercely resisted in vain, but the downtown continues to hold its own after getting itself on a good track during the early mall fight. Corning remains a national model of a renewed downtown with a robust local economy. Market Street is well supported by the local population, attractive to tourists visiting the nearby Corning Glassworks Museum, and is so much a part of the life of the community that downtown is just expected to do well. Change continues, not all of it smooth. When a new bridge was necessary across the river, demolition of the historic old bridge was fiercely fought by a broad cross section of local residents and business people. The bridge was kept, converted to a well-used pedestrian bridge, and recently a new park opened on the other end. One block of the backs of Market Street buildings facing the parking lot have been cleaned up and added a new dimension to the sprucing up activity.

Burlington and its small neighbor, Williston, continue to win probably the country's longest running Stop-the-Mall Fight. (The battle has now expanded to fighting a Wal-Mart and Sam's Warehouse Club.) In the meantime, Burlington has transformed itself from a struggling to a prosperous downtown frequently cited around the country as a model of downtown rebirth.

Ironically and sadly, Burlington and the whole state of Vermont may be the first to win the battle but lose the war. Wisely, Vermont has remained almost mall-free, certainly megamall- and regional mall-free. It is almost 20 years since the Pyramid Mall Company first announced its intention to build on the Williston cornfield. Largely because of the absence of massive malls and all the ancillary environmental degradation, demolition, and new development that accompanies them, Vermont has held onto its strengths, fared economically well, and remained a desirable vacation destination for more than enough people. But now Wal-Mart has targeted that state — Williston is the first announced site—and Vermonters are digging their heels in for another long and arduous fight.[41] The next few years promise to be most interesting as local groups build on the experience of fighting regional malls, gain wider support from public officials who see the unfortunate consequences of their existing area malls, and garner greater publicity through the successful resistance of communities such as Westford and Greenfield in Massachusetts.

Years ago, McDonald's was stopped from demolishing a historic New England landmark in Freeport, Maine. The fast-food chain that had no experience building anything but its rigid formulas learned how to occupy the landmark instead of demolishing it. Even in a few other places, McDonald's has shown it could adjust to innovative thinking. Maybe the same could happen to Wal-Mart. This multibillion dollar selling machine has gotten rich off the ruins of too many American downtowns while promoting itself as environmentally advanced because of its ecologically smart new building construction methods, designed by architect William McDonough. Yet, Wal-Mart executives have not yet figured out or else they don't care to do so that ecologically sound construction methods on an environmentally devastated site with destructive environmental, economic, and social impacts on surrounding communities may produce high cash profits but is not good corporate citizenship.

Finding a way to reinforce rather than replace existing downtowns with appropriately designed new or converted old buildings should be the corporate motto of the next decade. The "sprawlmarting" of America—whether it be with a Home Depot, K-Mart, Shopko, Target, Meijers, Costco, or others—is an extension of the transportation, environmental, and downtown mistakes described earlier. The history of this unfortunate and long-running tale are described in this book, but new attention must focus on these serious national issues.

Fundamentally, all of this is about economics, about strengthening the national economy from the bottom up, about recognizing that the strength of the nation is locally based, about acknowledging that national strength can neither exist nor endure without strength at the local foundation. Local, local, local. That is really where it is at. All eyes may be on GATT, NAFTA, balance of trade, balance of payments, and the like, but the real work is local. As Michael Porter notes in *The Competitive Advantage of Nations:* "The process of creating skills and the

---

41 The National Trust for Historic Preservation put the whole state of Vermont on the same most endangered list as downtown New Orleans because the state "is at risk from the potential effects of a national problem known as 'Sprawlmart,' which the National Trust defines as unplanned, uncontrolled, large-scale commercial development on the periphery of town that saps the vitality from traditional main streets and destroys open space." Trust President Richard Moe noted: "Naming Vermont...is an unprecedented step for us. While Vermont has been a model in enacting exemplary preservation, environmental and land-use planning legislation, its citizens are now being tested by big chain discounters and megamall developers to make these laws work. The potentially disastrous impact of commercial sprawl on the towns and countryside of this beautiful state—and in historic communities everywhere— is not only an economic but a quality of life issue."

important influences on the role of improvement and innovation are intensely local. Paradoxically, open global competition makes the home base more, not less important." What Porter refers to is more commonly being referred to as the "municipalization of the economy," or "localization philosophy" as real estate and economic consultant Don Rypkema calls it, or—my favorite—what Akio Morita of Sony calls "global localization."

This brings us full circle back to the primary importance of cities, a continuing reality despite erroneous assertions that communication technology is making cities obsolete. The old wisdom of Jane Jacobs and the new wisdom of Don Rypkema are again applicable. Noted Jacobs some years ago in *Cities and the Wealth of Nations:* "All developing economic life depends on city economies...all expanding economic life depends on working links with cities." Says Rypkema, "The decisive role cities play in the emerging global economy is absolutely unrecognized," adding that "cities will either innovate or they will decline and failure to innovate is never the fault of external conditions." Back to innovation, and as Rypkema explains it, localities have to pay primary attention to what they can influence. This works from the bottom up from the smallest source. And while a small downtown or a big city cannot directly affect NAFTA, it can affect how many new businesses originate on Main Street or in an urban downtown, and whether urban neighborhoods renew or decline. And Rypkema points out, this is both cost efficient and the way it works. He cites two interesting figures. An Urban Land Institute study noted that the costs of sprawl range from 40 to 400 percent more than compact development. And a survey of engineers, as Rypkema notes, reveals that most of their ideas come from *face to face contact,* something that happens best in cities, not on the "communication highway."

One of the most gratifying changes since publication of the first edition of this book is the growing recognition of the widespread impact of the community development movement, the embodiment of this book's primary theme, "Thinking Small in a Big Way." And while not enough people go as far as Rypkema to assert that "over the last 10 years it has been the nonprofit sector that has been the most effective in identifying and responding to urban problems," many at least are looking to more and more smaller local units for lessons to expand on. While the stories here are a good starting place to learn new lessons in redeveloping local economies, local neighborhoods, local downtowns, and local places, there are hundreds if not thousands of additional lessons to be learned. My hope is that readers will expand their way of looking at the world around them, perhaps look at things somewhat differently, and, most of all, apply the newly acquired wisdom to home.

Roberta Brandes Gratz
New York City
April 1994

Acknowledgments

Years of travel, interviews, observations, discussions, thinking and rethinking, writing and rewriting went into this book. During that time, scores of people all over the country contributed in countless ways. Many of those who helped shape the book are identified in these pages, but there are many others, not mentioned by name, to whom credit must be given.

First I would like to thank the editors with whom I worked at *The New York Post* from 1963 to 1978 for letting me roam New York City neighborhoods and probe city agencies in search of the stories that contributed to my understanding of the city. After I left the *Post*, one of those editors, Robert Friedman, provided critical encouragement and counsel, as I embarked on the first of many drafts of this book. Jason Epstein first supported me in the conviction that what I had to say about cities mattered. Jane Isay nurtured the book into a new incarnation. Finally, Bob Bender has been a model editor, caringly and respectfully strengthening the manuscript. Lynn Davis Lorwin first represented me and showed me how thin the line can be between literary agent and dear friend. And Elaine Markson came through with great insight and advice at the most opportune moments.

Grants from the National Endowment for the Arts and the New York State Council on the Arts were essential in giving me the freedom to travel, observe and interview. Just like some of the success stories in this book, those two seed grants were critical to making this book happen. A debt of gratitude also is due Irma and Frank Gratz who gave early financial assistance at a critical stage.

Much of the research and the first draft of the book were done in the Frederick Lewis Allen Room of the New York Public Library. When I started working in the Allen Room, I joined a group of writers organizing the Writers' Room, a writers' work space in New York City, separate from the library, that was to become the country's first urban writers' colony. There I wrote the bulk of this book; in both places I found a community of writers whose moral support, encouragement and friendship were of critical importance, especially during discouraging times. These are the writers whose friendship has sustained me: Nancy Milford, Judith Rossner, Lois Gould, Andrea Egan, David Lowe, Bernie Weisberger, Marjorie Iseman, Lucinda Franks, Victor Navasky, Susan Brownmiller, the late Madelon Bedell, Robert Caro, Eliot Asinof, Jack Newfield, Tony Mancini, Molly Haskell, Felicia Hirsch, Robert Spitzler, Eric Fettman.

Portions of this book were also written at the Virginia Center for the Creative Arts and at the Millay Colony. Ann Ellen Lessor, director of the Millay Colony, is particularly skilled at ensuring that a resident's colony stay is amazingly productive.

In the course of my work on the book, some of the people whom I met and profile in its pages have become close friends and partners in preservation and other ventures. In Ron Shiffman, Bobbie Handman and Lee Adler I found three citizen experts of the highest caliber whose wisdom permeates this book and whose friendship I treasure. And in Jane Jacobs I found a friend and exemplar whose warm encouragement and challenging observations were of immeasurable value. Some close friends, especially Nancy Cooperstein, Jordan Charney, and Carol and Burt Biderman, provided early and sustained encouragement. I cherish the memory of Doris C. Freedman, who understood so well the value of thinking small in a big way and whose mark on New York City remains indelible, and her husband,

Alan Freedman, who understood and encouraged it all. Their friendship is sorely missed.

Residents of many urban communities guided me to the high spots and low spots of their cities, sharing the insights that can come only from those who have struggled to strengthen their residential or commercial neighborhood. Citizen activists explained the details of their successes and failures. Professionals of all kinds offered insights and observations that cumulatively strengthened many parts of this book. In this largest group and not specifically mentioned in the pages of the book are Kent Barwick, Laurie Beckelman, Hugh Cosman, Fred Cawley, Rex Curry, Joan K. Davidson, Frances Edmunds, Jack Goldstein, Curt Hagedorn, Bill Josephson, Ellen Kanner, Lenore Loveman, Herb McLaughlin, George McMath, Dorothy Miner, Ruth Murphy, Sandy Lundwall Nance, Brad Paul, Steve Robinson, Stuart Stein, Brian Sullivan, Sherry Kafka Wagner, Diana Waite.

Earliest credit goes to my parents, Larry Brandes and Celia Gillis Brandes, through whose eyes and with whose encouragement I first explored New York City and learned how to think small in a big way.

Above all, I am grateful to my husband, Donald, whose ideas and wisdom are as much a part of this book as my own and whose love and encouragement have made the difficult periods of this project less arduous.

My daughters, Laura Beth and Rebecca Susan, have been a source of joy throughout this endeavor and, from time to time, have offered useful observations and insights.

For Donald, Laura and Rebecca

Contents

Preface

I was born in a city, New York City. And I was born in a neighborhood, the quintessential neighborhood—Greenwich Village, with its variety of people and architecture and its small-town friendliness. Forty-eight years later, I am very much a city partisan. It was not always so. It took living in the suburbs as a teenager to make me understand that I would never choose to live outside a city again. I understand the lure and appeal of suburbs, and Westport, Connecticut, where I lived, did have its charms. Both city and suburb have their attractions and styles, and I do not value one at the expense of the other.

It took my experience of fifteen years as a newspaper reporter for *The New York Post*—clocking more miles on the city's streets in that time than most pedestrians do in a lifetime—to understand the dynamic that makes a city work. At the *Post,* I reported on housing, urban renewal and community battles for survival, on small successes and large failures, on historic preservation and neighborhood revitalization. I saw government policies repeat the mistakes of the past because vested interests and misguided analyses stood in the way of appropriate change. And I saw neighborhoods rebuild themselves despite government-created impediments. What I learned about the rebuilding of cities, I learned first in the neighborhoods of New York and from the people who fought to save their turf. One can learn more from observing the survival efforts of one city block at close hand than from all the government reports and policy studies in the Library of Congress. One can learn more, as well, from the residents and users of a community than from any number of planners and theoreticians.

In the early 1970s, I began to report on and study the landmarks-preservation movement, first as it was evolving in New York and later around the country. Somehow this movement clarified for me—as it did for many others—why so many of our cities seemed to be hell-bent on self-destruction. People saw the bulldozer working overtime during the 1950s and the 1960s, erasing neighborhoods and architectural treasures that were the touchstones of their lives and the social fabric that comprises the human sinews of a physical place. The people who loved their city, the streets they walked and the neighborhoods in which they raised their families, had seen too much disappear unnecessarily, and they rallied to preserve what was left. They had seen buildings go down that were historic, beautiful or just plain utilitarian. They had seen them replaced by monuments to mediocrity and real-estate profits which were destroying, not reviving, cities. Preserving the urban fabric, weaving together the treasured old and the needed new, not being afraid to think small—that is what genuine revitalization is all about.

This book is an outgrowth of that experience, the city's and my own. It is a book about cities—their rediscovery, their rebirth, their durability. My personal experience is not unique. In many ways, it resembles the experience of millions of city residents. The suburbs still grow, but we are in a period of urban renaissance. People are moving back to cities or resisting the pull to leave, recognizing that experts prematurely pronounce cities dead because they don't understand what makes them live. We are in a period of reexamination and reassessment of what we have done to our cities. I hope this book will contribute to that emerging new understanding.

I have spent several years researching this book, traveling thousands of miles by car, train, plane, bus and foot. If I started out with a set of preconceived notions, I do not remember what they were.

Firsthand observation invariably shattered old myths and legends. I observed the successes and the failures, always in search of lessons. This book is about those lessons.

From large and small, remote and familiar illustrations, it is possible to draw lessons that are applicable to development patterns in almost every community in this country. The principles and patterns, for better or worse, do not vary greatly. For every illustration that I have included in this book, I am confident there are others to which every reader can point to illustrate the same lesson.

ROBERTA BRANDES GRATZ

Introduction

*The received wisdom of today belongs more and
more to experts who hold their licenses without
ever having asked themselves or having been asked
whether intimate experience with the subject at
hand might in any particular way be relevant to
their qualifications.*

—MURRAY KEMPTON, columnist

In a small town on eastern Long Island, an aging bridge spans a juncture where fresh marshland water flows into a large pond. When it was necessary some years ago to rebuild the bridge, the mayor sought financial help from the federal government, since the cost of repairing the bridge was more than half the village's annual budget.

Federal engineers, however, claimed that simply repairing the bridge would add no more than ten years to its life and therefore would not be cost efficient. Only by widening the bridge by two lanes, they argued, would long-term repair be possible. Adding two lanes, however, would require widening and straightening the curved road that provided access to the bridge and condemning adjacent parkland. This additional work would both disturb the ecologically fragile marshland and considerably escalate the project cost.

It is a familiar dilemma: A modest problem triggers an out-of-scale solution that can be achieved only at an unnecessary economic and physical cost. Local residents, sensitive to aesthetic and ecological issues, oppose the solution and are accused of opposing progress. Local elected officials rationalize the damage rather than reject a large sum of federal money. Proponents argue that the negative impacts are the inevitable price of progress. And the federal bureaucracy—rigid, regulation-heavy and remote—is unfit to respond to varying local needs.

For several decades now, large and small American communities have been facing this kind of Catch-22 development dilemma, too often making the wrong choice. Overscaled, overpriced projects are imposed where smaller, less costly, equally productive and more aesthetically satisfactory solutions would do. Things that should be built to last beyond a twenty-year mortgage, from individual buildings to whole neighborhoods, fall apart more quickly than what they replaced. The planned obsolescence that shortens the life of the automobile or toaster now threatens, as well, our built environment.

Unwittingly we have arrived at the Era of Waste.

But while the bad news of costly, unnecessary projects built in the name of "progress" is familiar to us, the good news is the hopeful stories of genuine urban rebirth, of modest developments making major impacts—stories, more often than not, representing people who are fighting back, overcoming the system, making a big impact in small doses.

This book examines examples of both urban destruction and urban rebirth, in order to learn the lessons of the past, to establish a framework in which to evaluate current and future proposals for urban change and to stimulate a nationwide reassessment of urban-redevelopment policies.

After World War II, decay of cities began imperceptibly, camouflaged by a heady postwar prosperity and a government-encouraged migration from cities to suburbs. Few understood where those postwar forces would lead. The Federal Housing Administration and the Veterans Administration programs, for example, subsidized homes for nearly fourteen million families.[1] New construction sped along in the suburbs and the federal highway program provided easy new access to the new developments. At the same time, the federal Urban Renewal Program in two decades after World War II demolished 404,000 low- and middle-income urban units, replacing them with only 41,580 units for the same population.[2] Millions of additional dollars from Washington poured into the suburban infrastructures necessary for residential and commercial development that would lure the middle class out of the cities. Millions also poured into the cities to rehouse the urban poor, at the same time segregating and ghettoizing our cities in new ways.[3] Too often, physical solutions compound instead of solve social problems.

Urban-renewal projects erased a significant portion of the densely built and highly centralized heart of urban America, caused huge social and economic disruptions in whole regions and accelerated the decline of cities in the guise of noble goals. In the 1950s and 1960s, few people in government advocated *reinforcing* rather than *replacing* existing neighborhoods, and no programs fit that goal. Today, advocates are many and efforts—mostly community-based—are laudable. But public and private support is meager in contrast to the big money that continues to pour primarily into the big, the overwhelming and the inappropriate.

Urbanism Repeatedly Destroyed in the Name of Renewal

It makes no difference whether or not one subscribes to a conspiracy theory of urban decay—a view which argues that political and economic forces on the one hand purposely allow or encourage decay in some areas so that, on the other hand, the right people or groups can profit later from the area's renewal. The fact remains that urban principles have been habitually violated in the name of "renewal" for decades, and enormous sums of money have been spent badly over many years with little that can be genuinely called success.

One has only to visit New York City's Coney Island, where once both a world-renowned summer resort and amusement area and a vibrant urban neighborhood existed. There a solid working-class, multi-ethnic community living in a mixed urban fabric was systematically undermined with an endless array of dismal but expensive government-sponsored housing mistakes. Now hardly a shred of evidence exists that a community once flourished within walking distance of the once famous amusement park, resort strip and excellent oceanfront beach.* Countless millions and every conceivable government program have been applied here. One local observer maintains that more money per square foot has been spent here to destroy a community than anywhere else. Today, Coney Island is an urban nightmare. The population is even lower than it was before it was "renewed" (59,000, down from 120,000). A segregated community now exists where once there was an ethnically and economically diverse one, and public subsidies are a permanent requirement of neighborhood survival. This site represents one of the largest investments in community rebuilding in the country *and* one of the nation's most visible failures. The cycles of displacement and alienation of the resident population are reinforced by alienating housing projects, isolated from jobs and disconnected from community institutions that foster stability. Coney Island is probably one of the country's best examples of "planned" destruction underwritten by public funds, a catalogue of every failed renewal program known to government.†

Most of all, Coney Island is a laboratory of lessons unlearned. As one drives along Surf Avenue, the neighborhood's central roadway, with spectacular views of the Atlantic just beyond the famous boardwalk, the eye follows almost in disbelief at a building sequence, a sample, it seems, of each government building program and design solution. There are red brick, yellow brick, cast concrete, cross-

* Today the once elegant hotels and restaurants are gone and the Coney Island amusement area—from West Tenth to Nineteenth between Surf and Boardwalk—is an amalgam of fast-food strips, individual amusement offerings and flea markets.
† The irony of Coney Island is that there are still entrepreneurs trying to bring life back to the amusement-park area, or what is left of it. The neighborhood may be gone, but the park still seems to have enough life in it to be rebuilt. Even the remnant community in this endlessly problematic neighborhood has enough life that could be sparked in much the same way as some of the communities examined throughout this book.

shaped high rise with grass all around, slab-shaped high-rise book-ends with grass in between, an S shape, a stepped-back and a V shape. Each represents a new solution to problems made worse by the prior solution, each reflecting no better understanding than the one before.

One can also look at New Haven, Connecticut, where every program since the 1950s has only compounded the problems meant to be solved. New Haven was one of the first cities to start and restart and continue renewing itself at great public expense. It is a model city in the application of government programs in which millions upon millions were spent with the problems growing larger and larger. Now it is Yale University's time to try. In 1987, Benno C. Schmidt, Jr., president of Yale, announced that the university would invest $50 million in endowment and other funds in New Haven housing, commercial and industrial development over five to ten years.

In their book *Restructuring the City: The Political Economy of Urban Redevelopment,* an account of several case studies of urban redevelopment in the 1970s, Susan S. Fainstein and Norman I. Fainstein review physical and social revitalization programs of recent decades in New Haven,[4] concluding that new tax gains were offset by expensive inducements to reluctant developers—"in constant dollars locally raised revenue was no greater in 1978 than it had been in 1962." Fewer new housing units were created than families displaced—"in fact, total new housing construction through 1980 fell more than 1,000 units short of demolition through 1972." The employment-base growth in new sectors was insufficient to offset contractions in the old sectors, and, although economic development did benefit business interests, "there was little evidence to show that New Haven's development program had not destroyed more jobs than it created."

In fact, the Fainsteins note, the "data about New Haven's residents and economy show that the city started out in 1950 in a position similar to that of other small northern manufacturing cities, and ended up in 1980 in the same place as they did." This despite all the money spent to avoid that fate.

Each piece of bad news is bad enough, but saddest of all is the

Fainsteins' observation that "the most important effect of the first core area projects and then those in the next ring was to produce a continuous flow of displaced persons, as much as one-fifth of the entire population of the city was uprooted between 1956 and 1974. Community social networks were in part destroyed by the very officials who sought to stop decay and make New Haven slumless."

Warnings Have Long Been Ignored

"Cataclysmic, automotive and suburban: these have been the pervasive characteristics of Urban Redevelopment in America," wrote Vincent Scully in his perceptive book *American Architecture and Urbanism,*[5] which, although published twenty years ago, seems as pertinent as ever. Scully described what was occurring at the time in New Haven as being reflective of this process. He described the "renewal" process by which low-income neighborhoods had been decimated by clearance, rebuilding* and highway construction and how following the announcement of the mere "intention of redeveloping" one neighborhood, known as the "Hill," "the disintegration of the district accelerated at once, and over the long interval of waiting which ensued, because the future was now uncertain for it." Then Scully noted:

> We can hardly be surprised that New Haven's own special riot during the summer of 1967 exploded in the "Hill," with this threat hanging over it. Though comparatively minor by current standards, the disturbance set up tremors that were felt as far as Washington, because New Haven had been heavily propagandized as a model city. The mayor of New Haven denied this title, and unlike the mayor of Newark, who blamed "outside agitators" for his

---

* Scully noted: "Redevelopment has demolished about 5,000 living units of the poor in New Haven during the past twelve years or so but has built only about 1,507, of which about 793 have been luxury housing and 445 middle-income, with only 12 low-income public-housing units, and 257 for the elderly, constructed during that period."

troubles, [Richard] Lee stated that it was merely "Urban America, 1967," which was at fault.

The pattern focused on by Scully continued, as the Fairsteins' more recent assessment indicates. New Haven applied all the conventional programs, built almost all the formula gimmicks, experienced all the ups and downs of most older cities although not many have the stabilizing anchor of a prestigious university, and wound up no better and no worse, except that it is permanently dependent on massive infusions of government monies.

Urban critic Jane Jacobs has observed appropriately: "We seem to have no ways of extricating ourselves from development traps because by now so many people, so many enterprises, so many governments and so many once vigorous cities, too, have come to depend on incomes contrived through city-killing policies and trans-actions."

In the 1980s, inappropriate and unnecessarily expensive schemes are still destroying our cities in the false name of revitalization. More modest, appropriate and creative alternatives exist that could achieve the pronounced goals with minimal, if any, damage. Invariably, the oversized and overpriced are promoted by the well-known and well-connected. Also invariably, the oversized and overpriced are fueled by large amounts of federal funds. It is a bankrupting cycle.

This book calls into question much of today's conventional development being done in the name of community rebuilding and renewal. It highlights the variety of small successes making a big difference on the urban landscape and advocates changing some of the ways in which we develop and preserve our cities. But it is not my purpose here to create new rules that can easily be transplanted into "plans" and "formulas." Instead, I intend to report on the forces shaping our cities, to examine the qualities that make neighborhoods and cities work and to identify criteria by which one can evaluate the development policies of any city.

The evidence is everywhere that there is a fundamental national problem underlying the crisis of our cities. As long as a permanent underclass and permanent unemployment exist on the present scale, fundamental urban problems will remain. Our economy no longer develops the jobs suitable for a critical portion of our urban population. The distinction must be made between different pools of labor—for example, those engaged in short-term construction jobs and those engaged in long-term production and service jobs. Whatever we do about rebuilding cities won't matter without more long-term productive jobs for the minimally educated and minimally skilled.

Recognition of this basic economic reality underscores the urgency of redirecting urban-development strategies and priorities. Much of the urban development criticized in this book exacerbates national economic problems. Many of the successful rebirth stories create people-building as well as product-building jobs without economically and socially destructive dislocation. The stories show that thinking small in a big way works.

Who Are the Real Experts?

In the years of research and travel that went into this book, I was staggered by how often I found things not to be what experts said. Over and over I found reality in contradiction to the prevailing expertise. Consequently, the overriding question in urban matters is: Who are the real experts?

Experts pronounced beyond redemption Seattle's Pioneer Square,* the city's original downtown—minutes from Puget Sound—which had been rebuilt after an 1889 fire swept through it. The brick, stone and cast-iron buildings, rich in ornamentation and detail, served the city well during the boom years of lumber and beyond but, like so many downtowns, had badly deteriorated by the 1960s. The robust and graceful buildings—large and small, loft and office buildings

---

* Pioneer Square is actually a small park at the gateway of the old downtown, but the whole area took on that name with the designation of the Pioneer Square Historic District in 1970. The historic district was forty blocks at first and later was expanded to sixty-five blocks.

alike—were mostly vacant except for bars, flophouses, missions and thrift shops. Experts declared the area of no use except as a raze-and-rebuild urban-renewal project. Citizens fought the bulldozer and fostered instead Pioneer Square, an interesting mix of offices, art galleries, restaurants, bookstores and boutiques in a variety of building styles and ages only a short walk from the waterfront. The concentrated diversity of Pioneer Square is urbanism at its best. Today, many cities search for a Pioneer Square equivalent.

An added significance to this story is that Seattle got the momentum of Pioneer Square—and other forward-thinking projects*—going without tax incentives and big Washington, D.C., funding programs, and at a time when city spirits were lowest and financial woes highest, notes architect Arthur Skolnick, the advocate who was most responsible for the vision of Pioneer Square and who successfully persuaded Mayor Wes Ullman of the merit of preservation. "Seattle needed a boost," Skolnick remembers. "After the high of the 1962 World's Fair came the bust when the bottom fell out for Boeing, Seattle's biggest employer. Seattle turned itself around by looking at its resources and dusting off its existing environment, getting to know itself again by recognizing what is unique about it."

Experts pronounced Manhattan's "Hell's Hundred Acres"—between Houston and Canal streets, from the Hudson to the East River—dead and thus expendable to make way for a highway. The once bustling center of light industry and manufacturing, located just south of Greenwich Village, was slowly losing some of those businesses in keeping with the shifting economy of postwar America. With the announcement of the highway, the exodus accelerated to almost stampede proportions. Experts pronounced the area and its buildings anachronistic. Many manufacturing businesses—probably with years of life left if they were not uprooted—left the city or closed

---

* This was also when Seattle created one of the most imaginative new parks, Gasworks Park, on a northern shore of Lake Union, converting an old gas refinery to a spectacular recreational site: demolishing some structures, turning most of it into an industrial sculpture, neutralizing the soil, converting machinery sheds into a kids' playground—turning an industrial eyesore into an urban delight.

up, taking the low-skilled jobs with them. Who cared to stay around to watch the building fall? Surely no new tenants considered moving into a neighborhood destined for demolition—except for artists looking for cheap, if temporary, lofts. The artists like their new neighborhood. They and other citizens challenged the explanations of experts and fought the highway with a fierceness and persistence that made it a textbook case. The highway was stopped by those citizen activists. SoHo (the acronym is from "South of Houston"), a vibrant mixed-use area brimming with many small innovations, was the result. Today, every city searches for a SoHo equivalent.

Experts predicted financial doom for the precedent-setting preservation of Boston's Faneuil Hall Marketplace and Pittsburgh's Station Square, two very different historic landmarks battered by age and neglect. Downtowns were dead, the experts declared, no place for bold and innovative restoration schemes that include a mix of commercial uses. Today, both landmarks are models of urban recycling and commercial successes, the envy of real-estate investors trying to turn them into magic formulas.

Experts questioned the business sense of the refurbishers of the Oviatt Building, an Art Deco masterpiece, and the Biltmore Hotel, a classic in turn-of-the-century elegance, both in downtown Los Angeles, and the creator of the River Café, the restaurant on a barge in the shadow of the Brooklyn Bridge. Those bold ventures are models of defiant entrepreneurism. Today, investors look high and low for comparable business ventures.

Experts ignored the Victorian Districts of Savannah, Galveston and San Francisco, while people moved in and rebuilt them into marvels of urban renaissance. Today it is difficult to conceive that there was a time when the splendid survivors of an era of grace and craft were not valued.

These success stories are the successes that "experts" considered inconceivable. These are the stories of innovative efforts the experts thought too small to make a big difference. But, experts to the contrary, these are the stories of significant change—genuine, appropriate and positive.

It is not that "expert" planners, architects, developers and government policy-makers don't ever offer sensible and appealing solutions to commercial decay or neighborhood neglect. Of course they do. They just don't leave much room for either the breakthrough of the unconventional idea or the contribution of the on-site expert, such as the neighborhood resident or businessman—the city "user" whose instinctive judgment sometimes is at odds with professionally developed plans. Genuine participatory planning, in which public input is desired, not just tolerated, is rare. Public meetings are many; acceptance of the public's preference is rare.

Too often, moreover, experts ignore how solutions to earlier problems sometimes cause new urban ills. Experts—such as planners and urban theorists—are faddish, even fickle. Planners, for example, once declared density* bad and the thinning out of cities good. Now density is in and thinness out, although a distinction between density and congestion is seldom made. Density comes when many people are in the same place doing things that gain strength from their interaction; congestion results when there are so many of them that interaction becomes difficult, access in and out unpleasant and frustration high.

Planners once decreed that urban uses should be sorted and separated. Now they say that they should be mixed and in "context," even if that "mix" is prescribed by formulas akin to shopping-mall planning instead of the natural development that evolves in a real place over time, and the "context" is a replacement, not an addition. Many of today's "expert" urban-planning and development problem-solvers are the very "experts" of yesteryear whose earlier "solutions" led to today's problems. They were as much the "experts" then as they are now. Being skeptical about experts is healthy.

I did not begin the research for this book with this view. Yet, as I followed the path pointed out by experts, as I found things not to be what they were describing and as I found stark contrasts between the

---

* Technically, density refers to the number of people per acre and overcrowding is measured by the number of people per bedroom.

real and the rendering, I believed the experts less and less, no matter how well-intentioned and/or well-trained they were. Scores of people *instinctively* know what is right and wrong with what they see happening around them, but are mystified by their disagreement with the professionals and intimidated by the experts' dismissal of their views. This book puts great stock in the "instinctivists," the "professional generalists," the "professional amateur."

So much is happening so quickly and in such a big way that alternative directions are urgent before we lose the opportunity to renew our cities and wind up only with the more expensive, less desirable option of replacement. We have not learned well from past mistakes.

For every complex, difficult problem, there is a simple, easy solution . . . and it is wrong.

—H. L. MENCKEN

Part One

THINKING SMALL IN A BIG WAY

Chapter One

PROCESS
IS
PEOPLE

■

An environment that cannot be changed invites its own destruction. We prefer a world that can be modified progressively against a background of valued remains, a world in which one can leave a personal mark alongside the marks of history.

—KEVIN LYNCH, "What Time Is This Place?"[1]

To visit Savannah, Georgia, at the end of March is to experience the kind of spiritual revival that any resident of a winter-ridden Northern city welcomes. Bright red and pink azaleas are everywhere, in little patches of front yards as well as in big clumps of city squares. The brilliant color of the bell-shaped flower is interspersed with the more subdued tones of pink-and-white dogwood in equal profusion. Savannah, with its 148,000 people on the south bank of the Savannah River, is a remarkable, open-space city. It doesn't have dull or unused areas of greenery. It has, instead, charming squares of varying size and character, each with a different landscape design and often a different purpose. Streets are rich in variety and full of pleasant surprises—an unexpected store on a residential block, fanciful mansions facing simple row houses, charming alleys or lanes with elegant carriage houses, small businesses and family backyards. And while it is a city filled with classic Southern architecture, its diversity of architectural treasures is limitless.

Many people think of this coastal city solely as a tourist attraction and mention it in the same breath with Charleston or New Orleans—travelogue towns, rich in Southern history. But Savannah has a robust and diverse economy and offers a lot to its resident population beyond its splendid beauty and heritage. Savannah was, of course, spared the fate of other Southern cities. Union General William Tecumseh Sherman reached Savannah in 1864, near the end of his "march to the sea" that left Atlanta and much of the Confederacy in ruin. When he reached this major commercial port, he sheathed his sword and sent President Lincoln his famous telegram: "I beg to present you, as a Christmas gift, the city of Savannah. . . ." Still, many an American city has been spared the destruction of war or fire only to be ravaged by senseless twentieth-century planning and development, justified in the name of progress.

Leopold Adler II, an energetic former investment banker in his late sixties and the driving force behind Savannah's revitalization, likes to say that "Savannahians voted down urban-renewal projects three times as a Communist plot." Many communities around the country rejected urban-renewal schemes in the 1950s and 1960s because they feared that with "government money" would come "interference from Washington." In so doing, Savannahians did for their city a favor comparable to Sherman's a century ago.

Savannahians did more than reject mindless schemes for doubtful progress. When downtown was at its nadir with almost total disinvestment and abandonment, they reclaimed abandoned and dilapidated downtown mansions and row houses of bygone eras, house by house, row by row, small bit by small bit. The rescued houses attracted members of a new upper-middle class, many the children of parents who earlier were encouraged to flee similar housing for the suburban promise. The city restored the historic waterfront that dated from the time when Cotton was King and brought its once bustling cotton warehouses to life again for commerce, retail trade and pedestrian pleasures. They replanted open spaces in the same design and spirit in which they were originally created. Then, with foresight and Savannah savvy, they set out to bring a similar new life to an adjacent neighborhood, the Victorian District, in a way which did not force out the urban poor. They recognized the value of the existing population, not just the historic neighborhood which that population occupied.

Historic Preservation Renews Downtown

The rebirth of this Victorian District, Savannah's first suburb, is a very late chapter in the complete Savannah revitalization story. It had its beginnings in the historic-preservation movement. The saving of historic buildings in many cities has been the earliest effort to revitalize decaying neighborhoods. Many of today's gemlike neighborhoods have pioneering historic-preservationists to thank for their rescue. The Victorian District would probably never have been saved, if preservationists—investment bankers as well as Junior Leaguers and the proverbial little old ladies in tennis shoes—had not mastered their revitalization techniques first in the restoration of Savannah's older downtown core. This earlier downtown effort started small and with a limited focus, the rescue of endangered historic mansions. In time, that effort broadened into one of the nation's best revitalization success stories. The impact is nationwide.

Downtown Savannah, two and a half square miles, is a designated national historic district, listed on the National Register of Historic Places. Its preservation started in the 1950s, earlier than that of most cities. Over two decades, more than one thousand eighteenth- and nineteenth-century buildings were restored and adapted to twentieth-century uses with an investment of $400 million.

Preservationists led by Lee Adler purchased and resold strategically located downtown property. He and other preservationists had to tap many different kinds of financial resources (friends, bankers, foundations) in order to buy property—commercial and residential—and resell it with restrictions that guaranteed its prompt restoration and long-term future. When they started, in the 1950s, the urban-renewal approach was riding high in national popularity. Anybody standing in the way of a bulldozer was criticized for stifling progress. Preservationists couldn't persuade people to save a building; they had to buy the property themselves. Through the buy-save-and-resell method, preservationists saved enough of downtown Savannah for a broad revitalization to take hold. This is the downtown to which tourists, planners and investors flock today.

A Model City

Downtown Savannah is a remarkable segment of city, splendidly laid out around English-style squares in 1733 by its English founder, James Edward Oglethorpe. Its basic layout is as appealing today as it was 250 years ago. The logic of the plan remains strong and is a textbook case taught in city-planning courses around the country.

Oglethorpe was a reformer in the British House of Commons who persuaded King George II that it was both good politics and good works to found a new colony to give worthy but poor Englishmen a new opportunity in the New World.* In 1733, Oglethorpe landed eighteen miles from the mouth of the Savannah River to establish Georgia, the thirteenth and poorest colony. He brought a plan to lay out a city around a series of small squares, an adaptation of the London he knew. The public squares could be used for defense in time of war or marketplaces in time of peace. They have been called justifiably the central genius of the plan because each became the quiet oasis or front lawn for almost every home—not unlike the common in New England villages. Around each square were forty house lots. The east and west sides of each square were reserved for public buildings, churches or important residences. Behind the rows of

---

* An early model public policy of giving poor people new opportunities.

houses facing the square were service lanes where carriage houses and servants' quarters were built later.

During the ten years that Oglethorpe remained before returning to England, only four squares were built, but his plan worked so well that subsequent leaders followed the plan until there were twenty-four squares in all, fanning south from the river's edge where commerce was concentrated. Twenty-one landscaped parks remain. Three gave way to highway "improvements"—new roads—and one of those was reclaimed and restored. Another, the site of the old City Market, was destroyed to make way for a parking garage in 1954 despite loud public protest.

Savannah prospered as a port, serving from its earliest days as the coast's gateway city. With Eli Whitney's invention of the cotton gin in 1792 near Savannah, prosperity was secure. By the middle of the nineteenth century, the railroad linked Savannah to inland routes.

Much of the original waterfront burned during major fires of 1796 and 1820, but fine homes of brick and stone quickly replaced them. During the period from 1800 to 1860, some of the most handsome structures were built. After the Civil War Savannah struggled for a while, but it eventually regained its position as a major cotton port. Prosperity continued until the boll weevil devastated the industry in the 1920s. The paper industry, specifically the manufacture of cardboard and paper out of Southern pine, brought new economic growth in the 1930s, but the paper mills located upriver from Savannah's center.

During the first half of the twentieth century, the economy mostly stagnated. Neglect set in, and new growth moved south of town to the suburbs in the 1920s and continued to do so through the 1950s, paralleling the population and growth shift of so many American cities, large and small. Some important downtown buildings were destroyed, but most were converted to crowded tenements or just left empty to decay.

Also, during the 1950s, some old commercial buildings gave way to incompatible new ones. And then, in 1954, the fine old City Market in the middle of Ellis Square was demolished for an ugly parking garage. Ellis, the third square to be developed in the city, had been the site of the public market from its founding in 1763 to its demolition in 1954. Its loss proved to be a turning point for the city.

Until then, there had been little organized preservation activity in Savannah despite the growing concern of a number of citizens. In the 1940s, one family, the Hillyers, officers of the local gas company, saved and restored thirty buildings in the area of the Trustees Garden, site of America's first experimental agricultural garden. Later, the property was bought by a statewide gas company, which still owns it. The subsequent destruction of the City Market and a plan to demolish the Isaiah Davenport House, an exceptional example of Georgian architecture built between 1815 and 1820, catalyzed the establishment in 1954 of the Historic Savannah Foundation by seven local women. These women and their counterparts in many American communities were the earliest front-line fighters for the preservation of our cities. For a long time, the task of saving the built environment from the mindless bulldozer *was* organized by women who cared early. Probably because those women were outside the power structure—even if their husbands were inside—so much was needlessly lost.

Downtown's Rebirth Started with One House

The rescue of the Davenport House was an important first, establishing the principle of saving a building at any price to get things started. The foundation raised approximately $20,000 to purchase the house, which had been used as a tenement for eleven families before it was abandoned. The foundation then restored it as a part-time museum and got another organization to use the basement for offices.

But in the mid-1950s urban-renewal fever swept the country. Demolition outpaced the capacity of the Historic Savannah Foundation. In 1959 the foundation did not have the funds to save Marshall Row, four excellent 1850s row houses built of "Savannah Gray" brick—a brick kilned from Savannah River clay—with marble steps leading to the parlor floors. Lee Adler got three other Savannah businessmen together and bought the property, and the Historic Savannah Foundation assumed the interest payments on the mortgage. The carriage houses that had stood behind Marshall Row had already been demolished. Adler first purchased the land under Marshall Row for $45,000. Then he had to buy the four buildings from a demolition company, which had acquired them for the bricks. There was a great demand for Savannah Gray bricks—which were no longer being manufactured—among builders of new FHA-financed suburban homes, and many old downtown structures were threatened. (Ironically, a parallel phenomenon was a catalyst for the historic-preservation movement in Charleston, where, in the 1920s and '30s, dealers razed historic buildings to obtain valuable wood paneling for which there was a growing market.) Savannah Gray brick was selling for ten cents a brick, compared to three cents for common brick. The demolition company paid $6,000 for the Marshall Row houses. Adler paid $9,000 to the would-be demolisher, who then asked him, "Where do you want the bricks?" Adler replied, "Just leave them standing."

In 1962, the foundation produced an inventory of the entire two-and-a-half-square-mile downtown area to illustrate the vastness of the historic resource and encourage its preservation. (Charleston had been the first city, in 1939, to do this.) The foundation also organized house tours and block parties and published brochures celebrating the heritage of downtown Savannah. Every aspect of preservation was sold as vigorously as Procter and Gamble sells soap, and the business community was persuaded of the untapped tourist potential. The foundation worked with the Chamber of Commerce to create a tourist and convention bureau, with a visitors' center set up in the abandoned 1860 Central Georgia Railroad Station.

Adler and the foundation also persuaded city officials to use Urban Renewal funds for conservation and preservation. The 1954 Housing Act in fact had authorized the use of such funds for housing rehabilitation, but government's preference is usually easy replacement, so rehabilitation never became a meaningful part of the urban-renewal program nationwide. In 1961, rehabilitation rather than replacement was still an unconventional notion. Actually, the city had little choice. Voters had opposed urban-renewal clearance schemes several times. The public forced local political leaders to be innovative and turn to rehabilitation as a means of gaining federal money.

Historic Savannah in 1961 bought and resold for restoration eight 1870s and 1880s row houses in the Troup Ward neighborhood. Then the foundation persuaded the city to use Urban Renewal money to buy and renovate thirty-six additional houses, many of them vacant, and resell them by making low-interest rehabilitation loans available to purchasers. This was, in a way, a forerunner of the homesteading programs that evolved in the 1970s, and it was one of the first programs in the country to use Urban Renewal funds for conservation rather than new construction.

Individuals Count

Lee Adler, friendly but tough, is unafraid to make his feelings known to anyone. His wife, Emma Morel Adler, who, like him, is a native Savannahian with roots solidly in the local aristocracy, is equally committed an activist, but more subdued than her husband. Emma Adler says with a laugh, "Lee jokes that we can't go to a wedding in this city where he hasn't sued everyone but the bride." In the early days of the Savannah preservation effort, it was necessary to take the battles to court.

Lee and Emma Adler got involved in preservation at a crucial time in Savannah's story. One of the seven forward-thinking women who founded the Historic Savannah Foundation was Lee's mother, Elinor Adler. Lee's great-grandparents were Savannah merchants and real-estate owners, and his grandfather was an important leader of Temple Mickve Israel. (This congregation was founded in July 1733, just five months after the first settlers landed in the new colony. Its present Gothic Revival building was built in 1878.) For decades, Adler's Department Store on the main shopping street was the city's retail anchor, until a fire in the 1950s destroyed it. For a while, Lee was in the family business, but he left it in 1956 to become an investment banker. After the fire, other Adler family members moved the store to a suburban mall, reopening it as a small boutique.

Emma's family continued to live downtown when many of her

friends' parents chose to leave. "My friends had to travel in for school, but I was the only one already here and I loved it," she recalls. "People were leaving for the suburbs to build more comfortable houses with central heating rather than modernize the ones they lived in here." Her father, president of a local shipping company and owner of Savannah real estate, had "an intuitive recognition of quality," she says, and he chose to keep the family in their spacious 1878 double house next door to where Grandma lived.

Lee and Emma Adler became preservation activists soon after their wedding in 1953—Lee in the Historic Savannah Foundation right after his mother helped found it, and Emma in the Junior League, an organization that gave crucial support to preservation. Later, Emma helped save Savannah's Massie School—Georgia's oldest surviving public school, an 1855 Greek Revival building designed by John S. Norris—and turned it into a heritage center, heavily used by Savannah's schools. Today the Massie Heritage Information Center has a most impressive permanent exhibit showing the elements of Greek, Roman and Gothic architecture and their influence on Savannah's architectural heritage. The center's programs are a model for teaching local history in a public-school system.

The Marshall Row success gave impetus to a new, aggressive preservation movement, but it was not until 1964 that a significant effort began. The Historic Savannah Foundation established a $200,000 revolving fund to purchase threatened properties and resell them to new owners who would restore them. The revolving fund later became a popular preservation tool around the country. The fund is constantly replenished as properties are bought and sold, even if it is diminished by some degree of loss.

"We sold the revolving-fund idea to contributors," says Adler, "first on the basis that buildings are worth money and shouldn't be discarded easily. We assumed a business approach immediately. We tried to think and operate just like a developer. And just like a developer who doesn't let go easily, we didn't, either."

During the next decade, Historic Savannah used its revolving fund to buy and resell endangered properties all over downtown. In the first eighteen months, it purchased fifty-four structures and sparked $1.5 million worth of restoration work. In almost every case, it was just in time, just before the bulldozer. When, for example, a local bank planned to demolish a valuable historic building to provide a customer parking lot, Adler persuaded the bank to hold off. Then the bank found another property suitable for parking, and the foundation bought the endangered building. Some of this real-estate activity incurred losses. Some of it was profitable. Foundation leaders recognized, however, that they had to assume the financial burden of showing the way to the practical use of old buildings or preservation would not be achieved.

The foundation stretched its limited funds by buying one of a pair of buildings or one in a strategic row, thus preventing easy assemblage by speculators who would demolish. Gradually, and with increasing momentum, the public, the banks and the business community started buying for restoration, not demolition.

By the early 1980s, most of the approximately 1,100 downtown buildings had been saved and restored at a cost of more than $400 million in private investments. By 1987, the annual tourist business exceeded $200 million in revenue, and overnight visitors numbered more than one million. This was greater than the payroll of Savannah's largest industry, the Union Camp Corporation, a paper company, which employed nearly five thousand people with a $100 million annual payroll. Privately sponsored restorations with conventional financing paralleled the efforts of Historic Savannah. This private-market activity would never have occurred without the groundwork of the preservationists. Inevitably, local residents are the only people able to rekindle private-sector confidence in the viability of urban neighborhoods as investments.

After his election in 1970, Savannah Mayor John Rousakis became one of preservation's many ardent converts. "I was one of those advocating the ripping up of squares to make way for new roads," Rousakis says. "Preservation gave the city new pride. The spirit was deflated. We had lost our Air Force base. A lot of property was for sale. Gloom set in. Many in the business community thought about moving south of downtown. As preservation blossomed, they changed their mind. When the city administration committed itself to preservation, too, the business community knew it wasn't just a pie-in-the-sky civic movement."

Adler chuckles at the mayor's words, for before this mayor cooperation with City Hall had not been easy. "Once Rousakis saw what was happening, he gave support to it," Adler says. "Now he loves to show everyone who comes to town what's been done."

Savannah has a remarkable track record of revitalization success. Inevitably, however, a number of modern eyesores—including an ugly hotel that replaced a vintage Victorian structure, and a dismal convention center—intruded upon the appealing landscape. The banality of the new structures stands in stark contrast to the city's predominant beauty.

Many positive things resulted from the city's physical rebirth. Savannah's economy is in good shape and port activity strong. Restoration was coupled with port expansion and modernization, so Savannah was competing nicely with other ports for container shipping. Military bases nearby added personnel. An aircraft manufacturer and an automobile assembly plant moved in. Paper mills, among the largest employers in the area, spent more than $30 million cleaning up the pollution that had been pouring into the Savannah River. The mills' odors still permeated the city's air, but expectations were that those too would diminish. Other traditional economic indicators pointed up for the city—bank deposits, retail sales, utility usage and new connections. The economy remained diverse, but tourism was a major economic contributor.

Twenty-five years earlier, Lee Adler was talking until he was blue in the face to persuade political and business leaders of the value of promoting tourism. Now it was the shrine at which almost all of them were worshipping. But while it is one thing to make the most of inherent tourist appeal while attending to the basic needs of a place, it is another if local concerns take second place to the deceptive appeal of the tourist dollar. Nowadays, too many communities are grasping at this new "solution" to complex ills.* Potential pitfalls associated with other outsider-oriented solutions are true of the tourist quest as well and constitute an issue worth a close look.

The Threat of an "Ice Cream Economy"

Providing amply and diversely for resident businesses must be a paramount concern of public policy, more than responding to the needs of suburban commuters, tourists or distant corporate executives. Too many municipalities seek to accommodate visitors at the expense of local residents and businesses. The downtown resident is one of the most valuable assets cities have lost during decades of outward movement. Only recently is the value of their presence becoming widely understood. A permanent consumer/user populace to support the stores, to work in the offices, to eat at restaurants, to attend the theater, to populate the streets, to make life interesting—this is what any downtown needs. Tourism, however, is viewed too often as a painless, clean, relatively recession-resistant industry that requires little in the way of infrastructure and that can help offset serious economic weaknesses. This is deceptive.

Several years ago, I attended a convention of the National Trust for Historic Preservation, an annual event attended by a higher proportion of local residents to public officials than many such conventions. I attended a workshop dealing with historic neighborhoods and tourism. Across the country, small towns and large cities were awakening to the tourist potential and were looking for ways to cash in. Since the Bicentennial, the rediscovery of our own rich history spurred national tourism to the point of tourist-mania. But at the tourism workshop I listened with a sense of impending doom as Frances Edmunds, the spearhead of the exemplar citizen preservation

---

* As *Planning* magazine noted, February 1987: "Tourism has, in fact, become a major factor in the U.S. economy, employing nearly 15 million Americans last year. State and local leaders have come to view it as a clean, relatively recession-resistant industry that requires little in the way of infrastructure and that can help offset the leakage of manufacturing jobs."

efforts in Charleston, South Carolina, warned disbelieving listeners how excessive numbers of tourist buses and crowds intruded terribly on the daily lives of residents of her historic city. Despite Edmunds' warnings, the big rush was on, and in the 1980s hotel/convention centers and other outsider-directed formulas, rather than the more appropriate projects and programs geared to the local populace, have become favorite downtown "revitalizers." The danger is that these projects either fail miserably or work so well that the outsiders overwhelm the local ambience, new hotels dwarf the scale of the historic locale, outside vehicular traffic impedes local movement, and residents and locally oriented businesses are replaced by tourists and tourist-oriented activity. Any place left primarily to tourists ceases to be a real place and eventually loses its appeal even to tourists. As Robert McNulty, president of Partners for Livable Places, wrote about the mushrooming tourism in the Fall 1981 issue of *Livability Digest,* which was devoted to tourism issues:

> . . . this demand has caused a growing sameness in our new architectural standards and tourist developments, which erodes the regional character and flavor that first stimulated people's desire to see different places. . . . As too many people congest our unique cultural areas at the same time, the unique sense of place diminishes.
> The blend of people, place, and visual character within our natural and built environments increasingly resembles a nonrenewable resource.

In my summer community on Fire Island, a thirty-three-mile-long narrow sliver of land off Long Island, New York, with the Atlantic on one side and the Great South Bay on the other, the tourist, or day-tripper, phenomenon grew to such overwhelming proportions in the 1970s that limiting the outsider influx was essential to stem the critical exodus of residents. A drain of the local populace was threatening the qualities that made the community worth visiting. After much controversy and many fierce political battles, we cooled expansion of tourist-oriented development and imposed visitor restrictions in order to maintain the village's character and charm. We became known as the "Land of No." Despite the shrill warnings of some business owners, however, tourists and day-trippers were hardly chased away and the businesses still thrived, but, most important, the exodus of local residents slowed and new families moved in. With good reason, residents fear the impact of tourists. "Tourists do not leave a city untouched by their presence," wrote the late urban-design professor Donald Appleyard. "A classic instance of the observer affecting the observed, the tourist, through his demands, subtly and sometimes drastically changes the character of a place."[2]

The phenomenon is international in scope. When fears of terrorist reprisals following the spring 1986 attack on Libya kept so many Americans away from Europe, tourism in Europe plummeted. The economic distress in England gave credibility to critics of a few years earlier who cautioned against the growing dependency on tourism as a substitute fix to fundamental economic weaknesses. *The New York Times* reported that in prior years the British press "was filled with foreboding at the onslaught" of American tourists each summer. "The *Guardian* warned darkly that Britain, given its heedless embrace of tourism as a substitute for its dying industries, was in danger of becoming an 'ice cream economy.' If the British were not careful, some cautioned, gum-chewing Americans, loaded with money and ignorant of history, might succeed in appropriating the country as the 51st state. One writer suggested that Britain should simply declare the nation the United Kingdom Theme Park Inc."[3]

Visitors should be accommodated without inappropriately interfering with a locality's essential flow and function. But an essential characteristic of a city is the existence of a multiplicity of uses whose continuation depends on one another. This implies balance. A balance in favor of local uses and users makes the best city.

Savannah Remains a Real Place

Savannah could have become one more tourist mecca, vulnerable to the vagaries of a highly volatile industry. Instead, that delicate balance is in place and its appeal to the resident as well as the visitor remains strong. That is one of the most important lessons of Savannah's metamorphosis. Historic preservation was a driving economic force in the city's rebirth, but a functioning place, not an antebellum theme park, was the result. The restoration process moved slowly, in small doses, initiated by citizens. Small successes made a big difference and reinforced and redeveloped the failing economy.

The hallmarks of Savannah's early metamorphosis are clear. Citizen activists prevented the city from being seduced by the misguided government "rebuilding" programs of the 1950s and 1960s. The city's basic urban fabric was restored instead to modern use. Savannah now has a clean, comfortable, elegant downtown of manageable size appealing to both residents and outsiders. But the most interesting chapter in the Savannah story has been the later rejuvenation of the Victorian District, a sizable low-income area. The energy that grew out of the 1950s and 1960s effort stimulated the same process in Savannah's Victorian District in the 1970s. The process had worked in one part of town, why shouldn't it in another? Just as Savannah was ahead of others in preserving its historic downtown core, so it led in preserving another architecturally rich area without displacing the poor who lived there. This more recent effort clearly confronted and skillfully answered some of the crucial urban dilemmas of the decade.

Chapter Two

SAVANNAH'S VICTORIAN DISTRICT

■

HUD is telling people in each neighborhood they have a problem unique to their neighborhood and to which government can not help. We thought we were alone, until we started learning from each other.

Bankers say people who want to stay in the city need a psychiatrist, not a banker. They are wrong. Appraisers going into old neighborhoods need two policemen with them to appraise each building—one with them while looking inside and one to stand guard outside.

*These are the people who give old neighborhoods a
bad name.*

—GALE CINCOTTA, Chicago activist, founder
of National People's Action, speaking at a
1977 Savannah neighborhood conference*

Victorian District is an appropriate name for the forty-five square
blocks (162 acres) of predominantly wood-framed houses that range
from the splendidly fanciful to the crisply elegant. The short, tree-
lined blocks contain a mix of clapboard or brick row houses and
freestanding two- and three-story homes. Some houses are sparse in
architectural detail. Some have porches, bay windows, turrets and all
kinds of ornamental trim, so popular in the late nineteenth century
when one could assemble a gingerbread fantasy out of a mail-order
catalogue. Some are brightly painted in bold color combinations,
rivaling those of San Francisco's and Galveston's quintessential
Victorian Districts. Small service and grocery businesses filling basic
neighborhood needs remain on a few corners. Empty weed-filled lots
where homes once stood are still noticeable, but their number is
slowly diminishing as infill housing is added to the area.

The Victorian District is now part of downtown but was, in a
way, Savannah's first suburb—dating back to the 1800s. It lies just
south of the older downtown. Much of Oglethorpe's original city
was rebuilt, after fires in 1796 and 1820, in brick and stucco to meet
a new building code that prohibited the use of wood-frame construction. The Victorian District, however, was south of the area covered
by that code, so that skillful carpenters were able to express their full
creative energy in wood.

---

* Under Cincotta's leadership, the National People's Action grass-roots and anti-
redlining campaign and lobbying efforts led to the Community Reinvestment Act of
1977, a significant law requiring financial institutions to serve the poor as well as the
rich. The act also allowed for community challenge of bank policies that negatively
affect low-income neighborhoods, forcing many banks to reexamine their neighborhood disinvestment policies.

For decades, the Victorian District was the home of Savannah's solid middle class. By the turn of the century, Savannah was the second biggest cotton port* in America and the largest exporter of naval stores. Shippers and cotton brokers lived in the lavish brick and stucco mansions downtown. The people who worked for them, the bank cashiers, store clerks and railroad workers, established themselves in the Victorian District. Then, like so many middle-class neighborhoods, the district fell upon hard times in the 1950s. Spurred by the federal government's postwar enthusiasm to encourage the search for the two-car suburban dream at the expense of the older downtown neighborhoods, Victorian District residents moved out to greener pastures. Their residences were left to uncaring absentee landlords whose goal was big rental income at minimal maintenance expense, a pattern common in neighborhoods of all our nation's cities.

The Victorian District became the refuge of the black poor, following a pattern typical of older urban neighborhoods. Two to four apartment units were often crowded into a house where once a single family had lived. Property investment, except for a scattered few resident owners, all but ceased. Bank investment fled. Political interest disappeared, except at elections. One by one, even the civic institutions moved out. By the 1970s, many of these architecturally solid houses looked like Tobacco Road, ripe for demolition and redevelopment, and daily were ravaged by vandalism or fire. The area was pronounced irreversibly dead by experts lacking imagination to see beyond the dirt, disuse and decay, and blind to the potential of the people in place. The federal government approved Savannah's designation for urban renewal and promised funds for demolition and development—a promise fortunately never kept. Unusual vision was required to look at some of these falling-down houses and believe they could be restored. Even today, with remaining derelict buildings side by side with lovingly restored residences, it is difficult to believe anyone dared embark on a rebuilding task.

* Savannah's Cotton Exchange was, in effect, the country's national cotton exchange, since prices were set here and in Liverpool, England.

Fresh from leading the successful drive to restore more than 1,100 residential and commercial properties downtown, Lee Adler turned to the Victorian District in the mid-1970s. Adler could recognize an urban trend as well as he could pick a good stock. He knew that the success of the downtown restoration would spread sooner or later. In fact, it already had.

In the 1970s, new practical considerations fostered a conservation trend nationwide. Environmental issues were already recognized when the oil embargo of 1973 caused many to rethink this country's over-dependence on the automobile. For anyone who could read it early, the handwriting was on the wall for suburban economics. High taxes, unending traffic, public-education woes, mushrooming home fuel bills and the expense and headache of commuting, all had helped to make the surburban siren song go flat.* The vitality and diversity of previously abandoned city neighborhoods was appealing once again.

Adler was not content to wait until it was too late to protect the district's resident poor. "Black people built a lot of this town," says Adler. "Some have lived in that neighborhood for thirty years. Yet with sensible rehabilitation, it was clear there could be a stable neighborhood for new and old residents alike."

Adler first tried to interest the Historic Savannah Foundation in shifting some of its interest and its revolving-fund money into the Victorian District. Resistance was firm. The downtown core was as far as the aristocrats of the foundation would go at that time. So Adler and other preservationists organized a nonprofit development corporation, the Savannah Landmark Rehabilitation Project, to focus exclusively on the redevelopment of the Victorian District.

As an activist in the national historic-preservation movement and a member of the board of trustees of the National Trust for Historic Preservation (from 1971 to 1980), Adler saw early that a price was being paid for preservation successes everywhere. The urban poor

---

* The lure of the suburbs will continue to ebb and flow. And although it is hard to imagine it not continuing in some form, the suburban appeal can never again be as overidealized as it was in its earlier stage.

were paying that price, although it was rarely as brutal and extreme as that exacted during the peak of urban-renewal destruction/ construction programs. Adler foresaw two equally grim futures for the Victorian District and its 3,200 residents—two options that confront all old neighborhoods. Deterioration would continue to the point where abandonment and demolition were inevitable. Or middle-class value hunters would transform the area to an upper-income sanctuary. Neither option would allow the poor to remain.

A Broad-based Group Is Formed

The Savannah Landmark Rehabilitation Project was organized in 1974 with a twenty-three-member board of directors—businessmen, bankers, ministers, social workers, a landscape architect, a judge, neighborhood residents and other civic leaders. From the start, it set an ambitious goal: to purchase and restore one third or more of the Victorian District's 1,200 units for low-income tenants, always a step ahead of land speculators and middle-income home purchasers. Savannah Landmark began a program of gradual rehabilitation that employed low-income residents of the area and provided appealing and affordable rental units to low-income tenants in the district. Slumlords were bought out and the abandoned units restored. In time, improvements became visible. Black and white middle-class families had already started buying in, but now the free market accelerated. By then, however, enough of the Victorian District was secure, so that low-income housing was guaranteed and no massive change disrupted either the social or the physical fabric of the community. With more prosperous buyers renovating the remaining housing in the area, eventually the Victorian District could be one of the most racially and economically mixed neighborhoods in the country.

In the beginning, Savannah Landmark leaders recognized the long-range nature of the goal and that it would be accomplished slowly, but they did not anticipate the kind of obstacles they would face. They had one great advantage, however, over most neighborhood preservation projects. Savannah's downtown was already a showcase for preservation. There was a very visible track record of economic and cultural gain. Support of local backers was easier to win, and there were already individuals willing to cosign loans for the purchase of property in the Victorian District. The local minority-owned Carver State Bank provided financing. In fact, the bank's vice-president, Joseph N. Bell, Jr., moved into the area. "I got caught up in the excitement just as Lee had earlier," says Bell. Bell bought and restored a two-family house and moved with his wife and child back from the suburbs. "I had wanted the suburban experience," Bell says with a smile, "but I quickly learned that it was not what I really wanted."

Savannah Landmark's clear advantages were not enough to avoid stumbling blocks. "The learning and gearing-up process took two and a half years," from 1976 to 1979, says Beth Reiter, the group's first executive director. Reiter graduated from the University of Pennsylvania with a degree in architectural history and is, like Adler, a native Savannahian. "In the beginning," Reiter says, "we had no staff, only students doing research on the district to gain the information necessary for government grant applications."

The National Endowment for the Arts provided the first seed money, a $17,000 matching grant for administrative and staff costs. Under the farsighted direction of Robert McNulty, the NEA's Design Arts Program in the 1970s seeded many similar long shots around the country that have since blossomed into full-scale rejuvenation efforts. NEA small grant programs and their state arts council counterparts illustrate well the catalytic value of small, often high-risk grants.* Small grants are flexibility money, and they help legitimize new groups, allowing them to grow and move on, says McNulty. "No one can milk the system with these grants and it is a small amount to invest in people's dreams."

Savannah Landmark sought from the mayor $1 million to rehabilitate fifty units. The mayor—not then an avowed preservationist—

---

* In many of the success stories in this book, small grants provided the seed money that began the process.

denied the request. He could not justify, the mayor said, spending large sums in one neighborhood when he had to consider all Savannah. The federal government was the next step. "Lee had good contacts in Washington," says Reiter, "but it took him fourteen trips to Washington even to get in the door at HUD," the Department of Housing and Urban Development. Through the grapevine, Adler and Reiter heard about the Urban Homesteading Assistance Board (UHAB) located at the Cathedral of St. John the Divine in New York. UHAB, whose role in the South Bronx efforts will be told later, is one of the varied neighborhood technical-assistance organizations that emerged with the neighborhood self-help movement in the mid-1970s. Reiter called the then director of UHAB, Philip St. Georges, for advice. "He warned me that HUD responds only to programs that can be cloned and repeated but often don't fit different local needs."

Savannah Landmark plodded through the government grant process, meeting, applying, pleading, arguing and succeeding. Eventually, the Victorian District became a favorite federal-government showcase. Savannah Landmark hosted a national conference in 1977 focusing on techniques of neighborhood restoration without displacement. From around the country came pioneers in preservation for low-income residents—bankers, neighborhood organizers, "instinctivists," architects and restoration specialists—to exchange expertise and experiences. Meetings were held in some of Savannah's historic black churches, with gospel singing enlivening each session. The three days of meetings were imbued with a spirit of determination. Although Savannah Landmark at that point had only just begun its work, the spotlight was on it. The conference brought together for the first time low-income neighborhood activists and historic-preservationists.

News of the conference and of the Victorian District reached the White House, and Rosalynn Carter came for a tour in December 1978. Savannah Landmark had worked out a three-part funding combination also being used in the South Bronx—a 3 percent federal mortgage for twenty years, a rent subsidy and a CETA (Comprehensive Employment and Training Act) labor-training grant. By 1978, eighteen buildings containing sixty-four housing units had been purchased or optioned. By 1980, the figure was 125 apartments. Three separate construction crews were working, and after the first eighteen months about half of the forty-six CETA trainees were placed in private industry. By 1982, Savannah Landmark had placed with private industry 65 percent of the two hundred CETA workers it had trained.

Success Is Difficult to Measure

After the first five years, Savannah Landmark's success could not be measured by a statistical count of rehabilitated housing units. Programming had adjusted and expanded to meet new needs or old ones that it had not been able to cope with in the earlier stages. Rehabilitation crews were doing work for neighborhood homeowners who had been granted low-interest improvement loans under a recently established city program. A program was established to work with tenants before their occupancy of a new apartment, to familiarize them with the mechanics and care of conveniences such as thermostats and modern appliances that they would enjoy for the first time. Savannah Landmark established a permanent headquarters in a renovated Queen Anne house in the Victorian District that would serve as a focal point for the neighborhood and provide meeting space for the growing number of community groups. It would be a resource center, a possible base for a newly formed food cooperative and a tool-lending service for homeowners. The do-it-yourself home-improvement fever had caught on. Twenty percent of the people in the Victorian District were limited-income homeowners. Many had the will and the talent to fix their homes but no budget to buy tools.

After five years, both a little and a lot were happening. Savannah Landmark leaders knew that they had a good start but a long way to go to achieve a genuine revitalization effort. If they didn't go further, they would have only seeded the neighborhood for speculators. It would have been only a pretty Victorian housing project for low-income people.

"A group like ours doesn't have to own everything," says Adler, "but unless a tremendous amount of property is secure you cannot say that you stopped displacement, and that is what we were determined to do."

The Savannah Landmark experiment was at a crucial juncture. It was time to push forward more aggressively or fizzle. Help had come from many quarters: individuals who had either cosigned loans or donated substantial sums, including Adler; the National Trust for Historic Preservation, Ford and other foundations; the city and Washington, both of which had granted prior smaller requests. Now Adler was pulling for something larger—260 units at once. It was a gamble.

"The trick" Adler says, emphasizing the significance of the point with a stab of the finger, "is to involve people so heavily they can't get out when the going gets tough. How do you think [Atlanta architect/developer] John Portman pulled off his Times Square Hotel deal?* Or, for that matter, all developers of both sound and unsound schemes? Just that way. Get enough people and institutions so committed, they can't pull out, only get in deeper. I figured that developers aren't so smart, so why can't anyone else do it that way? We had sixty-four units behind us, but it would mean nothing if we couldn't move on. And by now we certainly knew how to do it. Also, we had a thousand people on the waiting list for apartments, half from the neighborhood."

It took two years to put together a package of 260 additional units, of which 44 were new-construction infill housing on vacant lots, designed on a scale and in a style compatible with the Victorian District. Delays came from all quarters, not the least of which was HUD, where application forms kept getting lost and design changes were constantly demanded. HUD insisted tenants vacate at least 60 of the 261 units just purchased by Savannah Landmark, in order to be ready for renovation when the federal money came through. The

* This story will be told later in the book.

purchase of the units took place in 1980. Renovation began in 1982. That meant thousands of dollars in rent lost and apartments off the market. During that interim, because of cash-flow problems, Savannah Landmark was forced to sell some of its unrenovated units.

"If we hadn't lost those two years of rent," says Adler, "we would finally have an endowment." Delays also meant higher interest rates and construction costs, all of which nibbled away at precious funds. "We were dealing with layers and layers of paperwork and government people with no incentive to move things quickly," said Adler. "Middle-level people who are not on the local scene have no commitment to a project like this and show no willingness to take risks."

By 1988, the full three hundred units were completed and another two hundred were under way. Other groups or individuals had renovated an additional 150 units. "Nowhere," Joseph Giovannini wrote of the Victorian District in *The New York Times* (July 21, 1988), "is there a sense that the houses are owned and rented out by housing agencies: they look like family-owned homes in established neighborhoods."

Roadblocks Never Cease

Savannah Landmark had started in 1976 with an NEA grant of $17,000 and now had assets of $4.5 million. Not one conventional government program or one large developer or one overwhelming style had gained a dominant foothold. Helpful small pieces had come from everywhere possible. The city government was finally coming through with funds for street improvements, sidewalk rebuilding and tree planting. Corner stores—the 7-Elevens of the 1890s through the 1920s—were coming back, serving once again as community anchors. Area residents were getting a share of city home-improvement-loan programs.

Then the federal government created a new stumbling block. After Savannah Landmark, like other grass-roots groups in other cities, had creatively combined funds from three federal programs—the low-interest rehabilitation mortgage, the low-income rent subsidy, and CETA training funds for rehab workers—to get multipurpose programs moving, the entire national CETA program was killed when the Reagan Administration took office.* (In Savannah's case, when the CETA program was canceled, a downtown Unitarian church, Universalist Fellowship of Savannah, fortunately came through with a $27,000 training grant that for a while longer extended the life of the training component of Savannah Landmark's programs.)

"They told us it was a double subsidy, CETA labor-training money used for housing on top of a housing subsidy, and they didn't want to do that anymore," said Beth Reiter with a sigh of frustration. Of course, double subsidies for developers, like tax incentives combined with direct government funding, are a common technique around the country.

Roadblocks would continue in one form or another, and success would undoubtedly continue to build on itself. One could already envision the Victorian District in years to come. Rehabilitated housing for the poor would not discourage more affluent buyers and renters. Private-market renovations would follow in the wake of low-income subsidized restoration. Pride and high-quality maintenance would characterize residences of all incomes. Passersby would not be able to detect residents' income status or race. The end result undoubtedly would be a diverse, economically and heavily black but racially integrated community. It would happen without any divisive social conflict. And it would help stabilize adjacent areas—an immeasurably significant additional contribution.

The Process Spreads

There are many yardsticks by which one can measure the strength of an area's vitality. For some, the rejuvenation of an old neighborhood is almost impossible to recognize. It may be that some observers

---

* The discontinuance of the CETA program was considered a terrible loss by advocates of community-based self-help programs. When used creatively, CETA really nurtured people, who then benefited not only from the end product but also from the process. As an employment-opportunity program, it trained workers for the private sector. CETA did for neighborhood groups, one observer notes, what WPA did for artists.

require signs of luxury—well-kept mansions with highly landscaped surroundings and expensive cars on the driveways, hardly the signs of low-income occupants. Those same observers may be unable to discern a reawakening in any urban neighborhood where the residents are not primarily white middle-class. For others, only the presence of new construction is a positive sign. Too many people see new construction and *automatically* assume that things must be either good or getting better. Nothing could be *automatically* further from the truth.

At a minimum, one should recognize revitalization by small signs—fresh paint, a new roof or new windows, or other recent exterior improvements indicating property investment. Well-tended landscaping or flower pots reflect the care of residents. Social activity on the street—children playing, neighbors talking, the elderly sitting—reflects the critical sense of community. Local stores doing business demonstrate some degree of economic strength. These signs, and others often not readily or quickly visible, reflect resident interest and confidence in their neighborhood.

There is another important sign of the genuine renewal of an area. A neighborhood's new growth spurs good things to happen in adjacent areas. Genuine revitalization should spread if physical or psychological barriers don't stand in the way. By this most difficult standard, many conventional renewal programs fail. By this standard, however, many gradual, small-scale and sensitive grass-roots programs succeed; the revitalization of the Victorian District succeeded dramatically. In halting decay and achieving new growth, it inspired modest locally initiated upgrading in two adjacent areas—Dixon Park on the southeast side of the Victorian District and the Beech Institute on the northeast side.

Dixon Park is a predominantly homeowner community of modest single-family houses built in the late nineteenth and early twentieth centuries. Progress in the neighboring Victorian District encouraged community leaders to lobby downtown for public improvements. They succeeded in getting their small park, Dixon Park, rebuilt by the city. A focal point for the community that bears its name, Dixon

Park had been deteriorating for years and was of no use as a public amenity. Once refurbished, it again became a centerpiece of neighborhood life.

At the same time, Dixon Park won from the city a fair share of low-interest home-improvement loans for property owners, and reinvestment became visible. Residents developed a new awareness of the architectural value of their homes. Misguided demolition was occasionally still taking place, but after the area was designated a historic district and listed on the National Register for Historic Places residents began to understand the aesthetic values and architectural distinction of what they owned. These were meaningful advances for Dixon Park, enough to spark a community-improvement spirit that would grow with time. Dixon Park had experienced much less deterioration than the Victorian District. The rejuvenating energy here was percolating from within, sparked by the neighboring success. Outsiders were not needed to start things going here as they were in the Victorian District. If the Victorian District had been left in a continuing state of decay, decay eventually would have spread to Dixon Park. Its arrest in the Victorian District prevented that.

"Dixon Park was a truly grass-roots preservation effort," says Beth Reiter. "That is so important. We can impose and impose all we want, as we were doing in the Victorian District. But the truly grass-roots movement is what should be encouraged."

The metamorphosis of the Victorian District affected, as well, an adjacent deteriorated but deeply historic Savannah community called the Beech Institute Neighborhood, named after a school established in 1867 by the American Missionary Society for the education of black children. It is a Civil War–era community of about four hundred small wood-frame houses, many of which originally were and still are black-owned. In 1980, the area looked like an accumulation of fallen-down shacks. But this community had watched the transformation of the Victorian District and asked, Why can't we do something? The residents did not want it done for them by outsiders, but they did need advice. A grass-roots leadership was already in place with a singular leader in W. W. Law, a black postman in his mid-sixties. Many church members had moved away but still felt attached to the community of their birth. Neighborhood ties remained strong. Joys and sorrows were shared among many. Neighborliness ran deep, from assisting the ill to celebrating the accomplished. When word got out that an occupied house had been placed on the market, Law would personally appeal to the owner on the tenants' behalf, sometimes persuading him not to sell.

Law talks eloquently, and bitterly, of his Southern roots and slave heritage. He was an early civil-rights leader, played a crucial role in saving Savannah from the riots that swept other cities, and energetically developed a model black-heritage program in the Beech Institute Neighborhood, including tours of black historic sites.

"I had sense enough to realize how ideal this area continues to be for blacks," Law explained one evening. He was sitting in a splendid Victorian frame house that he had bought and restored for a black-history museum. "This area is near their churches, has five city bus lines and two major supermarkets, and is within walking distance of downtown shopping."

Law is a short man with graying hair and fierce pride. He resisted, at first, Savannah Landmark's willingness to help in the Beech Institute Neighborhood. Law's distrust of outsiders did not diminish easily. But after several homes were bought by white outsiders and the black tenants were displaced, Law reluctantly turned to Savannah Landmark. Savannah Landmark helped fill out grant applications, gain city support and secure financing to buy a number of units that would surely have been swept up by gentrifiers.

The outside technical assistance and the visible success in the adjacent Victorian District were working in the Beech Institute's favor. The Inner City Ventures Fund of the National Trust for Historic Preservation* granted the Beech Institute $50,000 to pur-

---

* This program was initiated in 1982 to address the displacement of in-place low-income residents in historic neighborhoods experiencing upper-income immigrations. This is an important program whose impact in small, local doses is growing nationwide. In 1986 the fund initiated a movement to get local preservation organizations to establish similar mechanisms, drawing on local contributions.

chase fourteen units and loaned an additional $50,000 to renovate them. The grant was based on Savannah Landmark's successful experience. The city provided an additional $50,000.

Law insists, perhaps correctly, that more important than the technical help of outsiders is his effort to educate resident home-owners to the value of their property. "They have to be the ones who want to stay," he says. Law bought and renovated two houses to set an example, and worked to attract new black property owners, steering them to buy vacant properties or persuading them to leave current tenants in occupied ones. At the same time, middle-income nonresident black investors were found to buy rental property for tax advantages. Investors included a pediatrician, a dentist and an op-tometrist.

Law had fashioned one more variation of the locally initiated and locally controlled revitalization process, as appropriate for the Beech Institute Neighborhood as Savannah Landmark's strategy was for the neighboring Victorian District. In every such case, more value emerges from this process than just a straight count of housing units. Everywhere, potential leaders like Law exist, and everywhere people exist to respond to the leadership of a Law. Law's efforts first slowed the losses and then turned the tide to a slow upswing. Sufficient positive movement was visible to persuade the Ford Foundation and HUD to fund the rehabilitation of one hundred to two hundred units under Savannah Landmark's guidance in 1987, a continuation of the process of spreading revitalization that included a new partnership between neighborhood groups—the Beech Institute and Savannah Landmark.

In three very different neighborhoods—the Victorian District, Dixon Park, Beech Institute—a true renewal took place, a process that was not and probably never could have been government planned or initiated. The process is one, however, which government resists responding to and nurturing in any meaningful way. Only the unswerving persistence of the resident leadership—the Lee Adlers, Beth Reiters and W. W. Laws—made this process happen. It bene-fited both residents and new arrivals. Spin-off problems, the unwanted side effects characteristic of big-scale construction projects, are minimized.

What happened in the Victorian District of Savannah and its neighboring areas is more than a lesson in physical urban rebirth. It is a lesson in everything that urban revitalization is truly about, including genuine integration and the stimulation of lasting economic and social diversity. When the emphasis is on urban process, each component has value, and it all leads to a result. When the emphasis is on a development, a building or a project, the product, not the process, is more important. And while the project may or may not be a worthy one, it should not be confused with the multiple elements of the genuine process. Savannah-style urban rebirth is worthy of spreading in many small doses in a big way. Perhaps best of all, this process also imaginatively addresses the most serious problem plaguing the upgrading of older urban neighborhoods around the country, the problem known as gentrification.

Chapter Three

GENTRIFICATION AND DISPLACEMENT

■

In England, where it first gained broad use, the term is "gentrification;"* in Canada, "white painting." In this country, the process is called "gentrification" and "displacement." The labels vary, but the phenomenon of new people moving into a neighborhood and old ones being forced out, and of the newcomers' new values dramatically altering the area's essential character, had by the 1980s become one of the most heated issues in the urban-revitalization movement.

Ironically, the new residents of "rediscovered" neighborhoods are precisely the ones that cities were losing painfully for decades. Their return is a hopeful sign that the mass urban exodus is over. New residents—whether they be young middle-income families or recent immigrants—add vitality to any neighborhood, just as the constant flow of new people, new ideas and new businesses is always important to the vitality of the larger city.

---

* The term first became popular in England to describe the process of middle-class sophisticates taking territory from working-class people.

Without a constant flow of new blood and new businesses, any community will stagnate. Economic growth follows with the increased patronage of local businesses. Newly improved property contributes to the surroundings, gives confidence in the area's future to neighbors and encourages longer-term residents to invest in their property. Some long-term residents who can afford the option of leaving decide to remain. (What is often called the back-to-the-city movement probably is in fact as much a stay-in-the-city movement, populated by people with options who decide to stay instead of moving to the suburbs.) New political strength reinforces community demands for services from City Hall. Thus the new residents often can be an asset. They are a necessary ingredient of any revitalization effort.

Many affluent newcomers and poorer long-time residents may eye each other uneasily and live together awkwardly. In time, many do learn to adjust. Some observers, however, view the new residents unequivocally as a menace threatening the stability of current residents. This is not necessarily the case. The arrival of new residents doesn't have to have a negative impact on old residents. When the new arrivals inhabit and improve abandoned property, purchase property from a homeowner looking to move, or bring new trade to local businesses, the impact is positive. But when a neighborhood experiences accelerated property sales and inflated property values, major reassessments and increased tax bills often follow, making it too expensive for residents of modest means to own their property. That impact is negative.

Solutions to this kind of dilemma exist. For example, tax increases based on increased assessments can be imposed gradually, with a reasonable yearly maximum and the balance—if there is one—deferred until the sale of the property. This way the long-term residents pay the increase if they cash in on the property value upswing, but are not penalized if instead they remain. Unfortunately municipalities eager for increased revenues and insensitive to any human cost tend to resist such solutions.

Unqualified opposition to gentrification puts critics in the curious position of advocating the "preservation" of the very low-income ghettos they profess to help. The gentrification dilemma is not simple. There are no easy solutions, but there *are* solutions.

The Rate of Change Is Key

The upgrading of any neighborhood has countless spin-offs, often as many good as bad. Streets get paved. Vacant property becomes inhabited. Maintenance improves. The police respond more quickly. The aim, however, should be to retain a larger percentage of present residents than of newcomers. The problem is not that the new people are moving in, but that residents and businesses are pushed out.

There is nothing inherently wrong in this privately financed upgrading process. In fact, it is good, because there will never be enough public money to do the proper job. *The problem comes with the rate of growth and the rate of change.* The trick is to cool the trend in some places and to heat it up in others, to avert speculation which neither adds to a neighborhood nor benefits its residents, but permits outside investors to make unconscionable profits. In Savannah, for example, a small, controlled dose of new residents is appropriate, tightly controlled as vacant units and empty lots fill up. The South Bronx and comparable large urban areas, on the other hand, with a huge number of vacant housing units, empty business sites and cleared acreage, can absorb a heavy dose of new business and residents, hopefully socially and economically integrated. This is where proper, sensitive government programs—small, gradual and manageable—can help. Yet government help of this nature is the hardest to come by.

It is, however, myopic to dimiss all new immigration as bad. Neighborhoods change. No one should want to protect the status quo of a deteriorated neighborhood. If all change is mislabeled as gentrification without distinctions, the problem of gentrification is not addressed, just ignored. Disinvestment, neglect, demolition-style urban "renewal" and abandonment displace more people, faster, than gentrification ever will.

Gentrification is primarily a problem in those neighborhoods where public policy abets accelerated speculation, does little to assist in-place residents to stay and, in fact, encourages the new investor with a variety of incentives but provides no encouragement for in-place residents to stay. Such shortsighted policy that doesn't apply available stabilization tools fails to recognize certain realities:

1. The displaced don't disappear. The issue of their poverty is not addressed. Separated from their institutional anchors, they become rootless and more alienated. They take their poverty with them to other fragile neighborhoods, intensifying the decline of their new location at great public cost. It is a debilitating process, both to the individuals on the move and to the neighborhoods that receive them. This process negates many of the economic and social opportunities that can result from gentrification if it is properly managed or regulated.

2. Displacement cannot be identified simply as a racial issue, because blacks, Hispanics, Asians and other minorities are increasingly part of the middle-class movement into older neighborhoods. Gentrification often is portrayed in racial terms, when it is most basically an economic issue—the impoverished and the working class versus the middle class.

3. Some of the reinvestment in neighborhoods on the upswing is by people already in that neighborhood before gentrification. Upgrading going on around these long-time residents gives them new confidence in their neighborhood and spurs them to improve their property as well.

4. In gentrifying neighborhoods, the continued presence of low- and moderate-income households obviously does not discourage substantial investment by new, often more affluent residents. The absence of adequate city services is more likely to discourage newcomers than the presence of lower-income residents.

5. The imbalance between rich and poor neighborhoods might begin to be addressed *if* marginal, low-income neighborhoods were viewed as a city asset worthy of attention and public investment, rather than ignored until gentrification takes hold. Cost is an unpardonable excuse; first, because in the long run *not* maintaining

low-income neighborhoods is more costly; second, because government remains too willing to invest large sums in big, new developments that don't make as much sense; and, third, because it is morally unacceptable.

6. The techniques to address gentrification problems exist in profusion. One has only to look at the number of grass-roots groups and foundations* sponsoring innovative urban efforts. The spectrum of techniques is broad and includes land-banking of abandoned housing for designated use (as Savannah Landmark land-banked units for future rehabilitation), subsidized rehabilitation of government-owned buildings for low-income tenants, tenant management and/or ownership, inclusionary zoning that guarantees provision of low-income units in any new project, "granny flats" that expand the use of old single-family homes too expensive for the long-term owner to maintain, an antiflip tax imposed on quick property turnovers at spiraling price increases, and other creative tax policies that moderate quick turnover and high profit-taking.†

Historic Preservation Gets the Blame

An unfortunate twist to the gentrification debate is the attempt to blame the popularity of historic preservation. In truth, renewed interest in the older, architecturally rich neighborhoods of our cities has been one of the most positive contributors to urban revitalization throughout the country. More new housing has been created in small doses (primarily rehabilitation) than through many heavily subsidized

---

* Several examples in this book underscore the extraordinary value of foundations as innovative risk-takers responsible for stimulating and nurturing some of the most creative change. Among those strongly supportive of grass-roots initiatives are the Local Initiatives Support Corporation (LISC), launched in 1980 with almost $10 million from the Ford Foundation and six corporations; the Inner City Ventures Fund of the National Trust for Historic Preservation; and the Enterprise Foundation, started by developer James Rouse. Creative seed grants from the National Endowment for the Arts and many state arts councils were often the first money invested in now fully matured revitalization successes.
† An antiflip tax, for example, would go a long way to moderate the real-estate practice of rapidly selling, reselling and reselling again the same property—one that starts out at a price reasonable enough to make moderate-income use possible—so that when the final owner decides to upgrade, ludicrous new rent levels are required.

new building programs.* Only where the safeguards against displacement, possible through governmental action, are not used is this accelerating movement a problem. New interest in historic neighborhoods more often has prevented the complete deterioration and disappearance of a valuable resource of the physical and social environment. "Among the thousands of tax-delinquent houses New York City has sold off during the past five years," reported Kurt Anderson in *Time* magazine November 23, 1987, "more than half have been bought by black and Hispanic homesteaders."

The absurdity of blaming historic preservation can be seen in a number of locales, but one example is Cincinnati's Over-the-Rhine. Over-the-Rhine, close to Cincinnati's central business district, once was a cohesive working-class neighborhood. As Phyllis Myers and Gordon Binder of the Conservation Foundation noted in a 1977 report:

> Over-the-Rhine has been torn apart socially and physically in recent decades by many forces. After achieving a degree of affluence, the Germans and newer Italian residents left for the suburbs. Into the housing came thousands of unskilled Appalachian whites, seeking jobs in the city. Displaced blacks from other neighborhoods were relocated here. The Findlay Market (Cincinnati's sole remaining open air market, with a distinctive peak-roofed building of 1902 vintage) deteriorated. Stores became vacant. In place of its former ethnic homogeneity, Over-the-Rhine became a series of fragmented sub-neighborhoods: business people who lived elsewhere, social service personnel, clergy, blacks, poor whites, elderly Germans. The indices of social malaise—crime, welfare, transiency, and vacancy—soared.

It is a story that could be written about neighborhoods in virtually all older American cities. Renovation of six hundred houses and three

---

* Neal R. Peirce and Carol F. Steinbach in a 1987 report to the Ford Foundation noted that in some locales 80 percent of new low-cost housing is being produced by community-development corporations. "With the federal government's construction subsidies virtually terminated," they write, "nonprofits have become the low-income housing industry in the United States."[1]

thousand apartment units with federal-housing-program funds could not reverse the tide of physical and social deterioration. In the mid-1970s the Findlay Market was refurbished, but, although it spurred some nearby upgrading, deterioration remained the prevailing trend. Then as the back-to-the-city and historic-preservation movements gained momentum across the country, middle-income professionals began trickling in. Pockets of gentility began to sprout in this neighborhood of twelve thousand residents* but 24 percent of the area's housing units still were vacant in 1981 (and vacancies were increasing still), according to a survey by the city planning commission. Encouraging new immigration into the area is sometimes automatically labeled gentrification. But can gentrification be an immediate problem with a 24 percent vacancy rate? Would not continued deterioration and decay of existing buildings displace more people, as it has done in the past, than gentrification? This vacancy rate, however, did not prevent neighborhood leaders from vociferously opposing all attempts to encourage further upgrading of the scattered architecturally appealing buildings, including the designation of a national historic district. (In 1983, after a four-year controversy, the area was officially designated a historic district and listed on the National Register of Historic Places.)

Instead of an enemy, the historic-preservation movement should have been viewed as a potential tool for a rebuilding effort in which public funding applied to the upgrading of housing for neighborhood residents *and* private investment by newcomers could work hand in hand to give the entire Over-the-Rhine neighborhood a new lease on life. In 1983, in fact, the Inner City Ventures Fund—the same National Trust for Historic Preservation program that aided the Beech Institute in the creation of affordable housing in historic buildings—with funding from the Standard Oil Company (Ohio), helped in the acquisition and restoration of four buildings, creating fifty-eight units for low-income residents and employing neighborhood residents to do the rehabilitation work.

* As of 1981.

Here gentrification, or the voluntary influx of new middle-class residents and property owners into a deteriorated neighborhood, is not to be discouraged. It wouldn't be a problem if the positive aspects of the neighborhood's character were respected and enhanced while efforts are also made to improve the negative aspects. The point is to welcome new middle-income residents while access to decent affordable housing is not lost to current residents who can't afford the luxury of movement by choice. If the assistance provided—whether it be by government, foundations, churches, financial institutions or a combination thereof—enables older residents to be part of the upgrading process rather than dislocated by it, gentrification benefits can be shared by all.

Gentrification *is* a problem anywhere, however, when it occurs in excess, causing large-scale evictions and displacement. But it does not have to be a problem if proper safeguards are taken, if ruthless, sweeping change is scrupulously barred. The intensity of gentrification can be controlled and disruption minimalized. This is one of the lessons of Savannah's Victorian District. There are two other places where this gradual and positive form of the gentrification process occurred, both of which happened before Savannah's Victorian District.

Lessons Are Everywhere

The rebirth of the Victorian District started with the vision and determined leadership of primarily one man, Lee Adler. Adler set the goal of human-scale restoration before knowing how to achieve it. He built on his experience with the historic preservation of Savannah's downtown. For that earlier effort, he had sought to learn from Frances Edmunds, head of Historic Charleston Foundation, in Charleston, South Carolina, renowned for its well-tended colonial history and its rows of carefully restored antebellum mansions; from St. Cláir Wright, head of Historic Annapolis, Maryland, a classic colonial seaport and state capital; and from Antoinette Downing, head of the Historic District Commission of Providence, Rhode Island, with its historic downtown commercial and residential areas remarkably intact because Downing has been battling on their behalf since the bulldozing 1950s.

For the later effort in the Victorian District, however, and its different set of challenges and goals—particularly the goal of assisting current residents—Adler went to Pittsburgh and Cincinnati to study techniques used to assist low-income residents. Adler knew in advance that there were no specific government programs addressing Victorian District needs, but he also knew that there were people and groups in other communities, like Pittsburgh and Cincinnati, achieving similar ends.

Cincinnati is a city that grew and flourished with steamboat traffic on the Mississippi and its tributary the Ohio River, on whose banks the city sits; a city that resisted the introduction of railroad service, believing that steamboat service would do just fine. Cincinnati prides itself in not rushing into new things without careful thought. Mark Twain once remarked that if the world were to come to an end he would rather be in Cincinnati, where everything happens ten years late. Unfortunately, however, urban renewal and highway building did not happen late and Cincinnati experienced a fair share of dislocation.

Cincinnati's Mount Auburn neighborhood, for example, a nineteenth-century suburb, was once a prestigious community of mansions and substantial row houses. By the mid-1960s, it was one of the city's worst neighborhoods, with a high crime rate, poor housing stock and a dwindling population.

Mount Auburn is a classic case of a neighborhood that suffered from cataclysmic change wrought by the combined impact of a federal highway project and accelerated suburban development. In the 1950s, Interstate 75 bulldozed through Cincinnati's West End, a down-and-out mostly black community. Encouraged by blockbusting real-estate practices occurring in downtown areas like Mount Auburn, some of the displaced West Enders relocated to Mount Auburn, filling vacancies left by whites moving to the suburbs, and alarming enough of the remaining whites to cause white flight. Between the 1960 and 1970 censuses, Mount Auburn's racial mix changed from 84 percent white and 16 percent black to 74 percent black and 26 percent white.[2]

A struggling, semiorganized Mount Auburn community, encouraged by a federal grant underwriting community activity, grappled with such pressing issues as drugs, crime, overcrowding, absentee ownership, blockbusting and racial conflict. Out of this process, focus on serious housing conditions increased.

"Housing presented a slew of interrelated problems, and the Community Council formed a housing committee to do something about them," Edward K. Carpenter reported in 1977.

> The committee found the problems easy to identify—deteriorating housing, abandoned housing, lack of control by residents, absentee ownership, inability of residents to deal with city government—but beyond the committee's ability to solve. The committee lacked what is known as clout: the prestige, skill and leverage needed to gain attention and financing. Committee members found city officials indifferent, banks timid. Corrupt private developers working on government programs in the neighborhood were hostile, absentee owners evasive, uncooperative.[3]

In 1967, a tough-talking, no-nonsense black community resident and early historic-preservationist, Carl Westmoreland, and eight neighbors converted the housing committee of the Mount Auburn Community Council into a nonprofit corporation, the Mount Auburn Good Housing Foundation, with a $7,000 grant from a wealthy former Cincinnatian. They bought and fixed up absentee-owned houses—75 percent of the neighborhood was absentee-owned—and either sold them or converted them into tenant cooperatives. Tenant cooperatives were the preferred mechanism, in order not to let control of the property leave the community. Included in their first targets was the most decrepit housing, just the sort most appealing to vandals and drug pushers. They bought and renovated storefronts and found new commercial tenants. They even bought a twenty-seven-room turn-of-the-century mansion in use as a brothel and converted it to an appealing office building, which drew a downtown law firm as its first tenant.

"It's our neighborhood and we decided that if we're going to live here, then we are going to own it," says Westmoreland. "We couldn't deal with the slumlords, so we bought them out. That gave us political clout. When we go to City Hall to talk about public improvements, we're not going like beggars. We're going as people who have done something in our community, and deserve some consideration that goes beyond charity."

One project of considerable impact involved a residential site known as "The Hole," where four hundred families lived in dark, deteriorated row housing along a hillside street. After a $3.1 million investment ($1.8 million by the foundation and $1.3 million by the city for public improvements), 150 families live in high standard and affordable apartments.

Slowly but surely, the corporation gained credibility within the financial and governmental community. Small grants of any sort were creatively mixed into rehabilitation packages for architecturally notable buildings. Local savings-and-loan companies were persuaded to sell properties with defaulted mortgages.

By the midseventies, the initial $7,000 grant had been leveraged into a $9 million nonprofit business with over three hundred rehabilitated housing units and several commercial buildings. The corporation had trained hundreds of unemployed, financed the start of small businesses and extracted improved services from the city. The housing foundation had also become one of the largest taxpaying property owners in Cincinnati.

Mount Auburn occurred early in the now well-recognized back-to-the-city renovation movement. "But there are so many neighborhoods like Mount Auburn all over the country," Westmoreland told an interviewer for *Preservation News*, the newspaper of the National Trust for Historic Preservation, in October 1977. "We are not even one of the best. The only thing unique about us is that most of the renovation is being done by the people who live here. People have recognized us for our effort and our willingness to help ourselves. That recognition has helped us so much."

Westmoreland was correct in noting that neighborhoods like Mount Auburn around the country were either happening or waiting to happen. Similar interesting developments were happening in Pittsburgh, on an even broader scale and with additional variations. "These restoration projects have been among the best-kept secrets in America," adds Westmoreland. "People mistakenly view preservation as an elitist activity, not as a tool to revitalize inner-city, low- to moderate-income neighborhoods."

Instinctivists Change City Policy

Pittsburgh is a classic blue-collar city made economically great by such barons of industry as the Mellon, Frick, Phipps and Carnegie families, whose descendants still remain the city's movers and shakers. At the confluence of two rivers, the Allegheny and the Monongahela, that form a third, the Ohio, Pittsburgh has an interesting and compact downtown, encircled by a diverse assortment of residential neighborhoods built up since the eighteenth century. Made prosperous by coal and steel and infamous by the smokestacks and soot those industries produced, Pittsburgh was once described by Charles Dickens as "Hell, with the lid lifted." After World War II, architect Frank Lloyd Wright went so far as to recommend abandoning it. In the 1940s, Pittsburgh tackled its air pollution problems with one of the country's first clean-air acts. Determined as well to clean up the city, Pittsburgh was a pacesetter in tear-down-and-replace urban renewal.

Ruthlessly, Pittsburgh ripped apart its urban fabric, clearing a vast portion of its commercial heart at the tip of the city, known as the Golden Triangle, for a very large and highly underutilized park and a series of dull and dreary buildings whose uses—office or residential—are indeterminable from their architectural appearance. Arthur P. Ziegler, Jr., a professor of English at Carnegie-Mellon University, and Jamie Van Trump, an architectural historian, were outraged by the city's "Renaissance" master plan of the 1950s and 1960s—the early urban-renewal projects that leveled so much of the heart of the near downtown and adjacent neighborhoods and that called for the demolition of many more blocks of housing in those neighborhoods. In 1964, Ziegler recalls, "we learned very quickly that we would have to engage in pitched battle with the authorities to prove preservation was a practical goal and that historic architecture could be a means for community renewal."

Ziegler and Van Trump organized the Pittsburgh Historic Landmarks Foundation (PHLF). The rescue of the 1894 North Side Post Office Building, a classic domed granite structure, was an early target. Scheduled for demolition, the Post Office was a landmark for one of the areas Ziegler and Van Trump sought to protect through a variety of techniques, including the building of community pride, for which historic preservation was a common physical denominator. After a major petition-signing campaign and by raising private funds, the PHLF acquired, restored and remodeled the stately building both as its headquarters and as an impressive local historical museum. Ziegler and Van Trump early understood that, as Ziegler explained, "restored landmarks serve as an educator for community residents who had not already realized the architectural beauty and value of their neighborhood." This was a significant and symbolic victory, early in the movement to preserve and reuse significant historic buildings.

More significant was the trail-blazing effort to save historic residential neighborhoods with inherent character and graciousness that were otherwise doomed to more expensive and socially destructive demolition and replacement by high-rise anonymity. PHLF, under Ziegler's leadership, creatively combined private funds with available government funding, much of which had to be refashioned to meet renovation needs. A $100,000 seed grant from the Sarah Scaife Foundation enabled PHLF in 1966 to buy, restore and resell its first vacant house at a cost of $53,000 and begin a revolving fund that allowed a gradual expansion of this process. With additional foundation grants, the revolving fund was expanded to $500,000. The city was pressured to refashion the urban-renewal plan to include a renovation strategy for several architecturally rich neighborhoods, one of which urban critic Jane Jacobs called "the working man's Georgetown." This effort turned into the country's first historic-preservation program for poor people and combined both home-owner assistance and low-income rentals. "We saved taxpayers $30 to $40 million through our investment and, more importantly, we saved neighborhoods," notes Ziegler.

In a 1972 article, Ziegler summed it up this way:

> The effort took us to Pittsburgh neighborhoods where we found hundreds of mid-to-late 19th century buildings that created potentially pleasing architectural environments. We studied the preservation methods of several other cities and concluded that while they had produced fine results, those methods wouldn't work in Pittsburgh. We questioned the morality of relocating almost 75,000 residents in the proposed preservation districts, and we simply had no idea where to locate an equal number of more affluent and informed citizens to replace them.
>
> We decided to analyze each neighborhood on its own terms, to study its history and demography as well as the architectural quality of the buildings. In making presentations to the residents, we emphasized the uniqueness and goodness of the neighborhoods—not the deterioration— and the need to save buildings as a significant cultural resource for the city. The approach was much more successful than that of the local Urban Redevelopment Authority, which stressed how bad the neighborhoods were and how it would be an improvement to buy the buildings, clear out the buildings and residents and sell the land to a major corporation for "redevelopment." We soon obtained considerable support in the neighborhoods and clout with the politicos.
>
> The series of programs developed by the Foundation evolved naturally, almost organically, from the prevailing situation in each neighborhood.[4]

One hallmark of this effort was its establishment of a variety of strategies—as opposed to a master plan—that could be applied in different combinations to any area in accordance with its physical and social differences. Another hallmark was its encouragement of and dependence on a genuine community-planning process. Neighborhood residents of all kinds gathered to identify problems, explore solutions and set priorities. Eventually, there emerged neighborhood associations that worked in partnership with the foundation and functioned separately to address the full assortment of local issues. Under PHLF's diverse techniques, new tenants or homeowners were drawn into vacant properties restored after purchase from absentee landlords. Buying and restoring the buildings in worst condition was the priority. Renovation of occupied rental properties was made possible through financial assistance to owners, permitting the upgrading of living conditions for existing residents and not just incoming residents. Loans were made available for resident homeowners of modest means to encourage them to upgrade their property rather than sell out and move; "Renovate, Don't Relocate" was the slogan.

Says Lee Adler, explaining why he went to both Cincinnati and Pittsburgh to learn: "Carl Westmoreland was the only one at the time doing this on a big scale. He already had completed nine hundred units. Arthur Ziegler was leading the way in every aspect of preservation and was the first to show that it was cheaper to restore than build new. He was also the first to bring whites into the vacant units of an historic neighborhood without moving blacks out."

Eventually, Adler built Savannah Landmark on the successes of Cincinnati and Pittsburgh as well as Charleston and Annapolis. Activists from as near as Columbus, Georgia, and Shreveport, Louisiana, and as far as San Antonio, Texas, and Philadelphia, Pennsylvania, came to learn from Savannah, as Savannah had learned from others.

It is crucial to understand that what happened in Savannah was not a duplication or replication of what happened in Charleston, Pittsburgh or anywhere else. The essential process in each place was *innovative, not duplicative.* The steps taken were small and gradual. In each place there were great differences allowing for the retention of local character, the avoidance of conventional development formulas and the critical involvement of neighborhood residents.

Enormous differences exist among the neighborhoods and grass-roots groups across the country exhibiting parallel revitalization successes. In fact, the specific differences between Savannah and Pittsburgh and Cincinnati and other areas are so dramatic that many observers fail to recognize the same rebirth process at work. The initiators in Savannah were affluent; in Pittsburgh they were middle-income academics; in Cincinnati they were poor. The housing stock in Savannah was Victorian wood-frames of notable design; in Pittsburgh, brick and wood mansions and worker housing from the eighteenth and nineteenth centuries; in Cincinnati, nineteenth-century row houses and mansions. The technique in Savannah was renovation for low-income renters by a nonprofit organization; in Pittsburgh and Cincinnati, it was a combination of rental and ownership.

Each defined a character and a methodology of its own. Each drew lessons from different places. Each invented solutions appropriate to its own environment and even exported its acquired wisdom to a different assortment of places. Each functioned as a separate urban forest that experts had pronounced hopelessly dead. Each grew again through the same nurturing process but with its own particular assortment of trees intact. None depended on large developers and none developed an ubiquitous uniformity.

The process in each locale reflected and respected its own place; it did not remove and replace what had been and could be again. It reflected the city itself.

Integration Without Conflict

The success of these efforts also addressed a goal that until recently was an objective of government policies: racial integration.

In the years since the riots of the 1960s, government officials struggled to devise programs that would lead to neighborhood integration. Resistance and backlash were inevitable. Oversized and poorly conceived low-income complexes, incongruous to their neighborhoods, created tensions and destabilized the physical and social fabric of many communities, making integration more difficult. Low-income ghettos proliferated. Many government leaders quietly gave up on integration as an attainable goal. The object was to produce the numbers—the quantity of low-income units, no matter where or how—to look good on an administration's record. In the process, tragically, the segregation of neighborhoods has been either reinforced or created fresh. This entrenched racial segregation is the biggest byproduct of decades of ill-conceived public-housing programs that erased the social and physical fabric of neighborhoods with the potential of stable change and created permanent low-income ghettos. It was a backward approach.

Had government instead revitalized older neighborhoods, with their usable stock of vacant or underutilized housing, and strengthened the existing social fabric, low-income residents could have been accommodated in a mix of income groups with minimal conflict and relocation. How quickly people forget that the abandoned or vacant housing of today usually was once occupied not only by low- but also by upper-income people, often within close proximity of one another. How shortsighted it has been not to recognize that these buildings may be ripe for renovation at a much more modest cost than the total rehabilitation or new construction that follows abandonment. Rehabilitated housing and public improvements add new appeal to a neighborhood. Such positive signals encourage people to remain. New residents with higher incomes invariably follow. They are often followed by new opportunities that allow the people in place to improve themselves as well—if, that is, they are not displaced instead. How easily all of this happens varies, of course, with the degree of public commitment. Yet it is essential if new residents are to be attracted to fill the vacancies of the departing. In this way, integration is facilitated with a minimum of pain. While building new public housing from scratch may be more short-run cost efficient, dislocation and deterioration are contained better through rehabilitation, thus making this approach better in every way.*

This kind of gentle change allows the preservation or establishment of social integration better than other approaches. Middle-income residents invariably resist the immigration into their neighborhood of visibly low-income newcomers of a different racial or ethnic group. Middle-income people do not, however, resist moving into a neighborhood that has a low-income, racially mixed population already in place. Conversely, in-place, low-income residents don't resent higher-income newcomers—in fact, they welcome them—so long as their own continuance there is not threatened. Thus, in this order—upper-income residents moving into a neighborhood with low-income residents in place—integration has a chance of smoother acceptance.

There is a neighborhood in New York City where, for years, I watched this staged economic integration happen while other areas in the city were in turmoil over integration-forcing programs. It is a high-rise area in lower Manhattan, just to the east of the Civic Center, where City Hall is the focal point. The oldest housing project is a traditional public-housing complex, the Governor Alfred E. Smith Houses, built in 1952 in standard fashion but not of overwhelming scale.† In 1961, another subsidized project went up, called Chatham Green, but this one was for moderate-income tenants and was directly across the street from the low-income complex. Designed by Gruzen and Partners‡ in an undulating snakelike curve, Chatham Green is surrounded by parking lots and seems lifeless in comparison to the public housing. People walk and children play in

---

* If done right and not as a result of inappropriate demolition and dislocation, new construction can be as good—properly scaled, well designed and well maintained. By this standard, appropriate new construction projects are hard to find. If the physical design—whether new construction or rehabilitation—integrates, social integration has a better chance.

† This public housing is well managed by the city's Housing Authority, resulting in a low tenant turnover and high overall population stability.

‡ This architectural firm has gone through a few restructurings since then and is now called Gruzen, Samton and Steinglass.

the dull open spaces of the Alfred E. Smith Houses. The dead spaces are brought to life by people. But no interesting activity can possibly take place in Chatham Green's parking lots. Following these two publicly aided low- and moderate-income buildings, a third residence building was built, Chatham Towers—a middle-income co-op with cantilevered terraces, skillfully designed in 1965, also by Gruzen and Partners. Chatham Towers won several design awards. Landscape architect M. Paul Friedberg added an extra level of appeal with terraced landscapings.*

For years, as I passed through this area on my daily trip to work, I couldn't help but wonder what would have happened if the higher-income component had gone up first and the city had tried to build the low-income project later. Undoubtedly, there would have been an uproar. The fear of new low-income neighbors would have provoked the upper-income residents to protest. In the most successfully integrated upgraded neighborhoods, the more affluent came *after* the low-income were in place. This is one reason why gentrification *can* be successful.

The Process Is Recognizable Everywhere

The rebirth process identified in Savannah, Cincinnati and Pittsburgh is not only a residential neighborhood phenomenon. Instead, it is an urban process relevant to a whole city. The hallmarks of the process, regardless of characteristics of the fabric to which it is applied, have been highlighted in the previous stories. Such hallmarks as innovation versus duplication, strengthening of local character instead of replacement, respect for place, building of big differences in small segments, meaningful involvement of local people, continuity of time, and careful and productive use of public funds can be applied generally and generously to any genuine urban-revitalization scheme. Perhaps most important in this rebirth process is the creation of improvement

---

* Ironically, the Smith Houses are a dull design but alive with people. Chatham Towers is beautiful but appears peopleless.

opportunities and growth potential for the people in place to have the chance to stay and become middle-income.

Savannah, Cincinnati and Pittsburgh exemplify these lessons. They illustrate the process through which incremental change has significant impact. Now it is useful to examine this process at work in an urban neighborhood that in this country has come to define urban decay—the South Bronx. Savannah and the South Bronx, for all their differences, reflect the same process. The revival process that worked in Savannah is applicable, in fact, to any area regardless of the area's state of decay or stability.

WINNING SKIRMISHES, LOSING WARS

■

*In a local community [in the United States] a
citizen may conceive of some need which is not
being met. What does he do? He goes across the
street and discusses it with his neighbor. Then what
happens? A committee comes into existence and
begins functioning on behalf of that need. . . . All
of this is done by private citizens on their own
initiatives. . . .*

—ALEXIS DE TOCQUEVILLE, *Democracy in
America*

The first thing that you notice about Kelly Street in the heart of New
York's South Bronx is its shape, a gentle curve with just enough of
a bend to allow the eye a full view of the nine modest turn-
of-the-century four-story row houses that line the east side of the
block.

Kelly Street is the only crescent-shaped block in an area where the customary urban grid prevails. Little beyond the eye-catching shape appears unusual about Kelly Street. There are solar panels on the roof of one building and a pleasant park at one corner. A block away is a well-maintained 7.5-acre park of rolling green lawn, trees, ball fields, walking paths and benches, created in 1986—the biggest recreational project in the South Bronx in a century. Within a few blocks of Kelly Street in every direction are small multifamily developments, ranging from two-story single-family row houses to five- and six-story garden-apartment buildings, and financed under different programs. The quality and appeal of these housing developments vary, but they all are appropriate in scale and need for the neighborhood. Around the neighborhood as well are colorful high-quality murals on the sides of buildings. On Kelly Street, most of the buildings have been upgraded, either with modest improvements or with full-scale renovation. These are interesting characteristics, but, in themselves, they are not startling; in recent years, such changes have become increasingly common in urban neighborhoods across the country.

Kelly Street, however, is an uncommon block with an uncommon success story. The story is instructive and moving, a success that would not be so unusual if this country were really serious about the genuine rebuilding of its cities.

According to all conventional wisdom, Kelly Street ought not to exist. It is the kind of block that no meaningful government program addresses, and that most urban experts would argue requires too much money to rebuild. In 1977, three vacant and abandoned Kelly Street buildings were scheduled for demolition by the city as the first step in a process that has wiped out many similarly beleaguered urban streets. To the untrained observer in 1977, there seemed every reason to bulldoze this apparently hopeless block.

At that time, there were no solar panels, no new windows, no garden and no playground. In fact, only a small number of people lived on Kelly Street, where there had been hundreds a few years earlier. Only three of the row houses were fully occupied, and just a few tenants were scattered among the other buildings. It was difficult to think of the block and its environs, a virtual stockpile of vacant buildings and rubble, as anything but hopeless.

A group of neighborhood residents knew better. They had only instinct to go on. They understood real hopelessness. They had lived with it in one form or another for many years. In their eyes, neither Kelly Street nor the three buildings scheduled for demolition were beyond redemption. They rallied to rescue the three vacant buildings from the bulldozer, argued with government bureaucrats and pleaded for the right to renovate the buildings themselves for their own use. They adopted a motto, "Don't Move, Improve," and organized the Banana Kelly Improvement Association. "Banana Kelly" had been a nickname coined by a Jewish immigrant living on the block in the 1920s when Kelly Street meant a step up in the pursuit of the American Dream. The "Banana" in the title still served well to identify the curved stretch of Kelly Street.

Three Buildings Start Things Going

Banana Kelly started with the three buildings. Today those buildings contain twenty-one comfortable apartments designed by the residents who own them.* The process that occurred will be examined later in this chapter. The rescue of the buildings was a small, catalytic step in the rebuilding of an area of 37,000 residents—an area for which experts offered no prescription other than demolition. Local residents knew that they could rebuild the neighborhood and with it the lives of many of its inhabitants. First they had to preserve what was there, rather than try to start from scratch. These people were tackling what the federal and local governments had been unable to accomplish through decades of urban programs which failed to use or follow the lead of the residents themselves. To understand the rebirth of the larger neighborhood in which Kelly Street is located and which grew stronger as Kelly Street grew stronger is to understand the validity of the microapproach to the rebirth of cities, an approach that relies on

---

* Some have since sold the apartment they renovated and moved on to reinvest their earned profit in another residence.

the small and the meaningful to do what the expensive and massive macroprograms have repeatedly failed to do. We have no choice in these budget-conscious times but to learn the lessons of our Kelly Streets.

Kelly Street should not be considered peculiar to either New York City or the South Bronx. Those who ignore its lesson because New York is "different" from any other American city reject an opportunity to understand the common issues contained in most stories of neighborhood decay and rebirth. The lessons of Kelly Street exist for all cities and for all citizens who view the erosion of their neighborhoods with alarm. The lessons should be particularly instructive to a government that for decades has ridden a roller coaster of urban-revitalization solutions which lurch between programs that do nothing and programs that are grandiose, wasteful, expensive and destructive.

We have already seen how instructive can be the stories of successes in Savannah, Cincinnati and Pittsburgh. There are many stories from which useful lessons can be learned. None of the others, however, takes place in the South Bronx, which symbolizes so well nationally the shame and the hope of our cities. Cities across America experienced many of the patterns of urban change evident in the Bronx. Elsewhere the scale of those patterns pales in comparison to the Bronx, but the substance is similar. To understand what happened first in this New York borough and later to examine closely what happened on Kelly Street is to understand the wasteful tragedy of urban America.

South Bronx as Urban Metaphor

The South Bronx is located only seven miles north of the elegant prosperity of mid-Manhattan. It forms almost half the borough of the Bronx—one of the five boroughs that make up the city of New York and the only one attached to mainland America. As the city's beachhead on the mainland, the Bronx provided a first step up and out for generations of the working class moving from the slums of Manhattan's Lower East Side to the American dream of suburbia along what political scientist Samuel Lubell has called the "Old Tenement Trail."

The South Bronx can stand as an exaggerated metaphor of our decaying, dying cities—"the legendary symbol of the despair of the 1970s," Michael Harrington has called it. The South Bronx is more than a place name. It is a condition of national urban failure. "It is both an area and a scare word," wrote John J. Goldman in the *Los Angeles Times* in July 1981. It is what any city or neighborhood can become if the mistakes of the past are repeated. Because the South Bronx *is* such a symbol, President Carter visited it in 1977, wanting to show that he cared about all cities. *The New York Times* editorialized: "President Carter took time out from the United Nations to visit the South Bronx as crucial to an understanding of American urban life as a visit to Auschwitz is crucial to an understanding of Nazism." Streams of politicians have continued to make campaign stops, and Hollywood helped make it a symbol of runaway urban crime with the movie *Fort Apache*. President Reagan visited the South Bronx in 1980 in order to point out the "broken promises" of the Carter Administration.

Photographs and news coverage have given people everywhere the impression that the South Bronx is like Berlin in 1945, a moonscape of emptiness. But 638,500 people* live there in more than twenty neighborhoods—more people than in Boston or San Francisco, in an area one third the size of Boston. Almost 1.2 million live in the whole Bronx.† If it were a city on its own, the Bronx would be the sixth

---

* According to New York City Planning Commission 1985 figures, about 293,000 people live in the inner core of the South Bronx, the area south of the Cross-Bronx Expressway. Another 177,400 live in the larger area north of the expressway and south of Fordham Road, and another 168,200 live east of the Bronx River and south of Tremont Avenue and the expressway. For federal-aid purposes, the city designated the whole area south of Fordham Road as the South Bronx. These figures reflect an increase of 16,500 since 1980.

† Susan Baldwin reported in 1980 that in one area of the South Bronx "the district population declined from 151,000 in 1970 to 100,000 by 1977, a loss of one-third in seven years. One-third of the housing stock was demolished in the past 10 years, leaving 755 vacant buildings standing as late as 1979."[1] Many of those buildings have since been demolished.

largest in the country. It is an area of striking contrasts, containing a few of New York's wealthiest residential areas and its poorest. And while pockets of persistence have miraculously survived, the Bronx is best known for its seemingly endless vistas of destruction. It is not all that way and was not always that way.

In the mid–nineteenth century, the rolling landscape, rich farmland and miles of waterfront provided a summer playground for Manhattan's rich and middle class. The Bronx became a borough of New York City in 1898, and in the first decades of the new century subways were extended there from Manhattan. Simpsons, Foxes, Tiffanys, Kellys—all names that now identify streets—and other estate owners sold their property to apartment-house developers whose buildings accommodated new waves of eager low-income immigrants.

The Bronx had—it still has—a lot going for it. All the ingredients of a well-functioning city were there. Small and large manufacturing companies employed the local population, providing them the opportunity to learn skills that many later took with them to the suburbs or to other cities. A wide mix of housing, from private homes to apartment houses, existed. A diversity of neighborhoods were manageable in scale and rich in local shopping. Open space was abundant and included some of the best parkland in the city. With 20 percent of its land area devoted to parks, the Bronx remains the greenest of the city's five boroughs. Good mass transit, with good access to it, was extensive. And, of course, there were Yankee Stadium, the Bronx Zoo and the Bronx Botanical Gardens.

The Bronx evolved in a classic urban way in response to a growing city. Between 1890 and 1940 its population expanded from 90,000 to 1.5 million. Building focused around elevated-train and subway stations as developers responded to the appeal that mass transit offered to potential new residents. Flourishing communities of German, Irish, Jewish and Italian immigrants replaced bucolic nineteenth-century villages. Courtyard apartment buildings and garden-apartment complexes replaced private homes along the Grand Concourse and in the western sections, while tenements and row houses abounded in the south and the east. In the 1930s, the height of Bronx growth, splendid Art Deco buildings proliferated, and even today the Bronx still probably has the largest, most impressive collection of Art Deco apartment houses anywhere.

For several decades, the Bronx exhibited many of the healthy urban patterns that critic Jane Jacobs vividly described in her classic books, *The Death and Life of Great American Cities* and *The Economy of Cities,* both of which did a great deal to shatter destructive myths generated by master planners and urban-renewal advocates and offered an alternative urban vision. Jacobs rooted her observations in the practical versus the visionary and abstract, the immediate versus the projected future, the small detail, not the large plan. What Rachel Carson did for our neglected natural environment, Jane Jacobs did for our built environment. The Bronx embodied the process Jacobs described to identify a viable city. It gave birth to as many new and small businesses with growth potential as it exported successful ones to new places, probably the most critical characteristic for urban neighborhoods. If a growing manufacturing company moved from the borough to larger quarters, a new small one was there to take its space and repeat the cycle. As long as new businesses had a place in which to start and grow, and as long as there were appealing housing opportunities for owners and employees, and public services met basic needs, the export-import cycle continued in balance and the borough thrived.

While the Bronx functioned this way in the 1920s, '30s and '40s, nobody gave it a thought. It was like a quiet, good worker who causes no problems. All eyes were on Manhattan and even Brooklyn; the unexciting Bronx remained out of the limelight. Reporter Peter Freiberg—who traveled by foot, bike or subway to every New York neighborhood in search of stories showing the value of on-site observation—wrote in a 1971 series of articles on the Bronx for *The New York Post,* the Bronx was the "forgotten borough," ignored by "downtown" and the rest of the country.

"Unlike Manhattan and even Brooklyn," Freiberg pointed out, the Bronx was "the setting for few novels—its writers moved away as soon as they could. Songwriters occasionally threw it a line, as in 'I'll take Manhattan, The Bronx and Staten Island, too,[2] but the name of the song, after all, was 'Manhattan.' Comedians mentioned the borough more often, because The Bronx could usually be depended on to draw a few chuckles."

Hunter College Professor Donald G. Sullivan has written: "As late as the 1940's, life in the South Bronx was predictable and social alterations were gradual; change was measured over decades rather than months. . . . Bronxites were ferociously proud of their borough . . . they were rooted to a sense of place that began in the home and extended toward the building, the block and the neighborhood."[3] Nothing too big happened too fast. The all-important seedbed function of the city prevailed where innovation and growth were the main source of developing the economy. Scattered throughout the Bronx were small highly productive economic and community units providing the larger city with the most really productive and fruitful activity. Each area was a distinct, robust and semiautonomous unit with local activity connected to the larger city and each with its own character. As long as change remained incremental, stability prevailed.

The Bronx survived the Depression, but not postwar prosperity. After World War II, all the policies that began to erode cities across the country began wounding the Bronx as well. Government policies encouraged the mass exodus to the suburbs where low-down-payment homes with large government-insured mortgages enabled many families to fulfill their dreams of a freestanding house in the suburbs. No comparable financing opportunities were available for those who preferred to pursue the American dream in the city.

The decline of the Bronx was not an accidental consequence of local residents moving to the suburbs in pursuit of the American dream, nor was it the *unintended* consequence of federal housing and transportation planning policies. Mortgage money and business investments moved out of the city, following the routes of new federally financed highways and new federally financed infrastructures, leaving behind the tax base, job opportunities, mass-transit facilities and the middle-income population in steady decline. Redlining—withdrawal of private resources—and the diminishment of public services and resources contributed significantly to decline.* The message of the government's loan programs was that the future was in the suburbs. City residents who stayed were mostly on their own in the search for mortgages and loans.

Herbert E. Meyer, in a 1975 article in *Fortune* ("How Government Helped Ruin the South Bronx"), pointed out:

> In 1945, the South Bronx had been a thriving industrial community. Its aging plants housed food processors, manufacturers of garments, cabinets, pianos and plumbing equipment, and even the American Bank Note Company, still the world's largest private manufacturer of stamps and currencies for foreign countries. Most of the employees of the industrial operations lived in the surrounding neighborhoods, and they in turn supported countless mom-and-pop stores—groceries, bakeries, dry cleaners—that in turn hired thousands of delivery boys, stock clerks, bookkeepers and the like.
>
> [Then, in the 1960s] upstate counties and other states, variously offering lower taxes, cheaper labor, or space for expansion, began sending industrial recruiters to lure New York businesses away from the city. By 1974, the South Bronx had lost 650 of the 2,000 manufacturers who were there in 1959 and 17,688 of the 54,037 jobs that they provided.

Businesses kept leaving and no new ones moved in or were born. Entry-level jobs, particularly for new immigrants, disappeared. Areas appropriate for new businesses were wiped out by highways and urban renewal.

---

* Not recognizing this threatens to distort any view of revitalization possibilities. All the federal housing funding in the world will not do a neighborhood permanent good without the presence of private investment—whether from the small homeowner or from local bank loans—and basic public services to make people want to remain.

Robert Moses Altered Everything

From the 1920s through the 1950s, Robert Moses, New York's "czar" in charge of highway building, urban renewal and much else, carved up the Bronx with roadways and in only *one mile* out of the seven-mile-long Cross-Bronx Expressway—which cuts right through 113 South Bronx streets, avenues and boulevards—bulldozed 159 buildings containing 1,530 families (5,000 people)* and countless small businesses out of their working-class neighborhoods, creating an instant slum. In *The Power Broker,*[4] Robert Caro documented the destructive impact on New York City of the Moses expressways and housing projects that drove businesses and population out of the city forever and in the process destroyed the sinews of the city. (Caro's Pulitzer Prize–winning book is one of the most significant contributions to the understanding of the politics of urban development.)

Moses was the nation's preeminent master builder of highways and massive urban-renewal projects in this century. He set a pattern in the treatment of our cities that, in large part, remains with us today. New York was, in effect, the unhappy standard-bearer for his ideas and manifest-destiny-style power, but his thinking went unchallenged in the rest of the country as well. Highway and other mammoth projects equaled a total repudiation of streets, pedestrians, social integration and human scale. Moses firmly established the vision of the American city seen from the highway instead of from the sidewalk, from the residential tower instead of from the block, and from the master plan based on rationality and efficiency rather than from the urban fabric that evolves naturally with its own unimposed logic. His entrenched antiurban policies continue to play havoc with many cityscapes. In New York, five city administrations held captive by Moses' power allowed mass transit to decay while highways and suburbs received attention and funding. To this day, crime (or the perception of it) and the poor operation of subways and

---

* Another section displaced 1,413 families, and that was not the full measure of uprooting due to expressway construction.

buses continue to keep residents out of mass transit and in their cars. Yet, ironically, so many of the city-dwellers who fled to the suburbs still find culture, excitement and jobs in the city, and their cars daily clog city streets.

In a *New York Times* story about Moses in 1987, anticipating the centennial of his birth in 1988, Caro told reporter David W. Dunlap:

> The mark of Robert Moses is much more than anything you can see physically. You have to analyze his influence in priorities because, for decades, he played a crucial role— and for many years, a decisive role—in determining where city resources would go.
>
> And for decades, he skewed spending away from the social-welfare aspects of city government toward the physical construction of the city. When you see his huge projects, you also ought to remember the way he treated the people who stood in the way of those projects.
>
> It would be nice if we could remember the wonderful and inspiring things that the young Robert Moses conceived and created—such as Jones Beach and the early parkways—without trying to falsify history by pretending that his overall impact on the city and, indeed, all the cities of America, was inspiring or triumphant. Because it wasn't.[5]

For decades Moses did more to shape the physical environment of New York State than any other figure in the twentieth century. He became a national household name, and his New York work became a model for the entire nation.* This was the postwar era when, as Professor Sullivan has written, "massive slum clearance efforts had captured city planning, and the era of the housing project began."[6] Block after Bronx block was "leveled to make room for those 'towers

---

* Ironically, with urban-renewal thinking acceptable again, reverence for Moses is on the rise. "He knew how to get things done," note admirers who don't want to sound as though they approve of what he did but want to make one believe how difficult it is to get good things done these days. Of course, this means the "big" things that are understandably difficult to be accomplished, usually because they are inappropriate and are widely opposed.

in gardens' in the name of the national housing goal of a decent, safe and sanitary home for every American . . ."

For the Bronx, this approach to urban problems was crippling. Sullivan adds: "By 1955, 'push-pull' entered the housing market. Push-pull is a term in sociology meaning people are both pushed from their old neighborhood by fear of newcomers and pulled out by their desire for better housing. This psychology created pressure on neighborhoods susceptible to weakened demand."

In the 1960s, hundreds of millions of federal dollars from assorted "urban improvement" programs poured into the Bronx, but failed to halt its rapid decline. For example, the South Bronx was designated a Model Cities area in 1967, and though more than $300 million was spent under that program, the decay accelerated. The most noticeable result of these and similar investments is what one observer called "planner's blight," vast areas of vacant land from which whole communities were ousted for new projects that never materialized. With its burned-out buildings, those empty spaces are the South Bronx's most significant scars. An estimated five hundred acres remain vacant in the South Bronx.*

In the late 1960s and early 1970s, one of the borough's favorite landmarks, Yankee Stadium, became the focus of awesome refurbishing plans that were supposed to cost the city $25 million and form the western anchor for a rejuvenated South Bronx—"the centerpiece of another New York City neighborhood renaissance," as a City Hall announcement boasted. When it was finished in 1977, the project had cost approximately $120 million, and not one penny of a promised $2 million had gone into improving the surrounding neighborhood. As a result, the area continued to get worse, since more businesses and residents fled. Baseball fans arrived just before game time and left immediately after. There was no reason to come early, and no reason to stay.

---

* As if this is not enough vacant land on which to make good new things happen, city demolition continues. From June 1985 to June 1987, *The New York Times* reported in the latter month, 436 buildings were demolished in the South Bronx, creating more empty lots.

Co-op City: Cataclysmic Change

Perhaps the most ill-conceived scheme meant to revive the borough—in fact it hastened its decline—was Co-op City, a 15,400-unit, 55,000-population government-subsidized apartment complex on a marshy three-hundred-acre site in the northeast corner of the Bronx, wedged between the Hutchinson River Parkway and the New England Thruway. Co-op City cost $413 million to build in the mid-1960s, and hundreds of millions more have been spent to bail it out ever since; at least $89 million in cost overruns added $8.9 million yearly to tenants' carrying charges. For three decades, Co-op City has been plagued by construction problems and financial crises. In the early 1980s it was undergoing a minimum $150 million repair, involving virtually a complete overhaul of every roof and facade and thirty-two miles of water pipes. By 1986, *The New York Times* reported, four hundred apartments were vacant due to major mistakes allegedly covered up by contractor payoffs to building personnel, $140 million additional state money was needed for construction repairs, $150 million was owed the state in back mortgage payments, and tenants faced a 31 percent increase in carrying charges over five years.[7]

Co-op City is the quintessential city-within-a-city, with thirty-five towers, six clusters of town houses, three shopping centers, three community centers, an impressive educational complex that even has its own planetarium, and twelve churches and synagogues. More people live in Co-op City than in some of the state's sixty-two counties. A monument to Robert Moses' philosophy of building big at any price, Co-op City—"the largest development in the United States and the largest co-operative apartment community in the world" at its construction—was to be a cornerstone of the borough's urban-renewal solution, the key to ridding the Bronx of all of its slums. Upon completion, Moses promised, the residents of these slums (Moses' definition of slum is open to question) could be relocated to Co-op City en masse, emptying older neighborhoods for urban renewal. The second wave would provide new areas for similar projects in a giddy cycle of improvement that would march around the city until every slum was erased—and every neighborhood with it.

It did not quite happen as Moses predicted, although an enormous shift in population was the result. When Co-op City opened in December 1968, thousands of middle-income families were vacuumed out of another section of the Bronx, the Grand Concourse, seven and a half miles south of the new development. The Grand Concourse, the proudest street in the borough, rivaling any grand residential boulevard in America, had been designed in 1909 with Paris' noble Champs-Élysées in mind. Some of the finest Art Deco apartment buildings in the country were built along this stately four-and-a-half-mile boulevard lined with trees, grass and appealing places to sit. The Grand Concourse was for the Bronx what Park Avenue was for Manhattan. A building boom there in the 1920s and 1930s followed the completion of the subway beneath "the Concourse," and it remained a prestigious address for the upwardly mobile. The D train brought new residents into the community just as the highways, years later, emptied them out. Before Co-op City opened, the Grand Concourse anchored the South Bronx's largest remaining prop of primarily Jewish middle-class stability. Nothing could have maintained that stability against the dual competition of the suburbs and Co-op City.*

Herman Badillo, then a Bronx congressman and before that the Bronx borough president, called Co-op City from the beginning "the single worst mistake of all."

When Co-op City opened in 1968, I wrote a series of articles about it for *The New York Post.* I interviewed scores of tenants who were just moving in. I thought that Co-op City was, by far, the most banal housing development I had ever seen. Jack Newfield and Paul Du

---

* "On Dec. 18, 1987, New York City officials turned over the last five vacant apartment buildings on the Grand Concourse to private developers for rehabilitation," reported *The New York Times.* After continuous decay and abandonment following Co-op City's opening, the Grand Concourse started coming back in the late 1970s and early 1980s.

Brul, authors of *The Abuse of Power,*[8] aptly described it as an "urban Stonehenge," but that gives its massive dreariness an aura of romanticism it does not deserve. Why would anyone *choose* to live in such poorly constructed matchbook layouts, with paper-thin walls and prisonlike hallways—an enclave dramatically isolated, divorced from the larger city? Why would residents give up row houses and well-designed apartment buildings in friendly, bustling neighborhoods? Then I talked to the tenants and felt their sense of hopelessness over the decay they had fled.

Nostalgically, they recalled how livable their neighborhoods once had been and spoke wistfully of the now shattered complex of family attachments and friendship links. They told of falling plaster, failing plumbing, erratic heating and other problems caused by landlord neglect. The apartments they wanted either close to or in their old neighborhood were too expensive, and financing for single-, two- and three-family homes there was unavailable. Co-op City appeared to answer all the problems of security, cleanliness and cost unsolved in the old neighborhoods. Government and private money was going into new projects or suburban developments, not into upgrading existing buildings. The unarticulated goal was to keep middle-income people within the city limits, not to upgrade existing neighborhoods. In their old neighborhood, there was little to attract new, stable middle-income families as old residents moved on. Instead, new, often poor, black and Hispanic families took the place of those who left.

Co-op City apartments, however, with the appealing parquet floors, limited but livable rooms and modest but modern kitchens, had the same poor quality of construction and design found in new Manhattan apartment houses. Still, the value for the price was demonstrably better than in the expensive downtown apartments.

Many of the Co-op City tenants knew their new neighbors from the old neighborhood, yet I was haunted by the way they spoke of their former communities. Their love for their former communities was strong, and if things could have been improved there, they said, they would have stayed. If their old buildings had been fixed up or if they could have obtained financing and bought a two-family house, or if they had thought that the neighborhood would not continue to decline, they would have stayed. They had no reason to believe that good things would happen. They saw banks and government interested only in the new projects like Co-op City. But they spoke wistfully of what they had left behind. They were not unlike residents of many urban neighborhoods resisting the push/pull effects of official policies and social change.

"People left the Grand Concourse not because they wanted the environment of Co-op City but because they couldn't stay where they were," notes historian Richard Rabinowitz. "Those new buildings had nothing to do with the way they wanted to live." In fact, the story of Rabinowitz' parents reflects the experience of so many of the new tenants of Co-op City and its smaller counterparts elsewhere in New York and other cities.

In 1948 the Rabinowitzes bought a two-family row house in the East New York section of Brooklyn. Along with most of the new homeowners of the community, they were in their midthirties and the husband was a war veteran. Two-family homes were the prevailing residential form, and a few small six-story apartment houses were comfortably interspersed. A strong commercial spine was within walking distance of the many still-carless families. This was a lower-middle-class district, whose residents were mostly small-store owners, teachers and civil servants—"the backbone of city life and with only one lawyer in the bunch," notes Rabinowitz. Although the community had some of the ambience of a suburb, working residents commuted to their jobs by subway.

The Rabinowitzes were very much involved in the community. They fought for and won a new junior high school, a community center and a public library, testifying at City Hall or Albany or wherever it was necessary. They gained traffic-safety improvements and upgraded street lighting. As a heavily Jewish community, they pushed and persuaded the Federation of Jewish Philanthropies to build a YMHA center with a swimming pool and a substantial educational-workshop program. The social network that evolved over time was strong, with lifelong friendships established among neighbors. "They all helped each other out in many ways," recalls Richard Rabinowitz. "They were in and out of each other's house daily, filling in for each other, watching out for each other's **kids**. It was all so automatic and matter of fact." And while relatives and some friends were moving to new Long Island communities, the Rabinowitzes and most of their neighbors, who had become their closest friends, made a conscious decision not to leave the city and their neighborhood.

Rapidly, it all changed. Blockbusting—that insidious tactic whereby real-estate brokers prey on the fears of a community by telling the residents that their quality of life and property values are about to plummet because blacks are moving into the neighborhood— started in the early 1960s, without interference from city government. Brownsville, a poor black community ("criminal elements," according to the blockbusters) to the west, which had not been a source of concern in the Rabinowitzes' neighborhood, was moving in, realtors warned. Letters, midnight phone calls, rumors. The sales started. The solid commercial infrastructure was decimated. The public investment that had been poured into the community—the millions in capital funds the city had spent in the 1950s—and the unmeasured private dollars and contributed efforts of residents was dissipated in no time. The house the Rabinowitzes had bought in 1948 for $14,000 they sold in 1968 for $21,000.

"They fled in the prime of their life, in their midfifties, the kind of people the city should always have as homeowners," notes Richard. First they moved into high-rise subsidized middle-income housing in Rockaway, not unlike Co-op City but on a smaller scale—and even less successful for them. "They were torn away from the moorings of their lives at the time they needed them most," adds Richard. "They were terrified in their new surroundings with dark halls and cinder-block walls and devastated by the reduction in their lives." Eventually, they and others moved on. The next stop was the suburbs.

"People are constantly forced in the prime of life or when they are old and anchored to be the flotsom and jetsom of society," observes

Rabinowitz. "Instead, they should grow old in places where they built something. They will never again live in as comfortable a space. Chances are my parents and their friends would have stayed another ten years and sold to people younger than themselves who would have kept the cycle going and they would have moved on, along with some of their friends, where retirement would have been their choice. This is a big loss, but we can't calculate the sacrifice of people or quantify the value of their investment. The problem is that whenever we begin to measure communities by statistics, we misunderstand the social values underlining them."

For many tenants, Co-op City and similar but smaller projects offered a last refuge—a way out of collapsing neighborhoods, an alternative to the suburbs for those who had neither the desire nor the means to leave the city. The United Housing Federation, sponsor of Co-op City, reported in 1966 that about seven thousand of the first ten thousand active applications for apartments had come from Bronx residents. But some observers argue that those people would have left old neighborhoods, perhaps to the suburbs, at whatever cost. That might have been true for some, but not for nearly as many, nor with such wrenching speed. Because of Co-op City, the Bronx experienced cataclysmic change and irreparable harm from which it has never recovered.

The Bronx had suffered less than many other urban areas during the Depression. "No urban area in the country," wrote historian Lloyd Ultan, "experienced more private residential development during that troubled decade, and the boast was often made that the Bronx was 'the city without a slum.' "[9] When the Grand Concourse exodus—to Co-op City and beyond—began, thousands of black and Puerto Rican poor filled the vacancies. The buildings they vacated elsewhere in the Bronx were emptied and eventually abandoned.

Herbert E. Meyer noted in his 1975 *Fortune* article: "The steady outflow of working tenants, of businesses and jobs became a hemorrhage. Within a year, the South Bronx began to burn."

"The point is that we created these dynamics that force large unnatural changes rather than incremental changes," says Ron Shiff-

man, an advocate planner who, in the twenty years of his work with
dozens of community groups, probably has done more than anyone
else in New York to put the ideas of Jane Jacobs into action. "If we
had taken the kind of investment committed to Co-op City and
improved the qualities of existing communities, we would have
reinforced the fabric" of neighborhoods that instead continued to
decline or disappear. The city, Shiffman adds, "only directed its
concern to keeping the fleeing middle-class within its tax boundaries
and not to improving the quality of life. It reflected a concern for the
physical fabric alone."*

One can only wonder what might have happened if the original
$413 million investment and further government bailouts had been
used instead to rehabilitate still salvageable neighborhoods all over
the Bronx. Few, if any, people in government in the early 1960s were
thinking of reinforcing rather than replacing existing urban neighborhoods, and there were no programs that fit that goal. As the decay
of the South Bronx became more publicized, awareness increased that
Co-op City had drained other neighborhoods of the middle class that
could have, if assisted in place, maintained stability.

All the "renewal" programs from either Washington or City Hall,
ostensibly designed to reverse urban blight, had only accelerated
decay. The "solutions" had become part of the problem. By the time
President Carter arrived in 1977, the scars were overwhelming.
Similar scars could be seen in almost every American city. Only the
proportions differed. The President stood amidst the rubble of
Charlotte Street in the South Bronx and was photographed. He
promised to pour millions into "revitalization." In the face of the

---

* Co-op City's bigness and the steady departure and aging of its original middle-
income tenants made it difficult to manage from the beginning. Decline has been
swifter than it might have been in less monumental structures, and crime has
increased. In fact, *The New York Times* reported in November 1987, Co-op City's
fifteen-member board of directors, which includes four blacks and one Hispanic
member, voted to initiate a marketing plan to attract more white residents in order to
preserve the community's ethnic mix. The white population had dropped below 50
percent, and concern increased that if the trend continued, municipal services would
diminish and deterioration would set in.

very long line of past mistakes, by 1977 revitalization should have carried a new definition. It did not.

In the decade between Co-op City's opening and Carter's South Bronx visit, many things had changed in New York and other cities that should have dramatically altered government programming away from the massive project to smaller, multifaceted approaches to neighborhood conservation. This did not happen. Government intractability continued. Dependence on the big and the new remained the rule. Yet something else was happening in our cities while public officials and experts were not paying attention. This new phenomenon occurred earlier in New York than elsewhere.

Building on Small Changes (Urban Neighborhoods: Surviving, Reviving)

New York—along with countless other American cities—experienced a rebirth of many of its neighborhoods, despite a critical financial crisis and the absence of government commitment to older areas. Middle-income families whose counterparts in the 1950s and 1960s bought homes in the suburbs bought cooperative apartments and brownstones in New York and, through a heavy dose of "paycheck financing" (no loans, no financing arrangements, just payments out of their weekly salary), invested limited funds and unlimited energy into transforming rundown mansions and modest row houses into modern dwellings with Old World charm. The lure of good housing values, quality design, spacious rooms, solid construction and friendly neighborhood living was enough to overcome some of the investment neglect of government and financial institutions. The energy crisis of 1973 prompted many home-seekers to reexamine the long-standing appeal of suburbia, where two cars and high oil bills were a fact of life. Resistance to sterile modern design stimulated interest in old buildings of architectural distinction, even if they were located in run-down neighborhoods.

People moved in. New businesses followed. New cottage industries sprang up, with the potential of growth. Vacant stores were rented. Community spirit revived. Local organizations formed around single issues—decent housing, chasing out drug dealers, graffiti-busting, anti-redlining or -blockbusting, crime watch—set sometimes limited, sometimes broad goals, eventually evolving into a widespread neighborhood movement. More than ten thousand block and community associations now exist, with equally vigorous counterparts in communities across the country. Pressures on City Hall eventually brought some recognition of the value of salvaging the old and shoring up troublesome neighborhoods. The landmarks-preservation movement stimulated that recognition and spurred awareness of the economic benefits of preservation in an era of shrinking resources. The neighborhood-preservation movement secured increased attention to social services.

Not all the neighborhoods stubbornly staying alive or gradually reviving were polished-brass restoration showplaces. Many were poor, working-class areas. Others were more prosperous. This survival and revival record cannot in any way be explained by the flow of federal-aid dollars.

Throughout the 1970s, city planners and policy-makers responded to the trend with glowing praise and a variety of highly publicized but minimally funded programs to assist neighborhood preservation. Political leaders mastered well the planning jargon to impress the public with their attention. But what had changed most of all on the governmental level was only the rhetoric. Conventional development approaches remained intact. Tax and zoning incentives were created to stimulate new office construction, while small businesses got crumbs. Office construction and white-collar jobs aplenty followed. Small businesses and small industry continued to struggle or be pushed out to make way for the new high-rise "factories of debt," as one writer called them. And massive investment was made in such new communities as Roosevelt Island and Battery Park City, with no comparable investment in existing neighborhoods. Housing and neighborhood abandonment continued at an alarming rate. Crumb-sized programs were directed at neighborhood decay, while major attention remained riveted on the massive proposals for new construction that made headlines.

Genuine rejuvenation stories rarely make headlines. But they were occurring, most notably in the one urban area considered hopeless—the South Bronx. Public officials had enough difficulty responding meaningfully to the movement of the middle class back to old neighborhoods; it was impossible for them to embrace the parallel developments in low-income areas. Yet the rejuvenation stories of low-income neighborhoods are the best lessons of genuine urban revitalization.

The Significance of Kelly Street

The South Bronx is this country's most awesome symbol of urban decay and despair. It epitomizes the plight of the nation's cities and dramatizes the failure of governmental policies. Yet the ten-block area around Kelly Street in the South Bronx is a story of urban rebirth. This tale would not have been notable in the decades when the Bronx functioned well, because there would have been nothing remarkable to observe. No President would have thought then to visit and no writer would have found anything unusual to report. When things were going well, the Bronx functioned the way cities function best. It grew slowly and in small increments, experiencing and accommodating change gradually and in manageable doses. But growth, change and continuous rebuilding do not happen naturally anymore. Only the massive and disruptive are popular with developers and with the government that encourages and sponsors them. So what makes the rebuilding around Kelly Street unusual is that it happened at all!

The achievement in the Kelly Street neighborhood is even more remarkable because the environs lacked the advantages of reborn middle-income areas around the country. The few tree-lined streets of run-down but architecturally pleasing row houses were not enough in the mid-1970s to appeal to a returning middle class. Few people owned their homes. Few parks were in condition to be oases of activity. Not enough industry was left to employ sufficient local residents seeking work. The delivery record of city services was dismal. In fact, few people were left in an area once filled with working-class families.

An abandoned, structurally sound housing stock, however, awaited renovation by homesteaders. Empty lots waited to be filled with do-it-yourself playground equipment, benches, lush vegetable gardens and picnic tables. Neighborhood businesses struggled to stay open in the hope that new customers would move into the area. Empty stores, as well, awaited modest new enterprises catering to basic consumer needs. Vacant, desirable industrial space was available for new industry to start small and grow. Mass-transit facilities surpassed those available in some of the best neighborhoods in the city. Most important, people were here who, as one local activist said, "wanted to get involved, who wanted to rebuild a neighborhood, who wanted to rebuild their lives." They had learned after too many disappointments that government could not be depended upon for sustained, meaningful help. Often, government simply stood in their way. They had to do it themselves, taking what help they could, but relying upon their own energy.

By now, many city dwellers understand what rebuilds a middle-income community, what brings back the middle income to old city neighborhoods or encourages them to stay, and what makes municipal leaders deliver the necessary support services. They have seen it happen in almost every American city. That the same process is at work in poor neighborhoods, however, is not as widely recognized. To understand the process is to know how to help it happen and to foster a genuine revival of cities. Indeed, if it can happen in the South Bronx, it can happen anywhere.

To visit Kelly Street over ten years, to see its vacant buildings renewed, to observe small changes making big differences, to visit the low-income residents and to walk around the area, is to understand how a neighborhood gets rebuilt. To talk with some of the first people involved—those who named their organization Banana Kelly—is to hear articulated the same visions, goals, values and determination so often voiced in middle-income neighborhoods. By appearance, Kelly Street now looks like a middle-income neighborhood.

Banana Kelly is one of several neighborhood self-help housing groups that sprang up in New York City's most desperate neighborhoods—and in neighborhoods across the country—in the mid-1970s. Some self-help groups did not begin with housing as their main concern. They may have started with a park, a school, an anti-redlining campaign or a security problem. But no matter what problem they started with, they eventually—inevitably—expanded into housing problems.*

Fighting government bureaucracy and intransigence, helping residents preserve their own buildings through cooperative ownership and cooperative labor, employing the unskilled to rebuild their community, enabling them to go on to new jobs, struggling to obtain meager foundation and government funding, groups like Banana Kelly created islands of hope where hopelessness once reigned. The results were sometimes modest, but a few were phenomenal. None of the results was enough, by itself, to stem the overwhelming tide of decay, but then these efforts were never nurtured or encouraged enough to be given the chance to try. These groups showed how the revitalization process *can* work and how thinking small can lead to significant improvements. Their successes challenged traditional urban policy. Banana Kelly is a significant story.

The Kelly Street Story Is Not Unique

Kelly Street is in a section of the southeast Bronx known for its proximity to the Bruckner Expressway, a favored escape route by car from Manhattan north to suburban Westchester County and beyond. It is light-years from such landmarks as Yankee Stadium and the Grand Concourse to the west and the Bronx Zoo and Fordham University to the north. But Kelly Street intersects a major South Bronx commercial and residential strip, East 163rd Street, where in the 1970s a few businesses survived the surrounding devastation.

---

* There was "the People's Firehouse," for example, a group of Brooklyn residents who were outraged when the city closed their neighborhood firehouse. They beat City Hall on that one, then branched out into housing, jobs and other working-class issues. Such small victories can have an enormous impact.

Near Kelly Street are several short streets—Tiffany, Fox, Simpson, Leggett—where neatly kept row houses have also weathered countless urban storms. Five blocks from Kelly Street is Southern Boulevard, the third-largest commercial strip in the Bronx. Nearby is a modern intermediate school, built in 1974. Also within short distances are busy thoroughfares, transit lines and the Hunts Point Market—a vital wholesale food depot, where much of the agricultural produce for the Middle Atlantic States is sold.

By the late 1970s, few people lived on Kelly Street. Some were still moving away. On the east side of the street stands a stretch of 1920s low-rise apartment houses, on the other the nine four-story row houses mentioned earlier. These small apartment houses and row houses are not unlike renovated buildings in other city neighborhoods.

Kelly Street was once a middle-income community, but by 1976 it was occupied mostly by people on welfare and the working poor. Landlords, banks, insurance companies and city agencies waited for it to go under. All around Kelly Street, one building after another had been burned down by vandals or arsonists. Absentee landlords milked the last penny from their properties, collecting rents but neglecting repairs, defaulting on taxes and, in the end, cashing in on the fire insurance. In the early 1970s, this neighborhood had one of the highest crime rates in the city. Junkies preyed on pedestrians at every corner. Five years later, even the junkies had left, along with the sixty thousand people who quit the larger area, leaving half the buildings vacant. The *Fort Apache* precinct—of Paul Newman movie fame—that includes Kelly Street had been transformed into *Little House on the Prairie,* one observer quipped.

But some Kelly Street residents liked their block and were trying to stay when I first visited there in 1977. Some had grown up there. Some had nowhere else to go. Yet the city did nothing to halt deterioration. Rather, the city seemed to help it along.

Two of the small apartment buildings on Kelly had been abandoned by a private landlord in 1975 when the block was still well populated. A community group organized the tenants, collected rents and used the money for needed repairs. Five months later, the tenants were notified to pay rent to the city, which had acquired the buildings through tax default. Some tenants kept paying the community group. Others paid the city. Some paid no one. Money for repairs dwindled. The buildings were sold at city auction to an absentee investor who informed the tenants that no repairs would be made until back rent was paid, even though most of the rent money had already been used for repairs and maintenance. The tenants refused to pay until the buildings were made livable. The community group could do no more without the rent roll, so it pulled out. Then the tenants started to leave.

Within four months, there was a fire, a new tax default, and the city again assumed ownership. Now the buildings were empty, beyond the incremental help that the rent roll could provide, and in need of complete renovation. Month after month, the same thing happened in buildings throughout the neighborhood. Some were still occupied, but tenants were leaving fast. By 1976, one side of Kelly Street was almost completely vacant.

One or two abandoned buildings is all it takes to initiate the cancer of abandonment. Once started, it spreads rapidly. In less than a year, Kelly Street looked like an urban wasteland. But one family refused to let Kelly Street die.

People Make the Difference

Frank Potts, a resident homeowner of Kelly Street, had bought his first building, one of the four-story brick walk-ups across from the apartment buildings, in 1963 and, over the next seventeen years, purchased four more and managed another for an absentee landlord. Potts worked as a plumber by day and a truck loader at a wholesale fruit company in the Hunts Point Market by night, managing the buildings with his wife on weekends. He, his wife and most of their five sons and three daughters and their families lived on the block and provided a rare example of resident low-income home ownership which contributes to the stability of neighborhoods.

In 1978, when everything around them looked hopeless, the Potts family was still there. "We couldn't give up," Mrs. Potts explained matter-of-factly. "Everything we worked for and everything we have is here. We'd sooner die than leave."

Frank Potts is a tall, heavyset, shy man who is a self-taught jack-of-all-trades. He left school after the sixth grade and has worked ever since. His grandfather taught him how to work a cotton gin in Weir, Mississippi, where he was born. At seventeen, in 1950, Potts came north to New York along with thousands of other Southern blacks. His wife, Frances—they had married the year before— followed six months later. By the early 1960s, the Potts family lived in a too-small apartment on Manhattan's Upper West Side. Frank Potts was working as a die-cutter during the day and a truck loader at night.

In 1963, when their Manhattan apartment seemed to be bursting at the seams, Frank Potts heard about a seven-room apartment available on Kelly Street. To get it, he had to buy the four-story building, but there was the dual advantage of an apartment and potential income. "We put our change together," Mrs. Potts remembered, "took out our seven hundred dollars savings" from the Carver Federal Savings and Loan Association. To that was added a $700 union loan and a $1,500 personal loan from the Irving Trust Bank (redlining* precluded getting a bank mortgage) to make the $3,000 down payment on the $25,000 purchase price. "We arrived with fifteen cents and one subway token left," Mrs. Potts said with a laugh.

"When we bought the house," she said, "and had our first pipe leak, my husband was out working, so I called the plumber. When the plumber came, I watched everything he did. He used a ninety-eight-cent can of Stop Leak, charged ninety dollars and was gone. When my husband came home that night, I described in detail what the guy did and we never had to call a repairman for that job again.

---

* The de-facto policy practiced by banks and insurance companies under which a red line is drawn around a neighborhood in which loans and insurance policies will not be written.

We did that with each thing that went wrong until my husband could do it all himself. If we hadn't done it that way, we couldn't have stayed. We didn't have the money to pay repairmen. We used to eat beans and rice one day and rice and beans the next until we started saving money. When you have your every dime in something, you have to learn that way."

Eventually, Frank Potts learned everything he needed to know about plumbing and then earned his living doing it professionally, working for people who couldn't afford a licensed union plumber. "If he had to take the plumber's test today," Mrs. Potts pointed out, "he couldn't pass the written part." In 1965, three years after their first building purchase, the Pottses bought a second four-story walk-up on the block. They had paid off the first $1,500 personal loan, juggled their income, obtained a new $1,500 personal loan and proceeded as they had with the first building.

By 1978, the Pottses had bought three more buildings and were the paid managers of another. One, which they had bought at a city auction, was still vacant and remained that way until they had the money to renovate. Another had had a fire and they were not able to renovate it either. In all, there were fifty-nine occupied apartments housing more than 250 people.

The Pottses easily rented their apartments. They enforced strict rules—no drinking on front stoops, no hanging around the hallways, no rent delinquency—and they carefully screened prospective tenants. Mrs. Potts, who carried out most of the business of landlording, watched the street carefully from her first-floor window. Despite this pocket of vitality, the city was planning to demolish three buildings adjacent to the Pottses' holdings.

"The Pottses' son Leon, today in his midthirties, started helping his father as a handyman when he was in fourth grade, and became a union plumber after high school. While the family watched the block crumbling around them, Leon remembers, "we talked a lot about what we could do. We had grown up here and wanted to stay, but we did not know how to go about helping things get better." They knew what it would mean if the city carried out its plan to demolish the three adjacent buildings. Once these were down, the rest would follow. They had seen it happen before.

Leon joined friends from the block in weekly basketball games at a nearby settlement house, Casita Maria. There he met Harry De Rienzo, a Casita Maria social worker living in the area. De Rienzo told his teammates about a neighborhood rebuilding effort elsewhere in the South Bronx, the People's Development Corporation (PDC), that had been under way for two years.

Big Value Out of Small Failures

The People's Development Corporation was one of the first of New York's varied grass-roots improvement groups to attract nationwide publicity and was in the vanguard of a national movement. It was the brainchild of one man, Ramon Rueda, a tall, handsome thirty-one-year-old with a fetching smile and enormous charm. Rueda was from East Harlem. He and a hearty band of like-minded determined friends selected a typically grim, threadbare South Bronx block on Washington Avenue, fifteen blocks northwest of Kelly Street, to be the cornerstone of a community-rebuilding effort.

PDC started by forcing the city to finish a sixty-unit renovation project that was 95 percent complete but on the verge of abandonment because of city litigation with contractors. After the project was ready and tenanted, PDC volunteers cleaned out and renovated another small abandoned apartment house and then another, installing solar hot water and income-producing garbage-recycling systems. Volunteers cleaned streets and vacant lots, creating a park in one of them with an attractive wall mural on an adjoining building wall. PDC organized a day-care center and established a new cabinet-making shop that employed the formerly unemployed who had learned carpentry skills while renovating the apartment houses.

News of what PDC was doing had spread. Harry De Rienzo, working at Casita Maria, was inspired by what he saw of it. PDC fell apart after five years, a victim of its own success, but not before it had served as an inspiration and model for scores of budding neighborhood self-help groups around the country.

At the height of its success, PDC gained the attention of government officials. President Carter stopped by for a look during his celebrated visit to the South Bronx in the fall of 1977 after visiting Charlotte Street. The spotlight of the national media was overwhelming. Overnight, PDC changed from a sincere, meaningful effort to the government's pet neighborhood project. Money poured in. PDC went from a $10,000 to a $5 million organization. Rueda, beguiled by publicity and invitations to speak around the country, was distracted from the rebuilding effort.

"Government was serving its own needs with PDC," said Anita Miller, director of the South Bronx program of LISC—the Local Initiatives Support Corporation,* started by the Ford Foundation in 1980 to channel foundation and corporate support into grass-roots groups working primarily in housing and economic development around the country. "Washington was warned that PDC did not have strong management capacity and should grow incrementally, but the warnings were ignored," adds Miller.

PDC crumbled under the weight of too much money too soon, too much internal disarray and too much outside attention. It left to other groups, born out of the PDC example, the work of achieving the long-term success that might have been PDC's as well. Banana Kelly was one of the acorns from the PDC tree. It learned well the lessons of PDC's mistakes. If PDC had *not* gone first, Banana Kelly might never have begun.

"PDC was a failure, but it had value," says advocacy planner Ron Shiffman, who helped both PDC and Banana Kelly get started.

---

* LISC is the same nonprofit lending and grant-making organization mentioned in the Savannah story and one of the crucial supporting organizations of grass-roots endeavors. It is now the largest private community developer in the country, having grown from a $10 million enterprise with funds from the Ford Foundation and four corporations to a $125 million concern with contributions and loans from 400 corporations, insurance companies and philanthropies. LISC "builds builders," one observer noted, by financially assisting the groups and individuals in place and on the job.

Shiffman also points out that PDC left behind some ongoing accomplishments: renovated buildings, a community organization that has rescued near-abandoned buildings through weatherization and management programs, the seeds for a neighborhood network that didn't exist before PDC's arrival. These accomplishments are hardly the full measure of the original PDC promise, but they are still giant steps forward from the area's earlier despair. PDC still exists today, but in a different form—it manages city-owned housing units and operates weatherization, adult-education and social-service programs—and at a lower energy level than its publicity-generating beginning. It is a modest, but useful, community force.

While PDC was flourishing, Harry De Rienzo told Leon Potts and his friends what it was doing. They talked about it after the Casita Maria basketball games and were stimulated by what they heard. "We were intrigued that they were rebuilding a block when ours was falling down," says Potts, who is as quiet and self-effacing as his parents and equally strong-willed.

To Leon's group, Kelly Street seemed the perfect place to make the same effort. Under the leadership of Harry De Rienzo, they formed a community-improvement association, named it "Banana Kelly" for the gentle curve of the street. They put up a sign on the front of one of the buildings announcing their existence and declaring: "Don't Move, Improve." Banana Kelly could build upon the Potts family and the tenants remaining in the five buildings. As the first step, Banana Kelly rallied around the three buildings on the block scheduled for demolition by the city.

Leadership Emerges

Harry De Rienzo has the outsider's vision and the insider's heart. Tall, thin, fair and blue-eyed, Harry is as Irish-looking as they come, his mother's legacy. He was born in 1953 in the Bedford-Stuyvesant section of Brooklyn, then still a predominantly white working-class neighborhood. His father's grandfather, an architect, had fled Mussolini's Italy and arrived in New York penniless. The next two generations followed the first De Rienzo into the building trades.

Harry's maternal ancestors came here in the late nineteenth century. They spawned generations of municipal employees, firemen and policemen. When Harry was five, his family moved to Long Island, where he remained until returning to New York to attend Manhattan College in the Bronx.

Harry had been writing poetry since the age of thirteen, but when he was college age he seemed resigned to fulfilling the family's ambitions for him by majoring in accounting. He hated it and by his second year, De Rienzo recalls, "I was into drinking and drugs and didn't want any part of the business world. I was a mess." He turned his back on drugs and then got involved with a campus social-action group, spent most of his time developing remedial-reading programs in various East Harlem and Bronx neighborhoods and became a community organizer. After he was graduated twelfth in his class in 1975, De Rienzo took a job at Casita Maria, working with neighborhood youth. That was where Leon Potts and the rest of the basketball team played and where the seeds of Banana Kelly took root. De Rienzo was to Banana Kelly what Ramon Rueda was to PDC, although they are opposite personalities. De Rienzo is quiet and self-effacing, determined to stay out of the spotlight. Eventually he assumed a more aggressive public stance, but his focus remained on the organization's goals, not his own stature. He perceived himself not as an innovator but as someone who would take what others started and do better.

There were fifteen or twenty in the original group that started Banana Kelly, but by winter 1978 only five remained. "The rest were still interested," De Rienzo says, "but they didn't believe it could happen. They wanted to wait and see."

While the skeptics waited, or walked away in disbelief, De Rienzo, Potts and a few others protested the city's plan to demolish the three buildings. They wanted to take the buildings off the city's hands and renovate them. They were willing to sacrifice, to provide some unpaid labor. They wanted to build low-cost cooperative housing that would not be a permanent burden on other taxpayers, as was massive subsidized new construction. They wanted to be their own general contractors, their own developers. They had no construction skills, but they knew that if they got the right supervisors and trainers, the job would be done. They knew, as well, that there was an endless resource of neighborhood people looking for just this kind of job opportunity. What Banana Kelly was proposing was trading labor for ownership—"sweat equity."

Under sweat equity—only one of the many local varieties of self-help approaches then being applied around the country—a group of prospective tenants buys an abandoned building for a nominal price from the city and, at the same time, obtains a below-market-interest-rate loan for the renovation. The partially unpaid labor of the group and the low interest cost keep rents affordable. The "sweat," or contributed labor, becomes the tenants' equity, and after completion they move in as taxpaying cooperative owners. No one was suggesting that sweat equity was *the* answer to neighborhood rebirth, just one of many answers.

Such a proposal was anathema to traditionalists resistant to creative risk-taking, even though other groups were doing it successfully elsewhere in the city.* Why bother with such a small and complicated effort when many more, mass-produced projects could be built on vacant land, much more easily? Banana Kelly's goal defied conventional wisdom. It was a page right out of American history, a new version of the Homestead Act of 1862 that gave pioneers 160 acres to support a family.

In her article "Go Urban, Young Man—American Homesteading 1862–1974,"[10] Sophie Douglass Pfeiffer points out that President Abraham Lincoln signed the Homestead Act of 1862 because he was "in favor of cutting up the wild lands into small parcels so that every poor man may have a home." Ms. Pfeiffer notes that the empty urban areas of the 1970s are not unlike the unsettled West of the 1860s, "desperate in its need for the courageous settlers." Horace Greeley, an ardent proponent of homesteading, extolled the reform in the pages of the *New York Tribune,* writing that it would "increase the

---

* It is still a program that is more popular than significant only because of its meager acceptance in public policy.

proportion of working, independent, self-subsisting farmers in the land evermore." Ms. Pfeiffer also notes that "the high tide of homesteading came not in the years after the Civil War but in the decade embracing World War I."

From the start, the government gave willing pioneers public land to develop the great open spaces of the West, on the condition that the homesteader remain on the land and cultivate it for five years. Labor in exchange for a place to live and a source of livelihood was a well-accepted bartering system at the time, promoting both the settlement of the frontier and the concept of the self-sufficient entrepreneur.

Actually, as a result of a coalition of neighborhood-based development corporations pushing for change, the urban homesteading concept already had gotten under way on a national level, though it was pitifully limited in scope. It started in the early 1970s in Baltimore, in Philadelphia and in Wilmington, Delaware, where city officials sold abandoned or tax-foreclosed properties that had fallen into municipal ownership. Under the Housing and Community Development Act of 1974, HUD initiated in thirty-nine cities a four-year pilot homesteading project that received 3,542 properties whose federally guaranteed mortgages had been foreclosed. The homesteader, committed to living in the dwelling for three years, was given a lease for a nominal rent (usually $1 a year) and a twenty-year rehab loan at 3 percent interest. Municipal programs followed this model but were also quite limited, since local governments prefer to simply auction the foreclosed properties and not get involved at all in a homesteading process.

In 1978, HUD expanded the homesteading* program, revising its prior limitation of single-family dwellings to include multiple dwellings like those found in most deteriorated urban neighborhoods. The first **two** groups on whom this program was tested were PDC and

---

* "Homesteading" and "sweat equity" are often used interchangeably, but "homesteading" is a generic program term encompassing individual homeowning programs. "Sweat equity" refers more to a deeper level of individual input, usually involving a multiple dwelling.

Interfaith Adopt-A-Building, working in East Harlem and on the Lower East Side. Banana Kelly wanted to follow the example of those who had gone before and to rebuild a piece of the urban wasteland. They wanted to be pioneers. For Banana Kelly pioneers, the shells of buildings were the equivalent of vacant land.

Instinctivists Know How to Learn from Others

De Rienzo sought out contacts around the city. He talked to Rueda and took the Banana Kelly group to see what PDC was doing. "When we saw those beautiful apartments," Leon Potts says, shaking his head in remembered disbelief, "we knew we had to start working on our own project." De Rienzo talked to community leaders, especially the most potent political force in the neighborhood, Father Louis Gigante, a city councilman for four years (1974–78). Gigante is a silver-haired Italian priest in a largely Puerto Rican community. In the late 1960s, he became an outspoken activist on behalf of his diminishing parish. He started as an insurgent politician and quickly learned how to court the friendship and favors of entrenched political bosses around the Bronx and downtown. By filling the vacuum left by the Bronx politicians who had turned their backs on Gigante's impoverished community as soon as the white middle-class voters fled, Gigante easily replaced them as the dispenser of jobs and favors in the neighborhood.

In 1968, Gigante established a nonprofit organization, SEBCO (the Southeast Bronx Community Organization), and through it he was bringing in large sums of federal rehabilitation subsidies* that were beginning to transform run-down buildings right around the corner from Kelly Street and on nearby streets. Over the years, Father G, as he is known from Hunts Point to City Hall, orchestrated

---

* Primarily Section 8 funding, the federal rent subsidy under which a tenant pays 30 percent of his or her income for rent and the federal government pays the difference between the tenant's payment and the market rent. When Section 8 subsidies were combined with tax shelters, outside investors gained enormous benefits. The program was terminated under President Reagan.

the construction and rehabilitation of more than two thousand federally subsidized apartments in the area, mostly along East 163rd Street but on some of the side streets as well. Through the sale of tax shelters to investors, SEBCO earned more than $1 million, which was returned to the neighborhood through church-sponsored programs.

"If I weren't here, it would be all devastation," Gigante says. "I pushed government to bring back something that was dead." While Gigante tends to take credit for everything good that has happened in that neighborhood, his accomplishments are impressive. "SEBCO showed that it was possible to rebuild a neighborhood with scale," notes Anita Miller of LISC.

Gigante opened crucial doors for De Rienzo in the beginning, helping him get appointments with the right housing officials and other downtown bureaucrats. The De Rienzo approach, teaching people to survive on their own, was the antithesis of Gigante, the patriarch, the one his parishioners depended on totally. But once it was clear Harry was not a threat, Gigante was helpful.

Through Rueda at PDC, De Rienzo learned about the nurturing groups around the city. Starting in the 1960s, this network of technical assistance provided the support services for neighborhood self-help groups that government didn't. The Pratt Institute Center for Community and Environmental Development in Brooklyn, headed by Ron Shiffman, who has been there since its inception in 1963, is probably the oldest and most effective neighborhood advocacy and technical-assistance group in New York City. Aiming to empower neighborhoods and their residents, not merely study them, Pratt Center offers a combination of architectural, planning and other technical services, government monitoring and policy analysis. A key resource for community groups around New York, Pratt Center is a model for more recent ones in other cities, and Shiffman is one of the wisest and most effective advocacy planners in the country. Pratt Center gave Banana Kelly early advice on the structural soundness of the buildings targeted for renovation and later gave architectural assistance. The Association of Neighborhood Housing Developers, an organization of twenty-three community-based housing groups, already experienced in not-for-profit small rehabilitation work in Harlem, the Lower East Side and around the city, helped Banana Kelly to obtain job money from the state's summer Youth Corps program and from the federal CETA program. The Urban Homestead Assistance Board (UHAB),* sponsored by the Episcopal Cathedral Church of St. John the Divine to assist self-help neighborhood-based renovation efforts, had learned how to put together proposals for low-interest loans from banks and the city. Philip St. Georges and Chuck Laven, then co-directors of UHAB, advised Banana Kelly where to get money and how to fill out the loan applications.

St. Georges remembers his first meeting with Banana Kelly. "We did with them what we did with every community group that came to us for the first time," he says. "We told them every reason why they wouldn't get what they wanted. We told them of all the hurdles the system provides and painted the grimmest picture possible. If they came back a second time, we knew they could make it, and then we would really begin to work with them."

Banana Kelly went back a second time. The goal was to rescue the three buildings scheduled for demolition adjacent to the Pottses' building. They had to save those first or kiss the block goodbye, so Banana Kelly made the three buildings the target for their sweat-equity homesteading package. St. Georges made it clear, however, that the dream would take a long time to fulfill.

While the rehabilitation plan was being put on paper, Banana Kelly started a garden behind Kelly Street in a lot where once there had been another proud row of apartment houses. It was a sizable stretch of vacant rubble, filled with the debris of demolished buildings. Banana Kelly cleaned it out, held block parties and planted an assortment of vegetables and flowers. "We needed to get something

---

* UHAB started in 1974 and was incubated in an office on the grounds of the cathedral, moving out in 1987 to its own office in Lower Manhattan.

going that was visible," De Rienzo says, "a short-term project that would draw in a nucleus of people and establish a track record."

"Few people in the neighborhood believed we would get anywhere until they saw the garden, with carrots, collard greens, potatoes, cauliflower and other vegetables," Leon Potts recalls. "There weren't many gardens at that time in the South Bronx," he adds with a smile to underscore what it meant for people to see that garden bloom in the spring of 1977. They also built a barbecue pit where summer cookouts became a block ritual.

"The important thing," says Potts, "was to keep people involved, give them something they could see and keep spirits up—all our spirits up. The garden did that. We could see things growing and believe that one day the buildings would grow, too."

Ten people showed up in September 1977 when Banana Kelly started cleaning debris out of the first of the buildings they planned to rehabilitate. (Ironically, they were working on the site on the day of President Carter's October visit to Charlotte Street, and they watched the motorcade pass right by them. The motorcade didn't pause.) Banana Kelly had been told they had to get the cleaning out started even before receiving assurance from the city that they would get possession of the building or financing to do the rehab work. They had to get a lot going on their own before anyone "downtown" would take them seriously. Each member knew, at least, that their unpaid labor, a minimum of six hundred hours, would count as equity in a rehabilitated apartment if those apartments ever materialized. It was a risk.

Banana Kelly learned quickly to cleverly and creatively manipulate the bureaucracy to fulfill their needs. Since there was a Kelly Street rat problem, they turned to the city's Bureau of Pest Control for dumpsters to cart away the debris from the interior demolition of the three buildings. They obtained a day's help from twenty National Guardsmen from the Engineer Battalion on mandatory weekend duty, who usually spent their weekends maintaining equipment. One Saturday the Guardsmen came with two bulldozers and three front-end loaders to clear the rubble-strewn lot that was to be transformed into a park. The landscaping and the play equipment were later fashioned by neighborhood volunteers out of donated materials or recycled debris. Banana Kelly even persuaded companies to donate excess cement, dumping it on future basketball, paddleball and walkway sites instead of their common practice of dumping it illegally all over the Bronx.

"It's hard to keep people involved," Potts says, "when you don't even know if you can keep your promise, so anything to show we were still moving was a plus. We had sixteen- and nineteen-year-old dropouts to whom we offered hope of eventual skill-training, but we never knew if and when that program funding would come through." Banana Kelly's first government contract was with the city to hire twelve high-school dropouts for demolition work. (Banana Kelly later hired and trained these youths for renovation work.)

"During the demolition period, we figured if we could just get them used to working hard every day, we would have done some good. Most participants believed it would still be a developer who would do the job. They had lived their lives with someone always doing it for them. Many of their parents were on welfare. The system told them that someone else will always do it for them."

The people downtown for years promoted the idea that some outside force would "help" the poor people (often in order to control them). Home ownership, whether in upper-, or middle- or low-income areas, fosters stability and pride in a neighborhood. Home ownership among low-income people counters this legacy of "benevolence" based on the idea that the poor are incapable of providing for themselves, that only middle-income people are capable of so doing. Sweat equity, of the type that worked on Kelly Street, is the epitome of self-help and self-reliance.

Chapter Five

UNDERSTANDING THE LESSONS

■

The gritty determination of many of the South Bronx's indigenous groups to build a more decent environment for themselves in the face of every conceivable obstacle, and even while some Manhattan-based urban "experts" preached a gospel of "planned shrinkage" to terminate city services to the South Bronx, was perhaps the most exciting, heartening story we found in America's devastated city areas in recent years.

—NEAL PEIRCE AND JERRY HAGSTROM, *The Book of America*[1]

In the fall of 1978, Kelly Street looked grim. True, the garden had bloomed. Buildings were cleaned out and ready for a sweat-equity reconstruction, but the bureaucratic delays in getting the necessary city loans were continuing a year after the proposal. One of the five

Potts buildings had had an accidental fire that left it a burned-out shell. One of the Banana Kelly youth workers, an eighteen-year-old, died, along with six other members of his family, in a fire that destroyed their apartment house a block away from Kelly Street.

Government-subsidized, developer-built rehabilitation around the area was continuing nonstop. It was a more expensive design and less individually crafted than what Banana Kelly sought, and it required permanent rent subsidies, investor tax shelters and developer profits which Banana Kelly's plans did not. The sponsor was Father Gigante's community group, using conventional private developing methods to produce rehabilitated units at subsidized rents. The potential for future problems with tax-shelter-dependent housing is real; as time on the shelter starts running out, the economic incentive to continue ownership diminishes, often leading to abandonment. Gigante's was one way to help rebuild the community, but Banana Kelly members felt there was room in the neighborhood for a variety of methods. Their proposal had initially fallen on deaf ears at City Hall. The city had first refused them a rehabilitation loan, on the theory that if there wasn't enough city money available to do the whole block at once it was better to do nothing at all. Thinking small in a big way was not government's style. Banana Kelly kept pushing. Finally, promises of financing had been forthcoming from the city, but in the fall of 1978 Banana Kelly was still waiting to take title to the buildings and to close its first city loan.

The block had other vacant and abandoned buildings in addition to the three scheduled for demolition. Banana Kelly went to work on them too. "We had six buildings cleaned out even though the city was only prepared to help us with three," De Rienzo says. "We were working faster than the city could respond. But we couldn't stop and wait for them to catch up. Four or five other groups in the area were waiting to see how we made out, before starting their own effort."

Even with a track record established by the more than a dozen neighborhood groups around the city—including PDC—not enough had changed to let this genuine revitalization process take root on Kelly Street. By the mid-1970s, do-it-yourself activism was very much in the air around the country. At the beginning of the decade, approximately one hundred groups were functioning; by the end of the decade, one thousand community-based development groups existed.[2] Self-help had long been attractive to grass-roots groups, but one fiscal crisis followed another and one budget cut followed another, and finally grass-roots self-help began to gain appeal in the halls of power, where large federal grants now were scarce. Because of new economic realities, the small local-based effort was an idea whose time had come. (Its gain in favor seems to rise and fall in accordance with bad and good times.) Yet the notion of neighborhoods taking their fate into their own hands still permeated the rhetoric more than the policy of public life.

A very real problem, however, was mushrooming in New York City, a problem which no official program adequately tackled and which was forcing government to respond to creative alternative solutions. An accelerated real-estate-tax foreclosure process had created an unmanageable deluge of city-owned buildings. This meant that thousands of occupied and unoccupied residential properties, like the three Kelly Street buildings, were falling into the city's hands. The city just couldn't handle the flood. Out of sheer necessity, the city developed, over the next few years, a number of programs based on community efforts which turned management control and some ownership over to tenants. At the same time, these programs helped the city divest itself of either management or ownership responsibility, kept tenants in their apartments and worked to get the properties on tax rolls by helping tenants to buy and manage their buildings.

The alternative management programs* were proposed by a coalition of groups—the Urban Homestead Assistance Board (UHAB), the Association of Neighborhood Housing Developers, the Pratt Center for Community and Environmental Development, and Operation Open City (a community-development group that had orga-

---

* Alternative management programs should not be confused with the buildings centrally managed by the city as public housing, not under alternative management and often criticized in the press.

nized years earlier around fair-housing issues)—brought together by Ruth Messinger, a member of the City Council from Manhattan's Upper West Side. The grass-roots origin is important to remember for two significant reasons: first, because the city now is so proud of its genuine accomplishments under these programs, even though the idea did not start with government;* second, because it illustrates the value to government of neighborhood planning efforts. The city eventually adopted the program promoted by neighborhood advocates, and, to the city government's credit, the program's success gained considerable attention and praise. Importantly, this success also shows what can result from creative responsiveness on the part of city officials, in this case then Commissioner of Housing, Preservation and Development, Nathan Leventhal, who saw no easy solution to the in-rem problem and was willing to give the community proposal a try. In fact, one of the community advocates, Phillip St. Georges, was put in charge of the programs. This partnership evolved slowly and painfully. In the meantime, neighborhood or tenant groups repeated the same struggle each time they wanted to save a building.

Traditional Planning Persists

Banana Kelly was challenging the system in every way possible, pushing for the first mortgage and job training money. De Rienzo wrote letters to public officials, reminding them of their well-publicized promises of help for the South Bronx. De Rienzo was trying to bend it to meet Banana Kelly's modest needs. Out of the system, however, was coming the First Step of a Plan—the byproduct of the presidential visit a year earlier. It was one more adornment of a splashy effort that, of course, would never materialize. That it did not materialize is fortunate. The history of earlier mistakes proves that anything is *not* better than something if that something is just one more big mistake.

* The idea was primarily the brainchild of advocacy planner Brian Sullivan of the Pratt Center.

The announced project was a $32 million, 732-unit moderate-income cooperative housing venture for Charlotte Street, the square block of bulldozed rubble where the President had stood in 1977 and from where the photographic image of the irreparable wasteland had been sent across the country and around the world. Predictably, the Charlotte Street proposal had elements that would camouflage its similarity to earlier errors. It was on empty land; no bulldozer would be needed. It was low-rise; no Co-op City towers here.

Critics argued, however, that the Charlotte Street Plan was too big, too expensive, in the wrong place, not linked to the employment needs of local residents, a guaranteed drain on working-class tenants from nearby neighborhoods, a continuation of the cycle of building up one area at the expense of others, a reflection of three decades of development thinking. All of those things were true and the plan had nothing whatever to do with genuine revitalization. The grass-roots efforts under way and in need of nurturing were inspiring, visionary and valid. Charlotte Street, however, was political reality. Ron Shiffman likened the Charlotte Street proposal to the planting of "one large tree in the desert so all the shade is in one place." Instead, he said, there should be "seedlings" planted all over the South Bronx. What a lot of seedlings $32 million could buy!

For more than a year, public debate raged over the Charlotte Street proposal. Leaders in other sections of the city understandably objected that too much financial commitment to the South Bronx would leave nothing for them. Residents of nearby areas let it be known that the project did not address any of their needs. Community leaders demanded construction jobs for the local unemployed, but unions refused guarantees. Washington and City Hall played a continuous game of one-upmanship, each expressing doubts about the other's commitment and competence. Members of both the New York City Planning Commission and the Board of Estimate, the city's primary legislative body, voiced endless reservations but voted in favor. They were taking what Planning Commission Chairman Robert F. Wagner, Jr., called a "leap of faith."

Washington officials promised that Charlotte Street was only the beginning of a $42 billion, seven-year federally funded effort. A larger, more comprehensive *plan* would be developed as Charlotte Street was being built. Skeptics charged that the scheme required government subsidies for which funding did not exist. No one was even discussing a meaningful program to deter continuing abandonment. Big bucks could be spent on conventionally designed and conventionally built new development, but there was no comparable commitment in the offing to spend money on saving what already existed. Eventually, fourteen months after the President's visit, the whole package fell apart. Criticism of the project kept trickling out of the Carter White House. "The President does not feel a building should be erected in a particular spot simply because he happened to set foot there," said a White House aide, prompting angry comments from City Hall. White House spokesmen were saying that they had never liked the Charlotte Street proposal in the first place—and, in fact, were embarrassed by it—but they weren't specifying what kind of program they wanted.

In early February 1979, the city's Board of Estimate reversed its earlier approval of the Charlotte Street proposal and voted overwhelmingly, against the mayor's publicly stated wishes, to defeat it. Deputy Mayor Herman Badillo, the administration's major proponent of the proposal, accused the mayor and other Board of Estimate members of not caring about the South Bronx at all. Mayor Koch said he would now rely on Edward Logue, whom he had appointed earlier to coordinate the city's South Bronx efforts, to come up with a master plan. Logue had honed his urban-renewal skills on New Haven, Connecticut, and Boston in the heyday of Big Plans, earning him glowing comparisons to Robert Moses. Logue said a South Bronx plan would take another fifteen months to prepare. The ball was now entirely in Logue's court. The city had been spared yet another costly mistake, another project that would drain vitality from areas needing help instead. But no one knew what would happen next.

Much of what had occurred in the eighteen months after Carter's visit was exactly what the people of the South Bronx expected. Year in and year out, officials had come, reacted and promised help, with not much to show for it. People greeted joylessly and skeptically the news of a bundle of money coming from Washington. They knew they would have to continue fighting among themselves for the crumbs while builders, bankers, planning consultants, lawyers and dozens of related professionals walked off with the cake. They knew instinctively what they needed: policies that favored tenant involvement, self-help, home ownership and entrepreneurial creativity. They knew they could get jobs in factories, where they still existed, but not on construction crews. Some knew they could start their own businesses, if only they had help. Many people in the South Bronx just wanted help in doing what they were already doing to save their neighborhoods. They wanted the obstacles to urban rebirth removed. But since such policies had never come before, why should they now?

Understanding the Bits and Pieces of Banana Kelly Success

One evening in the winter of 1982, a small seminar took place in an elegant nineteenth-century room of the Urban Center, in the plush heart of Manhattan. The Urban Center is the crowning glory of the Municipal Art Society, one of the city's oldest and most respected urban-design watchdog groups. It is located in what used to be the Villard Houses, the three 1880s McKim, Mead and White landmark mansions behind which a luxury hotel,* the Helmsley Palace, was built in 1979. There was a precedent-setting battle to get the powerful New York developer Harry Helmsley to incorporate the landmark into the new building. Most of the U-shaped mansion complex became part of the formal entrance to the hotel, with some of the incomparable interior rooms used as restaurants, cocktail lounges or public spaces, by far the nicest part of the otherwise new and gawdy hotel. One wing of the Villard Houses was rented to the Municipal Art Society and converted into the Urban Center, where exhibits and lectures related to urban-design issues are held. The controversy that

---

* Emery Roth & Sons were the architects for the new hotel and its incorporation of the existing landmark.

ended in this successful solution was one of the more impassioned debates on New York's controversial development scene. The victory established a new standard throughout the country for the combination of historic preservation and new construction. The Municipal Art Society was a leader in that battle, as it was in the fight to save Grand Central Terminal and, later, Bertram G. Goodhue's 1919 St. Bartholomew's Church, the limestone and salmon-colored brick Byzantine church with a gold-colored dome. And although its record for courage in the face of potent development pressures is uneven, the Municipal Art Society was, by far, the preeminent civic group on New York City's planning, development and urban-design scene. To gain its attention was to Arrive.

On this winter evening in 1982, the Urban Center seminar focused on Banana Kelly. Scarcely five years after its meager beginning, Banana Kelly was a "big deal," not only to "downtown" but also to anyone across the country aware of the growth of the neighborhood movement. Charlotte Street had failed and was slowly fading from the headlines. Banana Kelly succeeded despite everything.

Banana Kelly had finally, in 1979, secured from the city the three abandoned buildings. The twenty-one homesteading families moved in during the fall of 1981. The total cost of the three-building renovation was $540,000 (including job training for forty workers and apartment rehabilitation at $26,000 per unit), considerably less than either new construction or the $45,000 per unit for low-income (Section 8) developer-sponsored rehabilitation. Banana Kelly, however, accomplished much more than the rehabilitation of those twenty-one units, so much more that in retrospect the three buildings seem a mere symbolic beginning when, indeed, they were a major achievement. Even by conventional standards—those that depend on hard numbers but neglect to measure lives—Banana Kelly's success is impressive.

The Urban Center seminar coincided with an exhibition, "Urban Pioneers: Don't Move, Improve!" adopting Banana Kelly's own slogan and highlighting the achievements of Banana Kelly and similar groups around the state. The exhibit, which featured poignant before, during and after photographs, was organized and sponsored by the New York State Division of Housing and Community Renewal, which had given technical-assistance grants to self-help groups. It is difficult to cheer, without a heavy note of cynicism, a statewide program that is funded with a meager $8 million annually when billions continue to pour into big, ill-conceived projects. However, this was one of the first state programs of its kind in the country. Six years of funding totaled $27 million. The State Housing Department, in fact, was the first government level to respond with money to Banana Kelly's needs; its technical-assistance grants of up to $100,000 were indeed significant for the more than two hundred groups, including rural ones, around the state receiving them. That kind of drop in the bucket often makes all the difference in the world in the destiny of one community.

At the Urban Center, Mildred Velez spoke for Banana Kelly. A short, vibrant woman with jet-black hair and eyes, Velez was one of the Banana Kelly "originals" and one of its great strengths. Velez was born and raised in the Kelly Street neighborhood and ran the open-space and youth-training programs. Named in her honor was the Kelly Street corner park's Magnificent Milly Dragon, a creative piece of play equipment made out of recycled rubble such as pipes, rocks and rubber tires.* In 1977 she gave up a "promising but routine" secretarial job in a Wall Street law firm for fulltime work with Banana Kelly and became one of the homesteaders living in the first three buildings.

An informative package of brochures and statistics listed basic accomplishments: 21 units rehabbed; 186 units in city-owned buildings under Banana Kelly management, including 18 units newly renovated; 75 apartments with new windows and weatherized; 20 buildings sealed in preparation for renovation; technical assistance provided to local property owners. That was the traditional bottom

---

* That park, which had served as a catalyst for community involvement, eventually lost appeal. Community energy turned elsewhere, but it had galvanized people in the beginning.

line. But that night at the Urban Center, Millie Velez tried to tell "the story."

"We were looking to block deterioration of our neighborhood," she said. "We had our first meeting in September 1977, started gutting three buildings and waited one and a half years for approval of our loan. During that time, we cleaned alleyways, cleared rubble and planted a garden. Best of all, we drew people. The next year, we expanded to working on sealing vacant buildings for future renovation and weatherizing occupied buildings,* transforming them from houses where people had to live to homes where they want to live. We organized a food cooperative and recycled paper and glass for income. We trained, employed and graduated hundreds of high-school dropouts. We have our own expert construction crew."

The expressions on the faces in the audience—planners, interested members of the public, civic leaders—ranged from puzzlement to awe. Questions were forthcoming slowly, but few in the audience even knew what questions to ask. Most of the listeners didn't know how to begin to understand what really happened on Kelly Street. It was hard for Millie to explain.

"Did you have help or support from local merchants?" someone asked. "In 1977 the merchants wanted nothing to do with us," Velez replied with a laugh. "We were just a bunch of kids trying to do something. They didn't understand."

"How did you get rid of the garbage?" another asked.

"In the beginning," Velez said, "we put it out on the street, called the Sanitation Department and figured sooner or later they would pick it up." Eventually, she added, they got an interest-free loan from the Consumer-Farmer Foundation,† which was giving seed-money

---

* Under the federally funded weatherization program, the average fuel saving per unit was estimated at 20 percent. The per-unit cost was $1,200 in mid-1984. The program used mostly community-based contractors and provided entry-level employment for low-skilled neighborhood residents. It was one of the most cost-effective national programs. By 1984, Banana Kelly was the largest weatherization contractor in the Bronx.
† Founded in 1970, the Consumer-Farmer Foundation provides interest-free loans to low-income homesteaders trying to salvage abandoned buildings across the city. The

loans to homesteading groups. The loan was used to rent dumpsters to cart away garbage and construction debris.

In answer to other questions, Velez noted that the homesteaders pay real-estate taxes, that the waiting list for apartments is always full and that they are working closely with private, small landlords in the area, offering a bulk fuel-and-supplies buying program and management assistance with tax, eviction and repair problems. "We don't condemn landlords," Velez noted in serious tones, "we're here to help them. We've helped nine or ten landlords get back on their feet. Without us they might have abandoned their buildings." It was the first hint of a boast.

On this 1982 winter night, it was hard to remember the earlier struggle. The press release cited Banana Kelly's accomplishments in housing, economic development, energy conservation, Open Space, and community services. A large group from the 1980 Democratic National convention visited the site. David Rockefeller, board chairman of Chase Manhattan Bank, toured it and wrote a laudatory letter ("The success of Banana Kelly certainly demonstrates that one of the major strengths of the South Bronx is its people"), and over two years' time Chase Manhattan Bank gave a token $13,500 in grants. Pictures taken of Rockefeller on Kelly Street were used in the bank's April 1981 newsletter, "Chase News," to highlight what the bank was doing for distressed urban neighborhoods. Two other banks, Chemical and Morgan Guaranty, also gave grants. Five government agencies gave contracts, loans or grants. By 1982 Banana Kelly had administered a combination of $4 million worth of different programs and rehabilitation funds since its first youth unemployment contract in April of 1978.

---

organization is a successor to a milk-processing and -delivery cooperative of the same name. In 1972 the cooperative was transformed into a seed and emergency loan-making foundation aimed at housing revitalization in low-income neighborhoods. With loans ranging from $3,000 to $12,000, the foundation in twelve years has loaned approximately $2 million to several hundred tenant groups, helping more than 4,000 families to build and own low-income co-ops. In 1982, De Rienzo resigned as executive director of Banana Kelly to become vice-president and executive director of this foundation.

Yet a first-time visitor to Kelly Street could never visualize the full extent of what had transpired. This is as impossible as judging a newly built development project without having seen what was replaced. E. F. Schumacher wrote: "The modern tendency is to see and become conscious of only the visible and to forget the invisible things that are making the visible possible and keep it going."[3] "I can't even explain it to my students," said Ron Shiffman. Shiffman has probably done more than any other outsider to bring attention to Banana Kelly. "I first started coming in 1970," he said, "when one building after another was being abandoned. The substance of change here is what is important, not the slowness of the rate of change. Banana Kelly was not producing the apartment units as fast as the system prefers, but what they were doing supports genuine long-term growth. They were not self-sufficient and they may never be, but they were certainly less dependent. Banana Kellys should be able to grow like crabgrass everywhere, but they aren't."

Small Changes, Big Difference

The key to understanding the current neighborhood is to realize that without the effort of Banana Kelly it probably wouldn't exist today. Barren rubble might be where now a modest working-class community lives. In the classic movie *It's a Wonderful Life,* George Bailey (Jimmy Stewart) wants to commit suicide by jumping off a bridge until the Angel Clarence (Henry Travers) intervenes and makes him look first at what his town would be like if he had never lived. The view of the town and its people, impoverished and miserable in numerous ways, persuades Bailey that his life is worthwhile. Similarly, one must look at what might be true if the Banana Kelly story had not occurred.

The high-school dropouts—now trained, graduated and employed—would probably still be dropouts. The resident families of once deteriorating apartments would have kept moving like Gypsies as the cycle of arson and abandonment continued; instead, they either own or rent upgraded apartments. The neighborhood merchants, who were rapidly losing customers and probably never expected new ones to move into the area, might be out of business altogether. Paralleling the residential upgrading, new businesses were filling up some of the long-vacant stores. Others expanded, and some continued just surviving. On one nearby commercial strip, $4,000 key money was required in 1987 for a store that had been vacant only a few years earlier. Even fruit and vegetable peddlers returned to the area, a throwback to the 1920s and 1930s. Today's peddler is potentially tomorrow's shopkeeper.

The importance of the change is endless. Banana Kelly pulled and tugged at a bureaucracy that first ignored it and then gave grudging support. By the mid-1980s, Banana Kelly was not only noticed by the traditional spheres of power but in some cases participating in joint ventures with them. Together, Banana Kelly and Father Gigante's SEBCO renovated a vacant 1920s Kelly Street apartment house with sixty apartments, facing the three sweat-equity buildings. Banana Kelly's construction crew worked on the building, and Banana Kelly shared in the profits that usually go only to the private developer.

Small Thinking, Not Thinking Small

On a vacant site between Kelly Street and Father Gigante's 1909 church, twenty-four brick-faced two- and three-story homes were built in 1983 under the guidance of the South Bronx Development Organization, headed by Ed Logue. Clusters of town houses* were built in several South Bronx areas, with federal interest subsidies providing below-market mortgage rates—a rare example of a sensible government infill program, filling in empty space without bulldozing usable buildings to create that space. Logue has always worked best on empty land. In the South Bronx, however, the bulldozer is no longer needed. Five hundred empty acres are left over from "slum clearance" days. Logue was operating for four years with a staff of

---

* Under the federal Section 235 program, these homes were going to families with incomes between $14,000 and $26,000, who paid $4,000 down on a $50–$60,000 home. The program as a whole was killed under the Reagan Administration, but this batch of houses was allowed to go through.

about sixty-five and an annual budget of approximately $3 or 4 million. He had an assortment of programs in the works or on the drawing boards, such as channeling developer-built, subsidized rehabilitation into target neighborhoods and assisting some sizable businesses to expand. But the new-home program on city land with heavy government subsidies was his most publicized achievement.

The new-home program underscored the difference between thinking small, the creative lesson of Banana Kelly, and small thinking as exhibited in this program inappropriately aimed at the suburbanization of the Bronx. The density and lifestyle of an urban neighborhood is not conducive to ranch houses set on private lawns, characteristic of the suburbs but neither urban in character nor very efficient operationally. In fact, the row house, a uniquely urban style, happens to be one of the most energy-efficient building styles, one that is being emulated in more and more suburban communities around the country. A contemporary version of the brownstone or brick row house would have been a more logical style of urban infill housing and was used for some of the developments elsewhere in the Bronx under the same financing program.

While Logue was primarily focused elsewhere, Banana Kelly was expanding and transferring its self-help model—assisting small owners with management, establishing supplies- and fuel-buying cooperatives and contracting with the city to manage, weatherize and renovate city-owned buildings—to other blocks in the neighborhood, fashioning new variations of its own successful strategies as needs of others dictated.

Genuine Revitalization Spreads

Separate from Banana Kelly, a twelve-block district of 180 Victorian row houses was also on the upswing, only a stone's throw from Kelly Street and probably the most visually appealing additional change in the community. We saw earlier how Savannah Landmark's Victorian District accomplishments spurred or strengthened efforts in neighboring areas. Similarly, Kelly Street's rejuvenation indirectly aided the rebirth of this Longwood Historic District, designated officially in two phases, July 1980 and February 1983, by the city's Landmarks Preservation Commission because it "contains some of the best of the turn-of-the-century architecture that transformed the Bronx into an urban extension of Manhattan." If Kelly Street had continued to rot away, the decay would surely have spread to Longwood. The public and private institutions now aiding Longwood probably would have looked askance at helping an architecturally distinctive enclave unsupported by surrounding strength.

As David W. Dunlap noted in *The New York Times* in October 1982, this "tiny neighborhood . . . has little in common with the prevailing image of the South Bronx. [It is] a community born in the 19th century and composed of homeowners, of acquaintances who know every face on the block, of people who have lived in one house for 30 or 40 years."

Longwood houses are 90 percent owner occupied. Most of the black and Hispanic middle-class residents grew up in these homes. "We moved here forty years ago," says Thomas Bess, who organized a strong community association with neighbor Marilyn Smith, another longtime homeowner. "We gave up Harlem to move up the ladder to the Bronx," Bess adds with a smile.

The semidetached brick and stone houses with iron-gated alleyways, bay windows, wide stoops and varied ornamentation were built between 1897 and 1900. Longwood, the Landmarks Preservation Commission designation report notes, had remained rural "until the very last years of the 19th century—when plans for the IRT subway connecting the Bronx and Manhattan were made known."

Following the landmark-district designation of the neighborhood, Longwood homeowners were eligible for city facade-improvement loans. Previously, they had no financial resource for needed upgrading. The Local Initiative Support Corporation (LISC)—the private consortium of foundation and corporation money that had already helped Banana Kelly—the New York State Department of Housing and Community Renewal, and the Inner-City Ventures Fund of the National Trust for Historic Preservation which had funded Savannah's Beech Institute, all provided technical assistance, staff funding, and grants and loans to buy and renovate eight abandoned brownstones. Grudgingly at first, the Longwood residents acknowledged that Kelly Street was an encouraging model. "We were guilty of snobbism when we first heard about Banana Kelly," admits Bess. "After all, we were brownstoners. We came to recognize the strength our existence gave them and their existence gives us."

Other things were happening. A young professional family with children bought a Longwood home, the first new blood in years. An empty red-brick school between Longwood and Banana Kelly reopened as a community facility, including a branch of the Bronx Museum and government offices. By 1987, the family and children population of the area had grown sufficiently again for consideration of converting the building back to a school. Tiffany Plaza, a new outdoor gathering spot, with ornamental fountains of lion's heads made in Italy, an outdoor stage and trees, graces the front yard of Father Gigante's St. Athanasius Church. By itself, the 1909 red-brick church is a neighborhood landmark. Tiffany Plaza, so reminiscent of Italian piazzas with its Mediterranean white and pink walls, adds a touch of artistic whimsy.

The spectrum of change in the Kelly Street vicinity is a marvel of genuine rebirth. The area is a diversified urban forest, rejuvenating at its own pace and in its own shape. There is no "big tree keeping all the shade in one place." Earlier years of arson and demolition pruned the forest. Considerable open space remains. An overcrowded slum does not threaten to reappear. Banana Kelly consciously limited its own growth to manageable proportions, purposely taking on small bits and pieces and leaving room for neighbors to do likewise.

Change Did Not Stop

Ten years after the Banana Kelly effort began, much had changed. Frank and Frances Potts had sold most of their buildings to new investors and retired back to Mississippi. Occasionally, they return to Kelly Street to visit remaining family and old friends and to check on the one building they still own. Leon Potts has moved on as well, also leaving the community to work in construction elsewhere. Banana

Kelly went through a series of changes after Harry De Rienzo left. Now primarily a successful community-development organization, involved in the financial packaging, construction and management that few would have dreamed of ten years earlier, it continues struggling with city agencies over community-management programs. The cast of characters has changed. The leadership and the programs have evolved. But the revitalization process continues, shaped more by the needs of the moment than any highly developed plan worked out earlier.

"It has been demonstrated that even a slight improvement in neighborhood conditions has a snowballing effect," wrote former Deputy Mayor Robert Price, president of Price Communications Corporation.[4] And Neal R. Peirce and Carol F. Steinbach note: "When residents of endangered buildings or neighborhoods realize they can make decisions for themselves, attitudes and habits change abruptly. Crime, vandalism, and drug use plummet. Buildings that police once feared to enter become self-policing."[5]

In this organic process, circumstances change imperceptibly at first until eventually it is not a different world but a better one, one that never could have been planned to happen this way.

Sadly, it seems that in New York and other cities the neighborhood movement has come full cycle. Banana Kelly groups were modestly celebrated for doing what no one else dared do and in places no one else thought worthwhile at a time of slow private development activity. Community efforts reseeded the Bronx and other sites of urban decay. Change was accomplished, but its lessons are predominantly left ignored. A new initiative is now taking root in these reseeded areas. Cities are going into the real-estate business and will select a new set of players.

In New York, for example, with other cities likely to follow swiftly, city agencies are looking to give vacant buildings to developers, mostly for middle-income housing and out of the price range of the majority of people who repopulated the deteriorated neighborhoods of the 1970s. At the same time, proposals multiply to create housing for the homeless in oversized chunks to be imposed on fragile neighborhoods for whom stability is such a struggle. Proposals abound, as well, to turn over large swaths of low-income communities to middle-income housing too expensive for most of the community residents and guaranteed to inflate real-estate values enough to price them out. The system is still looking for and responding to the developers who can produce the "numbers," first and foremost. The nurturing of the next generation of Banana Kellys is not a priority of public policy.

Success Does Not Alter Public Policy

Genuine community involvement in the planning process is seldom seen. Lessons learned in the past ten years are being applied rarely. And applying the lessons of the Banana Kellys or other grass-roots successes to the current homeless challenge is hard to find as well. In fact, at the close of the 1980s the danger is that the plight of the homeless is tragically being manipulated in ways that will help others more than the homeless. Now, as Peter Marcuse, Columbia professor of urban planning, noted in *The Nation* April 4, 1987, "emergency assistance is the name of the game." Once again the housing errors of the 1960s and 1970s are in danger of repeating themselves in the name of the poor, providing windfalls for speculators, financiers, developers and construction-industry workers and, in the process, touching a small fraction of the problem. In June 1987, *The New York Times* reported:

> Some neighborhood housing experts believe a new crisis will evolve from the land speculation the borough is now experiencing. The profit margins on these buildings are slim, and the speculative prices do not reflect real value. . . . Once the speculation stops and these buyers become landlords, many may find their investment returns minimal and some may even have to dip into their own pockets to maintain the buildings.
>
> When this happened in the 1960s, buildings fell into disrepair, back taxes and maintenance problems mounted

and finally they either went up in smoke or landed in city hands. . . .[6]

The Banana Kelly strategy—it cannot be called a "plan"—guaranteed that at least the Hunts Point–Longwood section of the South Bronx was rejuvenated naturally, bolstering the existing fabric, not replacing it. Banana Kelly is an example of success that should have set a pattern but has not, that should have helped the city create public policy but has not. There are equally significant grass-roots efforts everywhere offering lessons that should be built upon but are not. Token public programs come and go with changing political administrations that make gestures to the relevancy of the many self-help mechanisms, but the notion of letting the Banana Kelly idea, or any of them, grow "like crabgrass" in the run-down neighborhoods of our nation's cities is nowhere meaningfully considered.

"It is hard to know what the right way to go is," notes Harry De Rienzo, "but the official directions are clearly wrong."

In fact, government provides generous advantages to big developments, advantages denied to or parsimoniously given to neighborhood-based efforts. The system is filled with contradictions that work against modest efforts. Government puts faith in developers who have failed in some earlier projects, but not in neighborhood groups that haven't had a chance to try. Big schemes gain support before they are even designed, but small efforts planned in advance to the last bathroom fixture beg in vain for attention. Developers of big subsidized projects often have lax accounting procedures, but the De Rienzos must account for every last nickel. Big projects secure bailouts when cost overruns loom, but little ones sink under the weight of the honest overrun.

To add to their burdens, community-based efforts also share common enemies. No one feels threatened if movements like these succeed or fail on a small scale. But when they achieve the unexpected, attract publicity and challenge conventional policies, opposition is automatic.

Unions, determined to protect the job opportunities of their own members and resistant to working with self-help groups, objected to the heavy reliance on unskilled, nonunion labor. When the CETA program was instituted in 1974 to train the unskilled and put to work the long-term unemployed, union leaders objected to its use for funding neighborhood labor. As long as these efforts were small and experimental, the unions were overruled. As the homesteading movement grew, the unions quietly threatened lawsuits, arguing that federal funds were being used illegally as a housing subsidy, not a training program. Government officials denied that union pressure affected CETA policy, but when the program was revised, in 1978, Banana Kelly and other neighborhood groups were told there would be no CETA money for their rehab labor. They would have to manipulate nonconstruction CETA funds, accept new red tape, additional bookkeeping burdens, construction-schedule complications and less money. Three years later, the entire CETA program was dead.

Unions were not the only ones to feel threatened. Developers feared the diversion of government funding into rehabilitation projects over which they had no control. They argued against expansion of community efforts, claiming that those efforts were inadequate to fill enormous needs and too time-consuming.

When union leaders and builders get angry, campaign fund-raising encounters problems. Elected officials don't find rehabilitation projects as appealing as grandiose new plans. They want the symbolic photogenic projects that attract press attention and show they are really *doing* something big. The time-consuming hassle required of small, meaningful plans may go unnoticed and unrewarded and thus is not worth the effort.

The Catch-22–type obstacles are unending for the Banana Kellys of our cities. Even worse, when success is achieved public officials minimize the gain and ignore the lessons. Over time, I interviewed countless government officials about the self-help neighborhood movement that was growing around New York and the country despite the herculean problems. All those interviewed lauded the varied efforts, admired the obvious perseverance, acknowledged the government-created problems. Many pointed out how they had helped where they could. At the same time, as if in unison, these government officials questioned the "significance" of the successes and doubted their real value in revitalizing any city. Few were seriously looking for ways to remove obstacles or to increase funding opportunities. Public officials loved to be recorded as praising such efforts, but couldn't see how to build upon the lessons.

One such official was Robert F. Wagner, Jr., then the chairman of the New York City Planning Commission, later deputy mayor under Mayor Edward I. Koch and now president of the New York City Board of Education. The namesake son of a former three-term mayor and grandson of a famous U.S. senator, Wagner had shown himself to be bright and articulate but unwilling to champion some of the issues he understood better than most public officials. He, like other public officials, was clearly in awe of efforts like Banana Kelly, yet puzzled about how to learn from it. "Yes, it is simply marvelous," Wagner said, "but the real question is, Can we replicate it?"

He was asking the wrong question. Invariably, however, this is the automatic official response. It is a question that misses the point about how cities grow and rebuild themselves. Such a question would be legitimate for any scientific experiment. The revitalization of cities is not a science; it is an art. It depends on creativity, variation, innovation.

Urban Revitalization Cannot Be Formulized

Many who seek cures for urban ills try to reduce the search to a pseudoscience they call "urbanology." For these "experts," solutions must be reduced to an exact repeatable formula in every neighborhood, in every city. That may be the logic behind the development of government programs, but cities cannot be approached this way. Cities don't evolve or revive according to hard-and-fast rules. Their problems, moreover, cannot be solved by rote. No two revitalized communities have experienced an identical chain of developments even though they have gone through similar revitalization processes.

An urban organism—a block, two blocks, a neighborhood or a whole city—must regenerate naturally to endure. Things must be allowed to happen and in a manner appropriate to a particular place.

Each neighborhood will be different, but each will have its own strengths, its own particular characteristics and people, and that will be the basis for future growth. Spread the news that this kind of thing can happen. And when other areas show interest, nurture and encourage them too. But no two neighborhoods do it the same way. What each locale needs, one observer noted, is "a public program of loose parts that can be assembled by circumstances, not on an assembly line."

This regeneration process cannot be mass-produced, and it is by no means easy. "Production by the masses, not mass production," is how E. F. Schumacher put it, although he was referring to specific economic functions. A good deal more attention and care are required than most governmental approaches are geared to provide. The complexity of the process requires more sensitivity than the easy way of letting one large redevelopment scheme engulf an area. Recognition must be given that residents—the unappreciated "instinctivists"—have indispensable knowledge of the strengths and weaknesses of their neighborhood. Thinking small and appropriately is respectable. Anything too big or too fast that often results in equally big and irreversible failures is avoided. The result, however, can be a true regrowth of the urban forest.

As this happens, each improving neighborhood becomes a visible example of what other neighborhoods can do, stimulating further renewal. This way, each neighborhood replicates itself, instead of others replicating it. If government chose to significantly aid and nurture this process, a more significant renewal would have a chance.

The "Unique Leader" Excuse

Elected officials and agency bureaucrats often either exaggerate their assistance to neighborhood groups or rationalize their lack of it. Sometimes minimizing obvious community group success is difficult, so instead they focus on the "uniqueness" of the leader. This occurred throughout my interviews about Banana Kelly and the scores of groups making waves in city after city from coast to coast.

In contradiction to the "unique leader" argument, LISC director Anita Miller, who worked with groups in dozens of cities, says, "You can find these leaders everywhere. The point is to cherish them when you find them and then walk away when they get too big for their britches. Actually, it takes more than charisma to pull and tug at the bureaucracy. Charisma is just not enough."

"The issue is not whether they are unique," adds Ron Shiffman, "but how to encourage these new neighborhood entrepreneurs. There are many people with potential. The challenge is to stimulate them, to give them hope and the technical knowhow so that they have a chance."

It takes the energy and intelligence of people to sow the seeds of change, no matter what the target. People, not institutions, make change, and there are competent and dedicated people in every city to fill the need. They are unusual, but not "unique." In one sense, the "uniqueness of the leader" argument is akin to the "drop in the bucket" excuse. It is true in the positive sense. The neighborhood movement is not unlike a network of small businesses, as Ron Shiffman points out. "Rueda, De Rienzo, Velez [just like Adler, Cincotta, Westmoreland and Ziegler, mentioned in earlier chapters] and all of them," says Shiffman, "are community entrepreneurs. Success depends only in part on their leadership. Some will succeed and some will fail. The trick is to nurture them all, not just a token one here and there."

At the height of PDC's success, Roger Starr, at the time head of the city's housing agency and now on the editorial board of *The New York Times,* said of Rueda, "I was impressed by his charismatic influence. But there was no way to expand on that kind of group without encountering the Peter Principle." But when I asked why other groups like it could not be encouraged to do similar things in neighborhoods all over the city, Starr replied, "You can't bail out the Bronx with a teaspoon. You would have to multiply by two hundred to make a dent." Exactly!

In fact by 1979 what had multiplied were South Bronx developers—the kind the city likes to deal with because they are conventional builders. (In February 1978, Mayor Koch temporarily
stopped city auctions of city-owned South Bronx properties after a
Daily News exposé three months earlier reported that speculators
were buying up land for resale to government-sponsored projects.)
They were receiving generous government subsidies for low-income
renovations. Many of these developers had unsatisfactory records on
earlier city-approved projects; so much for the kinds of things
government *can* guard against. By the later 1980s, the speculation
market was better than ever.

Thinking Big Is What Reality Is About

Former City Planning Commission Chairman Wagner was more
willing than most public officials to attribute considerable significance to the role of self-help groups in the revitalization process.
When asked why government then did not institutionalize the
encouragement of this movement, Wagner said it was "simple
bureaucratic convenience," an explanation that goes to the heart of
the problem. Wagner has always been good at articulating such
problems. While he was Planning Commission chairman and later as
deputy mayor, he was known as the "resident intellectual" of the
Koch administration. "We have not yet created the mechanisms to
deal with these groups," he noted correctly. "We've only created
mechanisms to deal with developers. You can get burned going to bat
for a local group, but you know that developers can deliver. That
makes life as a bureaucrat much easier, just as it is easier to measure
programs by the number of units they produce and to go with
someone who you know can get a building up even if it is not to your
liking. People in government prefer not to take risks. A developer
may be involved in a rip-off, but it can get covered up, whereas a
neighborhood group seems more vulnerable. Somehow big mistakes
get treated differently from smaller, well-intentioned errors." And so
the pattern continues.

Wagner described another Bronx neighborhood taking on the

challenges of revitalization. This community group had come to the City Planning Commission while he was chairman with a proposal to rehabilitate some three-story row housing. The area was one square block. Two sides had solidly built but abandoned row houses. Another side had a series of mostly vacant one-story stores, and the last had a vacant lot and three six-story old-law tenements (bathrooms in the hall, apartments with limited light and air). Wagner suggested to the neighborhood group that, yes, they could restore the three-story rows, but he asked them to consider a plan that would bring in a developer who could deal with the three six-story tenements. One of them, he said, was still in good shape, was occupied and required only modest rehabilitation. Rescue for the other two was deemed uneconomic. Wagner suggested demolishing those two and letting the developer build new three-story housing extending into the vacant parcel as well. It was a perfectly sensible proposal that combined recycling the old *and* erecting compatible infill housing. It also combined reliance on local people *and* a developer who would be responsive to their needs. But when I asked Wagner why such an approach could not be applied on a broader scale, he could not answer. Clearly, government sometimes knows how to do the right thing *in response to local initiative,* but does not know how to institutionalize a broader commitment. The exception remains a fluke. Wagner agreed. "I really don't know why that is true," he said.

Another planning official who had worked on the South Bronx explained, "It is too difficult and time-consuming to think small and work with these groups. Government has to look for the easier route, and that's the big developments. Thinking big is what this country has always been about."

Thinking big and wrong certainly remains true across the country. If anything, the continuing decline of the Bronx in the face of a long line of massive projects that failed to revitalize it should have proven by 1977 that big developments accelerate decline and dislocation rather than reverse them. A lot of people had gotten rich on those big developments, but few neighborhoods had prospered.

The basic urban-renewal approach of the 1950s and 1960s continues. The schemes don't automatically involve massive bulldozing and replacement anymore; too many vast bulldozed sites still remain from urban-renewal days. In many cases, projects are better designed. Some even include popular recycling of historic buildings. But in the 1980s they are still government's way.

Richard Kahan, who replaced Ed Logue as head of New York State's Urban Development Corporation in 1978, summed it up appropriately. Although he willingly championed his fair share of big projects, Kahan wanted to balance those headliners with incremental showpieces. "I can get the State Legislature to approve $70 million for a Long Island Cultural Center, $53 million for a new American Stock Exchange [a building which never got built] in Battery Park City, $375 million for a New York City Convention Center and $40 million for a Rochester Convention Center," he told me in the winter of 1982, "but I can't get more than a $12 million annual appropriation for small projects around the whole state. It is still easier to put a political coalition together around the big things, almost impossible around the small."

The urban-development histories illustrated so far have been stories of success. They reflect strategies and attitudes antithetical to mainstream urban-development thinking in this country. The philosophy underlying these tales of success will be examined in the next section and then contrasted with the redevelopment-and-large-scale-renewal philosophy.

URBAN HUSBANDRY

The Economy of Wisdom

■

Cities change or they stagnate. But how they change—how the rights of property are made to balance with the less tangible public interest—is one mark of civilization.

—BILL MOYERS, TV commentator[1]

The same rebirth process worked in both Savannah and the South Bronx, under starkly contrasting conditions. This fact underscores the strength of the genuine revitalization process. I call this process "Urban Husbandry." Just as husbandry means the care, management or conservation of animals, Urban Husbandry means the care, management or conservation of the built environment. The built environment is, in fact, a man-made ecosystem that stretches from individual streets within a city to the highways between cities. So far Urban Husbandry has occurred sporadically around the country. Where it has been applied, however, its success often has been remarkable. There are scores of other examples besides the ones cited in this book.

The fundamental principle of Urban Husbandry recognizable in the stories of Savannah, the South Bronx, Cincinnati and Pittsburgh is change that is gradual, natural, noncataclysmic and responsive to genuine economic and social needs. Too much does not happen at once in one place and by one public or private developer. Cities do not deteriorate overnight and, similarly, are not reborn overnight. Quick-fix responses at best camouflage problems and at worst exacerbate them. Cities respond most durably in the hands of many participants accomplishing gradually small bites, making small changes and big differences at the same time. That is the essence of Urban Husbandry.

There are many examples of gentle rebirth across the country, and their significance should not be undervalued. The big, new developments, however, get the publicity. Politicians love them. The small, scattered, multifaceted redeveloping communities often escape the notice of the media and, when reported, are depicted more as a novelty than as a significant occurrence. The predominant public impression of these community-based success stories is that they are minuscule compared to the predominance of new construction developments. It would not be surprising, however, if, taken collectively, all these small efforts occurring simultaneously around the country, whether in the creation of housing or in developing new businesses and job opportunities, comprise significant improvement activity. The impact of many small and scattered things happening may be difficult to measure but should not be minimized.

Several years ago, for example, studies by MIT economist* David

---

* In the 1979 study "The Job Generation Process," Birch and his associates at the MIT Program on Neighborhood and Regional Change showed that between 1969 and 1976 small businesses with nineteen or fewer employees generated 66 percent of all net new jobs, and that more than 80 percent were created by "start-up" firms from zero to four years of age. Large firms (five hundred employees or more) generated less than 15 percent of all net new jobs. The study also showed that small firms are four times more likely to expand than contract, and large firms are 52 percent more likely to shrink than to grow.

Birch revealed that more than 80 percent of all new jobs created in the national economy were generated by small businesses and less than 15 percent by the Fortune 500. Few similar comparisons and measurements, however, appear to have been made—or given widespread attention—between community-based development activity and large-scale new construction projects in the creation of housing.*

An article by William C. Baer focusing on "the shadow market"[2]— "the many processes that reconstruct the existing stock of housing by subdividing, merging, enlarging and generally improving it and that increase the stock by transforming nonresidential structures into housing," in other words, providing housing by means other than new construction—indicates that this activity provided "21 percent of the increase in the total housing stock from October, 1973, through September, 1980." As for low-income units, the shadow market significantly "accounted for one third of the low-cost units occupied by owners and half of the units occupied by renters." Looking at it another way, Baer wrote:

> The conventional view that additions to the U.S. housing stock occur through new construction needs modification. New construction is indeed the main source of additions, but it is becoming less dominant. During the 1950s and 1960s about 90 per cent of all additions came from new construction, but in the 1970s that source dropped below 80 per cent, reaching an average of 73 per cent in the years from 1973 to 1980. The shadow market accounted for the remainder.

Baer cites these figures to show that a significant option exists besides the standard: "The usual solution proposed to deal with the chronic

---

* It is more difficult to measure the number of jobs generated in such community-based developments as outlined in the stories of Savannah, Cincinnati, Pittsburgh and the South Bronx. The significance of those jobs should not be undervalued, however. Corporate job creation for commuting professionals is of less consequence to the economic and social well-being of moderate- and low-income communities than pockets of blue-collar jobs for local residents.

shortage of affordable housing in the U.S. is to build new housing, often with Federal subsidies to reduce the cost to the buyer or renter."

The main point here is that large-scale new construction is simply not the only way to add significantly to the housing stock. But unfortunately these construction figures camouflage dilemmas caused by the nature, not the number, of the increased units created by the shadow market. Too often, such as in New York City, for example, these numbers reflect accelerated, not gentle, change, where an inflated market, harassment patterns and conversion speculation result in gentrification with heavy displacement.

But even in New York City one can find an example of increased units without large-scale new construction and without the unfortunate side effects of rapid gentrification. This is New York City's alternative-management program within the Department of Housing and Preservation. The program—the neighborhood-based management of occupied buildings gained by the city through tax foreclosure, mentioned in the South Bronx story—was responsible in 1986 for the first increase in years in New York City's housing supply. According to an in-progress three-year study reported on in *The New York Times* in November 1987, the city lost 7,000 units between 1978 and 1981, gained 11,000 units between 1981 and 1984, and gained 37,000 units between 1984 and 1987. The 1984–87 increase was the largest since the 1960s. This gain was *not* because the program built new units, but because it prevented units from being lost. The rate of new units added to the market has remained fairly consistent at about 9,000 annually in the past few years. The difference is in the number of units saved—those units that would have been abandoned and demolished instead if deterioration had continued—primarily a reflection of the impact of the city's alternative-management program.

Gentle Change, Significant Impacts: Urban-Husbandry Hallmarks

It is difficult to measure the impact of the 1970s trend of carving new residential units out of historic buildings that were built for another purpose (mills, firehouses, city halls, factories) or of upgrading dilapidated survivors of earlier residential styles (Victorian wood-frames, brick row houses, Art Deco apartment houses, resort hotels). Regardless of the difficulty of measuring such scattered activity, its importance, both as a direct resource and as an indirect stimulator of other activities of value, should not be diminished. Urban Husbandry places the highest value on this kind of creative, dispersed upgrading.

Urban Husbandry also places great value on adjustability—adjustability in planning and design. Just as the urban economy has to be diversified and flexible to endure, buildings should be adjustable, like Toronto's St. Lawrence Neighborhood school (discussed later) and residential tower, which allowed for the adjustment in the ratio of the two uses. The varied and economically productive conversions today of the ordinary and notable buildings of earlier periods contrasts sharply with the obvious limitations of the oversized, monolithic buildings crowding today's urban landscape. Today one marvels at the conversions of old buildings that are now offices and residences or both. Office buildings are apartment houses, mansions are office buildings, manufacturing lofts are apartments, tenement apartments are small factories, everything from a barge to a barn is a restaurant, and even a granary has become a hotel. These buildings were not designed with flexibility in mind, but their manageable scale provided inherent adjustability and their design and quality construction provided inherent appeal. Is it possible to even imagine an alternative use for any of the sterile monsters of today that could well be the white elephants of tomorrow? The rigidity of the urban fabric now being created and the overwhelming scale of some of its highly publicized new buildings precludes even a semblance of the kind of flexibility required to weather economic ups and downs and systemic change. We are wiping out that legacy of adjustability piece by piece instead of reinforcing and reweaving to accommodate change.

Urban Husbandry Is a Merged Ethic

Urban Husbandry is not just the rescue and reuse of old buildings. It is not one more "new" housing or historic-preservation program. It is a multifaceted treatment of urban ills that conserves and preserves both the natural and the built environment, even if that built environment dates from the eighteenth or nineteenth century. The community-based development, historic-preservation and environmental-protection movements of the past decade have made a dramatic impact on the urban consciousness. Urban Husbandry draws and combines goals and strategies from those three movements. The Urban Husbandry ethic reflects all three.

This style of rejuvenation does not readily appeal to political leaders. It is not quick. It is not easy. It is not captured in one photograph, like one large development. It removes the lion's share of control and profits from the traditional power networks—realtors, developers, construction-trade unions, bankers, insurance brokers. It thus removes a powerful support of the political structure dependent on the campaign contributions of these lucrative sources.

This process transfers a good deal of the control from traditional power centers to communities. That is both the good news and the bad news—the good news because therein lies the secret of its effectiveness, and the bad news because that is precisely why its wide applicability is resisted. The resulting empowerment of neighborhood-based groups is quite threatening to political leaders, although it does not have to be. Essentially, Urban Husbandry is a process that works best for the people who live and work in cities. The lessons of its success offer strong clues to sensible cures for the problems of our cities.

While age and decay are natural to cities, as to all else, maintenance and care can hold them at bay. In Europe, where land and such materials as wood are in short supply, the husbanding of urban resources is an old habit. We, on the other hand, seem to wait until calamity comes, then throw everything away, start over and, when the pendulum returns, start over again, this time re-creating what was destroyed earlier.

Urban Husbandry is different from the earlier period of the historic-preservation movement which concentrated on saving and restoring single buildings as landmarks. Although culturally important, aesthetically enriching and often economically wise, this older preservation strategy, focusing primarily on isolated buildings, is sometimes of limited consequence to the surrounding environment. Under Urban Husbandry, old buildings in aging neighborhoods are renovated before new ones are built, not only because they are either architecturally notable or just structurally useful and socially valuable, but also because to let them deteriorate out of use is simply wasteful in physical and human terms. Thus, renovation before replacement— fixing the old before building new—is another principle of Urban Husbandry.

Social Investment, Not People Removal

In the reverse order, building new before repairing or stabilizing the old, deterioration of neighborhoods is not halted, only camouflaged. The social institutions and human relationships that define neighborhood cannot be either preserved or replicated with wholesale new development. These personal connections form the glue necessary to a sense of community—the extended family of church congregations or social clubs, the trust of the shopkeeper who knows the customers, the information networks formed in public spaces, school friendships among pupils, and encouragement of teachers who watch a child grow over time. People are rooted in neighborhoods because of these human factors as well as because of the more visible buildings.

Herbert J. Gans poignantly reported on this phenomenon in his classic book *The Urban Villagers: Group and Class in the Life of Italian-Americans,*[3] focusing on the shortsighted renewal policies that wiped clean the physical and social fabric of the West End of Boston. Based on the "middle-class bias of city planning and caretaking agencies," housing units were provided that, though "profitable for builders," were no substitute for the invisible subculture and intricate personal and social arrangements destroyed. Gans depicted vividly the inner working of a classic blue-collar community and conveyed how being forced to move "disrupts a family, disperses friends and relatives and imposes heavier financial burdens on slim budgets."

Some of today's worst social disaster zones were built to replace neighborhoods decreed slums not too many years ago. Many of those newer projects now require rebuilding. What was not recognized when those neighborhoods were erased—and what remains under-recognized and undervalued—is that the social subculture and the human networks were an integral part of the life of the former neighborhoods, equally if not more important than the run-down physical condition that new housing units addressed.

In 1972, Pruit Igo, a 1955 oversized, nonflexible St. Louis public-housing project, highly acclaimed for design advances,* was partially razed because of the difficulty and expense of correcting mistakes. Ten years after Boston's 1953 Columbia Point housing project was built, the oversized, nonflexible and unworkable 1,500-unit apartment complex was in decline. Now a $200 million redevelopment of primarily luxury apartments is replacing it. In Newark, two towers each with 200 apartments for poor tenants are being replaced with 100 town houses, also for poor tenants. In Dallas, 2,600 units of prisonlike public housing is scheduled for demolition, with tenants to be dispersed around the city in response to a segregation lawsuit. In Kansas City, five public-housing towers were imploded in 1987 to be replaced by town houses. In Boston and other communities, there are more creative responses wherein existing projects are remodeled by enlarging apartment size to reduce the number of units, upgrading a host of features and relandscaping for more communal use—a wise husbanding of a resource, instead of repeating the pattern of total destruction and total replacement. Other cities as well have projects that are either being dismantled and replaced (another kind of waste)† or are undergoing major remodeling before they even can be called old.

With many of these alterations, massive displacement of low-income people is accompanying the upgrading, just as it did when these poorly planned and oversized projects were built in the first

---

* The acclaimed innovations were the absence of interior hallways, outside entrances off outside corridors, and elevator banks for alternating floors.
† Unfortunately, in some places the motivation for dismantling past "project" mistakes is not the articulated welfare of the occupants but the increased value of the land the "project" sits on. The site may be valuable and the people residing there displaceable.

place. The last generation's renewal projects are being destroyed by the same problems that contributed to their deterioration because the root social problems are not addressed meaningfully. Buildings are being replaced without solving social problems. To uproot the residents of the 1,500* units (retaining 400 low-income units) at Columbia Point and rebuild it is to erase a bad building mistake *and* repeat an old social one. Planners are repeating the original renewal attitude that ignores the fundamental needs of the people the building program is ostensibly supposed to serve and excludes from the planning process those people who could contribute to the rebuilding of their lives, as well as buildings. Rebuilding the last generation's misdirected low-income projects into spiffy new upper- and middle-income enclaves may meet some standards of improved urban design, but not standards of social justice.

This goes to the core of another principle of Urban Husbandry: respecting the existing social fabric. Investing only in the physical structures of an area is not enough. By treating as invisible the intricate human relationships or disrupting the social and familial institutions, large new developments alienate the people of the area. Consequently, no matter how good the replacement buildings may or may not be, the neighborhood is not better, because the social fabric is in disrepair. People can adapt to appropriate change if the human institutions and social networks which root them in their neighborhoods survive. If the bulldozed neighborhoods had been rebuilt according to the principles of Urban Husbandry, slums would less likely be on those sites today. When new construction is in order, Urban Husbandry dictates that vacant spaces be filled first without displacing the social and institutional infrastructure. The design and scale of the new structures must harmonize with the surrounding

---

* Columbia Point residents claim that the destabilizing process was exacerbated by official management policy of leaving vacated apartments empty. The vacant units became hangouts for criminal elements, and remaining tenants became easy prey, making easier the final emptying out of the project for redevelopment. Coincidentally or not, the redevelopment interest in Columbia Point, a spectacular waterfront site, paralleled a decade of nationwide rediscovery of urban waterfronts.

area, instead of conflicting with or overpowering it. New housing alternatives must not be unaffordable to local residents. Urban Husbandry is what happened in Savannah, Kelly Street in the South Bronx, Pittsburgh and Mount Auburn, where redevelopment created new opportunities for both area residents and newcomers, not just newcomers.

The traditional government response to urban decay is Planned Shrinkage*: selectively abandoning old neighborhoods in unpopular areas of a city, while continuing to build new ones in popular sections; selectively allowing old parks and other public amenities to continue to deteriorate, while building new ones elsewhere; selectively allowing mass transit, old streets, sewer lines and other elements of a city's infrastructure to continue to decay, while building highways to encourage more of the cars that choke cities and creating new neighborhoods or "new towns" that require new infrastructures and the disruption of existing networks.

The Economy of Wisdom, Not the Economy of Waste

Urban Husbandry reverses those priorities and, predictably, is aggressively opposed by all segments of the politically potent construction/destruction industry. Because the Urban Husbandry ethic recognizes the big differences to be achieved with small increments, big infusions of funds are not a requirement for progress, and the boom-or-bust cycle of massive public spending programs is not its nemesis. Thus, Urban Husbandry works in both good and bad times, but it gains favor during periods of severe financial problems when money to invest in new large-scale projects is in short supply and modest efforts are the only game in town. The appeal of Urban Husbandry, however, should *not* be confined to periods of financial limits. As an economy of wisdom, it is always valuable.

One of New York's best periods of neighborhood revival, for example, occurred during just such a time of minimal new residential

---

* This is discussed in Chapter Seven.

construction. In 1980, when inflation went through the roof and interest rates soared, investment interest in new development in New York City, especially in Manhattan, was scarce and the new-building-starts index for the nation plummeted. Public officials and business leaders bemoaned the sad state of affairs. *The New York Times* in January 1980 published a three-part page-one series of articles entitled "No Vacancy" and outlined the drastic housing shortage caused by a standstill in new apartment-house construction. "The production of new conventionally financed rental housing has subsided to a postwar low," *Times* reporter Alan S. Oser noted. While this deceptively depressing trend continued, however, something positive was happening.

With the lack of affordable space in choice Manhattan neighborhoods, people were forced to look elsewhere, in neighborhoods that, in fact, had not had much infusion of new blood since the period of outmigration to the suburbs after World War II. These were areas in Queens, Brooklyn and the Bronx that apartment seekers and home buyers might not have considered if new housing had been available in the heart of Manhattan. Some people living in neighborhoods less in demand stayed by choice or because they simply could not afford to move, in effect helping to stabilize areas that might have suffered under the weight of a sizable exodus. These neighborhoods, in turn, had a better chance of appealing to newcomers.

In many neighborhoods this happened gradually, gently and without the dislocation caused by accelerated change and speculation. In others, the rate of change was too severe to avoid the excessive displacement caused by too much gentrification too quickly. Two things were thus happening simultaneously. The end result was that many fine, ignored neighborhoods—all suffering from different degrees of neglect or disinvestment—were rediscovered by value hunters who never would have arrived there save for financial pressure. Old neighborhoods that had been losing population for years, especially middle-class residents, got infusions of new people, new investment and new or increased stability. Urban Husbandry and the market were working on the most basic level, and working best in the neighborhoods where the urban fabric, though worn and frayed, had not been destroyed beyond reweaving.* Since the housing-industry depression was national, the same phenomenon occurred in older neighborhoods across the country, from Baltimore to Seattle, from Boston to San Francisco.

The condition of a city's fabric—its street life, human scale, architectural variety, cultural and commercial diversity and patchwork blend of old and new—is the key to its ability to weather economic shifts and social change. If the texture is destroyed, nothing is left but shreds and tatters. Urban Husbandry respects that texture by recognizing its ongoing social and economic value, and weaves it back to strength. It is more economical, sometimes faster, certainly more meaningful revitalization than the megadevelopments. When development comes in smaller, flexible doses, change continues as a constantly evolving process. The impact of its failures can be minimized or contained. The impact of its successes does not disrupt the surroundings by triggering overwhelming change.

Economic Development Is Process, Not Product

Urban Husbandry views the existing urban fabric as an economic asset. The construction/destruction industry argues that new buildings, new highways and all manner of big projects bolster the economy of the city. But the primary focus here is real estate and its development, not the city's economy and its growth. Economic development is really a process, not a development project or an end

---

* Abandonment and disinvestment under way in many neighborhoods did not cease everywhere. In some areas it was reversed, in others it slowed, and in still others, where the fabric was already irreparably damaged, it was unaffected. It should also be noted that it was during this period, approximately 1980 to 1986, that the city's homeless population—so apparent now—was growing, clearly the population first to lose in an upgrading neighborhood that provides no safeguards for its resident poor. In fact, the October 1986 *Real Estate Reporter* of the Real Estate Board of New York notes that 75 percent of the buildings constructed in Manhattan over the prior 15 years have been on sites previously occupied by single-room-occupancy units where many of today's homeless once lived. New York City's housing authority, in addition, estimates that in 36,000 public-housing units families doubled up during this period because of the loss of residence by family members.

product, a process of many different things, including venture capital, employment training, technical assistance and loans that build on the inherent strengths and indigenous talents of a work force and strengthens the outlets for those talents. That process, in all likelihood, includes development of some kind of real estate, whether it be the reuse of a large empty building or the construction of a building to house a growing industrial enterprise. That *construction project,* however, is part and parcel of the *economic development process,* and usually comes at the end of it, not the beginning.

David Birch's job-generation study mentioned earlier showed that most new jobs are created by small firms. Subsequent Birch studies continuously show that much job growth takes place in firms which are unable to afford the cost of new commercial buildings and, in fact, are the very firms most frequently displaced by this new large-scale construction. These threatened job generators, moreover, are often owned by local residents who have a stake in the community and who reinvest their profits in the local region and hire local residents.

Thus, another basic principle of Urban Husbandry is the nurturing of small businesses and the encouragement of new ones. Urban Husbandry fosters the expansion of existing businesses and avoids sacrificing the already diminishing manufacturing base offering the best employment opportunities to the semiskilled, urban population, for the sake of service-industry expansion that employs more suburban commuters than local residents. Too much functioning manufacturing and light industry is put out of business *unnaturally,* justified because manufacturing is reportedly dying. There is a difference, however, between dying of natural causes and having one's life terminated by outside real-estate decisions.*

---

* ". . . our manufacturing sector is now the most innovative portion of the U.S. economy," wrote Birch in *Inc.* June 1987 ("Is Manufacturing Dead?"). ". . . for every large declining company there are a host of younger, smaller, highly innovative businesses that are surging ahead—even in the oldest, most 'mature' segments of the sector. Manufacturing is hardly dead. It is bubbling with activity and innovation."

Joel Kotkin writes in *Inc.,* February 1988 ("The Great American Revival"): "Indeed, rather than dying, America's industrial base has actually been restructuring

Urban Husbandry nurtures neighborhoods so that the people who reside there benefit, mending the holes in the fabric—not creating new ones to fill. Institutions flourish by expanding the social, economic and educational opportunities for the neighborhood residents. Investment is directed to buildings and people, not just buildings. A new community center, library or recreation facility is often more important than one more housing project. Often, no construction is as important as the improvement of existing municipal services or schools.

Urban Husbandry does not have to be initiated by citizen groups outside government. That is the way it seems to happen, however, most of the time. But less important than sponsorship is the substance of the project.

Meaningful Public Participation and Debate

The best experts in a city are its users. The vision for a place should come from the community up, not from City Hall down. In the face of more and more inappropriate urban development, it is fashionable these days to call for more urban planning. Unfashionably, Urban Husbandry advocates less planning, at least the kind of planning ravaging urban America. Conventional urban planning, in fact, has been a major cause of the destruction of urban America. Too often, planning schemes are merely rationales for megadevelopment proposals of limited justification. There *are* commendable planning approaches that enhance rather than undermine urbanism. These alternative approaches, however, frequently do not prevail.

Of the hundreds of people interviewed for this book, the most

---

itself—painfully, at times unevenly, but ever so surely. Since the mid-1950s, the actual number of manufacturing jobs and the roles of manufacturing companies have increased even as manufacturing's share of the gross national product has gradually declined. But within the manufacturing sector, even greater changes are taking place. Between 1974 and 1984, large companies shed themselves of some 1.4 million manufacturing jobs, but during the same period 41,000 new manufacturing companies created enough new jobs to offset virtually all of those losses. As a result, companies with fewer than 250 employees now account for 46 percent of the manufacturing work force, up from 42 percent a decade ago. If the trend continues, small-scale manufacturing should pass the 50 percent mark by the 1990s."

astute urban observers I found—the people who best understood and advocated the genuine application of sound urban-development principles—were specialists or special-interest people, such as neighborhood housing leaders, historic-preservationists, mass-transit advocates, local merchants, park defenders/open-space promoters and specific project opponents who, in their articulation of what was wrong with a development proposal, frequently articulated innovative alternatives. Such individuals understand the urban organism from the inside out, from the street, not the drawing board, from the vantage point of how things work instead of an idealized vision of how things should work, from a specific human need, not an appraiser's book. By understanding and strengthening the parts, such people learn how to enhance and enrich the whole. It is a microview of a city. The macroview is the prevailing one, however, and that belongs to the bankers, the developers, and the city planners who, unfortunately for our cities, rearrange the parts to achieve the whole as they think it should be. It is urban change from the top down, and it destroys more than it rebuilds. It rests on the trickle-down theory of everything—housing, economics, planning. According to the trickle-down theory, the poor are supposed to get the remnants—housing, jobs and all else—from the rich as they move up and out. Urban Husbandry percolates up.

Planning Is Process

Under Urban Husbandry, the planning process has multiple starting points. A project may be initiated by the community, by government or by reaction to private plans from outside. A problem or set of problems is presented to the various communities of a city, and each community is assigned its fair share of that burden. The matter is solved by discussion and debate, not solved by fiat and friction. This contrasts with simply giving in to community opposition, letting the community avoid an issue and allowing the not-in-my-backyard syndrome to prevail. But this also contrasts with the common municipal approach of taking the easy, opportune way of dumping problems in big overwhelming doses on fragile neighborhoods.

Here is an example of how it could work. In the working-class neighborhood of Greenpoint-Williamsburg in Brooklyn, an old eight-building hospital was closed a few years ago because of a surplus of hospital beds created by the opening of a new facility not far away. The closed hospital complex was in sizable proportion to this primarily Italian and Hispanic neighborhood of single-family homes, small apartment buildings and factories, and anything that happened to the former hospital was bound to have a noticeable community impact. This community had experienced its fair share of negative change with young families moving away, accelerated storefront vacancies and the rest of the indices of decline. But starting in the mid-1970s and under the inspired leadership of the local Catholic church,* the neighborhood reversed decline. By the mid-1980s, residents who had considered leaving stayed instead and upgraded their homes, new residents and businesses were moving in, financial institutions were persuaded to grant improvement loans, small public grants were secured for modest physical improvements, and spirits were high—except with respect to the hospital closing.

Painfully aware of how fragile were the recent steps to increased stability, the community approached the city with a conversion plan for the former hospital that had been developed with the help of the Pratt Center for Community and Environmental Development, the technical-assistance and advocacy planning group led by Ron Shiffman that figured in the Kelly Street story. The community's plan—it was indeed a plan, but in a small dose—called for converting the hospital buildings to a multiuse facility, including a 200-bed nursing home, a group medical practice, apartments for elderly and for families, and a small shelter for the homeless. Busloads of community residents appeared at public hearings. Residents testified as to how the homeless men drifted around the streets and lounged around their neighborhood park, where residents now feared to enter. The city

---

* Led by Msgr. Walter J. Vetro of the St. Nicholas Roman Catholic Church, the neighborhood is a model of grass-roots problem-solving and locally led reversal of decline. Joseph Berger artfully reported on this success story in *The New York Times* August 25, 1986, in a story entitled "Parish Helps Save Neighborhood."

turned a deaf ear and gradually turned the facility into a shelter for seven hundred homeless men, a sizable population. Here is a prime example of lost opportunity in meaningful public-participation planning. The community's plan for the closed hospital was superior to the city's in every possible way. The city was looking only for a place to dump as large a portion possible of a citywide problem population. The community, in response, was willing to accept the seven hundred homeless men and spread them throughout the larger community so that no one area was overburdened and intruded upon, while accommodating some of those homeless in the converted hospital that would also have other uses as described.

If the city had followed the community's plan, that would have been a fine example of planning with *meaningful* public participation. I stress "meaningful" because the habit today is to measure public participation by the number of public meetings or smaller meetings with community groups. All the public meetings in the world add up to nothing if the public is not listened to and valued.

New and Large but Not Overwhelming

Although the preservation character of Urban Husbandry has been most emphasized so far, plenty of room remains in this approach for new construction on a large but not overwhelming scale. Size, however, is not the important standard; appropriateness is. Many large projects are inappropriate in scale, so the tendency to define "large" as inappropriate is understandable but not the point. So far, the best example of an appropriate large new construction project that I have found is in Toronto, Canada. It is a 44-acre area, adjoining the downtown commercial core, within walking distance of the Lake Ontario waterfront and assorted cultural attractions. It is a neighborhood with ten thousand residents.

When I first visited Toronto, in the mid-1970s, this area was still a desolate patchwork of dilapidated, mostly abandoned industrial buildings, junkyards, parking lots and empty space. One could grasp the extent of this vast dreariness from the back of the old St. Lawrence Market, a handsome brick shed built around the original

Town Hall of the City of York, Toronto's old center. The market is full of fresh produce, fish and meat—and shoppers. On the site adjacent to the market, a whole new neighborhood evolved—called the St. Lawrence Neighborhood. It is not a "project," but a genuine neighborhood—a network of streets, row houses, low-rise apartment houses, stores, offices, schools, recreational space and recycled industrial buildings. Down the middle is a spine of parkland that has both passive and active recreational uses and serves as a kind of urban common, bordered by its streets. It seems to attract both neighborhood residents and office workers. There is no shopping "center," just stores scattered in logically convenient locations.

Over the years, Toronto had many citizen-led battles against overscaled and bulldozer development. Scattered around the city are successful examples of unusual solutions that emerged from the resistance to "project building." Toronto had been forced to respond creatively by those neighborhood fights. It had *learned lessons* from earlier confrontations. For a while in the 1970s, the wise vision of a multicentered city dictated development policy. City-gouging expressways were killed, new commercial development was governed by the capacity of transportation facilities, downzoning averted an excessive proliferation of downtown megabuildings, and development was encouraged to spread itself around. Creation of the St. Lawrence Neighborhood occurred at that time.

I have visited Toronto several times in the past few years, each time going back to see the St. Lawrence Neighborhood evolve. Urban critic Jane Jacobs had brought it to my attention and had, in fact, taken me there in 1977 when construction had just started and explained what was going to happen. I listened skeptically, but then I saw it actually unfold over time in the way she predicted. I had not heard it officially explained by any city spokesperson until the World Cities Conference in Boston in the fall of 1980. Toronto Mayor John Sewell was there and told about this neighborhood at a panel on redevelopment of large inner-city neighborhoods. Years before his election as mayor, Sewell had participated in some of the Toronto development squabbles from the citizen opposition side. He had a healthy distrust for development companies and planners. He knew they were necessary but had learned that the way to get them to proceed beneficially was to force them to "take instructions from real people." Sewell was not threatened by what he called "people as decision-makers." In fact, he built on that support.

I already knew the essence of the story when I heard Sewell speak, but I was impressed by the way he told it, understanding fully the implications of what had been accomplished.

Instead of seeking a detailed Plan, Sewell said, the city sent planners out to ask people what they wanted, to study nearby streets and the buildings on them, to learn what made them flexible and workable. Then the city established a development *strategy*—as distinguished from a Plan—with guidelines but few rules. There were, Sewell explained, several fundamental notions behind the strategy.

"First, we wanted to insure the relation of this neighborhood to the rest of the city, so we extended the street pattern. The grid makes for clarity and integration. No planning decision made before that, none that I know of, recognized the grid as the most important characteristic of a neighborhood.

"Second, we set a guideline that buildings had to face the street. This is very straightforward. It was good enough for the nineteenth century, and it is still good.

"Third, we required human scale, an eight-story maximum height, which was new for Toronto.

"Fourth, we provided for architectural variety. Different architects designed different pieces, and we included a number of types of housing—mixed-income cooperatives and rentals—to insure a mix of different types of people without being able to tell the subsidized from the unsubsidized units.

"Fifth, we provided for a range of uses—residential, street-level stores, offices.

"This is the way cities have worked well. It was a means of extending the city so it doesn't look different from the rest of the city. Again, these ideas are rooted in the nineteenth century. It looks old, instead of spiffy and new." Sewell added with a note of irony, "It is not innovative, it looks like cities did in the nineteenth century." That is precisely why it *is* indeed innovative.

Jane Jacobs adds another wonderful irony to this story: "When the Federal Government got the plan with a request for money, they turned it down at first. They said, It is too old-fashioned. Actually, it was the newest fashion going. There hadn't been anything like that since projects came in, since the time of the Depression. Not everything about it is planned. The city encouraged flexibility. They said, It isn't a spaceship. It is not going off forever. It can be diddled with. It is right here on earth. Make these buildings so they can turn into different things. For instance, they put the school in an apartment house [in fact, there are two schools incorporated into residential buildings, the first time for Canada] and did the apartment house in such a way that if the school needs to be expanded, it can be expanded into the apartment house. If the school contracts, some of it can go back into housing. They deliberately did the houses so that in the future the street-level apartments can become stores, if the demand arises, or some of them can be thrown together [for something else]. This is a real city, not a spaceship. This is all very radical."

There are a few drawbacks, Jacobs concedes, but she accurately points out that they are of the correctable kind. There is, for example, a sameness to the look of it: all the buildings are of brick, with white-painted wood trim. Some of the design reflects the much-loved Victorian design of many of Toronto's old neighborhoods. What is missing, of course, is the patina of time and the small changes that come with the alterations people make as they adapt to and use their environment. Toronto is a brick city, and the white trim will probably—if the residents choose—give way to color and embellishment. "It is too much new building of one period in one place," says Jacobs, "but it is a piece of city. It is not a project."

An additional significant point, Jacobs notes, is that the development of the St. Lawrence Neighborhood "is staged. It has no set plans." The plans emerge according to "what needs present themselves. *It is an incredible thing for planners to admit that they don't know what will be needed in the future."*

A very expensive and chic private development, Market Square, followed the emergence of the St. Lawrence Neighborhood. Market Square is a few blocks away on the other side of the old market. It was built by one of Canada's biggest builders, Olympia and York—also active developers in the United States of the kind of "big" projects worshiped here.

Market Square is not big in the American sense, but it is surely big enough to be attractive on a purely-for-profit basis. It is one of Toronto's most expensive new developments. Market Square, like the St. Lawrence Neighborhood, retains the street grid, follows the eight-story height limit, contains stores on the street, is nicely landscaped. It is as inviting to passersby as to residents. It also has expensive restaurants, saunas, sports facilities and swimming pool, all favored amenities for those who can afford them. Yet it does not overwhelm the existing neighborhood which forms the center. In fact, it is a comfortable neighbor to the St. Lawrence Neighborhood on one side and the glass-towered downtown on the other. The owners' promotional literature boasts mostly of the features that make it an honest part of an old neighborhood. Certainly the owners should know what sells. Essentially, this free-market addition adheres to the same guidelines as the St. Lawrence Neighborhood, without any sacrifice. The difference is in the financial status of the residents.

Savannah's Victorian District and the South Bronx's Kelly Street are very different old neighborhoods where Urban Husbandry has been applied. Toronto's St. Lawrence Neighborhood, however, demonstrates that the principles of Urban Husbandry can be as sensibly applied to new construction as to the rejuvenation of old neighborhoods and that the process can be government-sponsored. The most basic principles by which the St. Lawrence Neighborhood was planned were not new, however. In fact, those principles had been applied in this country in the mid-1960s in an interesting New York City experiment in Greenwich Village. This experiment was a direct result of a neighborhood confrontation and a grass-roots planning effort, led by Jane Jacobs among others. Although the Greenwich Village site was not a cleared one, the goal was the same—knitting the new into the frayed old *without* replacing the old, with community residents in control of the choice of stitch.

An Early Infill Housing Precedent

The West Village Houses grew out of a community-led battle in the 1960s against a large-scale urban-renewal project in Greenwich Village, one of the first times a New York community triumphed over an imposed private-public project that would have destroyed a neighborhood. In 1961, the city announced a high-rise redevelopment plan for the far-west Village, bordering the West Side Highway between Christopher and Eleventh streets. The plan called for the clearance of fourteen blocks of apartment houses, older brick and brownstone houses, and loft buildings—deemed dilapidated, deteriorated, marginal, and "a no man's land" by a City Planning Commission study. A community-initiated study, however, showed that the area contained seven hundred families and more than eighty businesses employing hundreds of people.

Under the urban-renewal plan, a collection of tall apartment buildings would replace this low-scaled neighborhood, but after all the demolition and relocation there would have been a net increase of only about three hundred dwelling units. A diverse group of neighborhood residents, which later became the West Village Committee, fought the plan and, with Jane Jacobs—she had just completed her book, *The Death and Life of Great American Cities*—as president, hired their own planning and design team to come up with an alternative. That alternative, the West Village Houses, consists of forty-two five-story walk-ups that required no demolition or relocation and provided a net increase of 420 apartments. "Not a single person—not a single sparrow—shall be displaced" was their slogan.

The West Village Houses went through a tortuous history, including a mortgage foreclosure that gave its critics ammunition with which to minimize its accomplishments and gave its defenders ammunition with which to accuse public officials of subtle sabotage. Few publicly built projects ever came in on time and on budget, and this one was clearly no exception. It had so much going against it because of its totally unconventional nature and official disapproval (its community sponsorship alone was enough to disturb establishment circles afraid that the idea might spread) that it is nothing but a miracle that it was built at all.

In 1962, when this battle started, official thinking dictated that residential and commercial uses should not mix in the same neighborhood, that old buildings should be replaced with new, that to achieve middle-income housing the economy of scale favored high-rise buildings surrounded by vast public open spaces, not low-rise row houses with private courtyards. The West Village Committee challenged every one of those precepts and more. Anyone who walked the streets of the neighborhood and visited the residences, factories and artists' studios hardly could do otherwise.

The committee recognized that the neighborhood was strong and healthy and should not be disrupted by large intrusions, but that it could be enhanced by the filling in of a number of odd-sized and -shaped empty lots. These were weed-strewn and decidedly unsightly spaces left vacant when an old freight-railroad spur was demolished years before. Respect for existing scale and flexibility of design were basic goals. The plan, furthermore, was to be achievable without total site assemblage, so it could be contracted or expanded according to available land. No condemnation of private property ever would be necessary. The result: three basic floor layouts—adjustable in width and depth and thus usable on different lot sizes—for five-story walk-ups. Elevators were expensive and space-consuming, and brownstone and brick walk-ups had long been a rentable Village commodity. As in those older houses, the first floor was raised and a basement level was a few steps down. Wherever space permitted, top floors contained duplexes reachable by four stair flights. Each floor had either two 2-bedroom apartments or one 3-bedroom and one 1-bedroom, guaranteeing variety in family sizes. The orientation of apartments alternated on each floor, with a living room facing the front and a kitchen facing the back on one floor and the reverse on the next, "the idea being," Jacobs notes, "that at all times there would be eyes and ears of the neighborhood" attending the street and the backyard.

In addition, there was no open-air parking. Car space was provided in a nearby garage. There were separate and well-defined private and public spaces. The well-known hazards of supposedly private areas into which anyone wanders was thus avoided. Instead, communal street-oriented public spaces were provided, adding to the neighborhood's traditional lively street life. Both of these provisions were in total contrast to the prevailing design of the day, which provided for high-rise buildings surrounded by acres of "keep off the grass" open space and parking lots. One of the schemes provided that the ground floor could be either a store or an apartment, providing flexibility for changing times and needs.

This was the first in New York City of what planners now advocate as "infill" housing, new construction filling in existing open spaces without causing demolition. On every point, however, the West Village Housing plan was at loggerheads with the "experts" of the day. Today, it seems so simple, so basic. "The plan is deceptive," Jacobs says in retrospect. "A great deal of innovative and creative planning went into this. It was done so it could fit into all kinds of empty holes in the Village or elsewhere. We could see the holes coming in the city. This plan could be used on a lot as small as fifty feet deep. It alarmed city officials that we had something for which you didn't have to knock anything down. They were frightened enough about a neighborhood doing it themselves."

This plan was too radical for its time. Nobody wanted to build it. Opposition came from hostile city housing officials threatened by the unheard-of community demand for meaningful participation, as well as from private real-estate interests who objected to developable land being turned over to nonprofit community-designed housing.

Rachele Wall, a leader in the fight along with Jacobs and many others, had moved with her artist husband into the neighborhood the day before the urban-renewal plan was announced. An off-Broadway producer and a public-relations expert, Wall had no more experience or expertise for this battle than anyone else. Once involved, Wall never ceased, and she remains to this day an energetic defender of the Village, an early staunch opponent of Westway—the $2 billion-plus four-mile highway that was planned to go right by West Village Houses but was defeated in the courts—and a generous adviser to urban warriors all over New York. There have been so many energy-consuming battles since the 1960s West Village Houses fight that Wall remembers it with a measure of uncharacteristic dispassion.

"We could have established a community pattern that other neighborhoods would learn from, but the opposition made sure that didn't happen," she says. "They created delays, inflated estimates, kept construction people away from bidding, nibbled at the design. There was one roadblock after another, with unnecessary but costly delays. Every means of blocking the plan was put in our way, and new ones were invented. We never knew who was working against us, where buttons were being pushed."

Changing economics—inflation, escalating interest rates, the city's increasing supply of middle-income apartments—only exacerbated the political and planning obstacles. Two mayors came and went before the city's Board of Estimate finally approved construction in 1969 under the city's middle-income-housing program. A three-year bureaucratic bog-down ensued, doubling costs by the time construction began in 1972, almost ten years after the community proposal was made. Complications didn't end there. When the city plunged into fiscal chaos in 1975, the builder walked off the job, leaving the project incomplete and near bankruptcy. Federal subsidies were used to bail out two big privately sponsored faltering high-rise projects built elsewhere in the city under the same program. City officials said, however, that the same federal subsidies were unavailable to similarly rescue the West Village Houses, because nearby truck traffic and pollution violated federal environmental standards. The city foreclosed on the mortgage, canceled the original plans to sell the apartments as cooperatives, and sold the complex to the builder who had first abandoned it. The buildings were finished and turned into rental units.

After years of cost-cutting sacrifices of architectural niceties, the completed structures had a decidedly bleak exterior. One could make a list of the design flaws, with any one of its original promoters more than willing to point out some not easily noticed. Nevertheless, when the apartments were finally placed on the market, rental was immediate, with an unending waiting list and a low turnover—clearly signs of success. One passes through the neighborhood hardly noticing the West Village Houses. They actually fit better into this neighborhood than a high-style high-rise might. If anything, the West Village Houses, spread over six sites and slipped in and around older buildings, make an acceptable background for the infinite variety of noteworthy and luxuriously renovated old buildings, many of which would have been lost under the originally proposed urban-renewal scheme. Like the new housing units built in Savannah's Victorian District, this complex was meant to fill in the empty spaces, not intrude on a successful neighborhood.

In its planning and design flexibility and its potential cost-saving efficiency, West Village Houses was a trailblazer. Actually, it fulfilled the "two basic aims" set forth in the West Village Committee's 1963 published plan: "(a) to fulfill its promise both to Mayor Robert Wagner and to its own neighbor-members to improve and further develop the community once the threat of dictatorial redevelopment was lifted; and (b) to devise, as a public example, a practical means of adding harmonious planned housing *into* an existing community without any sacrifice of the people already there."

It was a Pyrrhic victory at best. Under the best of circumstances, citizen-led change is nearly impossible. The almost seventeen years of controversy and delay guaranteed that few lessons would be learned or transmitted. Nowadays, it is referred to—if mentioned at all—as a failed experiment. The "experts" made sure they were proved right, one observer noted. Says Wall with a wistful smile, "People don't want to get into the same kind of jam. How do you say to people that there is no truth in what the city said? We weren't trying to be entrepreneurs. We were simply spearheading concepts and ideas we thought could work and should be tried." An October 14, 1974, *New York Times* editorial applauded the aim of the West Village Houses "to prove that new development could reinforce the Village's specific attractions and life style rather than destroy them." It further noted that "although design was reduced to the lowest common denominator to keep the project alive, there is still much to commend in terms of appropriate scale, neighborhood conservation and well-planned apartments." But, the editorial concluded, the city bureaucracy's handling of the project was obstructionist and the West Village Houses are "unplanned monuments to a system geared to sabotage and a city determined to red-tape itself to death."

By the standards of many, the West Village Houses are not architecturally attractive and, in fact, may be viewed as plain at best. This only demonstrates that what constitutes neighborhood is often enhanced by aesthetics, but not necessarily. Aesthetics are too often used as a standard that in the context of neighborhood rebirth or stabilization is not the highest priority. Most of all, the West Village project fits the fabric of the city and its neighborhood. It did not disrupt the institutions and social networks of the community. The larger area remains diverse and exciting. Stability and reinforcement were the result, not accelerated change and alteration. Those are the characteristics that give this project value, aesthetics notwithstanding.

The only real failure attached to this effort is the loss of some of the population and manufacturing from the larger surrounding area. If the West Village Committee had prevailed on a larger front, some of this might have been averted. Nevertheless, the process worked because area people became engaged, debate ensued and real planning took root.

Our nation's cities have an overabundance of vacant space that could be filled in a manner appropriate to local needs and preferences before one more functioning building or neighborhood is needlessly plowed under at immeasurable economic and social cost. That is the common lesson in the stories of the Victorian District in Savannah, Kelly Street in the South Bronx, Mount Auburn in Cincinnati, Manchester in Pittsburgh, the St. Lawrence Neighborhood in Toronto and the West Village Houses in New York's Greenwich Village. The choice for the mildly frayed or dramatically decayed urban neighborhoods is more than between continued neglect or excessive upgrading through speculation and displacement. The failure to follow the innovative patterns so far described or of those being set in other communities across the country is a loss this country no longer can afford.

In the next chapter, the focus turns to the unfulfilled promises of prevailing policies. Those prevailing policies reflect the urban-development approach known as Planned Shrinkage. The failure of Planned Shrinkage is so real that we have nothing to lose in applying new strategies according to the principles of Urban Husbandry.

PLANNED SHRINKAGE

The Economy of Waste

■

Urban Husbandry is not the prevailing urban-redevelopment strategy among policy-makers. Instead, the urban philosophy known as "Planned Shrinkage," the antithesis of Urban Husbandry, dominates traditional development thinking.

Planned Shrinkage emerged as a term in New York City in the mid-1970s. Reduced to its simplest definition and as applied in New York, it meant that in a city that was shrinking in terms of people and resources—as was generally the case then throughout the Northeast and the Midwest—the shrinkage should be guided, or planned. City resources should be carefully allocated to reflect the reality of the shrinking city. How and where those resources should be allocated is the philosophical essence of Planned Shrinkage. Although applied to the specific circumstances of New York City in the early 1970s, Planned Shrinkage had generic application to almost all older American cities, most of which experienced similar debilitating changes after World War II.

Just as earlier urban-renewal programs had been associated with the philosophy of one man, Robert Moses, so the articulation of

Planned Shrinkage can be attributed to one man, Roger Starr, head of New York City's Housing and Development Administration from January 1974 to July 1976, and a *New York Times* editorial writer since 1976. Starr articulated Planned Shrinkage as a philosophical approach to urban redevelopment in a *New York Times Magazine* article of November 14, 1976, "Making New York Smaller." Although his specific focus was New York City, Starr provided the intellectual justification for minimal public investment in existing stock of older neighborhoods—whether in New York or elsewhere—and the planning rationale for maximum public investment in large-scale new construction projects. Now more than ever, Starr's arguments in that magazine essay are representative of the predominant urban-development thinking nationwide.

To Starr's credit, his article was an honest and open elaboration of what others already were thinking and doing, in effect beginning public debate. In part he wrote:

> If the city is to survive with a smaller population, the population must be encouraged to concentrate itself in the sections that remain alive. This sort of internal resettlement—the natural flow out of the areas that have lost general attraction—must be encouraged. The role of the city planner is not to originate the trend of abandonment but to observe and use it so that public investment will be hoarded for those areas where it will sustain life.
>
> Obviously, the few remaining families in a section that is generally abandoned cannot be forced out. Frequently, however, the distress is so general in such an area that whole tax districts can be cleared by taking properties for tax delinquencies. Unsafe buildings can be cleared. The remaining families can be offered relocation benefits to move to areas that remain alive.
>
> Federal housing subsidies can be used to encourage movement away from deteriorating areas; given the wherewithal to move to a better apartment, families begin to question whether the ties that bind them to a grossly deteriorated neighborhood are as important as they seemed.
>
> Gradually, the city's population in the older sections

will begin to achieve a new configuration, one consistent with a smaller population that has arranged itself at densities high enough to make the provision of municipal services economical.

. . . The stretches of empty blocks may then be knocked down, services can be stopped, subway stations closed, and the land left fallow until a change in the economic and demographic assumptions makes the land useful once again.

Critics of Planned Shrinkage speak of "hidden agendas." Defenders dismiss the critics as "paranoid opponents of all development." In truth, the objective or agenda is not so hidden and is clearly articulated in the last paragraph of the excerpt from Starr's article quoted earlier—"land left fallow until a change in the economic and demographic assumptions makes the land useful once again." Cleared land sits mothballed until private investment determines that it has value again. Planning and zoning then become the handmaidens of new development, not the tools of a democratic process or the shaper of appropriate change and the fallacies and contradictions of planned shrinkage are ignored.

Under Planned Shrinkage, one 1,000-unit development on one piece of cleared land by one large developer is preferable to ten neighborhood-based efforts each producing 100 units and an upgrading ripple effect around them. The poor are used as "ideological loss leaders," one observer noted. New megaprojects are promoted for jobs and taxes to fund the poor, while directly helpful programs are cut back or "shrunk" because the city can't afford them. Small-scale projects are occasionally applauded—if developed by private developers, not community-based developers. Highway and landfill development schemes are more worthy of large-scale public investment than a long menu of smaller, less expensive, innovative developments fashioned to meet critical local needs. Under Planned Shrinkage, the value of an incrementally upgrading neighborhood is not recognized until speculators or big-project builders declare it worthy of investment. Property values are the unspoken bottom line. Neighborhoods remain undervalued, regardless of their use, unless property values appreciate acceptably.

As writer Jim Sleeper pointed out in an unpublished manuscript, "Representing New York's Developer-Statesmen: The Life and Work of Roger Starr," prepared as a Charles Revson Fellow at Columbia University in 1983:

> [Starr never explained] how planned shrinkage might actually be implemented. He couldn't have believed seriously that Oklahoma stood ready to welcome impoverished black and Puerto Rican families. . . . He couldn't have believed that there were enough jobs elsewhere, given national employment figures.
>
> Nor could Starr have believed that the shanty-towns springing up in sunbelt cities offered better living conditions than did New York's neighborhoods. Or that the continuing influx of poor immigrants to New York—as many as during the peak years of the 1920's—could somehow be reversed, given horrid conditions in third world cities. . . .
>
> And since neighborhoods like Bushwick and Morrisania had been devastated by redlining, blockbusting, speculation, milking, and mortgage scams even *before* job-flight had undermined tenant income, how did Starr expect the neighborhoods he proposed to consolidate through "internal resettlement"—like Williamsburg or Soundview— to avoid a similar fate? What would keep them whole in a private real estate market abandoning low income properties? And how could resettlement be confined to them, anyway, and kept away from the softening rental markets of transitional white neighborhoods in the northern Bronx and southern Brooklyn?

Starr is a robust man with dark-rimmed glasses and a receding hairline that enhance his scholarly image. He is smart, articulate and a sharp debater. His observations can often be challenged—or interpreted differently from the way Starr chooses—but never dismissed. For years he ran one of New York City's most influential private good-government groups, the Citizens Housing and Planning Council. It was during his subsequent tenure as New York's housing chief that Starr called for the "Planned Shrinkage" of older neighborhoods to shift people out of the decaying populated areas and for the concentration of dwindling city funds on rebuilding and repairing areas of continuing strength. In so doing he infuriated advocates for the urban poor and the middle-class residents of troubled neighborhoods seeking more, not less, city help.

"I was denounced as a genocidal lunatic and enemy of man," Starr noted in the *Times Magazine* article, "for simply suggesting that the Department of City Planning should study" Planned Shrinkage. In public forums, in print and in private conversation, Starr always seems to relish being a provocateur of the public. Planned Shrinkage immediately appealed to those builders, bankers and policy-makers who wanted an excuse to begin withholding or continue to withhold money from neighborhoods they no longer considered profitable investments. Private financial resources have always been selectively invested in urban areas. That is appropriate. The criteria for public investment, however, ought not replicate those for private investment, where profit is primary. Public resources should fulfill public purposes and go where resources are not readily available, not necessarily follow and back up private investment.

"What I meant by Planned Shrinkage is that the shrinking of older cities is taking place," Starr explains, referring to the decades of out-migration of businesses and middle-income residents from the inner cities. "There isn't any question about that. The shrinkage of economic potential, the shrinkage of employment opportunities and the consequent shrinkage of population are taking place. Now, what I meant was that you have to plan for this shrinkage just the way you had to plan for growth in the days when everyone expected that these older cities were going to keep on getting bigger and bigger. A city with a smaller economic potential than New York has, compared to what it had fifteen or twenty years ago, cannot provide the services to the same number of people if they are stretched thinly over the same miles of street. They have to be encouraged to move closer, this smaller number of people, so that they can continue to be provided with services."

But Planned Shrinkage is more than an approach to handling urban problems. It recalls the concept of triage,[1] an old war term that sets priorities for medical treatment of the wounded by writing off the most serious cases and concentrating on the cases on whom medical attention has the best chance of success. On the federal level, triage works in an assortment of ways: program benefits are targeted through careful geographic designations, population standards such as income or education levels are set for program criteria, or criteria guaranteeing a preordained direction are established for funding qualifications. Variations of Planned Shrinkage and triage are used to rationalize assorted programs that shift public investment nationwide with dubious public benefit.

Cutting back on maintenance of New York's public-transit system to devote more resources to building New York highways parallels a national undercutting of a once proud rail system and the extravagant funding of a national highway network that has laid waste both cities and farms. Shifting institutional investment to the Sunbelt as if the Snowbelt were an anachronism parallels the shifting of public resources from older neighborhoods in need to more potentially profitable areas of investment interest. Subsidizing the infrastructure for new communities intruding on the rural landscape while neglecting maintenance and refurbishment needs of existing community infrastructures representing an existing public investment is not much different from underwriting new urban communities like Co-op City and Roosevelt Island (discussed later) while letting the South Bronx deteriorate past the point of minimum need.

Theory and Practice Don't Match

On its face, Planned Shrinkage sounds perfectly logical, as logical as Robert Moses' grand vision that if you bulldozed one slum* and rebuilt it, you could move people into the new neighborhood from

---

* Slums and discardable neighborhoods are always, of course, defined by distant experts instead of their residents and defined on the basis of buildings, not people.

the one to be demolished next and thus move across the city replacing one area after another. Starr defines the withdrawal of investment from troubled and needy neighborhoods as a sound targeting of limited resources, ostensibly meant to produce a healthy consolidation of the city. The results, however, are otherwise than intended.

Instead of a healthy consolidated city, an urban extremism emerges: increased abandonment of weaker neighborhoods on the one hand and accelerated investment in choicer areas on the other. Bad gets worse and good gets better. Existing residential communities, with whatever degree of cohesion and socially useful networking they experience, are either destabilized by an overheated real-estate market fueled by shifting public resources or abandoned as unredeemable. New human and economic costs for the larger society result, with the most visible manifestation of those costs in the homelessness epidemic that was barely in evidence a decade ago plaguing our cities today.

"The nation is at a crossroads on housing policy," wrote Christina Rossamondo in *City Limits* magazine January 1988, as part of her introduction to an article on the housing platforms of the presidential candidates. The condition of state and national affordable housing is grim. She noted:

> With the need for affordable housing greater than at any time since World War II, the federal commitment to housing for low and moderate income families is at its lowest point since the Great Depression. Federal spending on housing has plummeted to less than half the amount before Ronald Reagan took office—from more than $32 billion in 1981 to less than $13 billion in 1986. In the 1970s, the U.S. built or rehabilitated about 200,000 units of low and moderate income housing annually. Under Reagan, the country produces about 10 percent of that figure. Existing public housing is in decline, and it will cost more than $20 billion to repair and modernize these units.
>
> Authorizations for many federal housing programs will expire in the early 1990s, as will government contracts for assisted units with private developers. An estimated 288,000 Section 8 housing subsidies for new units could

disappear between 1988 and 2000, when contracts with
private developers expire. Another 750,000 Section 8
subsidies for families in rehabbed buildings will run out
between 1995 and 2000.

The current housing and homelessness crisis is often attributed to
drastic federal housing cutbacks in the early 1980s. In fact, as
Rossamondo indicates, federal outlays started tapering off in the
1970s under Nixon and Ford, became more significant under Carter
and were precipitous under Reagan. This progression paralleled the
application of Planned Shrinkage in the major older cities around the
country, such as Chicago, Detroit, Newark, St. Louis and Boston.
Thus, as the loss of existing units accelerated under Planned Shrinkage, there was less and less new investment for replacement. Neither
federal funds nor a private market were creating enough new
affordable units to match the consistent loss of housing over many
years. Investment was heading either out of cities or into new
megaprojects, like Co-op City, but not into existing neighborhoods
needing gentle doses for stability.

The two extremes also work on existing commercial and industrial
neighborhoods with their networks of independent businesses that
gain strength and efficiency by their proximity to one another.
Real-estate-value escalation that follows residential conversions or
office-tower assemblage can destabilize those areas just as badly as the
outmigration of businesses and abandonment that follow disinvestment. The final effect here is the loss of critical blue-collar jobs
suitable for an urban population and the gain of white-collar professional jobs, a large portion of which are filled by suburban
commuters.

Lower Manhattan neighborhoods, once filled with manufacturing
jobs in industries from printing to hatmaking and now dominated by
expensive apartments and offices, exemplify this trend. Few of the
country's older cities are without an old industrial or manufacturing
district either expensively upgraded or replaced with high-rise towers. And while national economic trends reflect the diminishment of

the blue-collar industries, urban-development policies exacerbate the trend by displacing those businesses prematurely.

Trickle-Down Doesn't Work

While the extremes that result from Planned Shrinkage apply to both residential and commercial neighborhoods, the impact is more easily recognized in residential areas. Planned Shrinkage would write off neighborhoods like Savannah's Victorian District, Cincinnati's Mount Auburn or the South Bronx's Kelly Street before their locally led rebirth. The people still living there would have to move elsewhere or struggle through. Certainly no new people were expected to move into such communities. Certainly no one living there was expected to want to stay. And certainly no one would be expected to want to recycle any of the area's discarded buildings. Low-income tenants must continue the destabilizing nomadic search for the affordable apartment and the appropriate job. Housing units are supposed to trickle down for them while the luxury market multiplies, fed by zoning and tax incentives. The trickle-down theory just does not work. Elliott D. Sclar, a Columbia University urban-planning professor, punctured the "trickle down" myth in a letter to *The New York Times* ("When It Comes to Housing, Trickle-Down Theory Is a Dry Well") September 10, 1987. The letter responded to an editorial supporting a controversial moderate-income housing-development project in the Bronx known as Tibbett Gardens. It said, in part:

> . . . For trickle down to work, moderate-income groups must move into new quarters and yield their places at a reduced rent to lower-income groups, while all else remains the same.
> But all else never remains the same. When higher-income households leave one set of units, they abandon both shelter and neighborhoods. Unless they are replaced by households of comparable or higher income, neighborhood services deteriorate and, because lower-income

households cannot afford rents to sustain the housing stock, it too deteriorates. Hence, without some form of public subsidy, the conditions of the poor are not improved by such actions. The history of the Bronx housing market bears much painful testimony to the process: witness the beautiful 1920s middle-class neighborhoods that trickled down around the Grand Concourse.

Trickle down also requires that the number of households seeking shelter remains constant so that demand does not increase with supply. This too has not been the case. Housing shortages cause people to double and triple up. When supply begins to loosen, so does demand. Before the poor get access to more desirable housing, the market requires that their social betters be satisfied. Trickle down also assumes that ill-housed moderate income groups outside the city's jurisdiction will not claim housing we hope will filter down to the city's poorest.

Between 1930 and 1970, when the city's population swelled by 1 million people, the needs of the poor were accommodated by more than 150,000 units of new public housing. Between 1970 and 1980, the city lost more than 800,000 residents, but the needs of the poor for shelter became dire. . . . Despite the apparent increase in supply caused by population loss, we have had higher housing prices and abandonment rather than trickle down.

Rent regulation* does not explain the result. The rent-regulated Upper West Side thrived while Bronx landlords could not collect amounts to which they were legally entitled under rent regulation because of the poverty of their tenants.

Harry De Rienzo, in his 1985 report for the New York Urban Coalition,[2] noted "the dramatic decline in income for the city's renters while at the same time, rent levels kept pace with inflation, increasing 24.5 percent in the last three years." De Rienzo points out

---

* Rent control is the popular explanation offered by real-estate spokesmen for neighborhood decay and housing deterioration. They never explain, however, why the same deterioration patterns occur in almost all the nation's older cities, including those without rent control.

that the cost of just maintaining (gas, electricity, etc.) an average two-bedroom apartment is $200 per month without taxes or the cost of money borrowed for a modest renovation of the space. With those extras the cost is $500 monthly, beyond the means of the population that is supposed to benefit from the trickle-down process.

The concept of Planned Shrinkage relies on either the trickle-down process or massive renewal projects to provide housing for the middle- and low-income groups. No room is left for the visions of the people who live amid the remnants of a bygone prosperity. It ignores the natural rebuilding potential of neighborhoods. Wrote Washington-based syndicated columnist Neil R. Peirce, after a New York City visit in March 1977 that included the South Bronx and other areas:

> When one tours New York's supposedly hopeless neighborhoods, the wrongheadedness of "Planned Shrinkage" is immediately evident. Many of the buildings are architectural gems. Most have sturdy, thick, brick walls that would cost immense sums to build now. In an energy-short era, the fact that they still stand is conservation in itself. They cry out for restoration—not abandonment.
>
> The capital investment that would be lost in abandonment of whole neighborhoods is staggering. Cheek-by-jowl with troubled residential blocks are schools, hospitals, firehouses and police stations. Water, sewer and electric lines are in place. Many of the neighborhoods are on subway lines, a few minutes from Manhattan, downtown Brooklyn and other employment centers vital to low-income workers. To recreate this massive infrastructure would cost billions of dollars.

(Peirce's 1977 article brought attention to low-income urban areas in a new way and was in large measure responsible for the awareness in the White House that led to President Carter's South Bronx visit. In the more than ten years since Peirce penned those words, increased acres of demolished tenements are visible in parts of the Bronx, the

Lower East Side and Brooklyn, a testament to the continuing prevalence of Planned Shrinkage. Much of the lost infrastructure must now be replaced and rebuilt at a cost of millions of dollars.)

Self-fulfilling Prescription

Planned Shrinkage amounts to a policy of government-sponsored redlining, the policy by which a bank, an insurance company or a government agency declared that no investment would go into a designated area. Diminished public-transit service, cutbacks in police and fire protection, reduced housing-assistance programs, curtailed sanitation services—it does not matter which "shifting of public resources" occurs first. The cumulative effect, as Starr wrote, encourages "internal resettlement." What Starr benignly refers to as encouragement is more like a no-choice proposition.

Forced-out residents don't disappear. They move into other neighborhoods, merely continuing the cycle and solving no problems in the process. New York City, for example, is experiencing the worst doubling up ever in its public housing. Approximately 43 percent of all public-housing units are now occupied by more than one family. Is it possible to consider that kind of planned shrinkage of the city, that sort of "internal resettlement," a wise consequence of shifting limited resources? Under Planned Shrinkage, people were supposed to move closer together for more efficient sharing of public services and resources. But when real-estate speculation overcomes some areas and abandonment engulfs others and not enough stable in-betweens are affordable to a large percentage of the population, doubling up and homelessness result. Community groups understand this in a way that policy-makers refuse to do. In many cities, whatever it is called, Planned Shrinkage is the essence of prevailing government investment and development policies.

In addition to the failure to support local renewal efforts, there is another enormous consequence to Planned Shrinkage. Support for the massive, expensive, permanently subsidized developments is commonplace. These big projects repeat decades of accumulated mistakes in new permutations. They are well publicized, editorially applauded in the daily newspapers and always hailed as a "corner-stone" or "linchpin" of some new revitalization effort. They revitalize nothing and only continue the cycle of drawing diminishing resources and energy away from existing neighborhoods into new ones. They don't "shrink" the city, as Starr prescribes, but "expand" it into newly created or redeveloped areas, in the case of New York City mostly in high-land-value Manhattan, and in its equivalent in other cities, offering more lucrative profits to developers, banks and unions and more political chips for elected officials. New York, like other cities, is loaded with such projects.

Roosevelt Island is an example. This new town of fifteen 14-story buildings on an island in the East River contains 2,138 (only the first of three phases) mixed-income housing units and a population of 6,960 people. The island is a two-and-a-half-mile-long, 800-foot-wide sliver of land between Manhattan and Queens. Roosevelt Island lost $86 million between the time it opened in 1975 and a 1982 state audit. The same audit predicted that it will probably cost taxpayers at least $236 million over forty years. The only easily calculable annual cost is the annual operating budget deficit, which in 1986 was $3 million out of its $7 million budget. Predictably, for all sorts of rational reasons this "instant city" bears no resemblance to its original 1971 Philip Johnson master plan for a heavily federally subsidized, economically and racially integrated community of 18,000 residents (1,000 more units are now under construction). Yet Roosevelt Island is applauded among traditionalists as one of the city's most successful "planned" development ventures.

There are many good and bad features of Roosevelt Island. When constructed, for example, the development marked a great break-through in good design for subsidized housing, smart discouragement of automobile use and the incorporation of appealing public amenities such as parks, community facilities and historic preservation.*

---

* A splendid job was done by noted preservation architect Giorgio Cavaglieri in restoring for public use a nineteenth-century country chapel, designed by Frederick Clarke Withers, and an eighteenth-century clapboard farmhouse, home of the

But where are the public-cost calculations of the new infrastructure, the increase in mass transit and in other essential services and the economic burden of maintaining the neighborhood convenience stores (a 40 percent vacancy rate persists) servicing the limited population? And where are the public-cost calculations in the elimination of a mass-transit system servicing the forty thousand patients and workers who were already there before redevelopment? A complex but efficient elevator system that carried vehicles up and down from the Queensborough Bridge overhead and five ferries that crossed the East River were eliminated, and an expensive cable-car system was erected. And even though the community that was created is racially and economically mixed, the critical issue again is where limited public resources should be placed.

Battery Park City is another case in point. After fifteen years and $200 million in state bond money, that new community on lower Manhattan landfill forged ahead in the late 1970s, applauded as an opportunity for increased investment in the city. Praised in the design and planning community for its wise and sensitive repetition of old urban patterns,* Battery Park City was built according to strict guidelines mandating buildings of varied shapes, sizes and materials to match the existing city fabric and meant to produce buildings that would look as though they had always been there. In fact, the tough guidelines underscore the view articulated by Stanton Eckstut, one of the guidelines' authors: "The more rules, the better the design. If you start with a clean slate, you produce a clean slate. Rules provide more information for design. Rules tell the architect *to* design, not *how,* and

---

Blackwell family who originally owned the island. Great opportunities were missed, however, in allowing to fall into ruin two unique landmarks—the 1856 Smallpox Hospital designed by James Renwick and the 1839 domed Octagon Tower built as a lunatic asylum and designed by Alexander Jackson Davis.

* In the 1986 Annual Report of Battery Park City, the following quote of mine appeared: "Battery Park City is the first new piece of city that is genuinely Urban. It connects to instead of isolating from the existing city, extends the proven Urban fabric instead of altering it and, in effect, succeeds simply because it repeats a tested pattern that evolved over time instead of redesigning it. Seldom is anything built today that reflects a learning from past successes and mistakes. Battery Park City reflects a learning of lessons."

encourage more thinking and more individual expression." This principle is true not only for new buildings on landfill like Battery Park City but also for sites defined by surrounding buildings or an unusual landscape. Valuing guidelines or the constraints that come with zoning laws does not denigrate designers. On the contrary, it is a great art to take what is suggested and make something creative.

With its 92 acres, splendid waterfront esplanade, public art, 6 million square feet of office space, 14,000 apartments and work force of 31,000, Battery Park City evolved according to a decidedly better "plan," with superior building "designs" than many prior monumental developments, and, in fact, was markedly improved because of the intense public debate that occurred prior to its final approval. Justifiably high marks are given for its traditional street grid and a serious effort to connect with adjacent areas instead of standing in isolation.

Battery Park City reflects another interesting and unusual happenstance. It benefited from the leadership of two very different men. The first, Richard Kahan, former head of the state's Urban Development Corporation, developed the successful final plan. Kahan understood the city and was committed to developing the kind of guidelines that mirrored the time-tested city fabric but also fostered good new design. The second, Meyer S. Frucher, formerly a vice-president of Blue Cross Blue Shield of Greater New York and now a vice-president of Olympia and York, succeeded Kahan and resisted the government-leader impulse to remake a project in his own image. Frucher recognized the value of what had been started before him and set out to make that vision work. He adjusted and embellished the vision instead of making drastic alterations. He lowered residential density, increased commercial space, added new public amenities and made room for the relocation of one of the city's special high schools—all sound adjustments, not major alterations.

The design of Battery Park City is a rare case of lessons learned, a case of building on an understanding of what has made a traditional urban area work, although it will probably never have the gritty depth of a neighborhood that evolved organically. Yet a critical lesson easily ignored at Battery Park City is that while millions are poured into this "re-creation" of an old fabric, comparative pennies go into maintaining the existing citywide fabric from which Battery Park City is copied and which needs no re-creation. And instead of that being the lesson of its success, Frucher and others are promoting the extension of Battery Park City north along the waterfront of Manhattan's West Side.

Regardless of how appealing such new places as Battery Park City and Roosevelt Island may be, some basic realities should not be forgotten. Both projects, like Co-op City before them, were heavily subsidized at the expense of areas of the city for which public funding was not made available. They received direct subsidies while services elsewhere were inevitably diluted. Citywide services, such as police, fire and education, were not expanded to accommodate the needs of these new communities. The new developments joined the many competing communities drawing on the same shrinking or expanding—depending on the municipal budgets of the day—service resources. Without the creation of these new communities, market demand and public investment might have been directed toward faltering older communities, providing the new energy necessary to reinvigorate stagnating neighborhoods and prevent wasteful deterioration.

But even more, perhaps, than Battery Park City or Roosevelt Island, Westway typified the Planned Shrinkage investment philosophy. Westway was the $4 billion, four-mile-long combination highway/development plan (*$10,000 per inch*) that, through landfill, would have created two hundred *new* acres of Manhattan. It was heavily promoted over the years in *New York Times* editorials.

In their vision of a grand new waterfront created by building a new highway under the new landfill, Starr and other Westway promoters boasted that this was an ingenious use of federal funds for local benefit. For many reasons, it was a deceptive promise. Federal funds would have run out long before the highway was finished, and other dollars would have been required to prepare the resulting mud flats into developable land. Promoting such an overwhelming project for the sake of federal funds is the height of the sell-your-own-grandmother policy. Arguing that Westway would mean the removal of vehicular traffic from city streets, proponents never addressed the fact that every new road built in recent years has, by its very creation, stimulated new traffic. The reality of highway building is that highways encourage further automobile traffic. From the beginning, Westway opponents advocated an adequate, less expensive rebuilt road along the West Side waterfront and a massive reinvestment in the city's primary mass-transit facility, the subway, which had suffered drastically during periods of maintenance cutbacks and concentration of public resources on expensive highway and road-building programs.

At its most basic, Westway was a battle over the wisest use of public resources in an urban environment. Only the courts, not political leaders, put a final stop to the construction of Westway, and then it was decided on the critical issues of environmental damage and governmental process, not the planning and public-resource issues that are so critical to the larger perspective of urban development. And when Westway was finally defeated,* little evidence emerged that the political/development establishment understood the wasteful and erroneous planning issues at its heart. Proponents had argued the need for more development, but they concentrated on an unnecessary project in a single site rather than turning their attention to a citywide effort of smaller, scattered renewal.

While the rest of the city languishes, grand schemes will continue to overburden Manhattan, New York City's cash cow. These projects make no sense, but they do make profits. Westway would not make sense even if the city were booming, but some of the other projects might be appropriate for growing cities that can benefit from large-scale development. This is not true of a "shrinking" city, unless the Planned Shrinkage philosophy prevails and older neighborhoods

---

* Although the Westway opposition garnered broad public support, the lion's share of credit for the victory belongs to one woman, Marcy Benstock, who, for more than a decade, doggedly devoted her life to fighting the scheme and vigilantly continues her watch on the city's water edge.

die while new ones are built. This, of course, is really a philosophy of selective expansion—the unspoken half of Planned Shrinkage. Where it prevails, the natural potential for regenerating existing neighborhoods doesn't have a prayer.

The stories examined thus far—from Savannah to the South Bronx—reflect the success of Urban Husbandry and the failure of Planned Shrinkage, but in both cases in residential areas. Now we shift to a national perspective on downtown business districts.

URBAN DISPERSAL

■

The chief deficiency in the creed of decentralization
was that when everybody moves to the country, all
the benefits of the country disappear.
—ROBERT A. M. STERN, *Pride of Place*[1]

I was born in Greenwich Village, and my family remained there through the first decade of my life. Our family story parallels that of millions of Americans and illustrates patterns of social change that altered the face of urban America.

Both of my parents were the children of immigrants, both born and raised in Brooklyn, both enthralled by the American dream as defined in the early decades of this century. I was the first of my family to be born in Manhattan, what may seem a dubious achievement now, but, for my parents' generation, moving from Brooklyn to Manhattan was a mark of accomplishment.

My father went into the dry-cleaning business, first learning the business by working for someone else, then opening his own store with money borrowed from the family circle, and expanding that business into a small chain of four stores in Greenwich Village. We lived in a spacious apartment on the south side of Washington Square

Park with windows overlooking the park through which my mother could keep an eye on me when I played there or beckon me if I overstayed my play time. I walked seven or eight blocks every morning to school, played freely and endlessly in the park, traveled uptown to museums and theaters, shopped Fourteenth Street for everyday things and Fifth Avenue for the more expensive special purchases. The city was an exciting place to be in. That was the 1940s.

We had a summer cottage—no heat or winter insulation—in Weston, Connecticut, in the heart of Fairfield County, one of those idyllic communities where comfortable homes were surrounded by woods, streams and lawns, and only a short drive from a Long Island Sound beach. Country living appealed to my father. For a boy who grew up on the streets of Brooklyn, learned to dive off piers in New York Harbor and played stickball in the street, the lure of the lawn, the rose garden and the swimming pond were irresistible.

Two things happening simultaneously would eventually cause my family to move to this paradigm of suburbia. Opportunity beckoned my father. The first strip shopping center, with the area's first branch of a New York City department store, had opened in Westport, the larger neighboring town to Weston. Across from that first shopping center, only minutes from Main Street, a second was about to open. The builder of the second center wanted to include a dry-cleaning store. The strip center of that time drew lessons from urban patterns and actually repackaged in a planned version the successful commercial mix that evolved spontaneously on urban streets. Developers went by a formula that included a mixture of service and specialty stores. Thus the builder wanted a dry cleaner to locate between the supermarket and the baby-clothes store, with the hardware, carpeting and other stores and the luncheonette to follow down the line. The offer was an irresistible business opportunity for my father.

In addition, my father hungered to build a year-round house. We had the land. Taxes were cheap. The schools were nationally acclaimed. And New York City was only one hour away by train, an hour and a half by car. Model homes were going up around Westport, a great lure to city residents, and my mother, an interior decorator, worked for builders, making the insides of the model homes as appealing* as was the larger idea of moving to suburbia. When in fact we built our own new home, it was a "customized" version of the split-level model.

While opportunity and suburban living were having a pulling effect on my parents, three negative forces that intruded on our balanced urban existence helped push us over the edge. The Greenwich Village building in which my father's main plant was located was condemned as part of a large urban-renewal project, devised by master builder Robert Moses, for which a sizable chunk of the Village's multifunctional, economically viable urban fabric was sacrificed for apartment houses set in green plazas. New York University, at that time still a manageable neighbor in a predominantly residential community, bought our apartment building and let it be known that all tenants would have to move to make way for university expansion.† In addition, underworld forces were muscling in on the small businesses, like my father's, located on Eighth Street, the central shopping street of the Village, and it was increasingly difficult for my father to remain independent.

This combination made the timing auspicious. So we moved to Weston, and my father, having sold what he could of the business in the city, opened in Westport one of the first cash-and-carry dry-cleaning stores in a Connecticut shopping center. The new store had all the most modern advances of the cleaning industry: on-premises operation, same-day service, shirt-laundering facilities—very different from his urban operation, where only one of the four stores was the actual plant, pickup and delivery were necessary, and same-day service was difficult. My father opened the store in 1953, and at the

---

* A deceptive trick my mother learned from her builder boss was to use small-scale furniture to deceive buyers into thinking they were buying more spacious rooms than they were.
† Years later, NYU's Bobst Library, designed by Philip Johnson, would rise on this site.

age of thirteen I was eager to work there after school and Saturdays. I spent many hours behind the counter working with my father, and I remember being amazed at how often new customers who came into the store knew my father from the Village. "Are you the same Larry Brandes, dry cleaner, that used to be on Eighth Street?" they would ask. They were former city customers, now new suburbanites seeking the same greener pastures as my father. Greenwich Village neighbors were moving to Westport. The exodus to the suburbs was in full swing. We were witness to and participants in an American phenomenon that was changing the face of America.

The Urban Exodus Did Not Happen Naturally

An unspoken national policy of urban dispersal evolved in this country after World War II. This policy, or set of policies, a phenomenon touched on in earlier chapters, unleashed forces outside of cities that require the energy of a whole city to combat. The specific manifestation of urban dispersal that is the subject of this chapter is the regional shopping mall. The regional shopping mall is not this phenomenon's only manifestation but is perhaps its most visual and obviously destructive one. The often lethal blow to cities by ever larger regional shopping centers parallels the earlier decades' impact on cities of the ever bigger highways, slum-clearance/urban-renewal projects and suburban-tract housing complexes. These developments, in combination with the swelling exodus of manufacturing concerns and corporate headquarters (for which there were no new ones in formation to replace them), caused an economic vacuum and decline.

Most of the phenomena that drain cities started during the post–World War II building boom, and as their momentum increased they devastated urban America. At first people left cities in pursuit of an ideal—the American dream of home ownership. Only much later could that departure be called urban flight—flight from urban frustrations, instead of or along with the search of a prescribed goal.

Some people argue, with some validity, that negative city policies, not external forces or national policies, prompted the exodus of residents and businesses from inner cities. This is a half-truth which omits the most important half: cheap land, low taxes and scores of federal funding programs for highway construction, insured mortgages and subsidies for water and sewer connections lured residents and businesses to the suburbs. Suburbanization became national policy. Federally funded change is not natural or evolutionary. City policies and changing urban populations did not by themselves catalyze the suburban movement.

In the face of outside threats, some cities became their own worst enemy, hastening the decline with misguided internal responses—i.e., "urban renewal"—to a genuine external problem. When downtown became vulnerable, the strong arm of vast urban renewal and slum clearance delivered the final blow. This, however, was not a simple matter of federal bureaucrats telling localities what to do. Many communities welcomed the federal infusion of money *and* the suburb-in-the-city vision that went with it. Some communities resisted. Savannah, as we have seen, was one. Some did not have the money or the energy to change. Others today are lucky to have what they didn't destroy in the days of bulldozer renewal.

Just as the pitfalls of urban renewal were ignored, so, too, were the implications of the bigger and bigger malls sprouting on the landscape. In recent years, crippled old downtowns, with empty shops and empty lots, have been everywhere destroyed by regional malls. The empty stores in the larger downtowns are more dispersed but no less real. When shopping centers were still moderate in size and scale, their effect on surrounding towns and cities was not so noticeable. Now their enormous size and merchandising appeal make their impact unmistakable. At least one downtown community near any regional center is adversely affected. Roads that once led to the center of town take shoppers instead to the mall.* Moderate-size shopping centers sometimes can bring new customers to nearby downtowns as well as to themselves, but not so today's large-scale regional centers.

* In the course of researching this book, my husband and I took many car trips over the years and were constantly amazed to see conspicuous signs for the latest malls but not a signage hint that there was a worthwhile nearby downtown.

The Law of Unintended Consequences

At the heart of the regional-mall problem is an unavoidable dilemma that keeps reappearing throughout this book, one whose recognition is basic to the understanding of what causes the decline of cities and what reverses that decline. Let's call it the Law of Unintended Consequences. At its heart is a simple thesis: Any action causes a reaction. Any *big* action causes a *big* reaction. Any change brings about a chain reaction of changes. Any *big* change brings about a chain reaction of *big* changes. In other words, everything we do has a side effect; the bigger we do it, the bigger the side effect. In the case of regional shopping centers, the side effect happens to be the decimation of the traditional downtown.

None of this means that change is inherently bad. Change is, in any case, inevitable, and it can be positive as well as negative. The heart of the matter is the nature and rate of the change, and the response to it. If the response fans a small flame into a full-scale fire, trouble is certain. Moreover, this is true whether the initial change is good or bad. Change—as we saw earlier with the issue of gentrification—can be positive if it is evolutionary and not cataclysmic. The issue is not a choice between preservation or change but between well-managed change and badly managed change. And, in fact, preservation is most basically a way of managing change.

At first, shopping centers emerged on the landscape in response to changes already under way. People were moving to the suburbs in increasing numbers, encouraged by generous government financing and construction programs. Government policies, however, were only tempting, not forcing, people to move. The front lawn and the backyard, the spare room and the two-car garage were understandably appealing. The suburban life and the home ownership that came with it became the ideal. Financing, far more easily available for new construction, made that goal readily attainable.

The population of the country was mushrooming. The postwar baby boom was in full swing. The small Main Streets and the larger downtowns responded and expanded only up to a point, and too often inappropriately, adding to their own decline. (I will explain what I mean by this in the following chapters.) The first generation of shopping centers—shopping strips facing a road with a series of shops and parking—served a need that was growing in proportion to the movement of people and real-estate investment.

This movement paralleled the dawn of a new era in retailing. Postwar America experienced the luxury of putting its creative talent to civilian rather than military use. Innovations in consumer products, packaging and promotion coincided with the trend to larger stores owned by national chains. National chains have no ties to downtown, no loyalty to a local community. Their profits are siphoned off by distant headquarters rather than reinvested locally.

The proliferation of products and services strained the fixed retail plant of Main Street that lacked the capacity to expand to meet new demands. Many businesses were ready and eager to take advantage of the larger space that new shopping-center stores provided and the easier access that new highways offered. Consumerism and Centerism went hand in hand. New was in. Old was out. Modernization was a national fever. So it would be for decades to come.

The Automobile Society Takes Hold

At the same time, of course, Americans had fallen in love with the automobile. The automobile was as much a reflection of status and style as it was an answer to the needs of an increasing mobile society.

"A mobile society that had established a new set of rituals focused on the drive-in anything, transferred the Saturday night rite of passage to the 'climate controlled' covered shopping mall in all of its frigid, canned-music-drenched, plastic glamor," Ada Louise Huxtable wrote in a 1976 *New York Times* article entitled "The Fall and Rise of Main Street." "On old streets, old buildings were torn down for parking lots, in a bleak, gap-toothed kind of mutilation. Main Street had become a sad, shabby relic, empty shopfronts alternating with faded displays that looked as if time had stopped on one of those 1940s summer afternoons."

The demise of Main Street as the activity and retail center of a community can be clearly traced to the rise of the automobile. Historically, sweeping social and physical changes follow transportation changes, whether in big cities or small, in towns or villages. In too many instances, these transportation changes, notably the elimination of rail and bus stations, meant death to downtown. "Now, only after trains no longer run as they did, do we appreciate how they balanced our community interests and our self-interest more happily than autos," wrote Newhouse News Service columnist David J. Jacobs in *Preservation News* in June 1987. Road bypasses were built with the idea of decongesting downtown, but in the process they accelerated the exodus of business to fringe areas.

Early towns, small cities and even early suburbs naturally evolved around railroad stations, shopping quarters or marketplaces where farmers once delivered on a regular basis. Such sites were logical centers of social and economic activity. The rise of the car and the highway brought urban dispersal and the proliferation of automobile suburbs that together form the spread cities of our metropolitan regions. Functions formerly found in the center went in a thousand different directions. Ironically, the old railroad stations that remain standing today are still a point of reference in their community, if not the transportation hub they once were. Many such stations, frequently architecturally distinguished, are being restored and recycled into creative new uses.

Before the dominance of the automobile, one of the special qualities about downtown was that it was geared to the pedestrian, in design, scale and ambience. Then came the shopping strips (like the one my father was in) on the roads out of almost every town and city across the country. They were mini–shopping centers with lots of parking; places to shop in designed to catch the attention of the driver passing by; big, overpowering signs shouting for attention but creating confusion instead, the result of trying to communicate with those in a car passing at forty-five miles per hour.

In its rush to compete with the strip, downtown did itself a lot of damage. Streets were often widened, shrinking pedestrian space and often destroying many fine old shade trees that commonly arched gracefully over main streets. (How ironic it is that tree planting is such a point of pride to mall developers.) Many distinctive and historic buildings gave way to parking lots—the old city hall, a Victorian hotel, a stately courthouse or a modest row of varied storefronts. With each building lost to a parking lot went an active or potential commercial use with which to attract more people to downtown. Unavoidably, the more cars a town or city tries to accommodate, the greater toll exacted from commercial and social activity. Displaced businesses and other activities either closed up for good or relocated out of town, taking their customers to the outlying strips. Downtown became an embarrassment, and property owners tried to compete with the strip by covering their facades with oversized signs, obliterating whatever gave downtown distinction and appeal. The result was visual chaos—an orchestra of screamers. Main Street merchants discovered unhappily that, although they could rig up their building to look like the strip, they couldn't compete successfully with it.

Along with the growing dominance of the automobile, consumerism blossomed in full force. No style, whether in a car or a dress, was good for more than two years. The notion that new was automatically good and that old was automatically bad, however, pervaded more than the consumer-products industry. Not only the toaster or the teakettle you were using was outdated and bad, but also the nineteenth-century row house or the early-twentieth-century apartment you lived in, the crowded streets you walked on or the busy park you played in. In short, the city in which you resided was a bad, messy, disorganized mixture of functions that got in each other's way, difficult to master and defying the kind of order that the new thinking extolled. The functions of life should no longer be all tied up in one place. That was the tiresome way of the city through the ages. Now, in the euphoric mood of postwar America, this could be changed. A tidy fragmentation was possible. Functions could be sorted out and separated, made clean and efficient, and where better to do this than in the wide open spaces outside the city? Life would be better if you lived in a house—so the thinking went—separated from neighbors by manicured lawns and from commerce by intricate road systems if you lived in one world and worked in another. Division by socioeconomic factors was an unspoken planning goal.

Cities: Drop Dead

Life would also be better if you could escape the growing problems of the cities—crime, dirt, alienation, high taxes, juvenile delinquency, minority poor, declining public schools. Achieving the new ideal and escaping the problem-filled old—this was the promise, and there were plenty of developers standing ready to build it for a profit guaranteed by the federal government. A frontier mentality prevailed—with its assumptions based on unlimited energy and unlimited growth—even though there no longer was an undeveloped frontier. Instead, it was a new era of diminishing resources and diminishing space.

The city was not the sole victim. The new order would be applied with equal savagery and inappropriateness to the rolling hills and farms of the undeveloped countryside as to the time-tested fabric of the urban core. By the 1950s, it was well under way. Bulldozers cleared rural forests and the heart of Main Street with the same abandon. Project builders worked in the city and mall builders in the country, and highway planners and city planners often seemed to be one and the same person. The result was urban sprawl. The lines of distinction between city and country were purposely obliterated. Little care was given to unique character, local flavor and economic rationale of either downtowns or wheat fields. The nation was rushing full speed in the name of progress to fulfill Gertrude Stein's observation "There is no there, there."

Planners, businessmen and suburb promoters, among others, declared cities anachronistic before cities had even begun to die. That diagnosis, cruel and wrong, on top of the vision of what should replace the city was the double-edged disease hastening the city's demise.

In 1958 Jane Jacobs wrote: "What will the projects look like? They will be spacious, parklike, and uncrowded. They will feature long green vistas. They will be stable and symmetrical and orderly. They will be clean, impressive, and monumental. *They will have all the attributes of a well-kept dignified cemetery.*"[2] (Emphasis added.) The irony of this new vision is that its goal was to clean and neaten up the city. Yet cities have never seemed dirtier and messier. Sanitation problems are always high on people's complaint list. Such problems cannot be designed away.

What Jacobs was describing were the scores of redevelopment projects then on the drawing boards of cities all across the country. The city was being remade according to antiurban values. Suburbia was the new refuge. Both notions were ill-conceived.

By the late 1950s and the early 1960s, the sterility of the homogeneous suburban environment forced residents to seek recreation in shopping. Malls sprouted fountains, art shows, seating areas and then restaurants, movie theaters and arcades in a clear attempt to emulate the once vibrant downtowns from where they were drawing customers. The mall was on its way to becoming the downtown for suburbia.

In 1956, Southdale, the first enclosed, climate-controlled complex of shops, stores and restaurants, opened in the well-to-do Minneapolis suburb of Edina. Designed by the late architect Victor Gruen, Southdale marked a major turning point away from the customary shopping center usually built along a main road with stores facing the street (the kind described earlier that my father's store was in) to the larger and larger enclosed mall—"Main Street in a space ship," William Severini Kowinski, author of *The Malling of America,* has called it.

In a speech to a 1978 meeting of the International Council of Shopping Centers, Gruen noted:

> It is hard to believe today, that at the time of the planning of Southdale the idea of creating a covered shopping center was so revolutionary, that all so-called "experts" warned my clients not to engage in such a crazy experiment, which they said was not only technically impossible, but would also be economically disastrous. It took in fact many years

after the successful opening of Southdale before anybody else dared to repeat the experiment of the enclosed shopping center which, as you know, has by today become practically standard, even for those locations where, because of pleasant climate, a so-called open shopping center would be preferable.[3]

By the 1970s, the local convenience shopping center had evolved into the regional mall that was often equal in retail space to the entire downtown it would supplant. At the beginning of the 1970s, according to the International Downtown Executives Association, regional centers were in the 200,000–500,000-square-feet range. By the end of the decade, super regional centers of one million square feet and more were common, and the center with two department stores as anchors had given way to the three- and four-anchor mall, while five- and six-anchor malls were evolving. Also by the end of that decade, there were 22,000 shopping centers of all types across the country, triple the number there were in 1965. Southdale, the first modern center, reflects the very evolution that followed its own establishment. When it opened, Southdale had two department stores and sixty-four shops and covered 800,000 square feet. Today it has three department stores and 140 shops and covers 1.1 million square feet.

Ironically, however, as the regional shopping centers devoured the rural landscape and grew to gargantuan size, something else was going on during the 1970s that by 1980 would be clear: Downtown was coming back. Now the new vogue was quite simply a rediscovered old one: Main Street. "Declared dead," Huxtable noted in her 1976 article, "Main Street refused to die."

The good old, much-maligned street—crowded, cluttered, full of unplanned surprises—was the place to be at. The old values of Main Street were again the coin of the realm. People wanted the small shops, the intimate scale, the one-on-one relationship with the butcher and the baker, the personal service of the local merchant who knew the family well, the tradition that came with the mom-and-pop store, and even the downtown department store—more personal and interesting than the mall, accessible to lunchtime shoppers, reachable without costly auto trips and, often, with salespeople who knew your size, taste and probably your birthday. The pendulum had swung back. These are qualities built over time and with a personal touch appreciated only when they are replaced by the cold plasticity of the new shopping center built at one time.

Malls Learned from Downtowns

What makes suburban shopping centers thrive is not mysterious, nor are the elements of their success inventive and new. Upon close examination, many of the characteristics the public now finds appealing in malls hark back to the qualities that were once appealing about urban downtowns. Old values, like old buildings, don't automatically diminish with age. And often they fade from the scene for reasons that have nothing to do with outlived usefulness. When Main Street was still strong, sometimes it all just hung together because of its inherent economic and social logic *and* the absence of overwhelming competition.

Activity and interest came naturally to downtown in those days. There was no replacement yet. Main Street was the community's front yard (in a big city, a neighborhood park or a shopping street filled the need), communal meeting place, site for festivals, fund drives, political assemblies and patriotic celebrations. In short, there was a lot going on downtown. There was always much to see and do there, *besides* going shopping. This old pattern—what Main Street and urban neighborhood-revitalization programs are renewing—lasted for generations and has faded only in our lifetime.

When I was a child living in Greenwich Village, Washington Square Park was the central activity site, and the whole city offered adventurous excursions. "The Park," as it was always known, was the meeting place, the focus of every activity from regular chess games to political speeches to guitar fests around the steps of "the circle," a massive fountain with spacious steps useful for seating. My grandfather and his cronies met on a park bench. My contempories met in the playground. People came and went in our neighborhood for every imaginable reason from shopping to entertainment and from education to health care, the way they still do in vital urban communities.

Later, when I was a teenager living in Weston, my friends and I often spent a whole Saturday "in town" in the nearby downtown of Westport. My mother, a city person to the core who hated being dependent on the family car and chose not to be the family chauffeur, would take me downtown on a Saturday morning and leave me for the day (or, if she had no reason or inclination to go, I would hitchhike in). I would either get a ride home or wait for my father to close his store and take me home with him.

There was always enough to fill a day—a little shopping, schoolwork in the library, a planned meeting with friends for lunch and the afternoon movie, an activity at the YMCA or just plain "hanging out"—much like the life described to me by friends who lived elsewhere, and not unlike teenage life in suburban shopping centers today.

School was not too far to walk to from downtown Westport, in case a football or basketball home game was on the schedule. Hitchhiking was an option. The favorite hangout was a drive-in Dairy Queen midway between Main Street and the shopping center where my father had his dry-cleaning store. Almost everything was in walking distance, as compact as one could hope for "in the country."

Today's shopping centers borrowed from that past. They built on and imitated the past, coopted and adapted it, succeeding only up to a point beyond which malls cannot go. The needs they serve have not changed with the generations. Downtowns can reclaim some of what those centers first learned from them; they can serve functions parallel to the malls' and still leave urbanism intact. The personality of a *real* downtown can never be achieved in a mall, above all because the stamp of the local populace is never stronger than that of the commercial (namely, national-chain) overlay. Malls don't have community input, the way downtowns do. Evidence of the local imprint is meager and superficial. Maybe the local blood drive or the Girl

Scouts set up an occasional fund-raising table and maybe a single bulletin board announces local events, but a mall is severely limited in how much a part of community life it can be. The local spirit in full strength and the symbiotic relationship between local merchants and community customers can be achieved only in a genuinely local setting—in other words, on Main Street or its equivalent downtown location. Local character is antithetical to the nature of a mall.

Lessons in Downtown Survival Are Many

The successful downtowns I have observed are not the ones that have responded on suburban terms, clearing their acreage to impose surburban malls—whether vertical or horizontal—in the heart of downtown, or transforming themselves into mere clusters of offices scattered among parking lots like their suburban competitors. Instead, successful cities have competed on their own urban terms, respecting streets and mass transit more than highways, restoring what's left of the city's time-tested fabric, weaving the new to fit the pattern of the old and evolving as cities always have evolved. This is another aspect of Urban Husbandry, which is as applicable to a city's commercial center as to its residential neighborhoods.

The following chapters focus on a series of communities and one national nongovernmental program that illuminate the changes wrought by the past twenty-five years of regional-mall evolution. The first story involves Ithaca, New York, and its suburban neighbor, Lansing, and outlines how one community, led by a feisty mayor, fought the building of a destructive mall and lost, but in the process woke up to the downtown changes needed to survive the mall, and succeeded. The Ithaca story highlights as well some downtown issues critical to downtowns of any size: the importance of public transit, the critical role of the downtown resident, the ripple effect that turns small changes into big improvements, the hidden costs of mega-change and the crucial difference that creative and gutsy local political leadership can make.

In Corning, New York, we will see a rational, undisruptive, frugal

and productive approach to genuine downtown commercial revitalization that is now being creatively applied to large and small
commercial centers everywhere. The Corning story also questions
whether it matters that revitalization begins with a public or private
initiator. We will also look at the impact of national developers and
national retail chains and the different community impact of local and
regional dollars.

Burlington, Vermont, successfully defeated the same kind of
suburban mall that Ithaca failed to stop, and it did so with the help of
one of the country's most forward-thinking environmental-
protection laws. The constraining development policies had not
interfered with the state's flourishing economy, but they did force an
examination of the consequences of megadevelopment that was
unusual for the 1970s. The Burlington story shows, too, how helpful
a watchful local newspaper can be. Also of interest in the Burlington
story are the good and bad manifestations visible in downtown of the
city's successful fight to save itself. Burlington must now deal with
some of the mistakes, but at least there remains a downtown alive
enough to have problems.

In the story of Pittsfield, Massachusetts, we see a more recent,
potentially more devastating phenomenon made insidiously worse by
an overwhelming infusion of federal money. Pittsfield successfully
defeated the outside suburban mall and then tried instead to impose
that defeated proposal on its revitalization-hungry downtown, almost
destroying itself in the process. Disaster was averted only because of
a battle waged by a hearty band of citizen protestors—such instinctivists as are applauded throughout this book—led primarily by the
kind of historic-preservationists so often in the vanguard of sensible
change.

All these stories illustrate how useful a revitalization tool historic
preservation can be. This is not automatically the case, however.
Historic preservation can be used to renew a downtown inappropriately as surely as the bulldozer can. A vital downtown neighborhood
was summarily destroyed in Albany, New York, in the name of
renewal for historic restoration. Good ideas can too easily be trans-

lated into bad formulas. Preserving what physically exists can be a tool for destroying a social and economic fabric that should be strengthened, not replaced.

The final story in the section is about the Main Street Project, a comprehensive approach to downtown revitalization. The Main Street Project is a program of the private, nonprofit National Trust for Historic Preservation and is so appropriately adjustable that it offers useful lessons for commercial centers of any scale, from small towns to urban shopping streets. It is a program that offers useful directions instead of easy answers, that values instincts of citizens as highly as expertise of professionals, that respects the inseparability of the economic and physical environment, restores the accumulated character of place and best exhibits the principles of Urban Husbandry.

Part Two

THE CITY REDISCOVERED

■

BIG STEPS, MODESTLY

The Stories of Ithaca and Corning

■

*Among shopping-center developers, it is assumed
that every element of the regional [mall] is
necessary to produce the internal dynamic that
causes it to spout money. The formula is so
unvarying that once the elements have been set in
place—once a department store or the developer has
done a market survey, once the land is under
option, once the companion department stores have
committed themselves—a well-established developer
might pencil in the names of some tenants before he
begins negotiating with them, the assumption being
that some credit-jewelry chains and shoe chains and
clothing chains will put a store in any regional
whose developer can produce a projection sheet with
acceptable numbers on it. If a regional is not
spouting money the way it was designed to, the*

developer can adjust what he calls "the mix"—the
way someone running an engine might adjust the
fuel mix. In time, he can cut the percentage of shoe
stores or increase the percentage of jeans stores. He
can try to persuade the weaker tenants that
everybody might be better off if some arrangement
were worked out for the remaining portion of their
leases—one of the generators for the regional's
internal dynamic being the principle that everybody
involved has a direct stake in the profitability of
everybody else. At this year's convention of the
International Council of Shopping Centers, which
was held not long ago in New Orleans, I
occasionally heard people refer to the regional as a
selling machine. It is a collection of stores only to
the extent that a station wagon is a collection of
auto parts.

—CALVIN TRILLIN in *The New Yorker*, July 28,
1980.[1]

The appearance of a retail mall on the nearby horizon of a small town or a large-city neighborhood inevitably disrupts communities within the mall's market reach. It is today's definition of cataclysmic change, as sure as slum clearance and highway building were yesterday's definition.

There are many large and small cities where the impact of a regional mall can be observed. In fact, there are few where it cannot. Consider Ithaca, New York. From the distance of more than a decade, Ithaca provides lessons that parallel those of scores of cities. Ithaca lost the battle against a regional mall but won the war to save itself. Ithaca's victory is a modest blueprint for downtown revitalization anywhere.

Ithaca is located in central New York state, 150 miles from Buffalo and fifty-five miles from Syracuse. At the 1980 census, the population was 28,000, or 50,000 when one counts nearby suburbs. It is surrounded by farmland. Ithaca's industry is education: the city is the home of Cornell University and Ithaca College, with a combined student population of 23,000.

During the 1950s, Ithaca experienced typical suburbanization and modernization. Change occurred there less dramatically than in many cities, for one simple reason. Ithaca's livelihood, education, remained economically stable. Its secondary industries of electronics and automotive-parts manufacturing also held their own. Ithaca weathered economic cycles well and did not experience the cataclysmic shifts of large-industry failures.

Still, people moved to the suburbs, turning up their noses at the Victorian wood-frame houses in town. Small shopping strips and shopping centers emerged on once thriving cornfields. Downtown was stagnating. Aged Ithaca neighborhoods and commercial buildings lost favor. The urge to modernize swept through town. First the aluminum-siding and then the plastic-front salesmen worked their wiles on downtown merchants. Varied storefronts exhibiting the design, individuality and caring of earlier eras were covered over or removed. Either shiny new and bland facades replaced them or garish, oversized signs were tacked onto the upper stories.

The city government was equally disrespectful of the urban fabric. Urban renewal was the current buzzword, and this city initiated its share of obliteration in its name, although municipal leaders rejected some drastic schemes that would have totally destroyed downtown. The early-nineteenth-century Greek Revival City Hall was demolished in 1966 to make way for a five-story parking garage—that dismal open-sided style of precast-concrete panels and no windows—that looks like a weather-beaten metal box and was unattractive even when the paint was fresh. A two-block stretch of State Street, the central commercial spine, was "renewed." At one end of State Street a one-story nondescript brick home of the telephone company replaced a block of varied buildings and uses. At the heart of State Street a new and larger department store replaced the city's nineteenth-century Italianate grand hotel, which had been vacant for years. The old department-store building was bulldozed and its sizable site, adjacent to the new store, remained vacant for seventeen years, one of the most common and worst vestiges of urban renewal. Nothing is more deadly to a downtown than a big empty space in its center that generates nothing—no economic activity, no taxes, no pedestrian movement, no visual interest. This is the missing-tooth syndrome, dismaying or devastating whether one small building is erased from a coherent row or a large parcel is razed in the center. Such vacant spaces at best prolong and at worst promote downtown devitalization and surely dim inherent revitalization potential.

Ithaca's downtown was in trouble.

The Rural Landscape Is Transformed

At the same time, the nearby town of Lansing, the southern part of which became the incorporated village of Lansing in 1974, surged with the growth that downtown Ithaca was losing. The push and pull between Ithaca and Lansing reflect a classic pattern of downtown decay and suburban birth that has occurred all over this country. Four miles from downtown Ithaca, Lansing remained a sleepy rural area until the 1960s, when a four-lane highway came in, followed by apartment developments, two shopping centers and three motels. Pressure grew for more access roads and sewer-line extensions through residential areas.

Lansing is in the middle of a rural county. By the 1960s Lansing was the fastest-growing area in the county. Town officials were delighted. They saw only a rising tax base, not the rising costs that would follow. Few people anywhere were measuring the costs of sprawl. Even today, one is hard pressed to find the kind of studies that examine the true economic costs of new developments necessary for any balanced evaluation of the litany of seductive goodies invariably promised by new development projects.

In June 1974, over strong objections voiced by Lansing residents, a major highway overpass was approved for Lansing—one that was promised to alleviate traffic congestion and improve safety but clearly was meant to facilitate development of a mall. A week later, a major regional-shopping-mall developer, the Pyramid Company of nearby Syracuse, announced plans to build at the overpass. There was an untapped retail market, the developer reported optimistically, not only in the county but within a radius of sixty to seventy miles of Lansing. That radius included not only Ithaca but also the larger cities of Binghamton, Elmira and Syracuse. Fifty percent of the market was planned to come from outside the local area. The Ithaca/Lansing community was about to get a regional shopping mall.

Lansing residents argued against approval of the mall's construction, but lost. The assortment of issues paralleled the development arguments heard in innumerable communities. Lansingites fought overpass and mall plans, for example, on the grounds that increased traffic would radically change the residential nature of the area. Overpass and mall promoters—just like highway advocates—countered that there would be no demonstrable increase in traffic. "Then why do we need the overpass?" residents asked, just as highway opponents ask why new roads are promoted if not to accommodate more traffic.

For years this has been the basic, unanswerable question in debates over new highways. It is the Catch-22 for which highway boosters have no answer. If there is to be *no* traffic increase, why spend public funds on new and bigger roads? If there *is* to be increased traffic—which there always is—then shouldn't the impact of that traffic be carefully considered? Every new highway or road widening continues to be promoted on the erroneous assumption that it will alleviate traffic. Experience has shown that instead it attracts new traffic. That is exactly what happened in Lansing. Lansing is now choking in traffic—as are its counterparts nationwide—and wrestling with the whole spectrum of problems that accompany that condition.

Public officials promoting the mall and the overpass, whether they believed it or not, offered the familiar refrain that development would bring new taxes and jobs. After construction, Lansing provided new street lighting for the overpass and ramps for safety reasons. In 1977 those lights cost the village almost $10,000, against the $1,025 received in new tax income. In 1988, those lights cost $18,300, against $33,045 in tax income from the mall. Also after the mall opened,* one third of the Lansing Fire Department calls came from there. Warnings of the hidden costs of development are always overwhelmed by the seductive arguments for lucrative new taxes and jobs.

Thousands of small communities and large cities across the country wholeheartedly embraced new development just as the Lansing officials did, only to understand in retrospect the illusive benefits as demands mounted for more police, fire or health services, streetlights, road and highway maintenance and other public services. In the past decade of feverish chase after the new-development treasure, awareness of the hidden costs has grown. In fact, according to planning journals, more and more communities today are mandating up-front, earmarked funding for requisite new roads and new water and sewer systems before developers are even given permits for new office parks, shopping centers or residential developments. Popularly known as exactions and impact fees, they signal a change from the days when such new developments as the Lansing mall were accepted as quick-fix solutions for everything.[†]

Although the Lansing mall was inevitable, its construction did not move ahead easily. There was one critical hitch, one that the feisty mayor of Ithaca knew how to use to delay construction. The one-year halt gave downtown Ithaca the time needed to start to pull itself out of its depressed state in order to compete with the mall.

The weapon was water.

Ithaca Fights for Itself

Ithaca's public water system, at the time, was the most logical source from which the Lansing mall would draw. Mayor Ed Conley refused

---

* The 550,000-square-foot mall contains eighty stores, ten restaurants and a movie complex.
† Inevitably, however, they are still promoted as quick-fix, all-encompassing packages of bonuses and benefits but in some quarters, at least, a healthy skepticism is growing.

to give approval of the extension of Ithaca's water supply to the mall.

Conley, a former city councilman, had won a five-way race for mayor in 1971 by nine votes. His platform: "Make Ithaca Happen Again." Later he was reelected by wide margins, becoming Ithaca's only four-time mayor. A robust man with a sharp wit and a quick mind, he identifies himself as coming from the hard-fighting school of Irish mayors.

Conley foresaw the damage to downtown Ithaca and was determined to fight the mall with whatever tools were available, in this case the developer's need for a water permit from the city. Local memories differ over which issues the fight rested on, whether water (the developer secured water from a nearby lake) or squabbles over permits and sewer extensions. Those specifics are not as crucial as the fact that the fight took place—and that the city of Ithaca and the village of Lansing were on the same side.

The fighting gave the city only one year, but it was symbolically important and stiffened the public's resolve to protect downtown. Downtown merchants who were considering branch stores in the mall got the message. Their buying public, both in surrounding Lansing and in Ithaca, led by Ithaca's mayor, would boycott if the stores opened in the mall.

Conley's strategy was a creative combination of psychological warfare, an assortment of very specific small-scale improvements and a large dose of public relations. Sheer bravado was an essential ingredient of everything the city did.

Publicly, Conley told anyone listening that the Pyramid Mall "would have no effect" on downtown. "I knew that was a lie," Conley now says. At a conference of retailer economists, Conley was told that without any of the Triple A National retailers—Penney, Ward, K Mart, Sears and Woolworth were the top five—downtown would die. Each chain, the economists noted, would spend more money on its own advertising for its out-of-downtown location than all the downtown small owners put together.

Conley set to work holding on to the skeptical local merchants, persuading them to work with the city at improving, not deserting, downtown—"jawboning," is how Conley describes it—and convincing them that "downtown had something good going on." He drew ideas from a diverse chorus of citizen activists—farsighted merchants, local garden-club members, historic preservationists, community representatives, nontraditional planners, and university academicians. There was no dearth of innovative suggestions, but someone had to channel the action.

Two blocks of State Street that were turned into a pleasantly landscaped pedestrian walkway became the centerpiece project, a rare case of a successful pedestrian mall that has withstood the test of time. While this was under construction, a feverish public-relations effort brought it proper attention. A contest was held to name it. "Everyone was calling it a mall or a plaza," remembers Conley, and neither seemed right. The final name: the Commons. A common is what almost every American town or city once had in its early history, and for good reason: the Common was the focus of city life, the center of public activity. So it was meant to be again. A media campaign to bring Ithaca residents and schoolchildren downtown to "Watch Your Community Being Reborn" worked so well that business was better than ever. Actually, this shouldn't come as a surprise to anyone who has watched spontaneous crowds gather at urban construction sites. But the effects were electric for still-skeptical downtown businessmen. Pedestrians have not stopped coming to the Commons since, the mark of its long-term success.

Retail sales during the year of construction increased 2 percent over the preceding year, but, Conley says with a laugh, "even that was a lie that worked." The increase was not much more than inflation— how much was due to inflation or to growth is unknown—but it made things sound better, and the public and the merchants perceived it that way. Significantly, considering recent downtown trends, it meant that downtown was at least holding its own.

With equal fervor, mass transit was improved and promoted. There had been demands to scrap the bus system as a cost-saving move. Conley saw its improvement as a necessary public investment instead and as part of the whole process of rebuilding downtown.

Free bus service and parking were instituted for big shopping periods, like Christmas, Easter and back-to-school days. New bus lines were added and old routes improved. The media were prodded to offer public-service announcements to promote transit use. Even the transit system's name, Ithaca Transit, was made into a conversation item, "Ride IT," signs read.*

Ridership doubled and then tripled as the cost per rider *decreased*. It stayed cheap. In 1967, a bus ride cost 25 cents. Twelve years later, it went to 35 cents (it is still there) with no loss in ridership. It was more of a bargain than it had been at 25 cents. (Also in 1979, parking fees went up for the first time in twelve years, from 10 to 15 cents per hour, where they have stayed.) Additional bus-ridership revenues offset increased expenses, although the deficit remained constant. Yet Conley viewed the deficit as an investment in the city's future. Cheap and efficient mass transit is so crucial to the survival and prosperity of cities that it is amazing that it is not the national urban priority. Conley also viewed as investments, not costs, the downtown parking garages that he caused to be built.

The Commons and mass-transit programs were the most visible municipal efforts. But many small things going on at the same time combined for equal impact. A municipal parking garage was built. The city was improving sidewalks and persuading property owners to upgrade their storefronts. Architects were hired by the city to provide free design assistance. City planners helped property owners find new tenants to fill vacancies. A downtown coordinator was hired by the city, which paid half the costs, with the other half paid by the local merchants' association. A sign ordinance was passed, with standards that allowed for the retention of some old nonconforming, even garish, but interesting and historic signs. Paint advice was provided free to property owners. One owner of a burned-out row of three buildings was ready to demolish them to make way for a

---

* Mass transit improvement and promotion of its use is imperative for genuine revitalization. One of the best promotional pamphlets I've seen produced was in Seattle where a transit service map was transformed into a promotional piece called, "The 2nd Car Owner's Manual."

doughnut drive-in. City planners showed him how the property could be restored instead and helped persuade a bank to finance the rehabilitation.

City policy discouraged repetitive and uninteresting street-level banks in prime locations and instead encouraged new retailing. "Retailing means taxes," says Conley. "Someone can go out of his way a few blocks for a bank, post office or telephone office, but shouldn't have to for a store."

New restaurants began opening, bringing new nightlife. Medical services had been leaving the city for the suburbs over the years, so the city bought an abandoned gas station and converted it into a three-doctor office facility, to give people one more reason to keep coming downtown.

Finally, in the early 1980s, plans were approved to fill the gaping hole on State Street with a mixed-use building, called Ithaca Center, having retail stores on the first of its four stories, offices on the second, and apartments on the third and fourth. The office space was designed flexibly so that if it didn't work out it could be easily converted to residential use. The result is aesthetically disappointing, with the ground floor interior a standard dull suburban mall in stark contrast to the interesting street outside, but Ithaca Center does not drain neighboring retail, nor overwhelm it. Since it has stores fronting on the street, the isolationist feeling of most malls is absent and the strength of the larger downtown minimizes the shortcomings of Ithaca Center. The design may be unimpressive at best, but, notes Cornell planning professor Stuart Stein, "it is a very urban place, with people sitting, reading and conversing, the only place in Ithaca where that is true." In its appeal to people, Ithaca Center compensates for mediocre design.

Conley, prodded by local preservationists who wanted existing buildings reused,* initiated a program to encourage the conversion to

---

* Despite a strong historic-preservation ethic in Ithaca, more than a decade elapsed after a 1975 fire ravaged the 1851 Greek Revival brick Clinton Hall before a purchaser restored the building, which once again is a productive mix of appropriate downtown

residential use of the second, third and fourth floors above the street-level stores in buildings adjacent to the new building under construction. Limited, but helpful, city funds were provided. This reversed downtown's residential exodus, replenishing the permanent population that downtown once depended upon and that must be depended on more than the transients who merely come and go as business or errands dictate. Many downtowns still have the storefront buildings that once housed residents above and could again, but too often this potential remains ignored. There really was a timeless logic to the historical pattern of development that produced a street-level store with residents above. It's a pattern as old as this country—older still, since it was a European import. The store below/apartment-above concept continues to work abroad and in many stable neighborhoods of American cities. As an idea, however, it ran into trouble with the ascendancy of the anticity vision which favored people working downtown but living in the suburbs. Today this is a rediscovered economic and social resource. The upper floors of downtown buildings are sprouting rehabilitated apartments and breathing needed new life into reviving downtowns.

Downtown Is People

The downtown resident is one of the most valuable and unappreciated assets cities have lost during decades of decline. A permanent consumer/user force to support the stores, to work in the offices, to eat at restaurants, to attend the theater, to populate the street, to make life interesting—this is what any downtown needs. As William H. Whyte, Jr., wrote in his enduring 1958 book *The Exploding Metropolis*[2]:

> The rebuilding of downtown is not enough; a city deserted
> at night by its leading citizens is only half a city. If it is to

---

uses—bookstores, ice-cream stores, a café, an art gallery and assorted offices. In the 1960s a similar private conversion of the turn-of-the-century 4-story De Witt Junior High School, a modest-version red-brick University Gothic, was the first preservation project to show that progress and change could come without demolition, and it earned a warm public response.

continue as the dominant cultural force in American life, the city must have a core of people to support its theaters and museums, its shops and its restaurants—even a Bohemia of sorts can be of help. For it is the people who like living in the city who make it an attraction to the visitors who don't. It is the city dweller who supports its style; without them there is nothing to come downtown *to*.

To its credit, Ithaca was not trying to entice residents into downtown "projects" of meager appeal. In the same 1958 book, Whyte offered an observation about projects then on the drawing boards that is no less true in the 1980s:

> They represented a design for living ideally calculated to keep everybody in suburbia. These vast, barrack-like superblocks are not designed for people who *like* cities, but for people who have no other choice. A few imaginative architects and planners have shown that redeveloped blocks don't have to be repellent to make money, but so far their ideas have had little effect. The institutional approach is dominant, and unless the assumptions embalmed in it are re-examined the city is going to be turned into a gigantic bore.

Thirty years later, how true Whyte's words remain! Choices are what the whole back-to-the-city and stay-in-the-city movements are all about. The choice to live in close proximity to shopping, work, and entertainment places. The choice to move freely, independent of a car. When more and more people started making that choice again—either to stay in the city or to return to it—look where they chose to live: the old discarded row houses or Victorian residences of the pre-suburban middle class; the vacant lofts of the one-time manufacturing businesses; even the abandoned firehouses, school buildings, police stations, department stores and office buildings built in the days when public and corporate architecture were worthy of the name. Some people *do* want to live *and* work *and* shop *and* spend leisure time in town, which is why downtown commercial and neighborhood revitalizations are inextricably bound together and should occur in tandem. The economic and social fabric of a city dictates the interdependence of residential and commercial locations and functions. If either genuinely improves, the other will follow. They should not be regarded separately.

The rebirth of Savannah started as a downtown historic-preservation effort—the rescue of mansions, public squares, the waterfront, and commercial buildings near the waterfront. Home and commerce were tied together through the common denominator of historic preservation. Revitalization would not have worked in Savannah or anywhere else if only mansions or commercial buildings had been rejuvenated. Any successful urban revitalization will have both residential and commercial activity in close proximity, even if it is not initially planned that way. This is a logical reinforcement process that reflects the nature of the city itself.

Ithaca's reinvigoration came in response to the outside threat of the regional mall it could not stop, but it came in a manner appropriate to its own personality and place. Conley set things in motion, but the momentum continued. New stores have opened around the corner and blocks away from the Commons, stores that reflect local tastes and are owned and operated by residents. Change is ongoing but appropriate.

Ithaca is the first sequence of the downtown–versus–the–mall story because it reflects modest lessons so broadly applicable and highlights a widespread current dilemma of communities forced to coexist with functioning malls. The fact that this scenario continues to replay itself over and over implies a lesson in urban change unlearned. Ithaca applied an assortment of strategies necessary for downtown survival. An interesting contrast, though also a dowtown success story, is offered by the town of Corning, only fifty miles from Ithaca.

History and Change Reinforce Each Other

Corning, New York, learned how to adjust to mall competition and to overcome natural disaster. The lessons of Corning, as we shall see, were exported far and wide.

A fundamental characteristic of genuine urban rejuvenation is the sharing of experience among communities confronting similar challenges, the importing and exporting of lessons, the learning from the teaching of other communities. This experience-exchange process is an informal one, and its informality is what makes it work so well, allowing communities to choose from the innovations and experience of others what is appropriate for them.

Adaptation, in contrast to copying, encourages the retention of local differences and avoids replication and sameness. The antithesis of this creative and flexible process of adaptation is the federal government's habit of taking one success, turning it into a formula, writing copious complicated and intimidating regulations and shipping it off to as many communities as will have it, without leaving room for local variation and flexibility. Another antithesis of the creative-adaptation process is the habit of many localities to welcome developer schemes cloned from somewhere else.

Corning, with a population of 13,000, is a classic company town—first for lumber, but since 1868 it has been the home of the Corning Glass Works, which moved there from Brooklyn, New York. A bucolic outpost in the thickly forested valley of New York State's Southern Tier, the city is situated on the banks of the Chemung River, which was the source both of Corning's economic birth and of its later near-total destruction. Following the 1972 Hurricane Agnes, the city was 60 percent under water. The physical damage was incalculable, and the spiritual scars were equally severe. A fledgling historic-preservation organization was left paralyzed in the face of such wholesale destruction.

Corning could easily have gone the conventional route of many communities ravaged by natural disasters. It could have leveled the remains and rebuilt itself in good textbook urban-renewal fashion. Elmira, fifteen miles away, did just that and stands today in dismal contrast to Corning. Instead, Corning channeled its one-shot flood-damage federal funds into new brick sidewalks and honey-locust trees for Market Street, the four-block-long commercial spine of the town. But the real turning point came with the involvement of Corning

Glass Works, whose leaders recognized that the revitalization of Market Street was as much in the company's best interest as the town's. Market Street contained a rich assortment of two- to four-story buildings, but no one was concentrating on encouraging businessmen to upgrade, rehabilitate or restore their property.

In 1974 the glass company donated $64,000 to start the Market Street Restoration Agency. Norman Mintz, a young preservation planner and designer with low-key charm and immense warmth, was brought in as director. With great skill, Mintz combined a large dose of diplomacy with an equally impressive design talent to set about providing free design services to Market Street merchants and owners.

Over 20 percent of the 125 storefronts were vacant when the agency began in 1974, and from one end of Market Street to the other there were unsightly remains of decades of misguided "improvements"—aluminum siding, garish signs and all manner of cover-ups of architectural details dating from the late 1800s through the 1930s. Mintz drew attention to the hidden assets of Market Street. The cornices, shapely brackets and array of gingerbread of the Victorian era; the large windows, leaded-glass transoms, glazed and unglazed terra-cotta surfaces and creative hanging signs of the 1920s; the Art Deco geometric patterns and inspired use of metallic ornament of the 1930s; the Carrara glass and artistic neon of the 1940s—all these stylistic differences were treated as valuable assets to be enhanced. Always with the merchants' economic self-interest in mind, Mintz showed them how to make low-cost improvements in their storefronts essentially by making the most of their building's particular design style.

"Merchants can be difficult, stubborn, independent and apathetic," says Mintz, "but gaining their confidence and sparking their enthusiasm is the key to any comeback."

There was a purposeful effort not to produce a "harmonized" look, to encourage the renovation of an Art Deco front with the same enthusiasm as an 1890 terra-cotta facade. The object was not to erase the layers of history but to restore them for modern use. The "prettified" look and the antique imitation were also discouraged. The ordinary building was treated with as much respect as the ornate. Many interesting and appealing Main Streets and large city blocks have that mixture of plain and fancy that imparts a character no modern superblock can achieve.

"Each Main Street is different, but the diversity makes it exciting," Mintz says. "The storefronts shouldn't match. The street is a stage to which they are a backdrop."

Through gentle persuasion and one-by-one examples, interest among merchants spread. The design help was free, but it was the merchant's own money that paid for the changes. Cooperation was voluntary. There were no elaborate incentives, no tax breaks and no cheap loans. The program was based entirely on good business sense. Small changes led to more small changes and to some big ones as well. The scale of each store, whatever its size, and of the total street was maintained. Mintz discovered many early elements—delicate transoms, opaque glass, Deco signage, cast-iron columns—buried beneath tacky wood and metal panels. Where this is the case, historically accurate restorations are often the cheapest, most attractive improvements shopkeepers can make, usually much to their surprise. Within a few years, close to 100 buildings were rehabilitated and approximately 125 signs replaced or added. Vacancies disappeared. Business on Market Street increased, and more and more of the perennial tourists to the Corning Glass Works and the Rockwell-Corning Museum of Western Art were shopping Market Street as well.

Actually the improved business of Market Street was more psychological than real, just as it had been in Ithaca. More accurately, business levels held firm despite the 1975 and 1982 national recessions, despite the hard times for the Corning Glass Works and its employees, and despite the loss of the major retail anchor, a hardware/furniture/housewares store that had served as the most important traffic draw. Market Street just held on economically, but the business climate was good, confidence was restored and growing, and vacant stores filled up quickly. As in so many revitalization efforts, attitude was critical. Confidence is hard to measure in dollars and cents, but its economic importance should not be underestimated.

"The most important lesson of the Market Street success," says Mintz, who has gone on to consult with many communities, "is that communities overwhelmed by all that needs doing can see that each step, no matter how small, is a positive move in the right direction and that each one of those steps counts."

What made this improvement process all the more remarkable was the existence of a huge regional mall only a short drive from downtown. The Arnot Shopping Mall, built in three phases, was started in the late 1960s and completed in 1983.* It is one million square feet and has five anchor stores. With the mall so close, Mintz approached the task of rejuvenating Market Street with a very simple premise: The main problem in downtowns is that the people there "fail to see the assets already in place. Downtowns suffer from an inferiority complex. When merchants see everything that is new and flashy going into the nearest shopping center, they think of downtown merely as old."

Undeniably, shopping malls offered a lot of things downtown did not, Mintz recognized, like the ability to arrive and leave in your own car, to park free, to feel safe,† to choose from wide selections often better displayed, and to do everything in an often enclosed environment protected from the vagaries of weather. But downtown had assets that the malls did not—a sense of place, a sense of community, streets suitable for the small, locally owned business, the service store and the quality shop, and of course the family-owned businesses of all

---

* Ironically, murals depicting the varied streetscape of downtown's Market Street decorate the interior of the Arnot Mall.

† Safety is increasingly an illusion. Michael Winerip, writing in *Nation's Cities Weekly*, March 28, 1983, reported: "With the general rise in crime over the last two decades, the suburban shopping mall has become a major police beat. . . . Most major metropolitan malls average a stolen-car report a day. The size of the shopping areas works to the thieves' advantage." A Sept. 10, 1987, story, "Shoppers Beware: Malls May Look Safe, But Some Lure Crooks as Well as the Crowds," in *The Wall Street Journal* reported crimes up in malls across the country—assaults, stolen cars, robberies, sex crimes and shoplifting—but noted that mall owners don't reveal such statistics and local police don't record them specifically by location.

kinds that command the loyalty of a buying public who delight in personal relationships. "The downtown of a hometown," Mintz says, "is always the social gathering place. Historically, if anything was happening, it was happening there. A parade, a special-day event, a fair, whatever it was, it happened on the street and the street belonged to the community. There were intangible values there that could not be replaced." All of that is what Mintz understood could be either built upon if it remained or rebuilt if it had been lost temporarily.

Mintz was working on a small scale, with sign changes and modest facade improvements and inexpensive investments, a fine-tuned version of the process under way in Ithaca. In Corning, the private sector was the initiator; in Ithaca, the public sector was the initiator.

Leadership Can Come from Any Quarter

This is a point worth stopping to ponder. We hear so much about how government is to blame for everything, that the best way to achieve development of the right kind is to encourage the private sector to do it. In many cases this is true, although not automatically. And, clearly, my bias—based on extensive observation—is for citizen initiative and citizen control with appropriate but modest government support. A strong local leader is a must, in any event. But it doesn't necessarily matter whether the leadership is public or private, if what is done is innovative and economically relevant to the locality. Arguing over who should do it distracts people from understanding what needs to be done. Deciding *what* is appropriate means asking, *For whom* is it appropriate—the developer, whose prime concern is the bottom line, or the community, whose prime concern is the quality of life? When a genuine balance is struck, the result is both private and public gain. They don't have to be mutually exclusive.

As for the strong leader, such a person can come out of a community, a business or a level of government, but what is critical is the value system that the leader is upholding. If government agencies exacted the right things from builders *without giving away too much,* there would be less public despair over government sponsorship. The real question whenever there is governmental involvement is: To whom are the governmental agencies or leaders accountable?

The regional mall *outside* a community interferes with the reinforcement process of public and private sectors *in* the community. The regional mall is a destroyer of a city from the outside, just as the creation of a new section of a city can be a destroyer from the inside when old sections are razed or left to decay. The outside force of the mall is as inappropriate and destructive as the inside force of urban renewal. Both forces sap strength from what exists and threaten its continued viability. Both development methods re-create expensive infrastructures, instead of building on past investments. Both waste limited financial, energy and land resources. Both involve private development and private profit, but it is the public investment that makes them work—in short, public investment for private gain.

Today, the building of bigger and bigger malls goes on. Now some of them are rising in the heart of old downtowns instead of outlying cornfields. The destructive cycle of the regional mall has come full circle, back into the downtowns the malls helped to destroy. Some communities resist successfully, as will be seen next, through court action or political intervention. But the critical issue, as will be shown, is how the victorious community pulls itself together to bring new strength to downtown.

OUTSIDE, INSIDE

Burlington and Pittsfield

■

The Mall's nature as a packaged environment for selling products by selling itself is appropriate to a city that dreams up, advertises, sells, manages and keeps track of things, while making less and less.

—WILLIAM SEVERINI KOWINSKI in *The New York Times Magazine,* December 13, 1981[1]

Battles against ill-conceived big development schemes, whether in an urban or a rural area, are rarely won on the merits. The promoters and supporters of inappropriate highways, urban-renewal projects, regional malls, or nuclear power plants rarely can be convinced by public opposition that the proposal is wrong. The partnership between elected leaders and developers, when it occurs, is usually too potent to be overcome by persuasion. The stakes are too high. Arguments on merit alone prevail with difficulty and not often.

Invariably, when these battles are won it is through a fluke—the intervention of a strong political leader, or a court suit that doesn't necessarily win the case but delays the project long enough to allow other considerations to intervene and kill it. In an act of desperation, communities have learned to call on any legal hook available to upset development projects that endanger their community. Often, environmental laws become the chief or only weapon in a struggle over a piece of real estate. Only through those laws, it sometimes seems, can the long-term aesthetic, environmental and economic impact of development proposals be considered.

In the late 1970s, Burlington, Vermont, and Pittsfield, Massachusetts, won significant regional-mall battles in just this way. Neither fight was won on the merits of the opposition argument. A technicality shaped each outcome. Burlington leaders learned from Ithaca's experience in not being able to block construction of the outside mall, and, in turn, they were besieged by callers from cities around the country seeking to learn from Burlington. Vermont's most prosperous and largest city, Burlington took advantage of a strong state law that had been passed years earlier for a completely different purpose. Pittsfield, on the other hand, was helped by the intervention of a governor willing to use a technicality on behalf of the opposition.

Vermont voters have a traditional aversion to restrictions on the rights of property owners. At the same time, however, they can be fierce in their protection of their lush countryside, still rich in well-used farmland and uncluttered rolling land. In the decade before regional malls appeared as a threat to anything, there was a different danger, the proliferation of second-home developments in southern Vermont—the summer retreat or the winter ski house. The second-home builders of the 1960s set the cornfield-bulldozing pattern for the suburban-mall entrepreneurs of the 1970s. In 1970, faced with runaway growth that menaced the essential character of their state, Vermont voters approved one of the broadest and strongest environmental-protection laws in the country.

Act 250, as it is called, aimed at the "unplanned, uncoordinated and uncontrolled use of the lands and the environment of the state of Vermont" and requires—beyond the standard local and state building permits—that commercial developments larger than ten acres meet ten strict environmental criteria. Factors for consideration include water and air pollution, traffic, municipal-service burdens, economic impact, aesthetics and conformance with local and regional development plans. In effect, Act 250 forces a regional perspective on the development-approval process and consideration of predictable and unpredictable results. In 1970 this reflected very advanced thinking.

The law contains strong words and strict environmental standards. In practice, however, it didn't stop or slow growth. In its first thirteen years of existence, only 2.5 percent of nearly 4,500 applications were denied under Act 250. The impact of this regulation, though, is greater than even these numbers imply. One cannot calculate the number of harmful or ill-conceived plans that were not even attempted because developers knew ahead of time that such plans would be rejected. Undoubtedly as well, Act 250 forces potential developers to be concerned earlier in their plans with the intent of the law.

Significantly, however, Act 250 was there to be invoked when necessary. Most important, Act 250 recognized that the state's environment was its strength, that to impair that environment was to impair the state economy. Pro–big-development critics of Act 250 predictably argued that it was an impediment to *all* development—a standard claim when development of any kind is restricted in the public interest.

Restraint Fostered Strength

In fact, Vermont did well during the 1970s, with the economy growing 15 percent. Its manufacturing sector grew, unemployment decreased and personal income rose at a rate faster than that of any other New England state during the period. While some shopping centers were built, Vermont was spared much of the commercial sprawl experienced in other states. Vermont central cities still contain the major portion of retail business. Vermont is one of the few remaining areas in the country that has maintained the historic, evolutionary pattern of central cities containing the major portion of retail business. Vermont survived well and, generally, escaped those same schemes that promised other areas so much but brought devastation instead.

Studies have shown a direct link between economic losses in downtowns and continued growth of shopping malls. These studies attribute the continued economic viability of downtowns like Burlington and Pittsfield to the lack of competing regional malls near them. Thomas Muller, principal research associate of the Urban Institute in Washington, D.C., pointed out in 1981[2] that during the 1970s regional malls were draining retail sales from downtowns nationwide and that central cities had a greater decline in sales than could be explained by changes in population or income. "Most CBDs [central business districts] registered severe losses between 1972 and 1977," Muller wrote. "Among the exceptions are cities without suburban malls, including Burlington, Vermont and Pittsfield, Massachusetts."

For many American cities like Ithaca, the realization that outlying shopping centers are destructive to downtown comes too late. For Burlington, that awareness came in time. When a mall proposal loomed on its horizon, Burlington was a fast-growing area with a bright future as electronics and high-technology companies like IBM (the state's largest employer) and Digital Equipment Corporation built new facilities there. Economic activity was strong, with these companies and others attracted by the open spaces, the celebrated ski runs and the pristine summers.

In 1976, Pyramid Mall Developers picked an 80-acre hayfield in nearby Williston (population 3,200; six miles from Burlington) for an enclosed retail mall: two department stores, eighty shops, no fewer than twenty fast-food outlets and 2,600 parking spaces.

(I should note at this point that it is purely by accident that Pyramid is the developer who figures so strongly in my examination of the impact on downtowns of regional malls. When I first started piecing together stories from around the country, I didn't know where I would find the kind of continuum on which I wanted to focus in depth. There are scores of mall developers of varying sizes producing similar projects of comparable impact. Many of them, for reasons that are obvious, concentrate in defined geographic sections. I began hearing about

Ithaca, Burlington and Pittsfield, and in a secondary way about Platts-burgh, Saratoga and Albany, New York, before I knew that one shopping-center builder was involved in all these sites. Pyramid owns twenty-one shopping malls, many of which inflicted grave wounds on nearby downtowns. As a whole, the story of the cities that succumbed or resisted Pyramid proposals embodies a telling chapter in the external destruction of cities. It is a story I knew I had to tell. Pyramid turned out to be the largest mall developer in New England, and, according to a February 1985 article about it in *Business/New York,* it is thirty-second in the country's top fifty shopping-center developers. Pyramid executives refused to be interviewed. Although Pyramid's approach is typical, there are similar mall developers around the country producing the same impact.)

Pyramid's proposed Williston Mall would have been the largest in Vermont—eleven acres of buildings, seventeen acres of parking, and room for expansion. As malls go, it was of medium size, but it was larger than the total retail space of downtown Burlington. It was planned to draw not only from Burlington's population of 38,000 and the Greater Burlington area's 100,000, but also to bring in consumers from all over northern Vermont and southern Canada. Burlington, a classic small city, the center of its region, a traditional urban meeting place and the state's financial capital, felt threatened.

Led by its mayor, Gordon Paquette, Burlington fought the development under Act 250. The Williston Mall was the largest to come up for state approval since passage of the law. Mayor Paquette cited the Ithaca story. He also pointed to Plattsburgh, New York, a city of 20,000 across Lake Champlain from Burlington, where downtown had been wiped out by surrounding mall development in the early 1970s, and he spoke of Manchester, New Hampshire, then almost a ghost town as a result of suburban malls. He even took Burlington leaders on a field trip to New London, Connecticut, a city which, after spending $30–50 million in federal funds on a downtown redevelopment project, suffered when a suburban mall opened nearby. With all of its improvements, there were few people in downtown New London. This struck a familiar chord for Burlington residents, since their own city was embarking on expensive downtown improvements that they hoped would improve business conditions. Creative downtown efforts would be rendered meaningless if the Williston Mall went ahead.

A Well-informed Public Makes All the Difference

Two years of public hearings followed Pyramid's first announcements. Experts who were called in by both sides delivered detailed studies of everything from economics to traffic to impact on local schools. Every detail was well covered in the local press, with unusually thorough coverage provided by an enterprising young reporter, Sam Hemingway (now an editor), at the *Burlington Free Press*. The press can make or break one of the projects in the degree it chooses to cover the details. (The story of the Portman Hotel in Times Square—now known as the Marriott Marquis—that will be told later in this book illustrates well how omissions by the press serve to enhance the developer's unchallenged claims and undermine public awareness and the opportunity for impact.) More issues than Burlington residents realized existed were brought to their attention in the steady news coverage that took no developer claim for granted and uncovered more issues than anticipated. The public was well informed, as was the District 4 Environmental Commission, which was empowered to approve or disapprove a permit for Pyramid under Act 250. The wide focus on Burlington's dilemma was probably the earliest and most thorough examination of the life-and-death struggle of small cities challenged by the fashionable big-development schemes that usually are so beloved by political leaders, retail executives, institutional lenders and, of course, the construction industry.

The story got national attention, and it was clear to Mayor Paquette and other Burlington leaders when they were swamped with calls from other cities that their fight held national implications. In the end, in October 1978, the Environmental Commission rejected Pyramid's permit application. The commission found, among other things, that the project would cause excessive traffic congestion, impose an unreasonable burden on Burlington municipal services and on central sewage facilities, not comply with development standards of Act 250, create excessive demand on the region's highways, and not conform with a duly adopted local or regional plan.[3]

The commission's detailed report is a textbook examination of the local, state and national effects of oversized regional malls and of the hidden economic and environmental burdens to be carried by the host community—and an example of the rigorous critical scrutiny to which megaprojects should be subjected but rarely are. It cited 131 road links in the region that would be congested by the Williston Mall, showed that new local costs would outweigh new taxes, and applied economic measurements to the case in a way in which Act 250 had not heretofore been used. The commission concluded that 40.1 percent of the total sales potential of downtown Burlington merchants, or $25 million, would be transferred to the mall. The resulting sales loss would cause a 10–14 percent decline in Burlington's property-tax base. The consequences of this are obvious.

Two main findings showed that the costs of scattered development that would continue after the mall's construction would outweigh its benefits and that the proposed scheme ran counter to regional plans for the area. Significantly, the commission gave important weight both to new service costs to be imposed on the new site and to economic losses to the existing area.

Burlington Turns Attention to Itself

Burlington had staved off the outside threat of a regional mall,* but the city did not stop there. With an accelerated timetable, an increased commitment and a new confidence, Burlington continued its efforts

---

* In the fall of 1988, ten years after the mall's defeat, a new Pyramid mall proposal—same size, same site, but redesigned and with increased landscaping—was wending its way again through the permit process. This time Pyramid had a partner, a condominium resident from Stowe, whose front-line position blunted local anti-Pyramid sentiment left over from the earlier fight. The environmental arguments against the mall were as strong as the first time around—intensified, in fact, because of the increased development in the area over the past decade. Burlington opposition remained strong, but many newcomers, some more sympathetic to malls, had settled in Williston and it was anyone's guess how the permit process would end.

to breathe new life into downtown. Pedestrian amenities, such as sidewalk resurfacing, landscaping and bench placement, were created. Mass transit was improved *and* parking facilities were increased. Vacant waterfront warehouses were rehabilitated for housing, shops and restaurants. Conversion of neglected or vacant spaces for housing—including subsidized low-income housing to minimize displacement—was encouraged, re-creating the twenty-four-hour population that downtown had long ago lost. Officials and citizens alike enthusiastically supported the restoration and reuse of the city's stock of historic and architecturally unique buildings, with new construction as an addition, not a replacement.

Downtown was marketed like a mall, and, in fact, in one unfortunate stroke, four blocks of Church Street, the downtown spine, was closed to vehicular traffic and converted into a pedestrian mall. While serving as a festive gathering place and useful site for public events, this artificial intrusion makes the city center too much like a mall, creating a separate and too well-defined shopping center. Businesses and buildings at the mall's edges and beyond are at a disadvantage competing with stores located on the four-block public stretch in which people gather. As with Ithaca's Commons, Burlington's Church Street Mall succeeds more because of the overall strength of downtown than because of any inherent appeal of its own. These pedestrian malls can be successful even where they are unnecessary to the success of a downtown. The danger is in attributing the strength of downtown to the existence of the pedestrian mall. As many times as I return to Church Street, I have yet to see any fundamental advantage to the closed street that cannot be achieved with limited vehicular traffic. The increased sidewalk activity—cafés, pushcarts, benches—can be accomplished with widened sidewalks and two traffic lanes, equalizing the full stretch of Church Street. The nature of a retail street simply is contradictory to the nature of a park.

Some 150 pedestrian malls—including transit malls—have been built in the United States in the last two decades. Most haven't failed outright, but few have lived up to their billing as the salvation of downtown retailing. Just about as many department stores and first-run movie theaters have closed in towns with malls as without, and just as many wig stores, fast-food places, and video-game arcades have opened up.[4]

Stories about communities returning vehicular traffic to closed malls appear now with more regularity. An article in *The New York Times* December 13, 1987, "Replacing the Downtown Mall with Traffic," noted that Eugene, Oregon; Independence, Missouri; Jackson, Michigan; and Champaign, Illinois, "have turned their malls back into streets again, and several other cities, including Chicago, Minneapolis and Decatur, Ill., are studying major redesigns of their downtown malls."

The pedestrian mall was one of the early planning gimmicks offered as a quick-fix solution for economically troubled downtown that does not address fundamental reasons for downtown inactivity. Most of these malls "failed to reverse the decline—and in some cases hastened it," noted Laurie M. Grossman in *The Wall Street Journal* in June of 1987, adding that those that have been successful "have the advantage of being near areas with inherently high pedestrian traffic—for example, in Boulder, Colo., near the University of Colorado and in Burlington, Vt., near the University of Vermont."[5] Many communities now recognize pedestrian malls as a design trap and are returning them to streets.

Quite simply, however, Burlington rejuvenated its downtown by building on its existing strength and special character, by combining small efforts with larger ones, by fitting in new construction comfortably with the old, and by addressing both commercial and residential issues for downtown. As development mushroomed outside, Burlington has weathered new changes well, and even the ill-conceived gimmick of the four-block mall in the future can either be undone, be reduced to a more sensible single block that would act more like a town square than like a shopping mall or be altered in another way. A strong downtown with its essential fabric preserved rather than replaced is still the best antidote to suburban retail competition, a lesson learned by Burlington but, as we shall see, not as easily by Pittsfield.

A New Twist in Pittsfield

Pittsfield's story adds a new dimension to this examination of outside threats to urban downtowns. The Pittsfield saga not only exhibits all the external perils in one neat picture, but presents a glaring example of a threatened city embracing a solution that would destroy downtown in the name of saving it; the so-called solution reflects an internal response as destructive as the outside threat. In a way not seen with Ithaca, Corning and Burlington, Pittsfield illustrates the destructive impact of big-buck federal programs intended to "redevelop" downtowns. And, probably most serious of all, this conflict exemplifies fundamental design and development concepts destined to kill as many downtowns in the future as have been destroyed in the past.

Pittsfield is a pleasant small city of 54,000, the largest in the beautiful Berkshire region of western Massachusetts. Its location, nestled in green foothills, has been at the same time its greatest asset and its biggest problem. A beautiful countryside has made the area a popular summer escape for residents of neighboring states, making tourism Pittsfield's second-largest employer (the largest is General Electric, with seven thousand employees).

Yet, in many ways, Pittsfield is a community, isolated from distant centers of commerce and culture (Boston is three hours away, Albany one hour and New York City three hours), with one newspaper, no local television station and a primarily summer-season culture based on the nearby Tanglewood and related arts festivals. In New England tradition, change comes slowly.

Its semi-isolated state has protected Pittsfield from the shock of accelerated change and overwhelming development. As in many other communities across the country, however, downtown deteriorated into drab dullness. In a misguided spurt of 1970s upgrading, a stretch of Pittsfield's commercial spine, North Street, was "renewed" (read demolished), producing a Hilton Hotel that dominates the skyline, combined with retail and office space. Adjacent are massive parking lots where blocks of a varied and useful assortment of buildings were demolished.

Historically, Pittsfield grew up as a rail link between Boston and Chicago, and it has remained attractive enough for an assortment of New England banks and insurance companies to maintain a steady base of operations there. In the 1980s, several developers showed an interest in Pittsfield, the county seat and reasonably stable hub of retail and other business activities. Without significant outside competition, downtown Pittsfield was holding its own.

In the mid-1970s, Pittsfield experienced a Pyramid regional-mall fight comparable to Burlington's, but with an interesting added twist. This proposal called for a regional center five miles south of Pittsfield, outside Lenox—a truly picturesque small town where bank presidents and the similarly well-to-do live without any desire to see their tranquillity disturbed by the kind of development they may judge suitable for the less influential. Shopping malls may be good investments, but they are not something one wants in the backyard.

As in so many American communities, Pittsfield residents were ambivalent about their urban center, regarding it with a mixture of pride and negativism. Downtown was unexciting but adjusting to contemporary merchandising and consumer needs. Yet Pittsfielders recognized that there would certainly be no future for downtown if a regional mall was five miles away. Logically, Pittsfield leaders opposed the Lenox Mall as vigorously as Lenox citizens, but for a different reason: they wanted to lure Pyramid to Pittsfield's own downtown. They wanted Pyramid to reconstruct downtown, to bring in the big department-store chains and, they thought, save the city. Thus the Pittsfield experience breaks down into two distinct stages: the first the now familiar fight against an outside suburban mall, the second the so-called solution which would have transformed the urban core into a suburban center.

Massachusetts Governor Michael Dukakis, on the one hand, showed a farsighted understanding of the negative impact on a city of a regional shopping center outside it, but, on the other hand, exhibited no comparable understanding of what is a proper down-town development response. As Neal Peirce noted in his syndicated column in October 1978, "Dukakis early recognized that not only Federal but also State policies had exacerbated 'scatterization' of housing business development to suburban and rural sites, wounding old city and town centers, and leaving disadvantaged citizens who needed jobs the most in declining urban neighborhoods." Dukakis understood that if the Lenox Mall were not stopped, Pittsfield, only five miles away, would be unable to remain the retail hub of the Berkshires and would become a "distressed area for 50 years."

Dukakis blocked the Lenox Mall in an unusual, precedent-setting manner. By an administrative order he denied Pyramid a crucial state permit, the one required for a curb cut. Without a curb cut—in plain English, a driveway entrance and exit—automobiles have no access to a mall. After decisively putting an end to Pyramid's suburban plan, however, Dukakis encouraged Pyramid to shift its building energies to downtown Pittsfield.

Defeated in Lenox but still anxious to get a foothold in the Berkshire market, Pyramid responded to the pleas of Pittsfield's leaders to redevelop downtown on a big scale. With Pittsfield's blessing, the developer proposed a plan that, in effect, would have wiped out downtown by converting it to a suburban mall. Historic character, lively streets, the ambience that makes a city, all would have been obliterated. In its effort to compete with the suburbs, the city was prepared to become one. Nineteenth-century buildings—like the ones bulldozed for the Hilton Hotel block—would have been ripped down to make way for suburban-style parking. Dull, win-dowless block structures preferred by department-store chains would have replaced the architectural richness and variety of existing buildings.

For years, Pittsfield's leaders had been unsuccessful in attracting a developer for the eleven downtown acres which had been cleared mostly for urban renewal. But eleven acres would never do for Pyramid, a company used to megamalls. Pyramid proposed a twenty-two-acre enclosed mall with 620,000 square feet of retail space (five department stores, eighty shops) and three thousand parking spaces, room for more cars than at Boston's Logan Airport. For this, 250,000 square feet, *half* of downtown's 500,000 *existing* retail space, would be demolished with not even a promise that the displaced businesses would be accommodated in the new project. Bulldozer targets included a block of buildings that housed some of the city's best specialty shops. Tearing them down would clear land *and* eliminate competition for mall occupants at the same time. Uncalculated were the uses and spaces that would be lost above the street-level stores marked for extinction and lost to the local economy.

Urban Destruction with a Federal Subsidy

Now, however, a new layer was added to this peculiar tale. A $14.2 million federal grant, the equivalent of half of the yearly gross retail sales of the entire city of Pittsfield, would make this mall possible. Ironically, the money was coming in under a federal program to encourage the revitalization of cities—the Urban Development Action Grant program. Created in 1977 by the Carter Administration, the UDAG program was intended to stimulate private investment in center-city development projects that ostensibly would not have occurred without federal support. Like its predecessors in earlier administrations (Urban Renewal, Model Cities, etc.), the expressed UDAG policy objectives were admirable and familiar: to promote private investment in cities, remove blight, create jobs and increase tax revenues. UDAG funds can be used to clear land, buy land and loan money to private developers. The primary difference between UDAG and earlier programs was the requirement of private investment money—guaranteed in advance—for any project to qualify for a grant. This provision was intended to diminish the likelihood of acres and acres of cleared land standing idle before a project was ready to go, a hallmark of earlier federal renewal programs.

A UDAG is a grant to a city which then converts it into a loan to a developer at below-market rates. The developer repays the loan to the city, not the federal government, and it is thus an indirect grant to the locality. It has been a favorite federal program among mayors attracted by the idea that their city benefits first from the construction project and then from the repayment of the loan to the city treasury. A cornerstone of the Carter and Reagan Administrations' urban policy, the UDAG program sanctioned projects too similar to the bulldoze/replace approach of past urban-renewal schemes. The unarticulated purpose of the program appears to be the moving forward of big, otherwise immovable projects. The leveraging of private investment became the primary criterion for a grant: *the substance of the proposal was secondary:*

The Wall Street Journal editorialized in 1987:

> There is no justification for the current UDAG program. It hands out federal tax dollars to big developers, who build hotels, office complexes, condominiums and shopping malls. To receive a UDAG, municipalities are supposed to prove that a project wouldn't be undertaken without the federal subsidy. A 1982 HUD study indicated that up to half of UDAG projects would have happened without the money.

This program became another case of government going for the big-buck Charlotte Street–style projects, with only an occasional Banana Kelly–style proposal squeaking through. The initiators of the genuinely innovative projects didn't have the resources to capture the attention of either the local or the national political/governmental network. Instead, a major hotel chain or some other corporate entity would propose for somewhere a "mixed-use" project mimicking a successfully completed project elsewhere. The dominance of national developers or corporate sponsors was guaranteed, and minimum room remained for truly indigenous efforts. Consequently, UDAG grants overwhelmingly went to shopping malls, convention centers and hotels and their garages* which often have an overwhelmingly

---

* Often, UDAGs covered a garage or other infrastructure expenses for which developers did not want to be responsible.

negative impact on surrounding areas. Even with some creative and small projects to its credit, UDAG primarily fosters inappropriate, formula-based and out-of-scale projects for cities, even where such projects are locally initiated. The destructive pattern of fashioning local projects to qualify for big infusions of federal money is encouraged, instead of solutions specifically relevant to the problem and scale of the city. "Good" and "sure" deals—bureaucracy playing it safe, taking no big chances—are favored over opportunities that carry small risks.

Instinctivists Prevail

If Pyramid had come up with a plan reasonable in scale, if the plan had not called for bulldozing so much of the remaining downtown that Pittsfield residents cherished, if it had not sparked a popular historic-preservation battle, and if the entire scheme had not been so large and financially dependent on a UDAG grant, the developer probably would have succeeded in plunking a suburban mall in the middle of the city of Pittsfield. The mall's proposed size guaranteed its demise. Pyramid went too far.

First the merchants organized. They understood that their businesses were threatened. Then came the taxpayer revolt. Private estimates contradicted official predictions that local costs (an $8.5 million city bond issue and $4.7 million in costs for street and parking improvements) would add only $1.27 to the tax rate. Private studies estimated a $5–6 hike. Different groups, each with its own reason for opposing this plan to transform Pittsfield, merged under a common banner and persuaded the federal government to deny the UDAG application. Then city leaders, a bit wiser after the Pyramid fight, sought out other developers willing to offer a smaller, sensitive proposal incorporating existing buildings and businesses.

Like so many of these hard-won battles against misguided development, the fight against Pittsfield's in-town mall was led by ordinary citizens—teachers, doctors, housewives. Many had never been involved in a civic fight before. None had any planning, architectural or other so-called expertise. Many weren't even sure technically why what they were opposing was wrong. Instinctively, however, they knew that the future of their community was at stake. They didn't oppose development or change per se. They just recognized that what was offered was *the wrong kind of development,* and they knew it would cost them in more ways than the experts were acknowledging. They were among the instinctivists who battle everywhere on behalf of rational and reasonable change.

While Pittsfielders were fighting to retain the essential character of their city, they latched onto historical preservation as a rallying point. Theirs was not an attitude of "preserve at any price." They simply wanted a smaller, more sensitive dose of change that did not remove a substantial segment of their historic downtown fabric, which had earlier been inappropriately and overwhelmingly abused. If that meant stopping development altogether until the right proposal evolved, that was just fine. Adele Chatfield-Taylor, a former director of the New York City Landmarks Preservation Foundation and currently director of the Design Arts Division of the National Endowment for the Arts, has written: "Historic preservation is not something you do to a piece of real estate if you have no other plans for it. Historic preservation is a form of paying attention, a device for recognizing and extending what has abiding value in the physical world. It is a framework for thinking about change."[6]

Often in these skirmishes, promoters of a development plan simplistically argue that the opponents are against any change and that progress will come to a standstill if those opponents prevail. The argument, cruel and wrong, serves well the proponents' purpose—to get the job done. Developers bemoan the difficulties of "getting anything done." This argument decidedly misses the point. There is a legitimate citizen resistance to grandiose schemes. Opponents want the implications fully and honestly explored, and want decisions made on the merits, not on the basis of politics, power and money. Usually, less disruptive alternatives exist. Change at any price is what is wrong.

Historic Preservation Incorporates Broad Issues

Pittsfield residents were fighting the whole concept of this downtown mall, but the most *visible* issue was the preservation of historic buildings scheduled for demolition.

Historic preservation, as we have already seen, became a favorite citizen tool during the 1970s to fight overwhelming change. Recognition of this reality does not denigrate the inherent value of historic preservation as a goal in itself. On the contrary, during the 1970s and 1980s the preservation movement raised the consciousness of the country to the physical and aesthetic values wantonly erased during the heyday of pave-over planning and fostered a new appreciation of our existing built environment. Many innovative developers have earned considerable profits recognizing the values that preservationists first brought attention to. Whole new—actually new old—industries and craft revivals have emerged in response to the increasing number of preservation adherents. Preserving distinctive and useful old buildings and putting them to a new use is a worthy goal on its own. Rarely, however, is that simply what preservation fights are about. The broad issues raised in these conflicts usually involve preservation of the city itself—its mix of economic uses, varied physical and social fabrics and human scale.

Like the anti-highway and anti–urban-renewal battles and other such citizen-versus-government conflicts, the preservation movement is overwhelmingly populated with untrained citizens—nonexperts, instinctivists. A long time passed and much was lost before the preservation ethic championed by citizen activists significantly penetrated the public consciousness. Business, finally, discovered profit in reclaiming urban treasures, only after the public vanguard led the way.

In fighting to preserve what was endangered, people were forced to think about what they didn't want to lose. By focusing first on the microelement (a building or group of buildings), they understood the macrocontext (the larger community and its social and economic systems). To save the particular, one has to understand how it fits into the general, unless, of course, one views the object of rescue as artifact. That is not the predominant historic-preservationist view. Thus, the Pittsfield preservationists opposing the downtown mall talked about scale, context, urban fabric, variety and texture—the full spectrum of relevant downtown issues—not just historic preservation. Preservationists and their sympathizers forced a reconsideration of what a city is and is not, and they fought to revive strategies compatible with and sympathetic to the essential nature of cities.

The centerpiece of the Pittsfield conflict was the future of five historic buildings on North Street (one of which had a fire of mysterious origin during the prolonged controversy) and their relation to the adjacent historic neighborhood surrounding the town square. What was really at stake was far more than five historic buildings. It was not enough to stop a regional mall *outside* the city; it was equally important to stop it from supplanting the city *inside* as well. In order for the city to be revitalized, downtown had to be preserved as downtown and not turned into a suburban center. The citizens fighting the downtown mall knew quite well that there was a real difference. They also knew that what should be preserved was not just a physical fabric, but patterns of business ownership and opportunity. The success of a rejuvenated downtown depends on bringing back people who have lost the habit of coming. Why, however, should those people drive past suburban shopping centers to patronize identical stores in a regional-mall ambience that happens instead to be in a city center?

After the mall's defeat, Pittsfield focused on downtown's reinvigoration by strengthening the existing fabric in smaller doses and by looking for diversity in growth, not just new retail. The corporate headquarters of a retail toy chain relocated to Pittsfield from nearby Lee and built a four-story, 75,000-square-foot building on two of the eleven acres of vacant city land that weren't half enough for Pyramid. Adjacent to it, on another of those empty acres, a local developer built a five-story, 112,000-square-foot office building. And the city built a 1,000-car parking garage. A downtown manager was hired to coordinate activities, special events and promotions that draw people.

Property owners and merchants were encouraged to upgrade their buildings and their window displays, and four local architects gave voluntary assistance to interested property owners. New stores opened and some old ones closed. Change continued, some good and some not so good. To walk down North Street today is to pass stores of both long-standing and new vintage, to see merchants of both an earlier generation and a younger one and to encounter the diversity of a viable downtown. More visible now than ten years ago is evidence of a growing artist and artisan population, with shows, performances and sales proliferating. Best of all, Pittsfield's downtown reflects its own character, not that of a suburban transplant. Some of that leftover urban-renewal acreage is still vacant, and the site of the big North Street fire is still empty, clearly ripe for a creative infill structure. Plenty of room remains for continued growth and change.*

Rebuilding downtown in a suburban mold is a danger encountered in cities across the country. It is a danger more easily understood when looking at a small city like Pittsfield than it is for a larger city like Atlanta, Detroit, San Diego or New York. The principles are the same, however, regardless of whether applied to a small or a large city.

The key to genuine revitalization and economic development is process, not product; incremental change, not instant transformation; modest local private investments, not massive infusions of federal dollars. These are the real lessons in the varying responses of Ithaca, Corning, Burlington and Pittsfield. The revitalization process initiated in these places rebuilt components of the urban fabric gradually,

---

* Ironically, Pyramid finally did build a regional mall north of Pittsfield. As of spring 1988, the mall is completed and, in fact, tenanted and stocked. It has been enjoined from opening, however, because it secured a building permit and proceeded with construction before requisite Environmental Impact Statements were filed. Several environmental problems—the planned access road passes through a wetland, the mall's water source is inadequate, the sewer system rests on top of an aquifer—must be resolved before opening will be permitted, which is not expected before late summer. Pittsfield downtowners are not worried this time around. Downtown has self-confidence, and, observers note, the mall is north of Pittsfield and the "high-end money lives mostly south of Pittsfield and would have to pass through us to go there and that is not likely to happen."

instead of imposing a new center, a new mall or any new gimmick that cataclysmically alters and fragments rather than reweaves and strengthens the physical fabric. Process is gradual, continuing, open-ended, not a finished product like a completed building or complex.

They did not all do it with the same degree of success. Some even included a few gimmicks—the pedestrian malls in Ithaca and Burlington. The gimmicks were of questionable value and quality but were not necessarily destructive, and definitely not overwhelming. And these gimmicks were reversible at a later time, if they were found to be a mistake. The overall effect, however, was natural, varied, gradual, interesting—and successful.

Chapter Eleven

AVOIDING WRONG LESSONS

The Remnant Complex vs. Small Improvements, Big Differences

■

By the diversity of its time structures, the city in part escapes the tyranny of a single present, and the monotony of a future that consists in repeating only a single beat heard in the past.

—LEWIS MUMFORD, *The Culture of Cities*[1]

There is a danger of extracting wrong lessons from the downtown success stories that have so far been described. Because historic preservation is so often an important catalyst for genuine revitalization, it is too easy to assume that historic preservation offers a magical approach to downtown revival, that everything should be preserved and restored, and that new construction has no place.

Historic preservation is fundamentally a way of managing change. More important than the retention of the old for old's sake is plain good common sense and the realization that even eyesores and discards can conceal economic and aesthetic value. Whether beautiful, historic or just plain practical, a building may be better reused than replaced. Common sense and good economics in the context of limited resources are what Urban Husbandry is all about. This is also what historic preservation is sometimes about, as much as the veneration of beauty and history. The recycling of old buildings has proven to be cost effective, labor intensive and a strong contributor to the stabilization and growth of a tax base—in other words, common sense. The reuse of an existing building may seem like a small project in contrast to a large-scale new construction project, but that smaller accomplishment can make a big difference within its context.

The danger, however, is that historic preservation can become an end in itself, in the name of which as much wrong can be done as right. The look of sameness that dulls the senses in a boring shopping center can be found as easily in a prettified restoration project such as La Villita in San Antonio—a remnant of an eighteenth-century Spanish community restored as a one-block spiffy commercial arts-and-crafts center—which strips the accumulated effect of time, whether good or bad, to achieve the historic accuracy of an earlier moment. La Villita, in fact, contrasts sharply with San Antonio's wandering, wonderful river—saved in the 1920s, by a group of gutsy and determined San Antonio women, from a federal flood-control plan that would have widened and straightened it. Now that river is a wondrous four-mile pleasure-filled stretch—called Riverwalk—crossed by pedestrian bridges, with footpaths on either side, lined with restaurants, shops, gardens, historic adobe buildings converted to apartments, nightclubs, hotels, cafés and a theater.* Here is where one sees the true mix and

---

* Consultant Sherry Wagner, who with her husband was active in the Riverwalk rejuvenation in the 1960s, points out that the uniqueness of Riverwalk came about

mingle of people, not at La Villita. Places like La Villita are gussied-up artifacts that have no relationship to the complex functioning of a city except as a curio, a museum piece, a useful tourist attraction. Artifacts of history, of course, have their place everywhere as cultural resources, but they should not be mistaken for a meaningful rejuvenation of a functioning built environment.

Overdone restorations are deadly. The goal should never be a romantic vision of a place-that-never-was. Realness is too important to sacrifice. Historic preservation should not be The Answer any more than urban renewal or new construction projects. A city is too complex for one answer. A vivid example of the inappropriateness of Historic Preservation as The Answer occurred in Albany, New York.

Urban Renewal Masquerading as Historic Preservation

In the early 1970s, the city of Albany sought to conserve and "revitalize" one of its oldest neighborhoods, a thirteen-square-block historic district of residential and commercial character. The area is known as the Pastures, a name that has stuck since the early seventeenth century, when it was set aside as a communal pasture by the city's Dutch founders. The Pastures sits at the south end of downtown and is not far from the Hudson River waterway that provided Albany with the natural resource for commercial prosperity during the nineteenth century.

Albany evolved in the classic nineteenth-century economic pattern, with shipping and manufacturing attracting workers who wished to settle their families nearby. The Pastures evolved simultaneously. Homes of wealthy businessmen stood side by side with modest tradesmen's and craftsmen's dwellings. Homes of free black citizens were scattered among them. Workplace and dwelling place were frequently side by side, and scattered throughout were structures housing a small store on the ground floor and apartments above.

---

without any master plans or design guidelines. Individual artists and crafts people were hired by the WPA to design and construct the paths, bridges and landscaping, given only the overall plan to work with. Variety prevails, but all the separate sections fit together quite naturally.

Gardens and open spaces dotted the area, and alleyways varied in width. Mostly, there were row houses of two or three stories, predominantly of red brick, with almost every architectural style from the late eighteenth to the late nineteenth century represented. Most of the Pastures' growth was completed by the Civil War, except for a large Victorian school built in 1871 that became an important focal point in the neighborhood and in the city's educational history, and a synagogue and a church built in the first few years of the twentieth century.[2]

In the 1950s and 1960s, the neighborhood, though in decline and by "urban-renewal" standards a "slum," remained socially and racially integrated. This is an important point. Classic urban neighborhoods evolved naturally with a social and ethnic diversity. In recent decades renewal has created segregated enclaves which only public policy could integrate. Then came the 1970s. The architectural value and the historic character of the Pastures were well appreciated, but the neighborhood was deemed in need of redevelopment. So the Albany urban-renewal agency set about to "preserve" the Pastures.

First, the city acquired all the land and every building and relocated out of the area every family and every business. When the neighborhood was empty, "selective" demolition of the shopping strip followed. Buildings the city deemed "insignificant" (nearly half the structures in the district), including many workers' houses, most of the outbuildings and most of the block-long strips of commercial structures, were bulldozed. The surviving buildings were "mothballed," with the heat turned off and the windows boarded up. Instead of selling the properties to individuals who would rehabilitate and reuse them, the city let the Pastures sit in desolation while it tried desperately to find a single developer to "do" the neighborhood. To add insult to injury, the city made plans to build copies of the remaining houses to fill in the empty lots where older-style historic houses once stood. Physically, the neighborhood was only partially bulldozed, but economically and socially it was killed completely just as surely as if it had been fully demolished.

This kind of "preservation" is as much an example of neighborhood destruction as is any land-clearance project. Even if the city had succeeded in finding a developer and salvaging the project before the cold and the damp completely destroyed the surviving buildings, the "new" Pastures would bear no conceivable resemblance to the organic neighborhood which had evolved there over the prior 250 years. The real place ceased to exist when its last resident was trundled off to a distant housing project. The best that could be hoped for was the survival of shells of a few historic buildings dotted around in a landscape of parking lots and infill houses.

Throughout the 1970s, many individuals sought houses in the Pastures to restore and live in. They didn't care that the area had not been fixed up and made pretty. They wanted an affordable home that they could improve on their own. Their offers were rejected.

In 1980, Albany's Pastures neighborhood was still vacant. The only change was the abuse that time had wreaked on the vacant buildings whose lack of inhabitants guaranteed continued decay. Scattered buildings were destroyed by arson. The 1871 school, a neighborhood cornerstone, had burned in a fire in 1979. A creative scheme had been drawn to develop that school building into a new community center, but now that plan was history, too.

By 1980 the urban-renewal agency was no longer looking for one developer for the entire neighborhood, but it was still rejecting individuals. Instead many developers were being sought to do one block or a few blocks at a time. There was a new proviso: 50 percent of the units would have to go to low-income families.

Today, which buildings are restored (some are historically inaccurate, according to some preservation experts) and which, if any, are built new to look old is difficult to discern. The area looks more like a sanitized suburban enclave—plenty of parking opportunities included—than an urban neighborhood. Pedestrians are few. Whatever character of place had evolved over time out of the indigenous social and economic mix has been "preserved" out of existence.

Ironically, on the north side of the Albany Mall, that space-age government center that can be seen from fifteen miles away and which was developed under the governorship of Nelson A. Rockefeller, another historic district was reborn in the classic natural pattern, by renovators buying empty houses and, building by building, regenerating the neighborhood, as they tried to do in the Pastures. An active and vocal historic-preservation group was organized to stave off inappropriate bulldoze-and-replace schemes, and some small government funding was obtained for individual projects. What government cooperation was achieved was won only by struggle and persistence. City officials watched the rejuvenation. Some marveled at it and even uttered grudging words of praise. The success here, however, had no impact on the south side of town. Nothing changed in the Pastures.

The rejuvenation successes examined earlier demonstrate that it is possible to preserve and restore the physical fabric without resorting to fake history and period pieces. The genuine maintains the *continuity of history,* as in Seattle's Pike Place Market or Portland, Oregon's, Old Town district, both preserved historic places with real and current mixed functions. The artificial re-creates a frozen rather than an evolved place, and sometimes—as in San Antonio's La Villita or the Pastures—it is hard to tell whether it's "real" old or "fake" old. The former has the potential to endure over time; the latter, reflecting the fashion of one moment, like the shopping center, quickly fades and appears dated.

It has always struck me as sad that Americans find such pleasure in the three-quarter-scale tidy replica of Main Street in Disneyland, but don't recognize or appreciate the real thing in their hometown. Sometimes—and equally unfortunately—after a trip to this expensive, prefabricated and romanticized past, visitors return home to "restore" what is left of the real past, only to concoct a forgery. In Dallas, Pensacola, Los Angeles, Houston and elsewhere, there are landmark "parks," sites to which threatened buildings have been moved, like so many porcelain antiques on a shelf. That is as fake as Disneyland. It is history under glass, museum artifact, not a living form of historic preservation.

Equally ludicrous are the new "old" theme reproductions. Whether it is a Wild West town, a Victorian, Colonial or pseudo-sixteenth-century Tudor, they all have the familiar sanitized look of the mall. Only yesterday, modernization fads destroyed so much. The salesmen of tile-and-stucco in the thirties, plate glass in the forties, asbestos in the fifties and aluminum siding in the sixties should not be succeeded by the prepackaged revivalists of the seventies and eighties, or of any design vogue—whether sleekly modern or chicly historic—that gives only the illusion of economic improvement. There is simply no such thing as an "authentic reproduction."

Some wide-area restorations come out looking rather good despite their overly "unified look," such as Newburyport, Massachusetts, with its singular brick architecture and uniform signage. They may succeed as tourist attractions and give new economic life to an area that was formerly in trouble. They do well during visiting seasons, but a local economy based on tourism is vulnerable, like the company town solely dependent on cars or coal. Such one-note economies don't have the diversity necessary to weather the ebbs and tides of fashion or the national economy. An attractive facade easily hides the absence of economic substance. Setting for a goal a historical theme or a singular time period cuts off the organic development of a community and substitutes a stage set. It is formula thinking at its worst. The most successful rehabilitation projects don't even look "restored" at all.

The Remnant Complex

Another wrong lesson easily extracted from downtown preservation success stories is infinitely more subtle. The restoration of a historic area often obscures the fact that what is being restored is of only meager meaning to the larger context of the whole city and is of a scale too small to remain or become again a significantly productive patch of the larger urban fabric. I call this the Remnant Complex. Meager pieces of urban fabric are being rescued, restored and celebrated as if the city itself had been rewoven back to full strength. Too many cities are suffering from this Remnant Complex.

Cities like Louisville, Fort Worth, Atlanta, San Diego, St. Louis and countless others show off a few blocks of a restored downtown when the rest of downtown is too much of a bulldozed, rebuilt nightmare. In Louisville, it is six square blocks of Main Street cast-iron buildings. In Fort Worth, it is Sundance Square, a two-square-block area of twelve buildings restored to their turn-of-the-century appearance adjacent to a multilevel enclosed mall, with an ice-skating rink* as centerpiece, that monopolizes downtown retail activity.† In Atlanta, it is a few blocks of the old commercial downtown, now known as the Fairlie-Poplar District. In San Diego, it is the Victorian Gaslamp Quarter, which never had a chance to be more than a remnant, overwhelmed as it is by the adjacent Horton Plaza—a massive mall that combines the worst of a Mediterranean village, Disneyland and voguish historicist architecture to produce what is considered the prototype of the next generation of mall, more amusement park than shopping center. In St. Louis, it is La Clede's Landing, a nine-block waterfront remnant of nineteenth-century warehouses and factories not bulldozed when so much of the economic heart of the city's downtown was demolished to construct the Saarinen Arch, erroneously hailed as a symbol of a resurging St. Louis. (More recently, St. Louis demolished some of the city's most important turn-of-the-century commercial architecture—architecturally irreplaceable and economically useful—to create a broad vista of the arch from downtown.) The story is repeated endlessly around the country. Such cities cling to bits and pieces, rejoice in their salvage—pitifully few pieces that there are—and then let megastructure blight and parking lots‡ dwarf those remnants. Some of these remnants work better than others and some provide a

---

* Ice-skating rinks seem to be a favorite Texas mall centerpiece, with other cities like Dallas and Houston also having them. One supposes the developers and designers were repeating a popular feature of Rockefeller Center or maybe they thought they were bringing in a bit of Northern urbanism.

†According to an article in *The New York Times* Jan. 1, 1988, "A Twist in the Revival of Downtowns," by Katherine Bishop, "Jesse Torres, the city's chief planner, said at least 25 percent of the retail space facing the square remains vacant and has been painted with a facade depicting 'a typical street scene' of ersatz businesses to minimize the effect of reality." Other reports indicate that the vacancy rate is even higher.

‡ "A parking lot," Chicago architect Harry Weese reminds us,[3] "is only the threat of a future building."

semblance of a functioning urban neighborhood. We deceive ourselves into thinking, however, that we are revitalizing our cities when
we preserve patches of architectural gems and forget to save the urban
fabric into which those landmarks are woven.

Bigness Has a Place

The most successful revived segments of cities I have found in which
historic preservation has been a primary rejuvenating tool are big
enough to sustain assorted economic activity, varied in age and
building type and under the influence of many redoers working over
a period of time. Again it is thinking small in a big way, where
bigness has a place.

Three very different city segments illustrate this lesson of rebirth.
The first of them is best known as a tourist mecca: New Orleans'
Vieux Carré, the area of the original town laid out by the French. At
the height of highway mania, an expressway that would have
separated the district from the Mississippi was planned and successfully opposed. The famous French Quarter has a reputation for being
touristy and tacky, overcrowded and overcommercialized. But, for
all its razzle-dazzle and tourist-meccaism, the Vieux Carré is still a
real place. Within a stone's throw of vibrant-even-if-tacky Bourbon
Street are an abundance of streets on which everyday life is no
different from that of scores of other city neighborhoods. There are
a commercial life and a residential life, sometimes on different blocks
and sometimes mixed together, but everywhere life goes on twenty-
four hours a day.

How can this be in one of the most celebrated historic districts of
any city? Why isn't it just one long series of expensive boutiques and
quiche-and-fern restaurants? How is it that real people can still live
here, side by side with the high-pitched entertainment and tourism,
just as in a well-functioning old-fashioned city with a diversified
economic and social profile? Granted that zoning, historic-
preservation and urban-design guidelines are all strict. Granted that
the inherent aesthetic appeal of the area's architecture is splendid. And

granted that it started out with the advantage of being a legendary place. All of these reasons may contribute, but none of them can answer the questions satisfactorily. Many cities, after all, have areas with these features. What makes the Vieux Carré so special and what makes it function so well is its size. The Vieux Carré is approximately *eighty-five square blocks* of the original city, primarily filled with original eighteenth- and nineteenth-century buildings but with many modern additions, some appropriate and others not. Actually, some of the most genuine buildings of the old quarter can be found on the side streets just outside the business core. Property owners and merchants there never had the money to make inappropriate cover-up changes, and the city when applying funds for capital improvements focused on the "main" areas of downtown. Overall, the quarter is a real place founded on real ongoing economic and social activities. Functions for the local populace are more critical than attractions for the tourist.*

A Highway Is Defeated and a Neighborhood Is Reborn

A similar lesson can be drawn from New York's SoHo, the area rich in cast-iron loft buildings that is now the envy of every city with an old and underutilized manufacturing and warehouse district. The twenty-six-square-block SoHo district is a collection of building types that lends itself exceedingly well to the rich mixture of uses that is uniquely urban. Expensive boutiques, restaurants and specialty shops have proliferated, for sure, yet small-industry and light-manufacturing concerns—those not priced out—coexist with artists in residence, pretend artists in residence, professionals and high-priced restaurants and shops. SoHo incubates and nurtures new and growing businesses related to the fine and commercial arts and the fashion industry. This is the kind of economically critical, bedrock

---

* This threatens to change in the near future, if an overscaled aquarium project gets built right on the edge of the district; it would guarantee to exacerbate already troublesome traffic and air pollution problems. Aquariums seem to be the newest development gimmick.

area that too many cities have either bulldozed entirely for office centers and housing or are rapidly losing piece by piece.

No one should mistake SoHo for a brilliant stroke of city policy. Few remember when the Lower Manhattan neighborhood then known as Hell's Hundred Acres was considered expendable. Manufacturing was dead, The Word of the day declared. The nineteenth-century loft buildings containing light industry were anachronistic. In the 1950s and 1960s, a planned expressway would have wiped out not only this area that was to become SoHo but also the vibrant neighboring communities of Little Italy and Chinatown. They too were declared no longer of value by expert urban renewers. Once the roadway was mapped, the future SoHo became a corridor for disinvestment.

In 1969, however, after years of fierce controversy, the anti-expressway forces won, and the city moved to allow artists to work and live in industrial buildings.* Then, in 1973, SoHo became the first commercial neighborhood in New York City to be officially declared a historic district by the Landmarks Preservation Commission. The rest is history. The artists and galleries already there were safe and were joined by others. Boutiques, specialty food shops, restaurants and New Wave fashion entrepreneurs followed. SoHo developed a vitality that urban experts declared unthinkable fifteen years earlier.

Fashionable as it may be to criticize SoHo for its high-priced chic, SoHo is a genuine urban place, one of the major focal points of the city where folks from Wall Street, the East Village, Park Avenue, the suburbs and abroad come to eat, walk, shop, live, do business or be entertained. Below the surface glitz, an active and trend-setting fashion center functions, creative newcomers can be discovered and a significant representation of the serious art world makes its home. The crowds may be overwhelming on weekends and some of the businesses may be pretentiously voguish, but SoHo's rebirth has a

---

* There has been some suggestion that this one act of preservation created more useful housing units in New York City than scores of city housing programs. This is true.

significance unsurpassed by any easily identifiable urban commercial district.

An artist friend, sculptor Walter De Maria, argues that SoHo's availability to the art world assured the continuance of New York as the art capital of the world, an identity that had taken root in the 1960s. "Fifty-seventh Street and Madison Avenue were stagnating, choking on caviar, if you will," he says. "SoHo opened up the kind of spaces the new art required, more generous in size than most uptown galleries. This energized the art world, and, in fact, Europeans started looking in their own cities for comparable loft-space areas." Art-world experts may dispute that claim, but the truth remains that old warehouses and cast-iron buildings *everywhere* were regarded with new interest and the object of innovative new uses after SoHo's trailblazing birth.

In the years since, the SoHo phenomenon has spilled over to almost every underutilized loft area in Manhattan and several in other boroughs. Other cities as well are transforming commercial areas into residential neighborhoods or new variations of commercial districts. Everyone now understands the glories of high ceilings and flexible open spaces.

Smallness on a Big Scale

A third example* of this rejuvenation of scale is the Skidmore Old Town section of downtown Portland, Oregon, an approximately twenty-block concentration of cast-iron buildings with carefully and colorfully embellished facades that had degenerated into a skid-row district after freeway ramps were scheduled to go through. After the ramps were canceled following citizen resistance (just when contracts were going out to bid), an upgrading process took root and gradually returned it to a vibrant area. One farsighted importer and property owner, William Naito, started refurbishing historic structures for use

---

* Other examples can be found in many cities: the warehouse districts of Minneapolis and St. Paul, the North End of Boston, Galveston's cast-iron district known as the Strand, Denver's Lower Downtown, etc.

by his retail business. Artists, architects and assorted businesses, residents, art galleries and restaurants followed, making the area function for Portland the same way the SoHo community does for New York.

Sadly, the Vieux Carrés, the SoHos and the Old Towns of our cities are rapidly diminishing. Some that haven't fallen under the bulldozer of earlier "renewal" programs are being rediscovered and gradually rejuvenated. The real trick is, first, to make the citadel of power in every large or small community aware of the potential of the useful areas that remain, and, second, to extract a commitment to rejuvenation through "process," not "development"—through a process that includes participation of a spectrum of willing "small redoers," from individuals to small developers, instead of development only by project developers, and that also includes innovative strategies which involve more than physical rebuilding. That, in fact, is the consistent lesson of the string of revitalization stories just highlighted, starting with Ithaca. All these stories and the earlier ones of Savannah, the South Bronx, Cincinnati, Pittsburgh and Toronto underscore the appropriateness and success of the genuine rebirth *process* in contrast to misleading redevelopment *projects*.

Process as Program

Since the 1970s there has quietly emerged a program that brings this revitalization process on a wide scale to communities seeking alternatives to devastating change. With impressive results that defy standard measuring criteria, the Main Street Project of the National Trust for Historic Preservation has slowly grown since its inception in 1976 into one of the most successful national redevelopment programs.

The National Trust for Historic Preservation is the only private national nonprofit organization chartered by Congress to facilitate public participation in conserving the built environment. Its basic purpose has been to care for some historic houses and to encourage the preservation of historically and culturally important buildings through education and programming. But in recent years the Trust has devised a number of small programs, such as the Inner City Ventures Fund mentioned earlier, that spur general revitalization efforts in many communities. The Trust receives a yearly budget allocation from Congress but is run independently of government and depends more on private donations and membership fees for financial support. Many preservationists criticize the Trust for not being a stronger advocate for preservation issues. The Main Street Project is one of technical assistance and, therefore, does not fall into that category.

The Main Street Project started as a small experiment in the Midwest, funded by private grants. Mary Means, the sharp, peppery former vice-president of the Trust and the first Main Street director, calls it "the project that wouldn't die." During the Trust's earlier efforts to help preserve historic buildings in downtowns across the country, its staff recognized that more than buildings were in trouble on Main Street and that the government solutions being offered were usually more harmful than beneficial. Everyone—whether a resident, a merchant or a public official—was looking for a quick-fix solution to the assorted and interrelated problems of Main Street. If only Sears, Penney or another anchor department store would come back downtown. If only there were enough parking downtown. If only Main Street were turned into a pedestrian mall. None of these "if onlys" could possibly live up to expectations. Too much had changed, and what was wrong could not possibly be addressed by the one-note solutions of the conventional projects popular around the country.

"We wanted to take Main Street out of the glass display case and break the dangerous habit of localities waiting for the federal Brinks truck to pull up full of big solutions dependent on the latest funding fad sweeping Washington," explains Means. The idea was to reverse the trend of handing responsibility over to government and putting it back to where it started and always belonged—in the community.

A three-year demonstration program began in 1977. The first test communities were chosen carefully. Only three Midwestern communities (Galesburg in Illinois, Hot Springs in South Dakota and

Madison in Indiana, reflecting variations in population, architecture, geographic features and economy) struggling with commercial neglect and physical decay were picked to be models out of the seventy entries in a ten-state competition.

A general approach or strategy—not a formal plan—was created to be applied with variations appropriate to each local community. Very importantly, since historic preservation was a unifying aim, the underlying purpose of all effort was *reinforcement, not replacement*. In looking for solutions for a particular Main Street, for example, Trust staff studied in detail the nuances of that specific downtown, the economic forces that had shaped it over time and those that were current. Consultants analyzed a community's architecture, planning, landscaping, real-estate economics, marketing, public relations and merchandising. Strategies appropriate to the peculiarities of that place were developed, including doses of physical refurbishment, economic restructuring, image promotion and merchant organizing.

A project manager was either sent to live in the community or hired from within, to stimulate the "rejuvenation" process and to persuade local property owners and merchants of the economic value of the suggested small investments—just as Norman Mintz did in Corning—either in the physical improvement of the store or in merchandise-display and marketing changes. The Main Street program offered the tools, but whether or not the tools would work was entirely up to the community itself. The self-help characteristic was never diminished. Design advice and technical assistance were given free. Low-cost storefront improvements were suggested. Experts advised on the retaining and strengthening of key retail operations, on recruiting and starting new businesses, and on promoting residential conversions of upper stories to increase the downtown population. The economic impact of gradual changes was studied. Trust staff closely monitored gradual changes and transmitted lessons to other communities.

Some of these principles seem so logical and matter-of-fact today that it is difficult to realize what a breakthrough this program was at its inception.

Through a project film, a manual and Main Street conferences, information was transmitted to the more than four thousand small and large communities that sought advice from the Trust. For the first time, historic preservation was used as a revitalization catalyst in a far-reaching way, another example of thinking small in a big way. Sometimes the accident of what is left downtown after a hundred years is what is new, exciting and unique. A preservation approach forges an understanding of the relationship between the aesthetic and the economic. It begins by looking closely at the microcosm, not the macrocosm. Close up, everything looks different. A more fine-grained understanding flows from looking first at the micro instead of the macro.

But within the Main Street strategy, buildings are viewed as pieces of a whole physical and economic fabric as well as of individual value. Ellen Posner, writing about the Main Street Project in *The Wall Street Journal* May 28, 1985, noted: "Buildings are powerful magnets, and they can provide those important intangibles: a strong sense of place and the promise of a civic life." From the restoration of buildings, Posner notes, has come the restoration of the specialness and personality of downtowns.

Posner summarized the process this way: "In each town the kickoff for the Main Street Project tended to be the restoration of a single building. As people walked or drove by to watch the work and read about it in the local newspaper, the feeling that 'something' was happening downtown caught on." (Like what happened in Ithaca during the well-publicized creation of the Commons.) "Then, one by one, usually as property changed hands, and as new businesses moved in, other buildings were restored."

Appropriate Change Encouraged

Change in this context is subtle. This became apparent when I visited Madison, Indiana,* one of the three Midwestern model communities

---

* My visit followed the three-year program, so I had no point of comparison.

chosen for the Main Street demonstration project. Madison is a shipping, industrial, retail and medical center on the Ohio River in southern Indiana, forty miles north of Louisville, Kentucky. Madison's five-block main-street commercial core is a classic assortment of low-rise nineteenth-century storefront structures of red native brick, adjacent to a substantial residential historic district of Federal and Greek Revival homes. Upon entering downtown Madison, I saw nothing unusual. There seemed to be a full assortment of community-service businesses, from barbershop to luncheonette and from movie house to bookstore. No indications of big changes were apparent, and only a few hints of change at all. There were a few new-looking small buildings, a few old ones that looked spruced up and a few businesses that looked like new entries on the retail scene. Mostly, however, what was noticeable was Main Street's variety of services and retail stores, some industrial businesses and government offices, a modest park, and banks and civic institutions. Only after a long conversation with John Galvin, then head of Historic Madison Inc., the local preservation group, and also head of the merchants' association, did I become aware that considerable change had, in fact, taken place.

What had been ailing downtown Madison, as Galvin described it, did not sound unusual. Postwar sprawl drew livelihoods and liveliness away from Main Street. Four-hundred-foot bluffs between the old downtown below and the new commercial strips above created a natural dividing line. The bluffs isolated the old from the new, causing downtown to suffer economically. But the bluffs also protected the downtown below from bulldozer development, in effect freezing it until the gradual change of the Main Street effort took hold. The active merchants' organization, Galvin noted, spent most of the time arguing over whether inadequate parking and erratic store hours were the cause of the economic ills. Merchants avoided, however, discussing poor merchandising, uninteresting window displays, cumbersome signage. They sought easy answers.

Despite the apparent down-and-out condition of Madison, everything was in place for the right kind of change. A varied assortment of buildings remained. The merchants' association was, at least, functioning. Pride in local heritage was strong, with an effective preservation movement having a noticeable impact on the restoration of historic homes.

"Like all part-time efforts," Galvin says of the merchants' association's work, "someone was needed with expertise to pull it all together," to be the critical leader. A Main Street coordinator was provided for Madison by the National Trust when Madison became a demonstration city. That coordinator was Tom Moriarity, a preservation architect who had been working for two years as executive director of Historic Madison Inc. "The real advantage of that coordinator," says Galvin, "was that we finally had a full-time person to go up and down Main Street discussing designs, marketing problems, promotion, signage and other things with each business-man."

Moriarity served as a Main Street advocate, persuading some businesses not to move out and organizing a search committee to encourage new businesses to move in. Where appropriate, financial advice was offered and store owners were given design help with modest upgrading efforts, starting with simple and inexpensive painting and sign-changing. "The subtleness of the restorations was startling," says Galvin, "but it prompted people to see things differently, and to realize that they could do manageable things to make a difference and that it could look natural without being cute."

Because the Main Street strategy is made up of so many components—from giving design or merchandising advice to individual merchants to encouraging appropriate public development—its stamp on a community is not easily discernible. An outsider visiting Madison had to have known that this program was functioning to understand that change was gradually taki..g place. Natural without being obvious or cute, attractive without seeming forced, fixed without looking "fixed up" or even without looking as if it had been "broken," is exactly as it appeared when I visited. What was also not obvious was that during the prior three-year effort at least half the merchants had upgraded their businesses, some owners had converted previously unused upper floors into apartments, adding a new population to downtown, six new businesses had opened, and the vacancy rate had settled down to below the ten percent national average.

More than $2 million had been invested in downtown, a major boost to the economic base, but, Galvin noted, no one considered the three years anything but a beginning. The rejuvenation was meant to continue, with the National Trust's program having served its purpose as a modest catalyst.

Formula Thinkers Intervene

During its three-year beginning, the Main Street program caught the attention of many, including Washington officials desperate for new and visible solutions to the growing problems for which no easy answers were working. Means met with government representatives in 1980 to discuss expanding the program with government funds. During the first three years, the program had a budget of $800,000. Means was asked how much more was needed to go big and national with government help. She said an additional $500,000 and was laughed at. "Ask for five million," she was advised. "The government will never pay attention to half a million."

"They wanted us to take it really big," Means said acidly. "They had caught the melody, but didn't understand the music."

To its credit, the Trust resisted. It expanded the program itself, again relying on foundation and corporate grants. A National Main Street Center was established in Washington, D.C., and small doses of support were gained from seven federal agencies—the Departments of Housing and Urban Development, Transportation, Commerce, Agriculture and the Interior, the National Endowment for the Arts, the Small Business Administration.

This time the program included five communities in each of six states: Colorado (Delta, Durango, Grand Junction, Manitou Springs, Sterling), Georgia (Athens, Canton, La Grange, Swainboro, Waycross), Massachusetts (Amesbury, Edgartown, Northampton, Southbridge, Taunton), North Carolina (New Bern, Salisbury, Shelby,

Tarboro, Washington), Pennsylvania (Easton, Jim Thorpe, Titus-
ville, Uniontown, Williamsport) and Texas (Eagle Pass, Hillsboro,
Navasot, Plainview, Sequin).

Twenty-two of the thirty communities either had a mall within
twenty miles (and many are much closer than that) or were awaiting
the groundbreaking ceremonies of one. In fact, at the first training
session, in Washington in January 1981, the Main Street Center took
the thirty project managers on a field visit to an enclosed regional
shopping center, as part of their training in financing, retailing,
design, marketing, historic preservation and organizing downtown
development commissions and merchants' associations. "The trip
was not a souvenir-shopping spree," Means says. "We wanted them
to understand fully what they were up against."

This national effort sought to go wholesale instead of retail. The
Trust understood it could not work with thirty communities the
same way it had worked with the demonstration three. The goal,
therefore, was to train others to do it. Thus, state program heads
became what Means called "secondary trainers." Organizing this
way had another advantage. State programs and public-policy decisions often work at cross purposes. The highway department plans to
widen Main Streets or to connect towns with an interstate highway
on which shopping centers will be built, while urban and rural
departments struggle to revitalize the Main Streets that the highways
will undermine. If, however, awareness of the statewide Main Street
strategy can permeate all departments, conflicts may be minimized.

Thirty-nine states had applied to be included in the expanded
second three-year demonstration program. "The application process
itself started a dialogue between those states and their communities
that had not occurred before," notes Means. "Many of the thirty-
three rejected states started their own programs based on our
three-year model."

Most important for Main Street, however, many participating
states initiated new programs for small-business management, marketing, retail recruitment and downtown promotions—the assortment of tools downtowns need to compete with killer malls. As a

result, more than one thousand new businesses were formed and $147 million was invested in rehabilitation and new construction.*

Ad-Hoc Change Is Not a Dirty Word

A coherent but flexible vision of how the whole downtown fits together—not just the physical image as reflected in a development plan or a building project—is the heart of this genuine renewal approach. It is a self-help program in the best meaning of the term, with the National Trust acting as nurturer, not financial Santa Claus and builder. The essence of the program is found in the already existing economic, social and physical place, and the highest priority goes to the cumulative record of what is there. Incremental change is preferred to anything too big for adjustments.

The Main Street approach relies on hundreds of decisions—what conventional planners and developers denigrate as "ad hoc" change. Room is left for tinkering. Pieces can be canceled, changed or expanded without threatening the whole. It is not momentum oriented the way major development projects are. And while leadership is called for, public participation is meaningful. In the process, the community is reempowered to take back responsibility for itself. The community comes out stronger as a whole, is better able to weather new change, good and bad, social and economic, and is more self-reliant, even if not self-sufficient. Realistic goals, not the grand, one-shot solution, are the bottom line. It is Urban Husbandry at its best. And because it encompasses many small—and some large—things happening over time, it cannot be easily defined, like a development project.

---

* The statistical accomplishments are as significant as the visual. Business starts in the network towns outnumbered failure by a ratio of two to one (1,004 starts, 448 failures). Twenty of the original towns formed new downtown organizations, and eight more strengthened existing organizations. More than 650 facade renovations occurred. More than 60 new construction projects occurred, representing $84 million in investment. Nearly 600 rehabilitation projects, including new signs, storefront renovations, interior improvements and conversion of upper floors, were completed, representing more than $64 million in investment. Nineteen of the cities organized business-recruitment programs or methods to attract developers and investors.[4]

The Main Street strategy, as Means says, is "economic development within the context of historic preservation." This is not without irony, she notes, because early in the program those with an aversion to preservationists did not recognize the economic underpinning of the program.

Economic development is one of those much-abused terms indiscriminately invoked to sell oversized building schemes. The Main Street program, however, is creative economic development in the real sense of strengthening existing and developing *new* long-term contributors to a local economy. Mutually reinforcing small things are initiated, not mutually exclusive big ones. The assimilation of change takes place over time, in small doses. Time allows for trying something and, if it doesn't work out, trying something else before being locked into an inflexible plan. As Mary Means notes, "Downtown did not decline in three years and it certainly isn't going to be revived that quickly."

For decades, Means points out, "small towns and cities adopted the failed solutions of big cities. Big mistakes trickled down, and that's how many small towns got into trouble." Now, she notes, the reverse is happening. Larger cities and neighborhoods within large cities are looking to learn lessons from the Main Street program, even though it started small and focused first on small towns. In response to the urban interest, an additional program was initiated in 1982 involving downtowns of medium-sized cities and neighborhood business districts in medium and large cities.

The urban challenge is different and more complex, just as cities are different from and more complex than small towns. Yet the leadership of the Main Street Project already has learned some clear lessons significant to a broader examination of urban revitalization. A percolating-up process works where the trickle-down process has failed.

A major difference in the larger urban areas, notes Scott Gerloff, who replaced Means as project director in June 1983, is that "reliance on government is more ingrained in cities. Whatever program government offers, they take," a new streetlight program, a tree-planting grant or facade-improvement loans. Whether the available program is appropriate does not seem to matter.

"There is more to keep track of and understand in an urban community," adds Gerloff, "more levels of power to keep up with and a lot of decision-making circles that are not always readable." Urban business districts are more project oriented. "Ribbon-cutting is their only definition of progress," Gerloff adds, so development-oriented advisers are brought into urban districts at an earlier stage than in smaller communities.

The Main Street program has moved from small town to large city gradually and carefully, learning from its experience at each stage and building on its success. One wonders whether, like a true catalyst, it can cause change and then disappear by going out of business. Instead of disappearing, the program is, Gerloff says, "maturing. We are no longer just a catalyst but a provider of technical assistance, a national presence, an adviser, an information source. We still have to deal with innovation and change. The need now is to stay ahead of things."

None of the regenerating communities examined in this look at recent decades of urban dispersal have finished. Plenty of room remains for new things—good and bad—to happen. Vital communities with an intact physical fabric can withstand change. These communities are already well grounded in a grass-roots urbanism necessary to handle the dynamic unleashed by new situations.

CULPRITS

*Although even small communities are sometimes
guilty of causing serious erosion, generally as a
result of ignorance, this is trifling in comparison
with the devastations caused by gigantic groups
motivated by greed, envy, and the lust for power.
It is, moreover, obvious that men organized in
small units will take better care of their bit of land
or other natural resources than anonymous
companies or megalomaniac governments which
pretend to themselves that the whole universe is
their legitimate quarry.*

—E. F. SCHUMACHER, *Small Is Beautiful*[1]

The lending institutions that bankroll regional malls and the national
chains that tenant them epitomize the power of national or international corporate capital over local destinies. National retail chains and
lending institutions are culprits in the urban death-cycle, just like the
federal government and the banks, insurance companies and regional-
mall developers identified earlier. Investment money is so mobile that

national entities hold local development policies hostage. Capital moves to the area of least resistance; the fewer the environmental controls, and the more flexible the zoning authority, and the lower the wages standard, the better. If resistance or demands are too strong, moving to a more welcoming locale is always an option. In the case of many manufacturing companies, the move often is offshore. Frequently, moreover, the first result of a corporate merger is the closing of local plants or branches. This bankrupting disinvestment/ reinvestment pattern has left scars throughout the country.

In the 1950s, when the suburban population was growing by leaps and bounds, when unlimited land and cheap energy made things look as though they would continue that way forever, sound business sense led department-store executives to follow their customers to the suburbs with suburban "branches." But, like many trends that develop a larger-than-justifiable momentum and eventually become self-defeating, the suburban growth of department stores got out of hand and became destructive.

First, as noted in the stories of Ithaca and Burlington, retailers fled downtown like a plague had descended and developed a city-be-damned attitude that left little room for the flexibility necessary to reverse a pattern. New signals that the public was rediscovering the appeal of urban downtowns were ignored. And, second, retail chains ceased to follow population movement and instead, through their location and development policies, began to lead it.[2] In less than three decades, the shopping centers that had started as small strips of stores serving a limited market—some with a supermarket anchor, others with a small "branch" department store—evolved into gigantic selling machines containing as many as five or six department stores with 1.5 to 2 million square feet of retail space in one controlled and rigidly planned environment. The impact on the landscape has been monumental. Raymond L. Trieger, vice-president for property development at R. H. Macy Properties, has noted:[3] "The mistakes of merchandising can be remedied in short order. Goods can be marked down and marked down again until the full stock is sold. But the mistakes of real estate cannot easily be removed from the landscape."

Department stores and national chains abandoned the cities that had first made many of them prosperous, and they never looked back. Some were less damaging, by opening in the suburbs without entirely abandoning their urban locations. We have seen that retailers were helped in their move to new suburban locations with the tax dollars of the urban residents they left behind, through the federally financed highway- and infrastructure-building programs. More important, however, they continued this pattern long after the 1973 energy crisis and other evidence made it clear that cities still have a future. Even when the energy-saving potential of cities brightened urban prospects and automobile dependency dimmed the appeal of suburban centers, many retail chains clung to their twenty-year-old practice of abandoning downtowns.

Regional centers create another kind of problem for the localities they affect. National or regional developers build them and home-office loyalists manage them with minimal commitment to local concerns. Similarly, national-chain tenants export their local profits to distant headquarters. Worse, national chains often put out of business locally owned businesses whose profits would have been retained or reinvested in the community.

When national chains supplant locally owned businesses, an entire community is damaged, not unlike the destruction suffered during the corporate merger and takeover process that wipes out home-based industries. Wrote syndicated columnist Neal R. Peirce in December 1981:

> Headquarters start looking for ways to maximize the profits of subsidiaries, and duplicate staffs are an inevitable target. Then everyone else in the city starts to suffer. Bank accounts, legal work, insurance, advertising and accounting services are transferred away. From the United Way to the arts to downtown development, essential leadership is lost. With job losses and property abandonment, everyone's taxes escalate. The 1981 business merger boom . . .

is like an arrow aimed at the economic health, government solvency and civic leadership of every city in America with businesses that might be ripe for takeover.

Peirce also notes that acquiring corporations often milk the new property like a "cash cow," investing that money elsewhere and eventually shutting down the weakened plant. The acquiring conglomerate may set unrealistic profit or market shares for the subsidiary to achieve, closing the local plant if it fails the challenge. "By contrast, home-city company owners accept good years with bad and may be satisfied with much more modest profits," adds Peirce.

Peirce quotes a 1980 national survey of corporate takeovers by the antitrust subcommittee of the U.S. House of Representatives' Small Business Committee:

> Conglomerate mergers do not create new productive resources and rarely develop new markets. The rates of job creation, productivity and innovation slow after independent companies are absorbed . . . the national interest may better be served by strengthening the role of independent businesses in the economy, as they are the most productive, the most innovative and the most prolific job-generating sector.

Nationals Stifle Localities

When not siphoned off from a town or city's economy, locally spent dollars can recirculate through local businesses and banks many times before leaving the area. When the regional center and its national tenants intrude, the cash flow is intercepted before those local dollars work their way through the local economy. Short-circuiting of local dollars can devastate a community. Thus, the developers of regional malls, the retail chains that prefer them to downtown locations and the big institutional lenders that love to finance them all have life-and-death power over small cities or sections of larger cities. They abet the cycle of big eating little, driving out local concerns and leaving a trail of abandonment behind at great public cost.

The situation gets worse as additional implications are considered. As the older retailing centers are threatened or discarded, communities turn in increasing desperation to state and federal governments for help, seeking millions of new-development dollars. This becomes a domino progression of decay for which government and taxpayers never stop paying.

Chain stores, more than anyone else, kept alive the continued growth of the kind of regional mall that Burlington defeated and dimmed the prospects of downtown revival when that revival was most logical. By the 1980s, some sizable retailers considered downtown opportunities only where the city provided "incentives" (huge public investment) and if large sites were available (urban-renewal powers). Department-store executives were willing to come downtown only if they could bring their suburban scale and design with them. Mostly, however, they were interested in the middle market—areas outside medium-sized cities like Burlington and Pittsfield—that had been largely overlooked in the first decades of shopping-center proliferation.

Chains continued to operate on the premise that big is automatically better and, in the process, ignored a countertrend. Consumers were beginning to return to the smaller, personal stores—where available—that Main Street historically offered. This trend did not go unnoticed by the more perceptive developers. James Rouse, who gained a national reputation creating shopping centers, commented on a 1978 *MacNeil/Lehrer Report*: "People really would like the intimate, across-the-counter contact with people who run their own stores. They would like to get away from the prepackaged distribution centers that many stores have become, [so] a highly personal, small, intimate, lively marketplace would have very deep human appeal."

Tastes changed and the appeal of the human-scale Main Street was on the rise, but national retailers clung to a vision that offered only the bleak destiny of the dinosaur. By the early 1980s, growth had leveled off and changed directions. A shrinking supply of suburban land, growing competition from refurbished downtowns, and proliferation of both outlet and discount stores and small neighborhood centers all contributed to changing patterns. Instead of downward adjustments in size, the responses to these changes seemed to bring even bigger developments. Now it is common to find the newest regional mall as part of a "mixed-use" complex of office park, luxury housing and entertainment center. The climate-controlled, self-contained fortress just gets bigger and bigger.

Smallness Regains Appeal

By the dawn of the 1980s, small stores in urban neighborhoods were rising in popularity and proliferating* as people chose to shop closer to home. The return to localism and to neighborhood shopping was fostered by the apparent policy of national stores of providing less and less sales help per square foot of selling space. Why wait forever to make a purchase in a big store when someone behind the counter in a smaller shop is there when you enter? While the business and financial pages of newspapers and magazines ran frequent stories of the economic woes of the national chains, rarely did a reader find any reference by retail executives to changing tastes of consumers. Onward they pushed with plans for new malls, looking back downtown only when the rare opportunity of a large site presented itself. They did not know how to think smaller.

Often a random observation tells us more than complicated statistics. Here is a personal story that makes the point. A Brooklyn friend told it to me over lunch one day in the winter of 1981. He, his wife and their three children live in one of those wonderful Brooklyn row-house neighborhoods that had naturally regenerated itself while experts still saw urban renewal as the future. With the new, young residential population came new, small businesses and retail shops run by young entrepreneurs—the future mom-and-pop generation. For years my friend had celebrated his children's birthdays with festive parties in their five-story brownstone, and for years he had

---

* I watched this happening in my Manhattan neighborhood in the 1970s, marveling at how many new local stores were opened by first-time merchants, many of whom were women.

watched the pile of presents all come in the familiar package of Abraham & Straus, Brooklyn's biggest (and homegrown) department store. By 1981 that assortment of presents had come through an interesting cycle of change. Not one was from A & S, even though A & S, downtown Brooklyn and much of the whole borough were enjoying a well-publicized renaissance. All of the presents now came from popular new stores in the neighborhoods in which the children lived. Most of the stores were owned and operated by local residents. Most were recent additions to the retail scene, but had already become landmarks, and clearly the future was theirs. And, in fact, my friend, who held a prestigious real-estate job, reported that A & S executives had been grumbling recently that business for them was better when Brooklyn was still in a state of decline. During that decline, those smaller businesses disappeared in great numbers. With the renewed popularity of city living in the late 1960s and 1970s, new young residents and small-store entrepreneurs reversed that trend.*

For national retail executives, however, formula thinking remains entrenched. Replicate, replicate, replicate. Why wrestle with the creative challenges of knitting retail outlets into the existing fabric of an interesting and time-tested downtown? It was easier to start from scratch in an empty cornfield, just as it had been for urban renewers to start with blocks and blocks of empty downtown space. But retailers are no different from the lenders who finance them. Bankers take the same "safe course" in lending, following closely the national retailing pattern, denying loans to independents whose proposals are innovative and contrary to familiar patterns.

Formula Thinking Can Be Devastating

A classic instance of this straitjacket thinking of national retail executives occurred in Brooklyn's Flatbush section. Flatbush is one of those many slowly but surely reviving communities rich in an

---

* In addition, the construction of a pedestrian mall on A & S's street in the late 1970s disrupted retail business there for a protracted time and chased away many customers who never returned when the mall was completed.

attractive stock of residential and commercial structures, ranging from nineteenth-century mansions to Art Deco apartment houses. Flatbush Avenue, once the business thoroughfare of the heart of Brooklyn, remains the commercial spine, a reasonably solid retail center dominated by moderate-priced goods in block after block of small and medium-sized stores. It may never again flourish as it once did, but a steady upgrading on the avenue has been occurring for the past few years,* confidence among businessmen is growing and the number of vacancies is at a minimum.

The star of Flatbush Avenue is a former movie theater, the Flatbush Kings, a hodgepodge of Art Deco, Renaissance and Baroque decoration—call it 1920s lavish—with a spectacular marble lobby, sweeping staircases, and brass, bronze and oil-painted ornament to rival the best of 1920s movie palaces. Built in 1928 as the 3,800-seat flagship of the Loew's chain, it is one of the last pre-Depression movie palaces to be built in New York and remains one of the best of its kind in the country, remarkably intact and unvandalized, despite the fact that it closed its doors as an entertainment center in 1978. Since its closing, it has had a complex and beleaguered history, but it remains standing, through the diligent efforts of a remarkable community organization, the Flatbush Development Corporation. Although the Kings fell into city ownership through tax foreclosure, the Flatbush Development Corporation remains the city-owned theater's guardian and has looked for years for developers interested in converting it into something functional. Unquestionably, with the right creative instincts, someone could turn the Kings back into an economic magnet for the community. Even more than its glorious architecture, what makes it attractive as a development opportunity is that it backs up to three major department stores, already a strong retail magnet.

The bizarre aspect of the struggle to save and reuse the Kings involves a national toy-store chain that at one point was almost

* In 1972, a major shopping mall opened farther down Flatbush Avenue, devastating the already fragile shopping street and postponing for at least a decade any significant chance for revival.

persuaded to be a major tenant. A plan called for the total removal of the street-level seating and the conversion of that level into shopping space, with the highly embellished and spacious balconies adapted to restaurant and small retail uses, including a small movie theater in the second balcony. Although returning the 3,800-seat theater to its original use would have been the ideal solution, this alternative had realistic possibilities, and the toy chain was interested. But the chain planned to insert on the ground floor a 40,000-square-foot box, a precise replica of its usual shopping-mall configuration, so that, once inside, a customer would never know that he or she was in an old movie palace instead of a suburban mall. There was no interest on the part of the retailer in exploring the possibilities of making this one of the most exciting shopping and entertainment experiences anywhere. The only way this national retailer would even consider using the space was to use it according to its national formula, and even that idea was not attractive enough to make the project go.

There is an additional twist to this unfortunate tale. A subsequent proposal for the Flatbush Kings provided for converting it to assorted retail, restaurant and entertainment uses and connecting it through walkways to the existing three traffic-generators that already back up to the theater—the two national department stores and the one strong local retailer—a creative redevelopment proposal with extraordinary possibilities. Lenders, however, resisted. Lenders could be found willing to finance this proposal only if both neighboring national department stores signed a fifteen-year lease. One store said yes, but the other said maybe. No lender would participate without both.

The Flatbush Kings still languishes, a missed opportunity with enormous regenerative potential for a sizable slice of Brooklyn. I have watched the Kings sit for several years now, suffering the damage of inactivity and vandals. Only recently, however, have I come to understand two additional reasons for its neglect—beyond the lender-formula resistance—that parallel downtown problems in many cities, regardless of size.

The first problem is the Brooklyn inferiority complex. Brooklyn-ites, for all their apparent bravado and chauvinism, struggle with a self-image problem caused by its location across the bridge from Manhattan. Brooklynites refer to Manhattan as The City, and even highway signs alert Manhattan-bound drivers to the direction of "The City." For the Flatbush Kings, this Manhattan complex translates itself into a concern among neighborhood and civic leaders that Brooklyn cannot sustain a third theater (the Brooklyn Academy of Music and Brooklyn College are the two main entertainment centers, featuring mostly classical productions) for live entertainment. A third theater for a borough of 2.3 million people! Only someone with no confidence in either the programming of the two existing theaters or the cultural taste of the Brooklyn audience would be so negative to the idea of a new and different entertainment menu flourishing in the Flatbush Kings.

In fact, as a positive 1986 feasibility study pointed out, in the 1950s and 1960s Brooklyn "was a center for popular music entertainment." Only three theaters in all of New York City (Beacon, Radio City Music Hall and Felt Forum, with the renovated Apollo coming in) and others outside the city now offer such popular entertainment, the study pointed out. Ironically, packagers offer Brooklyn residents transportation and tickets to New Jersey and Long Island entertainment events.

The second problem endemic to Brooklyn but with broad implications concerns the New York development community. To New York developers, Manhattan is the only game worth playing. They are more likely to build in Houston or on a New Jersey hayfield than to cross the bridge to another borough. When Manhattan developers do cross one of the bridges, it is usually for a back-office or Manhattan satellite project, layered with government bonuses and subsidies. In this respect, major New York developers are for New York what national developers are for American cities in general.

The refurbishment of old movie palaces as spectacular as the Kings is not uncommon around the country: the Fox in St. Louis, the Fox in Atlanta, the Majestic in San Antonio, the Proctor's in Schenectady, the Paramount in Oakland, the Ohio in Columbus. The list is endless and each has become a catalyst for downtown rebirth in the city in which they are located.

National retail executives, lending-institution executives and large developers respond in these instances no differently—no better, no worse—than government policy-makers and planners. It is safer to invest in formula designs for everything than to respond to imaginative new proposals.

A Boston Success Changes Everything

An instructive example of genuine local redevelopment can be found in Boston. It is one of the best-known redevelopment successes in the country. In the late 1960s, Boston architect Benjamin Thompson, former chairman of the Architecture Department of Harvard's Graduate School of Design and the founder of Design Research, Inc., a retail chain selling contemporary furnishings and housewares, had a vision for restoring an historic area of downtown Boston through a combination of landmark preservation and revitalization of a diverse assortment of small retail uses. Thompson proposed a combination of small special-food places, outdoor cafés and seating areas, flowers, trees and "all those little things," as Thompson has said, "that frighten great economic minds and many city planners."

The site he had in mind in 1966 was adjacent to the historic Colonial meetinghouse Faneuil Hall, a short walk in one direction from the waterfront, to which little attention was then being paid, and a short walk in another direction from the hub of Boston's commercial and government center. On this site were three parallel 500-foot-long brick-and-granite buildings designed by Alexander Parris and made possible in 1826 by then Boston Mayor Josiah Quincy (later president of Harvard College). By the 1950s, after more than a century of heavy commercial use, the three abused and deteriorated buildings were, as so many historic landmarks are, emptied of activity and threatened by urban-renewal clearance.

Vigorous public protests averted demolition. Boston officials liked Thompson's unsolicited plans, but that was not enough. An expert consultant's study showed that it wasn't financially feasible. The "downtown is dead" syndrome still prevailed, as did the first rule of mall-marketing, dictating the inclusion of at least one anchor department store.

In the early 1970s, Thompson went to shopping-mall developer James Rouse, who, having never lost faith in the strength and appeal of cities, responded to the vision and agreed to do it. Resistant lenders were no less dubious, and now a national economic slump added to their original negativism. Rouse was certainly a developer with a track record. He was already one of the nation's most successful creators of suburban shopping centers and was nationally known as the builder of the "new town" of Columbia, Maryland. The success and merits of Columbia are debatable, and I am not one of its fans. Clearly, however, by developers' standards it was an achievement. Rouse, in other words, was a bankable commodity, but when he offered a plan that diverged from the acceptable formula of the day, one that chose a downtown site rather than a rural meadow and promised no retail anchor, even he had to search hard to find a lender. Rouse raised most of the money in New York and had to go to no fewer than twelve Boston institutions for the last few million.

The success of that project is legendary, and the idea of the "festival marketplace" became the development formula of the 1980s. Ten years after its 1976 Bicentennial opening, the Faneuil Hall Marketplace—popularly known as the Quincy Market—with fifteen million yearly visitors, had "become a symbol and magnet of Boston's revival, and an influential model of urban rehabilitation elsewhere," wrote Colin Campbell in *The New York Times* (August 16, 1986).

Pittsburgh Does It, Too

A parallel experience occurred in Pittsburgh, this time involving one of the nation's most successful historic-preservation organizations instead of a developer. The Pittsburgh History and Landmark Foundation, as described earlier in this book, had been building an impressive record of landmark-restoration and neighborhood-revitalization projects since the mid-1960s. In the mid-'70s, PHLF president Arthur Ziegler sought to transform the landmark 1901

Pittsburgh & Lake Erie railroad station, with its lavishly ornamented interior intact, and its surrounding forty acres into a mixed-use commercial center. "Pittsburgh's nearest fashionable shopping district was in Manhattan," quips Ziegler, explaining the rationale behind the project, "and Pittsburgh's last tourist came in 1946." A market study by "experts" concluded that Pittsburgh was the wrong city, that the station was in the wrong location, that PHLF was the wrong organization as developer for this wrongheaded project. Then the study added that if the first phase went ahead, maybe it would support financing of $50,800 and maybe gross $300,000 annually.

Ziegler was proposing an urban-renewal program unlike any the lenders had encountered ever before, one that would preserve, not destroy, one that planned first to reuse the existing five buildings on the site, which required no demolition, no relocation of residents or businesses and no further land acquisition. Furthermore, it was one of the largest adaptive-reuse programs in the country undertaken by a nonprofit organization. Local lenders, despite respect for PHLF's commendable local reinvestment efforts, refused loans for the estimated $70 million first phase of the project, concurring that the project was on the wrong side of the river, in old buildings and in an area that had not been included in the master planning of the city during the previous one hundred years. It was as if Ziegler was speaking a foreign language when he tried to sell his idea of developing the site in manageable stages. "Like a city," Ziegler said, "we would let it grow by itself." His intention was to appeal to "hometown folks first, with tourism extra," a significant thought considering the proliferation of so-called revitalization projects around the country designed first for the tourist and only second for the "hometown folks."

In the end, the development got off the ground with a $5 million seed grant from the Allegheny Foundation, a trust of the Scaife family, and a $2 million investment by Detroit restaurateur Charles A. Muer. It includes a five-hundred-seat restaurant in the old terminal's spectacular grand concourse, with a stained-glass vaulted ceiling, stained-glass arched windows, and a marble staircase, all of which have long been considered one of the great remaining American Edwardian interiors. Also on the site is a nineteenth-century industrial building remodeled into office space, a turn-of-the-century railroad warehouse turned into shops and restaurants, a shiny Art Deco diner (moved from a demolition site in Pittsburgh's East Liberty neighborhood) occupied by a cooking school, a three-story office building restored for continued office use, a unique outdoor museum with a remarkable collection of industrial, railroad and architectural artifacts, and, alas, a three-hundred-room hotel of banal design—"a big box and a big blooper,"* admits Ziegler. But from day one, Station Square, as the total complex is called, has been a resounding success. The $300,000 gross that the "expert" market study projected turned out to be $3 million in the first year, just from the restaurant.

Perhaps most significant, as Ziegler appropriately boasts, "we changed Pittsburgh's mind about its own market. We dispelled the myths that no one eats out at night, that no one stays out at night, and that no one wants to be at a railroad station at night." (Brooklyn could learn from Pittsburgh!) Station Square has turned into a genuinely reinvigorating project for Pittsburgh and an important catalyst for similar rejuvenation schemes. As sole developer, PHLF will convert the profits into an endowment for its revolving fund to underwrite local housing restoration for low- and moderate-income families, educational programs and other preservation projects. Station Square, furthermore, although developed by a not-for-profit organization, is paying full taxes.

A Conventional Developer Learns Serendipitously

My favorite example of this pervasive shortsighted investment policy is found in Los Angeles. More than the substance of the case makes it so appealing. I'm sure the reason it is my favorite is that it takes place in Los Angeles. Downtown Los Angeles—the original

---

* The hotel has since been redesigned and reportedly has the highest occupancy rate in the city.

downtown predating the area's freeway sprawl—is one of the best-kept urban secrets in the country. There is more of a "there there" than in the downtowns of many overcelebrated cities like Atlanta, Louisville, San Diego and others. The central spine of this area is Broadway, a primary shopping street of the Hispanic community, enlivened by bustling crowds and Latin music pouring from busy stores. More than just Broadway, however: there are streets overflowing with pedestrians, shops, offices, lofts, small and large businesses, active movie palaces, a single-room-occupancy-hotel area, a jewelry-trade district, a little Tokyo, artists' studios and galleries in an old warehouse district, and an assortment of building styles from the 1880s to the 1950s. This old downtown is a short walk but a mile of mind-set east of all the new interior-oriented steel and glass buildings that hug the freeway side of downtown. Many Los Angeles residents have never been to that downtown. Only recently has the vanguard of artists, loft dwellers and real-estate bargain hunters who also precede the experts begun to rediscover the area.

In 1977, developer Wayne Ratkovich purchased the 1927 Oviatt Building near Pershing Square, the only downtown park and once the focal point of the LA financial district before post–World War II multicenter growth in the city left the old downtown mostly abandoned. The Oviatt Building was "priced as a parking lot" (100,000 square feet at $400,000), Ratkovich recalls. On his way to see the building for the first time, Ratkovich studied the numbers and decided to buy it. "You didn't need to be a genius to see that the numbers worked," he says.

He was pleasantly surprised to find in the building signed Lalique glass on the elevator doors, shimmering geometric metal grillwork, English oak doors and marble floors, and an elegant penthouse apartment where Oviatt lived. Ratkovich made plans to renovate the building for office use, and set out in search of bank financing.

"Many local bank executives remembered the building from their youth," says Ratkovich, "remembered its ornamental appeal, loved the fact that I planned to restore it, wished me lots of good luck and told me to come back when it was finished and rented to talk about financing."

Ratkovich had been in the development business in another firm; this was his first project as a new firm. His experience had been with industrial projects, renovation of large and small factory buildings. Just as the Faneuil Hall Marketplace was the first historic-renovation project for Rouse, so was the Oviatt the first historic building for Ratkovich. In the end, he succeeded in securing the financing through nonconventional means, but, Ratkovich says, "it took a lot of convincing."

Even Ratkovich underestimated the success of what he was planning to do. "The vision," he says, "was a low-cost job that was more than a coat of paint, but limited." He did one floor. It rented so quickly that he reassessed the plan for the rest of the building and moved instead full scale ahead on a major renovation and careful refurbishing of the old architectural features. It still rented quickly, filling up with a variety of tenants, especially, says Ratkovich, with "breeder law firms, newly formed firms with young partners who didn't feel they had to be in the newest building monument in town."

Ironically, the Ratkovich purchase of the Oviatt Building followed right on the heels of the resounding success of the Biltmore Hotel renovation in 1979 one block away by architect/developers Phyllis Lambert and Gene Summers, another creative venture that the investment community thought doomed. Lambert, who persuaded her father, the late Samuel Bronfman, to commission Mies van der Rohe to design the Seagram Building in New York, and Summers, a former associate of Mies van der Rohe, restored the outwardly reserved 1923 red brick hotel with its lavish Spanish and Italian Renaissance interior, moderating its past exuberance through muted colors and van der Rohe furnishings that gave the restored landmark a modern overlay. The hotel and a new and elegant restaurant, Bernard's, were instant hits. (In 1986 the Biltmore was bought and restored again, this time with the ornately detailed interior returned to the 1920s décor.)

"The Biltmore," says Ratkovich, was viewed by the real-estate community as an "independent happening because it was a hotel" and did not stimulate any reassessment of the office-renovation market. There was also an incorrect assumption that Bernard's drew only a hotel crowd, Ratkovich adds. So when Ratkovich and Bowers announced a new and expensive restaurant for the ground floor of the Oviatt, the financial community viewed them as crazier than when they first embarked on the renovation of the offices upstairs. The ground floor had once been occupied by a fashionable men's store. Elaborate wood paneling and cabinetry were still in place. The interior, cabinetry and all, was refurbished for reuse as a restaurant, but expert consultants warned that it would never make out because it would be totally dependent on a lunch crowd with a heavy turnover. "This restaurant was a purely entrepreneurial venture at street level," notes Ratkovich, "which was very different for LA." The Rex was an instant hit and is considered one of the finest restaurants in LA. It does three times as much dinner business as lunch, and Saturday night is its biggest night.

The Oviatt Building, says Ratkovich, "turned a lot of heads and awakened and excited a lot of people." New attention was paid to existing buildings downtown, with the market in those buildings getting stronger. Ratkovich went on to do other historic and architecturally special buildings. Financing was more readily attainable, not, says Ratkovich, because lenders recognized the economic potential and aesthetic appeal of these subsequent projects, but because he gained credibility with the Oviatt success.

Tales like these are common. Small businessmen and homeowners with no reputation or track record probably are hurt more than the examples given here and have no recourse when conventional financing is unavailable. One can't even begin to measure the opportunities denied to creative projects. Equally significant, however, are the cases of established developers unable to find support when they diverge from the expected. If they have no chance with the new and different, who does?

The lenders, like the retailers—in all their blatant inflexibility—only epitomize the tragedy of formula thinking. Their death-and-life power over cities is frighteningly real. Their investment and development policies destroy cities at the same time from within and without. Innovation should be more bankable than the routine formulas lenders now favor. Without a major change in formula-minded investment thinking at retail and lending institutions, creative new solutions to urban ills will prevail only despite them and against all odds.

Chapter Thirteen

STREETS HAVE VALUE

■

*The rich street life is no frill. It is an expression of
the most ancient function of a city—a place for
people to come together, all kinds of people,
face-to-face, and there is far more of this congress
here than in the bland shopping centers being touted
as the new downtown.*

—WILLIAM H. WHYTE in *New York*[1] magazine,
July 1974

The life of a city begins and ends on the street. This is a very simple notion, but it is so crucial to everything about city development that it is important to consider it for a moment.

The street is an ancient invention. What modern designers and planners have had so much difficulty accepting is that *streets continue to work*. The grid layout of streets has a logic that is timeless. City functions and people are integrated, not separated, providing a fundamental ingredient for economic and social integration. A grid arrangement ties a whole city together, rather than dividing it into carefully differentiated segments. The problem in recent years is that too much urban redevelopment has been designed by people who can't leave a good thing alone, who insist that they can do better, who aspire to improve but destroy instead. The results are streetless civic centers, cultural centers, shopping centers, convention or sports centers, all standing apart from the city itself with purposeful arrogance. Today, unfortunately, the pervasive pattern of planned development is to alter beyond recognition the existing environment, rather than acknowledge the value of what exists and weave into it the desired new.

Nobody is better qualified than the user to understand the virtues of a city street, especially the street that has evolved over time and not all at once according to some lofty design plan. Contrast, variety, detail, surprise, drama, nooks, compactness, mixture of functions, nothing static, nothing boring—these are some of the things that make up a lively, well-functioning street. The ingredients of an interesting and vibrant street are a microcosm of the larger city. The most lively and famous streets, it can be observed, are not "developed," "built" or "made." They evolved, resisting cataclysmic change, withstanding fads, adapting incrementally and clinging to the character of place. No individual or company produced Chicago's Michigan Avenue, Boston's Newbury Street, Los Angeles' Rodeo Drive, Philadelphia's Market Street or New York's Madison Avenue. Consider the following description of Madison Avenue by *New York Times* architecture critic Paul Goldberger:

> It is disorganized, it is erratic, it is full of different styles and different sizes of buildings. It has almost no buildings that stand on their own as distinguished works of architecture. Yet to walk on Madison Avenue in the 60s and 70s is to have one of the great urban experiences of New York or any city: it sums up the potential of city life as few places anywhere manage to do.
>
> Madison is a street above all—it is not a mall, it is not a plaza, and it is not a highway. It is a street of shops on

sidewalks, and if that sounds quite ordinary, consider for a moment how few American cities do have such streets. The experience of strolling, of window shopping, and of observing one's fellow urbanites doing the same things, is one that most American cities have relegated almost entirely to the indoors, all too frequently to places with glass elevators and waterfalls and parking garages. The very essence of Madison Avenue is that it has none of these things. It is a convenient street, but it reaches the very highest state such a street can, at least this side of Europe.

No recent redevelopment schemes come close to achieving the urban qualities Goldberger describes. Planning and designing a dream city according to some ideal are easy; but it takes real creativity to rebuild an existing and functioning city that just needs maintenance and strengthening. American cities are pockmarked with the results of megaplans that not only ignored the essence of the street but obliterated it in the rebuilding process. In recent decades we have seen varied manifestations of centerism, from housing projects to new towns in town. Nowadays, the most common manifestation is the creation in an urban downtown of a mixed-use, self-contained project with a combination of any number of bankable components, all adding up to something one step up from a regional shopping mall. The malling of downtowns has replaced urban renewal as the ultimate formula for rebuilding cities, even for those that don't need rebuilding.

Eliminating Streets Eliminates Urbanism

No matter how many interior design elements in suburban malls are drawn from historic arcades, the anticity nature of malls is too fundamental to overcome. "At its root, the essence of a suburban place (no matter what its location or how many cafés it boasts) is that it is conceptually a point in space, discontinuous from all else," wrote James Sanders.[2] "People drive to it, park, use it, get back in their cars, and drive away. Those using the mall make a deliberate decision to do so; no one is 'just passing' to get somewhere else. The malls remain detached from all else around them. Their use, in a word, is conscious."

The first thing a suburban mall does when superimposed on an urban downtown is eliminate the street. Every other design decision pivots around this first fundamental *mis*step. Thus, by this very singular design feature, the mall is antithetical to downtown.

The importance of the street to a city cannot be emphasized enough. The street, in fact, is the most important thread in a city's fabric. It knits the city together *as* a city. To kiss the street goodbye is the kiss of death for a city. As Peter Wolf wrote in his 1974 book *The Future of the City:* "The urban street is a starting place. It has been a large physical and social part of all cities throughout history. . . . In nearly all cities at all times the street has been conceived of as communal space, as everyman's turf; as the market, the place of assembly, the first place of business to be used by all of the people. Simultaneously, it is the pulsating, often fluctuating border between the private, public and administrative domains of which all cities have always been composed."[3]

As Grady Clay noted: "In nineteenth-century novels and plays, the street epitomized democracy-in-action. It stood for an open society, with freedom of access at its very core and foundation."[4]

Eliminating the street removes the one factor that singularly and permanently defines a city—or a section of it—and from which all other characteristics emanate. Whether as the main street of a one-street town or one part of an enormous grid in a big city, the street is the focal point where people and commerce meet, market, mingle and mesh.

Self-contained malls have no streets. They have pedestrian passages between parking lots and store entrances. Those passages have a distinct and limited beginning and end. Streets, on the other hand, link all the mixed functions of a city. Through the streets, the connections work. A mall separates, divides, disconnects, isolates. This kind of mall is appropriate *only*—when it is appropriate at all—if it is placed in an undeveloped field where it is reached by car and where it doesn't intrude upon an existing physical fabric. As Robert A. M. Stern notes: "The suburban mall . . . has no necessary relation to an existing town; all that is needed is a cross roads, preferably between two super highways and plenty of space for parking."[5]

Connectors Versus Centers

Some urban retail malls do integrate with their surroundings. The ones that work well are passageways between places, not destinations in themselves. They function like streets, not centers, and have an urban logic that is clearly different from the suburban-style isolating mall. They stand out as exceptions and illustrate the inappropriateness of the alien suburban-style fortress.

One of the earliest and rare urbanistically successful of the recent generation of in-town malls, and certainly one of the largest, is Eaton Centre's glass-enclosed Galleria, a 531,000-square-foot multistoried mall connecting two downtown Toronto department stores. The all-new-construction Eaton Centre, built in 1977 and designed by Eberhard Zeidler, has many entrances, contains access to two subway stations, and has continuous retail activity around its exterior on the street, so pedestrians move freely to, from, around and through it without feeling cut off from the surrounding city.

In San Francisco, Crocker Center, a three-story block-through galleria with an impressive arched entryway at the base of a thirty-eight-story office tower built in 1985, is a surprising deviation from current custom, which produces either boxlike malls that are warehouse look-alikes or spectacular interior atria, at the base of new towers, that keep themselves secret from passersby. The sun-drenched Crocker Center atrium/passageway makes complete sense when one understands that it was designed by Skidmore, Owings & Merrill as a *connector* between the Crocker Bank's new office tower and its landmarked early-twentieth-century headquarters across the street. The Crocker Center Galleria gets people to a place other than just a place to shop in, and, although it is unfortunately organized like a mall—fast foods clustered on one floor, etc.—instead of an urban street, it does not function like a final destination, a world unto itself.

In London, the Leadenhall Market, around the corner from the high-tech stainless steel Lloyd's Bank Tower, is a wonderful arcade at the intersection of four streets, three of which are covered with an arched glass buttressed roof. A butcher, florist, hardware store and other neighborhood service businesses exist comfortably amidst all manner of restaurants. A lunchtime crowd stands in the street while shoppers move above and pedestrians pass through on their way somewhere else.

Milwaukee's four-block-long Grand Avenue Mall, designed by the ELS Design Group (Elbasani, Logan & Severin) for the Rouse Company, is one of the best urban malls I've seen, clearly because it is a restoration and extension of an old shopping arcade rather than a new, isolating center. The historic 1915 arcade (Holabird & Roche) is restored and merged with a new one formed by creating a new infill structure that connects the interiors and the backs of six disparate existing buildings. The result is one continuous space that is obviously a combination of new and old, with minimal upset to the existing avenue. From the street, one hardly knows that the assortment of side-by-side buildings is one connected retail extravaganza. The only new external component is a 100-foot-wide glass entryway that fills a gap created earlier by demolition of a building on that site. Visitors enter from several points along the avenue as well as from the parking garages constructed at the rear. Because of its clear connection to the existing street and because it is part of, not separate from, that street, the Grand Avenue Mall served as a genuine catalyst for rebirth of Grand Avenue and had a ripple effect on downtown Milwaukee, just as the Eaton Centre Galleria spurred rebirth around it. Milwaukee's active, architecturally diverse and pedestrian–oriented downtown was reinforced, not diminished, by the Grand Avenue Mall.

Appropriate urban malls are not *in* a city, like a shopping center, but *part of* the surrounding network of city streets. They resemble arcades, an historic urban form found in Europe before being introduced to this country in the last century. The European version, as Robert Stern points out, were "chiefly mid-block passages squeezing through buildings to connect important institutions . . . a commercial distraction on the way to the theater."[6] Arcades reflected the good retail sense that dictated the placement of shops along links, connectors, and shortcuts between busy streets or notable destinations, generators of the steady flow of potential customers passing by.*

Providence, Rhode Island, and Cleveland, Ohio, still have two of the best remaining historic arcades, and both have been refurbished in the past decade. The 1827 Providence Arcade (Warren & Bucklin)† with its Greek Revival columned front can be regarded as an early Temple of Consumerism. Its three-story skylit interior, however, with a good collection of retail and restaurants, resembles a street more than a formula-planned mall and pulls pedestrians in and through to connecting streets. Providence, a compact city of 175,000 with a downtown of twenty-five square blocks, was passed over during the urban-renewal bulldozer days. Also to its enormous benefit, Providence experienced an early vigorous historic-preservation movement, spearheaded by an energetic, determined woman, Antoinette Downing. There is cause for concern, however, when Providence Mayor Joseph R. Paolino, Jr., tells *The New York Times* in March 1987, "one of my dreams is literally to change the skyline of the city—to build as high as we go." The Providence Arcade and the rest of downtown Providence could be strangled by that kind of vision.[7] The 1890 Cleveland Arcade (Smith & Eisenman) links two streets and two office buildings. Its impressive 300-foot interior, with its ornate ironwork, massive skylit roof and fifty-four gargoyles holding light fixtures in their mouths at each end of the ceiling's arches, is unusually large, five stories high, with professional offices on the top floor. The large scale enhances the space without overwhelming its surroundings.

---

* Not all cities appreciate these early marvels of commercial architecture. In April 1985, the 1883 Springfield, Ohio, Arcade, a four-story, 340-foot-long shopping area under a peaked skylight, was demolished in order to have an empty site with which to lure a new developer of an undetermined project. Preservationists fought for three years to persuade public officials that this old edifice could bring new life to downtown, as similar arcades have done in other cities.
† Restoration designed by the Providence architectural firm of Irving Haynes & Associates.

Many of today's new urban malls claim links to historic arcades and galleries, most notably Milan's 1865 Galleria Vittorio Emanuele, built to commemorate the end of foreign occupation. A grand street covered with a dramatic glass roof, the Milan Galleria is lined with all kinds of shops and cafés, is open at all hours and is a street connector in the best sense. Laid out like a Latin cross, the long stretch connects the public square with the great cathedral, and the shorter stretch connects two streets.

"Today, shopping centers with only two skylights and a small arch over the front door claim kinship with this most famous of shopping arcades . . . most try to copy the glass roof and large, central courtyard, and neglect many of the other elements that make the Milan Galleria such an exciting place," *Dallas Morning News* architecture critic David Dillon has written.[8] About the only similarity between most of the new ones and their supposed antecedents, however, is the often used design elements of arched entrances, vaulted interiors and skylit roofs. Such introverted retail centers as Chicago's Water Tower Place, Boston's Copley Place, Houston's Galleria and their scores of imitations around the country have nothing to do with urbanism, are merely glitzy and glossy descendants of suburban predecessors and have the same deadening impact on surrounding downtown retail activity. An abundance of extravagant and bubbling fountains, polished brass or marble and glass-boothed elevators reflects their upscale tenants. Copying some of the design elements of earlier successes and marketing them well is not the same as making a place function as well as its models did. Most of the malls currently being inflicted on American downtowns have two dominant characteristics—they are isolating and automobile oriented, just like their suburban antecedents. They start and end with total disregard for the urban street.

Automobiles Are Still Killing Cities

Malls are products of the age of the automobile. Mall design, in all its permutations, has been defined by the car. If there is one lesson above all others that should have been learned since the highway-through-the-city fights of the 1950s and 1960s, it is that to redesign cities to accommodate the car is to redesign cities out of existence. The car and the city are natural enemies. To experience a city, one must be able to participate in it, to walk the streets, take public transit, and to drive in a car or a taxi as an alternative option, not a single choice. To experience the suburb is to drive.

How to deal with the car has been a development design problem since the early decades of this century. No matter how one views the car—with love or with hate—one can't deny its dominating influence. The problems have come with attempts to reshape cities to accommodate cars.

As Peter Wolf noted in 1974:

> . . . The embrace of the automobile as a structuring mechanism for cities reveals a misguided infatuation with a device of the late industrial revolution, whose *real utility for people is non-urban travel*. [Emphasis added.] This has not yet been fully understood. Brilliantly promoted by industry and by government programs, and possessing universal allure, the inherent anti-urban qualities of the automobile are still not generally recognized. In America and around the world, planners systematically repeat the drastic mistake of building and rebuilding urban areas for automobiles rather than for people.[9]

Sadly, this remains true, though increased attention to pedestrian amenities distracts public attention from the extensive vehicular accommodating that continues.

In recent decades, automobile-oriented, anticity projects have intruded upon, if not destroyed, sections of almost every city, wiping out streets and urbanism in their wake. City-dwellers invariably have resisted, with uneven degrees of success. Some battles, after much destruction, have been substantially won. For example, the impulse to drive massive highways straight through the hearts of cities is somewhat behind us.* That impulse, however, reappears in more refined schemes now, so sugarcoated with high-style architecture and public amenities that it is hard to tell a new highway proposal from a land-development scheme, as was noted in the earlier discussion of New York's Westway. Highway promoters have so skillfully camouflaged the destructive highway component that the public is often deceived.

But it is not only highway building that kills urbanism. It is a rare American city that does not have a mid-twentieth-century civic center, cultural center, convention-center/hotel complex, or the like—all cousins of the suburban shopping mall—sitting like an alien blob either in its middle or at its edge. Despite the different functions and uses they serve, these "centers" have common characteristics. They sort out and separate functions. They clean up and "redesign" the city fabric. They interfere with natural and appropriate urban change. They diminish pedestrian pleasures, but try with varying degrees of failure to make car access easy. They are blatantly anticity, but they are always promoted as the centerpiece of a new city-rebuilding effort. Predictably, such antiurban projects start out by eliminating the street.

Unsurpassed Urbanism: Rockefeller Center

Rockefeller Center stands in defiant contrast to this trend, which, of course, it predates. The lesson to be learned from Rockefeller Center's incomparable urbanism is lost on its imitators. Because it is often used to justify and promote centers of another kind, Rockefeller Center deserves to be better understood. The nature of its greatness

---

* A sad and ironic exception, for example, is the Presidential Highway in Atlanta that unnecessarily tears through viable and historic communities to bring visitors to the Carter Library. And, just to assure the world that the highway impulse does not die either in the city or in the countryside, comes the news that Pennsylvania wants to build a twenty-mile highway through the heart of pristine, historic Amish farmland, wiping out thousands of acres of the most productive land in the country, ostensibly to relieve tourist and truck traffic. After much public protest, including from the usually separatist Amish, the location of the planned roadway has been shifted to the edge of this area. No matter. Damaging impact is unavoidable.

and the differences between it and unsuccessful imitations have been obscured.

In one crucial way, Rockefeller Center is unique. It not only respected the existing street system, it even added a street. Rockefeller Center (not including the 1960s additions west of Sixth Avenue) covers three square blocks (twenty-two acres) from Fifth to Sixth Avenue and from Forty-eighth to Fifty-first Street. Rockefeller Plaza—the extra street—runs almost down the center on a north-south axis between the two streets. It was not there before the Center was built.

Jane Jacobs cites the significance of this "extra street" in a brilliant chapter, "The Need for Small Blocks," in *The Death and Life of Great American Cities*.[10] As a concept, it is the antithesis of "centerism." "Streets and opportunities to turn corners must be frequent," she writes. Rockefeller Plaza does that for the very long blocks between Fifth and Sixth avenues.

> If the Center's buildings were continuous along each of its side streets all the way from Fifth to Sixth Avenue, it would no longer be a center of use. It could not be. It would be a group of self-isolated streets pooling only at Fifth and Sixth Avenues. The most artful designs in other respects could not tie it together, because it is fluidity of use, and the mixing of paths, not homogeneity of architecture, that ties together city neighborhoods into pools of city use, whether those neighborhoods are predominantly for work or predominantly for residence.

When in Rockefeller Center, one does not feel removed from the rest of New York City, but instead very much a part of it. One feels *at* the city's center, not *in* a "center"—except, of course, there is a cohesiveness to the original thirteen buildings, which are among the finest examples of Art Deco architecture that exist. (The new towers built on the west side of Sixth Avenue are not Art Deco but of the dreary style of most of Sixth Avenue office buildings constructed in the 1960s.)

Rockefeller Center is simply and wondrously a collection of thirteen buildings containing a varied assortment of urban functions, designed by an assortment of architects but built by one developer over a number of years in three square blocks. *Thirteen* buildings in *three* square blocks *and* open spaces like the skating rink and the promenade! What a lost art! If three city blocks were built on today, New York or any other city would be lucky to have as many as two megabuildings per block; more likely each block would be one structure. Rockefeller Center is the kind of urban bonanza that will never be seen again. It stands in silent testimony to a time when real-estate money built with vision, instead of by formula.

A tightly knit concentration of tall and short buildings, Rockefeller Center contains two hundred shops and service businesses, three theaters, restaurants, nightclubs, and the captivating skating rink and Channel Gardens. It has an unsurpassed underground concourse that ties all the buildings together and provides easy passage to mass transit, without draining the street of pedestrian activity. Even though it is big, it does not overwhelm. Rockefeller Center is many centers: radio, television and written press, entertainment and shopping, culture and commerce, international and local business. It was an idea born in the boom days of the 1920s, but built during the bust days of the 1930s, and not all at once, and not as originally planned. More than anything else, Rockefeller Center reflected the prevailing positive view of urban life. It celebrated urbanism, instead of apologizing for it. It was designed before the romance with the city began to wane.

Rockefeller Center's final form evolved over time as plans and conditions changed. It was supposed to be built around a grand new opera house, but wound up as a large, piecemeal commercial development that has successfully weathered the ebb and flow of economic change and varied tenants. Subtle and progressive adjustments were made during the entire decade it took to design and build it, and in every decade since, without doing any damage to its architectural and urbanistic integrity.

As Rockefeller Center's creator, John D. Rockefeller, Jr., said at the 1940 celebration of the Center's completion: "It was an idea that never worked out—and that's the central bit of dramatic action, the twist in the plot of this story of a vision and an ideal. This huge business and cultural development is an end result that was not dreamed of in the first place."

Billed as a "city within a city," Rockefeller Center works more like a neighborhood, a precinct, a district, relating well to its surroundings. It works within the natural order of the city, not against it. It contains small blocks with activity on every exposure. There are no dead, blank walls. The assortment of architects, with Wallace Harrison as primary architect (there were about a dozen in all), who contributed to its overall design accepted and respected the constraints of the site established by a street system.

Rockefeller Center contains probably the most exciting open space—the skating-rink plaza and Channel Gardens—ever to grace a commercial development, but it was never meant to bring the country to the city by creating unusable, open and windswept plazas. It is a "center" that derives security from its multiplicity of activity and day- and nighttime use. It is accessible and inviting to all, intimidating to no one. It is designed first and foremost for the pedestrian, not the car. Its most enduring strength is, perhaps, that it became and remains a place to go to, just for pleasure. Rockefeller Center invites the pedestrian in, as easily as it lets the pedestrian out. Its clearly definable set of buildings are distinct from their neighbors, but not totally different or alien from them. It is the essence of urbanism. And, it is architecture at its best. It works.

Perhaps most significantly, Rockefeller Center was designed and built when mass transit—the subway—was the wave of the urban future and the romance with the car was limited to the countryside. Beneath Rockefeller Center is a transportation hub as important as the pedestrian-oriented surface. Probably because the Center's primary orientation is to mass transit, a pedestrian hardly notices the entrances to a parking garage unobtrusively located on Forty-eighth and Forty-ninth streets. Unlike the grill-sided parking garages of too many malls, the Center's parking facility is unnoticeable. Also unnoticeable to the average user is a reportedly elaborate and efficient underground truck delivery system, again with an almost hidden entrance. This is, perhaps, the most important lesson of Rockefeller Center, since, unlike too many of its followers that can't survive without massive parking facilities attached to them, Rockefeller Center was designed for the pedestrian and the transit user, a critical urban definition.* Accommodation for cars and trucks, however, also was realistically provided.

Observes architecture critic Suzanne Stephens: "Rockefeller Center not only added streets to New York's grid and created two pedestrian levels, both connecting with different modes of transportation, but kept much of the retail traffic perpendicular to the flow of Fifth Ave. traffic—not parallel to it (and therefore competitive with it)."[11]

Like the urban arcades discussed earlier, Rockefeller Center also performs as a gathering place. It is midtown Manhattan's front yard, town center, village square and common all in one place. The urban malls with pretenses of Rockefeller Center heritage—the Town Centers in St. Paul and Minneapolis, the Omni in Atlanta, the Gallerias in Houston and Dallas and all of their ilk—bear no resemblance to Rockefeller Center except in giantism and imitative and out-of-place amenities like skating rinks. Moreover, these pretenders, both urban and suburban, function unmistakably as private places, with all the controls that that implies. In contrast, Rockefeller Center is a private place that functions like a public space, excluding no one and relying on its heavy use to discourage the domination of undesirable uses.

In contrast to Rockefeller Center, enclosed malls keep out people by policy, as easily as they keep out weather by design. "Someone walking through downtown may be a citizen, but someone walking

---

* The mass-transit link in places like Toronto's Eaton Centre or New York's Citicorp is critical to their functional success. A passerby has no visual hint of what is in Citicorp, nothing to lure one in from the street. Within a few years after its opening, merchants in the Market at Citicorp complained that after the novelty wore off, no one knew what was inside and that tens of thousands of people walk by daily and think it is just another office building. Now it is primarily an agglomeration of restaurants and is a popular lunchtime destination.

through a regional, the shopping-center people maintain, is a customer," noted Calvin Trillin in his 1980 *New Yorker* article on shopping centers. This raises grave freedom-of-speech issues, as "centers" of all kinds limit public activities, even though many of them have become the only site that comes close to being a public place for a community. Of course, the construction of most of such centers has been partially made possible with public funds. Yet an irreconcilable contradiction remains when a privately owned, privately controlled space makes claims to being a public space.

Architect and writer Victor Gruen summed it up this way:

> The segregator succeeds in robbing the hearts of our cities of one of their most essential qualities: variety and small-grained differentiation. He makes impossible the accentuation of cityscape by landmarks. He undermines public spirit in solely residential districts; and, just as he brings into existence city areas that are alive only at night, he succeeds in creating other areas that are ghost towns from the close of office hours until morning. The segregators are destroyers of urbane qualities and of urban activities; by making human communication as difficult as possible, they keep people away from other people.[12]

As enclosed malls and centers proliferate, their separateness increases and with it a sanitized and segregated society. This characteristic, perhaps more than any other, contradicts the claimed design connection to Rockefeller Center. It is a supremely private space that looks, feels and acts like the ultimate public space.

Another significant feature of Rockefeller Center, and the one that clearly distinguishes it from subsequent imitators, is also a functional one. The genius of Rockefeller Center is that it functions well *both* as a "center"—an organized complex of buildings—and as a cluster of independent buildings, all of which are functionally as much a part of the surrounding city as they are part of the Center. Pedestrians, office workers, shoppers and the like experience it as part of the city as well as part of the Center. Rockefeller Center, however, has a remarkable visual unity, despite the varied bulk and height of its buildings and despite the absence of symmetry in the total layout. It is a total complex, even though people experience its parts separately. Some of the parts of Rockefeller Center are jewels in their own right, but their greatest appeal remains as parts that equal a remarkable whole.

The lessons of Rockefeller Center's most winning qualities have been lost in the fifty years of attempted replication. As architectural historian Vincent Scully notes in his book *American Architecture and Urbanism:*[13] "None of the [developments] put together in the 1950s and 1960s come close to it. Indeed, . . . all [of those developments] seem to indicate in their various ways that Americans can no longer put the center of cities together at all but can only destroy them. The new spaces tend to be disintegrated rather than shaped."

The urban "centers" which followed Rockefeller Center bear no resemblance to it. Even the next generation of Rockefellers misunderstood their father's dream while claiming to follow it: Nelson, as governor of New York State, with the Albany Mall; John III, with Lincoln Center; David as head of Chase Manhattan Bank and reshaper of Lower Manhattan with the World Trade Center and Westway, the failed highway/development scheme; the Rockefeller real-estate organization with San Francisco's Embarcadero Center. All of these "center-style" developments and many of their clones in other cities miss the genius of Rockefeller Center as an integrator, not segregator, within the city.

Lincoln Center: Urban Devitalizer

I live near Lincoln Center, one of the earliest separatist centers, a trend-setter for marbleized entertainment centers that look more like giant mausolea than seats of culture.* Lincoln Center is a self-contained center without streets, without any connection to its surrounding urban fabric, without anything to relate to its neighbors.

---

* This discussion of Lincoln Center as a physical presence is not meant to reflect in any way on the quality of its cultural activities.

It sits alone in isolated glory and could just as well be in the Mojave Desert.

Civic, cultural or shopping centers like this are alien schemes imposed on the texture of a singular place. They don't mend torn pieces of urban fabric. They destroy what exists. They replace. They are imbued with revitalization attributes they don't deserve. Their promoters use them to promise what can't be delivered. When the promise does not follow construction, few care enough to look back to recognize the mistaken assessment.

Lincoln Center is one of those developments given inappropriate revitalization credit. It did not stimulate the rebirth of Manhattan's West Side. The myth of such impact is gaining increasing acceptance for the simple reason that it is often repeated.

Since my return to New York in 1960, I have lived in three locations on Manhattan's Upper West Side, the polyglot area from Fifty-ninth Street, where midtown ends, up to 125th Street, where Harlem begins, and bordered on the west by the Hudson River and on the east by Central Park. All the West Side areas in which I have lived are among the "improved" areas whose rebirth has been popularly attributed to the construction of Lincoln Center. While it has been responsible for starting many things—especially some imitations in other cities that look worse than the original—Lincoln Center is not the cause of the West Side's renaissance. This erroneous claim would be harmful enough if confined to New York. But the Lincoln Center revitalization myth has been used around the country to gain acceptance for similar antiurban, separatist cultural centers.

The Lincoln Center idea was born in the early 1950s. The site was selected when "urban renewal" was still at its height. Ground was broken in 1959. The first building (Philharmonic Hall, now Avery Fisher Hall) was completed in 1962 and the last in 1966. The dates are significant. They predate by many years what is currently identified as the rebirth of the Upper West Side. That renaissance did not truly take root until the midseventies. ("Renaissance" is a term I use here reluctantly, because by now the West Side is so "renaissanced" that it is almost homogenized, and that has never been my criterion to measure urban rebirth. But there are also many ways in which the West Side rebirth is truly genuine.)

The West Side's renaissance began in the same way and about the same time that a renaissance took root in many urban neighborhoods across the country. "The city" was a rediscovered choice for many people deciding where to live. Economics and auto dependency caused a reassessment of the suburban lifestyle. In urban neighborhoods, value hunters found inexpensive, down-at-the-heels rowhouse bargains that the energetic young could "do over." With this housing opportunity came some suburban amenities—the barbecue, the swing or sandbox, the garden—all in the backyard or at the park around the corner.

All over New York, not only in the West Side vicinity of Lincoln Center, "brownstone revival" neighborhoods emerged slowly during the sixties and by the eighties reached unspeakable heights when real-estate values shot through the ceiling and speculators began to reap benefits from what neighborhood residents had begun in the absence of real-estate professionals* and had achieved gradually. Chelsea, the West Village, Murray Hill, Clinton in Manhattan, and Cobble Hill, Brooklyn Heights, Park Slope, Fort Greene in Brooklyn—none of those New York neighborhoods had Lincoln Center as a stimulus, to say nothing of the row-house neighborhoods in other cities that were experiencing a renaissance about the same time. Yet in areas without any Lincoln Center, rebirth was happening, although at less inflationary rates, at the same time as on the West Side of Manhattan. It was the natural, regenerative urban process, described earlier, taking hold.

What all those neighborhoods had was good-value housing stock; diverse populations that appealed to those seeking alternatives to static, one-class living; a sense of neighborhood where people easily get to know one another; the assortment of locally run stores that

---

* Neighborhood renaissance often began as well without help from institutional lenders. Paycheck financing and borrowing from family was the route many urban pioneers followed.

provide a welcome shopping experience; accessible mass transit; diminished need for the increasingly expensive car. Such attributes made all of those neighborhoods—including Lincoln Center's West Side—so appealing. They still do.

"The draw of the West Side is natural phenomena that have nothing to do with Lincoln Center," says Sally Goodgold, a perceptive community leader and chairman of the City Club of New York. "It is an area with the best transit in the city—five bus and two subway lines. One is never more than a block from a park bench and a tree, and the whole area is sandwiched between two great Olmsted parks. That is the real mystique of the West Side, and it was here before Lincoln Center. It just wasn't discovered by overwhelming numbers because other areas, like the East Side, were more popular. The West Side has always had more to offer than the East Side, but for a long time that fact was like a big secret. Then, when the East Side got too expensive, many people were forced to consider the West Side, and the secret was out. Maybe Lincoln Center helped them know it. Is that necessarily good?"

Goodgold argues further that many of the upscale features of the West Side were already in place *before* Lincoln Center. "Upper-income families always lived on the West Side, on Central Park West, West End Avenue and Riverside Drive and in pockets of side streets. There may have been more of them on the East Side, but they were always here too. Now there are more of them. Artists too have long lived in the many beaux-arts buildings, with their thick walls and high ceilings."

Many New Yorkers and out-of-town visitors like Lincoln Center. They like the convenience to mass transit, the cleanliness and security, and the crowded excitement that occurs when all performance spaces are active at once. They don't see the emptiness between performances. Many are not turned off by its banal architecture or offended by its floating isolation (pedestrian access is basically limited to one side, Broadway, and a contemptuous blank wall on its "back" side isolates a public-housing project on Amsterdam Avenue).

Few remember, and probably fewer care, that Lincoln Center replaced 1,647 families and 383 businesses in 188 buildings, many the same kind of brownstones for which people are eager to pay extraordinary sums today. The past recedes from memory all too quickly. We are accustomed to accepting change in the name of progress without taking a questioning look backward.

Many people might not think it significant, but it should be noted that Lincoln Center has killed all remnants of neighborhood for the thousands of us who live in its immediate shadow. I can't eat at a neighborhood restaurant before curtain time without waiting on long lines. The streets are constantly overrun with honking vehicles, most with Connecticut and New Jersey license plates. The congestion is unpleasant at least, unbearable at worst. My nearest supermarket—as opposed to small, high-priced convenience food stores—is seven long blocks away. But I *can* buy ballet memorabilia, sheet music and expensive gourmet foods. I can feast my eyes on a dismal collection of new apartment houses that fetch thousands per month for a one-bedroom unit. What virtues have endured in our neighborhood—and there are some—have done so *despite* Lincoln Center, not because of it.

Again Victor Gruen summed it up nicely:

> This concentration of culture in one segregated spot is a psychoanalytically interesting confession of the feeling that our cities are so hostile to culture that only by putting culture behind figurative barbed wire can it be protected from the vulgarity of urban life. Besides, this practice denies enrichment through cultural activities to the rest of the city, giving it the stamp of pure commercialism.[14]

But my purpose here is to quarrel not with those who like Lincoln Center but with those who attribute the West Side's renaissance to Lincoln Center's creation. Lincoln Center did not rebuild a neighborhood. It tore it down. Lincoln Center did not remove blight. It just spread it around. New buildings don't erase problems, they just shuffle them from one place to the next. When the West Side was ready for the natural revitalization process to take hold, it did so. It would have done so without Lincoln Center.*

What Lincoln Center did was renew public interest in the West Side. But, as we have seen throughout this book, interest in and commitment to an area can occur in many more modest and innovative ways than massive new construction projects that require enormous public subsidies.

Lincoln Center was no more a natural descendant of Rockefeller Center than any of the overcelebrated urban retail malls are the logical stepchildren of the elegant arcades of the nineteenth century. Nor was Lincoln Center the catalyst for West Side revitalization. It was, pure and simple, an urban-renewal scheme cooked up by Robert Moses and John D. Rockefeller III in the monument-building heyday. This kind of urban-renewal program has long since been discredited. It is time for Lincoln Center to be viewed for what it is—an island of culture imposed on an urban context, and nothing more.

Isolating centers of any kind should be understood as inimical to downtown revitalization. But let's take a closer look at how thinking small in a big way can revitalize a commercial area in a city.

---

* One occurrence can hardly be called a trend, but it will be interesting to see if any other performance companies follow the lead of the Detroit Symphony Orchestra, which decided in 1988 to move out of its modern all-purpose hall with nightmarish acoustics but a good address, back to the 1919 Orchestra Hall that cellist Pablo Casals called "an acoustical marvel, a gem among the world's concert halls." Orchestra Hall's functioning in a run-down neighborhood could help stabilize and improve the area. One would not expect this to happen at Lincoln Center, but it could happen at other contemporary concert halls around the country.

OLD AREAS FLOURISH ANEW

■

A city doesn't get its character from brassy new hotels with space-capsule elevators gliding up the walls.
Nor does character come from Astrodomes or from phallic monuments to architectural egos.
Character comes from people, from the past, from tradition, from the interplay of human forces and emotions in the process of daily life.
It springs from the bazaars and marketplaces, the why and how cities began, where people could meet, buy, exchange, communicate, work, carouse, steal, fight, love, relax, be entertained and learn.

> *The marketplace is the city and the city is the*
> *marketplace and the character of a city is the*
> *measurable evidence of its markets, their continuity*
> *and their vibrance.*
> *Where those marketplaces are still closest to the*
> *people, to the streets and squares where they began,*
> *one finds a city deep and rich in character.*

—IAN MENZIES in the Boston *Globe*, March 24,
1976[1]

City malls do more than interrupt the natural urban flow so fundamentally dependent on a street system. They run counter to some
other essential characteristics of the city.

A city is not the creation of one person or one developer at one
frozen moment in time. Nor should it be. A city is an evolutionary,
ever changing organism. It has no clear beginning and no clear end.
It has something for everybody, because it was created by everybody.
The imprint of both powerful leaders and anonymous residents shape
a city. Its character is never permanently defined and shouldn't be,
certainly not by one person or corporate group, and certainly not all
at one time. That is not the urban way.

The city, in essence, is adjustable, various and decentralized. The
mall is the antithesis. Created in one act, by fiat, under single control
and formula guidelines, a mall is no solution for revitalization of
downtown. Calvin Trillin has noted: "Among the disadvantages a
traditional downtown has in trying to meet the competition of a
regional—obvious disadvantages in location and parking facilities and
design—is the handicap of not being a machine. Nobody owns
downtown. Nobody can adjust the mix."[2]

There is much a city can learn from the *operational* and *merchandising*
aspects of regional shopping malls that can be useful in revitalizing
downtowns. There are ways to learn, as the Main Street Project
illustrates, without suburbanizing downtown. To learn from and
adapt what is useful and appropriate, however, is different from

315

producing a carbon copy. The first means tinkering with the urban process; the other means erasing and replacing it.

The Main Street Project offers strategies to renew downtowns with appropriate adjustability, variety and respect for localism that contrasts so sharply with formula malls. On a more dramatic scale, developer James Rouse, in collaboration with Cambridge architect Benjamin Thompson, demonstrated at Boston's Quincy Market another strategy to make downtown lively, varied, economically innovative, and integrated with the city's physical and social fabric. And while the Main Street Project had to learn from the merchandising and operational aspects of regional malls, Rouse was in the enviable position of having developed many of them, learning those lessons firsthand.

The Rouse/Thompson Combination Was Brilliant

Rouse, a pioneering spirit with the vision and courage to take risks, was the first major developer or retailer to understand that the old patterns of downtown activity did not die because they outlived their usefulness. Rouse figured out how to learn from those patterns, just as downtown renewers had learned from shopping centers. In interviews after the success of Faneuil Hall Marketplace, Rouse pointed out that he studied vibrant downtowns for clues to what makes them function well. Even before Rouse's involvement, architect Ben Thompson and his wife and business partner Jane Thompson first proposed bringing beautiful but derelict buildings back to life by recycling the buildings into a new project, the essence of which would be "individual proprietorship with immense chaotic variety," Thompson once said. Their proposal, which they brought to Rouse after its initial acceptance by the city, was to make the *place*—a historic site—the anchor to draw the public. Purposely, they excluded national chains (this has not remained true) and a big retail anchor, a radical approach at the time. Instead, they called for a collection of small shops privately owned and managed by Bostonians, set in a lively, convenient, entertaining and historically interesting environment. Rouse responded, but his company colleagues and institutional lenders had to be unstuck from the conventional retail and lending formulas this project set out to change. Jane Thompson notes:

> It was quite presumptuous to make a plan committed to no national chains or anchors. . . . It later began to dawn on us that we had found a substitute for the deadly department store anchor: the food market in its totality. The collection of about 50 individual vendors of victuals and ready food created an event, a retailing critical mass, that acted as a central draw as powerful, in its variety, as the department store.
>
> This was especially powerful in Boston because of its authenticity: Quincy had been a food market and about 20 of the vendors were the originals from the old market. They were real people in the mom and pop sense—we worked with them, designed their new stalls, bought their goods, became friends. The essence was in those roots and those owner-operated businesses. . . . The interactive aspect of marketplace shopping must not be underestimated.[3]

Rouse and architect Ben Thompson set the pattern for the next decade of lively urban rebirth at the Faneuil Hall Marketplace when it opened in 1976. There are 150 specialty stores, markets, cafés, restaurants, food stands and apparel, gift and furniture shops in the three buildings—more than most whole Main Streets and more than many urban-neighborhood commercial strips. This marketplace combines the management techniques of the mall with the ingredients of a small-scale lively marketplace on a historic site that has served as a market since its construction. The central domed granite Quincy Building designed by Alexander Parris was erected in 1825 as a meat-and-produce market under the guidance of Mayor Josiah Quincy; thus the popular name for the market. The adjacent Faneuil Hall, built in 1742 as an assembly hall, also had served as a market, but the market function had outgrown the building. The private construction of two parallel rows of forty-seven five-story granite-faced warehouse buildings followed the Quincy Market building.

When, for the first several times, I visited the Boston Marketplace in 1977 and talked with some of the tenants, I was puzzled by their grumblings about the Rouse Company's management. Rouse, of course, had brought the tough management practices to this extraordinarily urban complex. This meant minimum-forty-page leases, surcharges galore and a commitment by the tenants to remain open six or seven days and nights a week. For many of the small businessmen who had opened there—for some it was their first time in business, for others it was a branch of a shop elsewhere—many of these practices were alien and troublesome. Rouse's rationale was that there were certain imperatives to successful management that would ensure a continuing flow of customers. These imperatives included long hours and a visible security system; a highly efficient, well-staffed sanitation system; a sophisticated retail advisory staff available to merchants whose business was sagging; design control and advice; a full schedule of public entertainment so that public events and street life were as much a draw as the shops; coordinated advertising. Each tenant shared in the benefits and the burdens.*

What made the Faneuil Hall Marketplace so genuinely special was the basic framework of historic preservation, of building new within the context of old, of recognizing the potential of what exists no matter how abused and shabby it might be, of celebrating character of place, craft, human scale and pedestrian pleasures. Similar successes of varying quality had been achieved in San Francisco's Ghirardelli Square (a former chocolate factory) and Seattle's Pike Place Market (a farmers' market threatened in the 1960s by urban renewal and saved and strengthened by citizen resistance), each of them an ad-hoc innovation. Part adaptation, part improvisation, the Faneuil Hall Marketplace is the essence of innovation accomplished on a grand scale with grand public relations to match and opening in the year of the Bicentennial, when heritage was suddenly rediscovered. The whole country noticed.

* Unfortunately, the onerous burden on all tenants of the cost of maintaining the public and common spaces at such a high level has been too heavy for some tenants, and some of the original retail balance and urban spirit has been eroded.

Site Constraints Breed Creativity

Not all credit should go to the "redoers" of such spirited urban sites. Notable successes like Ghirardelli Square, Pike Place Market, Station Square, Quincy Market, Harborplace (Baltimore) and South Street Seaport (New York) (the last two both Thompson/Rouse collaborations that followed Quincy) are as much a tribute to their unique settings—either historic buildings* or spectacular sites, often on the water, or both—as a result of originality and creative risk taking. In fact, the most interesting design work in recent years is evident in projects starting not with an empty lot but with the challenge of adding on, fitting new into old, adapting and knowing when to do the least. The current vogue of rediscovering waterfronts is very much a reflection of this. By definition, each waterfront site is automatically different and, because of the nature of the site, has to be handled differently by the redoer or redoers of each. Even if, in some cases, one developer does several—like the Rouse Company at Quincy Market, Baltimore's Harborplace and New York's South Street Seaport—the unique qualities of each site guarantee differences. Quincy Market was a total recycling of historic buildings, Harborplace a totally new construction, and South Street Seaport a combination of new and old.

Recently I served on a task force charged with recommending a reconfigured roadway along Manhattan's West Side waterfront following the defeat of the infamous Westway. Along with a roadway recommendation, we were asked to explore potential waterfront development options. Task-force members and community representatives traveled to several waterfronts to learn what others had done. The most unusual features, invariably those unique to the site, were the ones the group responded to the most strongly.

In Baltimore, it was the pedal boats in the protected harbor and the vast, lively, pedestrian-filled open space and accessible water's edge.

---

* A spectacular historic building is no guarantee of success, as evidenced by innumerable tasteless and tacky conversions. The consolation, however, is that at least the building remains standing so that a future owner can treat it properly.

In Boston, it was the recycling of a wide variety of historic buildings, including wharves for housing, and the development of new low-rise housing with an impressive mix of public benefits. In Toronto, a children's summer toy-sailing pond turns into a winter ice-skating rink, canals wind in and out of the Harbourfront, creating interesting sites at each turn, a nineteenth-century ice house has been amazingly recycled into a dance theater, and a former warehouse shed serves beautifully as artists' work space/gallery/art school in one of the most innovative projects I've seen anywhere in my travels. In Vancouver, a grand convention center/exhibition space imaginatively designed in the shape of a ship in port presides over a spectacular waterfront without overwhelming it, proving that innovation can be packaged on a grand scale. Across the bay at the terminal of Vancouver's Seabus—a waterborne mass-transit marvel—an almost empty pier with only a simple gazebo at the end exists within a stone's throw of a mix of modest housing and commercial developments and a splendid public market/shopping arcade with waterfront public space. And on Vancouver's Granville Island, theaters, art galleries, restaurants, an art school, a cement plant and other cultural and industrial uses coexist in recycled buildings on a onetime all-industrial site. The scope and variety of innovative projects is endless.

What New York officials learned from these travel experiences is hard to know. The jury is still out on this one. To the credit of task-force chairman Arthur Levitt, Jr., chairman of the American Stock Exchange, community leaders were brought into the process in a way not often seen in New York—despite the fact that of the twenty-one-task-force members only three (including me) were not city or state officials. Only because of the genuine public input was a compromise struck on one of the longest-standing and most divisive issues in the city for over a decade. The public seems to see a waterfront with an assortment of public and private recreation uses. City and state officials seem locked in a view of this waterfront as the site of future megadevelopments. Instead of viewing such an appealing waterfront as an investment, public officials speak only of the costs. Overspending on an enlarged road is not regarded in the same way as overspending on the public open spaces. Ironically, all along the inland side of this waterfront—once the site of the West Village Urban Renewal Plan mentioned earlier in the book—is an urban laboratory of examples of how to recycle and build new with respect for site and scale.

As William H. Whyte observes in *The Social Life of Small Urban Places:*[4]

> It is significant that the cities doing best by their downtowns are the ones doing best at historic preservation and reuse. Fine old buildings are worthwhile in their own right, but there is a greater benefit involved. They provide discipline. Architects and planners like a blank slate. They usually do their best work, however, when they don't have one. When they have to work with impossible lot lines and bits and pieces of space, beloved old eyesores, irrational layouts, and other such constraints, they frequently produce the best of their new designs—and the most neighborly.

Sometimes there are thin lines of difference between genuine and artificial revitalization. And, although I make an effort throughout this book to examine differences that I have observed, I seek to offer no easy answers to measuring what is genuine and what is not.

Urbanism Personified

I, for example, like the Faneuil Hall Marketplace. Many don't. Some observers say it is our consumer culture gone wild, a glorified shopping center, too artificial. Some of that—to a degree—may be true. Preservation purists argue with some of the design details and charge the whole scheme with being too prettified. Architects and designers of all kinds cite things that could be done better, from the choice of windows to the assortment of trees. Some of that may be true, too.

In fact, before architect Benjamin Thompson and developer James Rouse ever got their hands on the three Greek Revival market buildings, the city of Boston made some misguided improvements in the name of historic preservation. Gradual facade changes, ornamental additions, altered rooflines—the collection of gradual changes over time that made the complex look like a series of separate buildings—were removed (over the objections of many, including the Thompsons) to return the whole complex to its "original" style. Not only was the layering of history thereby indiscriminately removed, but the end result is an overall look of historic sameness which many discerning observers criticize. Maybe the single-pane windows are historically inaccurate and maybe there are trees where none existed originally. Complaints about historical inaccuracy and commercial excesses pale in the shadow of this ultimate people place and economic regenerator, a triumph of natural urbanism.

Aesthetic purists miss the point. Faneuil Hall Marketplace, warts and all, exemplifies urbanism at its best. Take, for example, the assortment of businesses. Side by side are the common and the unique, the chic and the cheap, the practical and the pleasurable, the chain and the first-time entrepreneur, the big and the small, high culture and low, the mass-produced and the handmade. Is that not the retail combination that once made downtowns interesting and successful? Whether it is 100 percent historically accurate in its restoration, its greatest achievement is the economic regeneration.

At Faneuil Hall Marketplace, one can have a serious business lunch as easily as a picnic. When it opened, one could visit a branch of the Boston Museum of Fine Art that eventually was replaced by stores, to the loss of the market's diversity. One can enjoy a staged performance, from magicians to musicians, or sit alone on a park bench to read a newspaper. One can pick up fresh fish for dinner or indulge in a calorie-filled delight. I, for one, had not had the pleasure of a good cotton candy or a jaw-breaking jelly apple since my childhood visits to Coney Island.

For sure, Faneuil Hall Marketplace is not, as some critics charge, like a suburban shopping mall. There is nothing "centerist" about it. One can stroll through the whole thing, easily entering or exiting from or to the civic center, the North End or waterfront areas. Like

Rockefeller Center, it is a connector to the surrounding city, not a separator. It is well defined without being contained or confined. Pedestrian passages both radiate out and flow in from the larger city without a single controlled set of entrances and exits. This is a downtown crossroad between commercial, residential and cultural uses, easily accessible from near and far by nearby public transit. For some it is the front yard of their nearby neighborhood; for others, a relief from their out-of-town suburb; for some, a tourist mecca; and for others, a retreat from the office.

The Faneuil Hall Marketplace also differs from suburban malls in its tenant mix. Although there are more chains than in the beginning (some start-up businesses have since become chains) and probably more than is desirable for depth of character, the merchandising atmosphere is not a formula mall. In August 1986, for the tenth anniversary of the Market's opening, Ben Thompson wrote a memoir in *Boston* magazine, recalling:

> Our plan was to keep as tenants the oldtime vendors who were the heart of the marketplace, together with other colorful local people. We wanted real proprietors who would run the kinds of establishments where you could meet the guy who makes the clam chowder and the one who bakes the bread. We didn't want national franchises; we wanted Boston voters and taxpayers—people who were part of the community, Sox and Celtic fans. Developers have problems with that attitude. They like banks or the telephone company or even a Hyatt hotel to take huge chunks of space. And such options were actually considered. . . . Nonetheless, we opposed institutional tenants. They may have made development sense, but in this special case they did not answer the responsibility to Boston's historic heart.

Although high fashion and slick operations dominate, the atmosphere remains of the urban market, a place of interesting aromas and social surprises, of gaiety and seriousness, romance and business. And, as in ancient open markets small and large, changes are possible and inevitable. For although this market was developed and is managed by one development company, it feels more like an ad-hoc affair, so many small creative pieces comprising an interesting whole.

Pushcart Urbanism

Perhaps the most creative economic feature of Faneuil Hall Market-place is the assortment of pushcarts. What a truly urban feature! Scattered about or interspersed with small booths serving similar functions are about thirty year-round carts inside, and an additional twenty-five outside from May through October, but their significance is greater than their numbers.

Not long after the market opened, Rouse told *Architectural Record* editor Mildred F. Schmertz:

> "We wanted to create as many independent tenants as we could, so we decided to give small merchants a chance with pushcarts. We hired a bright young woman who went all over New England identifying artists and craftsmen and small entrepreneurs with narrow specialties. She worked on 900 prospects for those 43 pushcarts, evaluating and recruiting them. We designed the carts and provided boxes and baskets to hang on them. Our standard lease with a tenant is 43 pages long and requires the merchant to have a lawyer, accountant, contractor and architect. So we created a one-page lease so that somebody could bring in his silk-screened whatevers and in a week or so he could tell if they would sell."[5]

Isn't it from pushcarts that so many of today's retail giants sprang? Wasn't the pushcart for many the entry level into the national economy? Wasn't that the starting place for the man or woman with the dream of the entrepreneur but the empty pocketbook of the immigrant?

Actually, the pushcarts started almost serendipitously. In Thompson's earliest plan, he included pushcarts in order to accommodate the nearby Haymarket vegetable vendors. Developers looking at the scheme, including Rouse at first, did not seem to take the idea seriously. But as the July 1976 opening day approached and the Quincy Building was short on tenants and real merchandise to show and sell, a substitute activity generator had to be found to give a more finished impression. Thus the idea of the pushcarts was brought forward again, and, as Jane Thompson recalls, "We put on them everything and anything we could round up." The significant lesson of the pushcart idea, she adds, is that "a small not truly original idea is successful because it accomplishes the right thing and answers a social/urban need."

The retail pushcarts were the most innovative feature of this market success story, and it has spawned similar pushcart areas in many retail centers around the country and Canada. The best descendants of the Boston model, in fact, are the marketplaces that include pushcarts—something Rouse included in both the Baltimore Harbor Place and the New York South Street Seaport markets that followed. The pushcart area, dominated as it usually is by local entrepreneurs, invariably is the one section with the best potential for variation from the national retailing formula that pervades shopping malls. The local flavor makes the difference. From Baltimore's Harbor Place to Toronto's Queens Quay Terminal at Harbourfront,* pushcarts and changing open stalls are, in fact, what often guarantees that markets don't calcify into boring formula centers.

I feel frustrated, for example, when I visit London's Covent Garden, because the vendors in the open stalls are not the same every day and I don't know what craftsman I might have missed the day before or the day after.† The pushcarts are the most interesting feature of places like Toronto's Queen's Quay which may be models of interesting nonisolating design but lack for meaningful attractions

---

* This is a conversion of an old warehouse, a project of Toronto's Olympia and York Company, designed by architect Eberhard Zeidler, who also did Eaton Centre and Ontario Place.
† On my last visit, however, I sensed from some of the vendors that the daily rentals were rising out of reach for the more unusual, just-starting-out artisans I had encountered a few years earlier.

beyond standard mall retailers, except for pushcarts and a few interesting attractions, usually related to food. Seattle's Pike Place Market, the renovated turn-of-the-century farmers' market whose long-term tenants and neighboring low-income community were fiercely protected by citizen advocacy groups,* has both a changing vendor area (an institutionalized flea market) and one of the most genuine food markets anywhere (probably because of its age and evolutionary character). A good food market—the primary tenant of the central Quincy Market building and the main feature of the Pike Place Market—is a guaranteed draw, as urban farmers' markets have always been. Some markets without pushcarts—like the Lonsdale Quay at Vancouver's Ferry Terminal, a three-story arcadelike water-front retail arcade with a farmers' market and outdoor restaurants that connects well to both an adjacent hotel and the inland area—achieve the same sense of realness by letting the food market dominate. The spirited, unplanned activity of a market achieves some of the same vibrant social interaction as the often unsuccessfully copied Italian piazzas. Traditionally, in many European cities and towns the market is physically and socially central to the community's public life, the glue that keeps people coming together, open and accessible to all, exclusive to none, drawing people for business and pleasure but, most important, just drawing people.

In their book *Public Life in Urban Places*,[6] Suzanne H. Crowhurst Lennard and Henry L. Lennard note:

> The markets are lively, with a constant buzz of con-
> versation. . . . Local residents shop there several times a
> week, using the market place as an extension of their living

---

* In 1987, the Pike Place Market was awarded the first Rudy Bruner Award for Excellence in the Urban Environment. The award, intended as a teaching tool examining the nature of successful urban change, was established by the Bruner Foundation of New York to "bring recognition to excellent urban places and encourage learning about their inevitably complex creation." The deciding factor in the market's selection was its "avoidance of Chocolate Chipification. Pike Place Market is reality." The $20,000 award was used for the market's health clinic, child-care center, food bank and senior citizens' center.

space. They pause during shopping to chat with strangers, meet friends or acquaintances, and stand talking in groups. . . . The market place is a favorite location for people watching, and for impromptu street entertainers. More formal concerts, festivals, historic pageants and special seasonal markets often draw participants and observers from a larger region who come to celebrate together.

The value of the urban marketplace in public life as a site for the constant, not occasional, exchange of goods can be significant.

In recent years, for example, New York City's historic Union Square, the East Fourteenth Street site of so many famous speeches and demonstrations, has been transformed. Millions of public and private dollars have been poured into the area's revitalization. As is true in most current reborn neighborhoods, the upward momentum of this one started with its discovery by adventurous tenants seizing the opportunity to gain spacious, appealing and economically reasonable quarters in what was considered a down-and-out commercial neighborhood. After the area was well along on the upward trend, the city responded with public encouragement that included a multimillion uplift for Union Square Park. Nothing about the redesigned park is as successful as the Greenmarket, as the farmers' market at the north end of Union Square is called. The Greenmarket predates all the other renewal efforts and was nearly pushed out by city officials with the upgrading.

Economic Incubators Are Critical

While markets can be central to the democratic lifeblood of a community, pushcarts are both a symbolic and a true return of a primary economic function of cities, incubating the new small business that eventually, with growth and success, will contribute to our national economy. In an article entitled "Putting the Horse Before the Cart," Jon Laitin reported in *Venture* magazine in February 1985:

For today's budding merchandisers, pushcarts have again become a first step toward the American dream. Reintroduced in 1976 at Boston's Faneuil Hall Marketplace, the carts are proliferating at shopping malls across the country. The phenomenon offers entrepreneurs an opportunity to test the retail waters with a minimal investment, and for some the carts can lead to shops that ultimately produce millions of dollars in sales.

Seasoned pushcart vendors compare the hands-on experience and assistance from mall managers to a college course in merchandising. Weekly leases, low rents, and ideal locations, they say, keep risks low and the potential for profits high. While the cost of renting pushcarts has increased since Faneuil Hall charged $10 a day, pushcarters pay only an average of $200 a week or $1,000 a month, and a 10 per cent fee of weekly sales over $1,500.

Laitin went on to report that several of the entrepreneurs who started on a pushcart at Quincy Market have advanced to major manufacturing and twenty-five have opened retail stores. An earmuff seller whose production started on her kitchen table expanded her line to woolen clothes and now supplies pushcarts and retail stores around the country. A pushcart vendor of wooden toys went on to open a men's-clothing store. A purveyor of merchandise for lefthanded people expanded to sell her specialty items around the country.

Local Economy Benefits, Not National Chains

More than just an incubator, the Faneuil Hall Marketplace is a stimulator of the local economy in a genuine sense. Observed Boston *Globe* columnist Ian Menzies in April 1979 in an article in *Country Journal* magazine:

> . . . in the thousands of words already written on the marketplace since its reopening August 26, 1976, one interesting aspect has been overlooked—its evolving importance as a window on New England, a reflection of a region's ways and skills. More than a third of the goods

sold in the marketplace are made in New England, the handiwork of the individual looms and workbenches of Maine, New Hampshire and Vermont, western Massachusetts, Rhode Island, and Connecticut, the products of cottage industries and small cooperatives. And, of course, there is the produce of New England's soil and sea—lobsters and apples, cod and corn, clams and blueberries.

This is what cities are really supposed to be economically—the spawning ground for the new and the innovative. Was not that the key before we reached the point where now we seem more intent on luring existing businesses from one place to the next and back a few years later, instead of nurturing the new and the growing? Cities compete among each other to lure the headquarters for the same company, when stimulating the birth of new ones has far more beneficial spin-offs. A transplanted business has a fragile connection to the locality, in contrast to the company born, nurtured and matured there.

Not every rejuvenation scheme has to be, nor should it be, on such a grand scale as the Faneuil Hall Marketplace. Nevertheless, following the remarkable success of the Boston marketplace, many developers were eager to imitate Rouse and many communities looked to a Rouse-type project as the "gold mine" and answer to their prayers. Sadly, "to Rousify" even entered development jargon. Mimicking solutions is not the same as learning from success, as we can see in the contrast between Rockefeller Center and its presumed descendants.

Beyond its commercial innovations, the most important value of the Boston success was, in a way, psychological. The skeptical were convinced that downtown commercial life is still possible and that downtown has a future. The success shook lenders' confidence in their anticity investment policies. The major problem in getting the project off the ground, Rouse explained after the opening, "was a state of mind that people have about the American city." There was, he added, "disbelief that it could work. . . . So our biggest single problem was to make people believe that this could succeed."

The staggering success sent planners and designers back to the drawing boards. It gave people much to ponder. The ingredients of this success make great lessons but defy replication. The Thompson approach, Jane Thompson has noted, "evolved from our rather unorthodox amalgam of professional experience (including forays into education, journalism, retailing, and restaurant operation), influencing whatever we do in planning and architecture and our view of what an ideal city should be." Jane Thompson also explains that they knew from the beginning there was no formula with which to revitalize the market, "no single existing prototype of the rich dynamic urban place we envisioned. Yet there were *fragmentary sources.*" The Thompsons learned from what they saw everywhere, from what they understood of the past and the present, and from urban examples both American and foreign. They looked to the American tradition of county and state fairs, the urban tradition of neighborhood markets, and the foreign markets they visited from Marrakesh to Helsinki. Added Jane Thompson, "Any successful realization would emerge, we believed, from countless small, subtle and complex details in a new combination, to form a total environmental experience of indigenous character."

Quincy Market Shattered Formula Thinking

Quincy Market has been badly imitated. Even the Rouse Company and Rouse's newer Enterprise Development Company have turned it into something of a "Festival Marketplace" formula, a routinizer instead of an innovator, which actually works only when the application has such a recognizable local stamp that it is not really a formula at all. The good news, however, is that, ten years after its success and overimitation, awareness has increased that there are other innovative ways to inject "life" back into downtowns. Variations of the market should still be considered where appropriate, but not to the exclusion of other ideas, especially risky new ones.

The Quincy Market is a model of urban innovation in the same way as Rockefeller Center is. An example of urban fabric *mending* in contrast to urban fabric *replacing,* Quincy Market offers endless lessons in Urban Husbandry.

The Rouse/Thompson understanding of urban rebirth that we see in Quincy Market is the antithesis of a development formula that began gaining in popularity at the same time—this one conceived by Atlanta architect/developer John Portman and as antiurban as any development concept could be. While the Rouse/Thompson design signature was open, street-oriented pedestrian activity, the Portman signature was self-contained, inward-oriented buildings with vast, busy and ivy-laden atria disconnected from the outside world.

The "Portmanization" of America

In the 1970s, John Portman was the country's new whiz kid of architecture, with a number of his splashy hotels/office/retail complexes either built or on the drawing boards in Atlanta (the Hyatt Regency and Peachtree Center), San Francisco (Embarcadero Center), Chicago (O'Hare Airport), Los Angeles (the Bonaventure Hotel), Detroit (Renaissance Center). Portman was welcomed by cities hard pressed to find any developer willing to invest and build downtown. For a while, his design ideas seemed fresh when architectural creativity was anything but. Portman was willing to take on the urban challenge when many viewed cities as the wave of the past. Atlanta was the new urban star, and Atlanta was the city John Portman was building. His Peachtree Center, Hyatt Regency and Peachtree Center Plaza set a new standard.

As the atria-oriented design formula proliferated, a critical view recognized confusion and deception beneath the glitz and the glamor. The most complicated cities in the world seem easy to grasp in contrast to the confusing public and retail spaces of Portman-designed developments. Columnist George F. Will, writing in *The Washington Post* in November 1982, called it "The Great American Lobby Crisis."

> . . . Indications of decadence are rife, but nowhere more
> so than in modern hotel lobbies. In such lobbies it is

possible to suffer vertigo as a result of the architecture and decor, and it is well-nigh impossible to find a quiet place to sit while waiting for the vertigo to pass.

Atlanta's Peach Tree Plaza has a lobby that Lewis and Clark could not have found their way across. Actually, the concept "across" hardly applies. It is a trackless waste in the fourth dimension. . . . In Detroit, there are, I'll wager, delegates—shells of their former selves—left over from the 1980 Republican Convention, wandering with blank stares and broken spirits along the endless concrete ramps and corridors that fill the cavernous space that should be the lobby of the Renaissance Plaza. The men nominated in Detroit should base the MX missile in that lobby. The Russians will never find it. . . .

The confusingly designed lobbies symbolized larger design problems in Portman projects. Like suburban shopping centers, these inward-bound spaces tried to put inside four protective walls what flourishing cities offer outside. They stand apart from the city, like alien islands, drawing the city's lifeblood inward as shopping centers draw it beyond the city limits. This vision remains at the heart of too many downtown schemes across the country. It is the Planned Shrinkage way of addressing urban needs as surely as Quincy Market is the Urban Husbandry way. Quincy Market leaves room for continued change and adjustment, for new ideas to grow into middle age, for eccentricities and individual expression of tenant merchants. The Portman formula leaves room for nothing but what is decreed from a central drawing board.

In every imaginable way, these approaches to urban redevelopment contrast with each other: one responds to its site, the other creates it; one is intimate and personal, the other reflects the impersonality of the formula; one is flexible and spontaneous, the other rigid and predictable; one reflects a fluctuating degree of localism, the other is devoid of it altogether; in one you feel a part of the particular city, in the other you feel like Anywhere, U.S.A.; one is democratic, the other exclusionary; one is genuine urbanism, the other a sanitized package; one reflects a love of city, the other is anticity. As many lessons can be learned from the Quincy Market about what to do with urban problems as can be learned what not to do from Portman projects. The two approaches symbolize two extremes of downtown development in urban America today.

The Portman project we will look at in detail in the final section of this book is the construction of the Times Square Marriott Marquis, also known as the Portman Hotel. This is the one urban disaster highlighted in detail in this book. The significance of the tale has many dimensions. The construction of the Times Square Portman Hotel, with the accompanying destruction of the historic Helen Hayes and Morosco Theatres, epitomizes the Portman formula and is a New York story only in its location. This is a classic urban-development struggle that has its counterparts in many cities. The ten-year history of the Portman Hotel's development embraces major changes in architecture and urban-design thinking, and it parallels, as well, the growth and maturity of both the landmarks-preservation and the urban-conservation movements.

Part Three

THE TROJAN HORSE

Big Plans, Big Mistakes

THE PAST
OVER AND
OVER
AGAIN

■

*There is no present or future, only the past
happening over and over again—now.*
—Eugene O'Neill, *Moon for the Misbegotten*

Times Square is unique. It is both the symbolic and the real heart of
the country's theater world, the ultimate theater district. It is the
Broadway to which George M. Cohan gave his regards. It is the neon
strip that Las Vegas imitated. It is the place where the New Year
begins for the nation when the ball drops from atop the former Times
Tower. It is the soul of the city that relishes its image as the cultural
beacon of the nation. It is the magnet to which every tourist is drawn,
and tourism in New York City's economy is second in importance

only to the garment industry—Times Square's neighbor immediately to the south.

The Theater District has always been a predominantly low-scale area of small interests and large surprises, where the new stands cheek by jowl with the old and where legitimate businesses operate next door to the disreputable. A special mixed-use character accompanies the dominating theaters and restaurants, but clearly the entertainment nature of the district predominates, and many of the ingredients of that area's mix, from offices to studios, are entertainment related.* Glittering gaudiness has always marked the area, and any effort to "clean it up" into antiseptic dullness misses the point.

"People can still walk through Times Square day or night and pick up a feeling of being in contact with the energy of a whole city," wrote Tony Hiss in a perceptive 1987 *New Yorker* article.[1] "Many of Times Square's businesses are family-owned and have been around almost as long as the theaters. . . . Most of the established businesses in the Square still cater to a middle-class and family crowd, and an increasing number of these middle-class customers are Black families, Hispanic families and Asian families. . . . Times Square is now on its way to becoming the first fully integrated American entertainment center."

Any urban neighborhood is infinitely more complex than it appears. This is particularly true of the Theater District, located roughly between Sixth and Eighth avenues from Fortieth to Fifty-third Street. The varied uses encompass a broad spectrum of entertainment-related businesses and many unrelated ones. Theaters, restaurants, ticket brokers, souvenir shops and small hotels are obvious. Less obvious are more than a dozen theater-related unions that are headquartered here, along with agents, producers and managers; musical instrument sales and repair shops sell to all levels of the music industry; teaching studios of all kinds are scattered throughout, although their number is rapidly diminishing. This

---

* More movie tickets are reportedly sold in the theater district's fourteen first-run movie houses than in all the rest of the city's movie theaters combined.

assortment of commercial and retail business, all spin-offs of and important to theater, depends on an inexpensive rental market not available in the high-rent midtown business district farther east.

Times Square is and always was something of an illusion—Damon Runyon *Guys and Dolls,* three guys *On The Town, Forty-second Street.* Many people look for that illusion, only to be disappointed and downright critical if they don't find it. Like the chorus girl, so appealing from afar but disappointing from the first row, this neighborhood is as flawed, human and aging as any other.

Yet the strength of the Theater District is that it sustains the illusion despite reality. It never loses its appeal to the New York native and the tourist alike. The district sustains this illusion *only* because of the theater and the theater's dominating presence. Audiences take the magic of the theater home, and the theater experience becomes the urban experience.

No Protection Against "Progress"

Over the years, and until the Times Square/Theater District became ripe for development schemes, the illusion sustained the district. It never needed defending. By the 1980s, however, the Theater District was one of the last Manhattan neighborhoods not yet under a development siege. No area exhibiting this neighborhood's vehicular congestion and clogged mass-transit facilities can be labeled underdeveloped. When city officials labeled the area underdeveloped in the early 1980s, however, they meant that not as many large office towers had yet been built there as in other areas of midtown and that the city was willing to make generous concessions to developers willing to build them. The Theater District became the new frontier for development. For the first time, it needed protection. Twenty-one legitimate theaters had been demolished since the 1940s. Theaters had become an endangered species. Whole blockfronts were being assembled for megaprojects.

Varying accounts of Times Square history reveal that speculators—conventionally called "investors"—bought Theater District land in the 1950s and 1960s in anticipation of a series of master plans sponsored by the city for the area. The name of the game was "Wait to see what happens." "Deliberate neglect, as a number of unscrupulous developers have discovered over the years," notes Hiss, "has a powerful perceptual effect: dirty, broken, or boarded-up windows, peeling paint, and a sagging cornice are painful to look at; consider the word 'eyesore.' " Under these circumstances, the district never had a chance to regenerate naturally. Some impending Plan was always in the wings to set things right. Despite this planning brinkmanship, scores of positive small things happened: new restaurants, building conversions, upgraded retail stores. There had long been room for something large, but not overwhelming, to complete a balanced equation of change.

Real-estate and political leaders promoted the misguided notion that only large-scale new building plans bring significant renewal. In New York, economic health is erroneously measured by the level of new construction. Few challenged the validity of the idea that massive new projects are necessary to revitalize a problem neighborhood.

The massive project that did invade Times Square, the Portman (now the Marriott Marquis) Hotel, highlights almost every wrong principle possible in urban-redevelopment schemes in any city. Even more, this battle evolved into a metaphor for clashing values and competing visions nationwide. The drama began to unfold long before it caught the public eye.

Planning and Zoning Changes Clear the Way

In the late 1960s, New York initiated incentive zoning—a tool that later gained popularity throughout the country. The idea was to give builders extra rentable floor space on a site in exchange for providing public amenities that might otherwise be too expensive to be in the builder's own interest.

In 1967, a special theater district was created to encourage—through such bonuses—development projects that would "save"

Broadway from decay and loss of theaters.* A builder could obtain extra bulk for a new building if it included a new theater. For each new commercial theater, creation of a new, nonprofit theater was required. This was an innovation. This provision, in fact, resulted in the construction of the Circle in the Square and the American Place Theatre, both nonprofit and both theatrically more successful than the commercial Minskoff and Uris, whose construction triggered the creation of the two nonprofits. But there was no bonus for *saving* existing theaters or, for that matter, *any* worthy existing structure.

The first important old building to be lost under the new incentive zoning was the regal Astor Hotel, replaced in 1973 by the corporate headquarters of a company, W. T. Grant, that would, in a few years, go bankrupt and vacate the new building. This die-stamped, glass-walled office tower is named, as if to mock the past, One *Astor* Plaza, and is worthy of the worst on Sixth Avenue to the east, the boulevard of textbook dreary architecture. The developer of One Astor Plaza was given extra floors because the building included the 1,650-seat, flashy and fundamentally flawed new theater, the Minskoff.

At Fiftieth Street and Broadway, another banal black steel office tower went up, graced by a lifeless, windswept plaza and containing another dismal theater, the 1,933-seat Uris. (It is perfectly fitting that both the Minskoff and the Uris theaters were named after real-estate developers, breaking the tradition of honoring talent connected directly to theater. In 1982, right after the loss of the Helen Hayes and Morosco Theatres, producer Alexander Cohen initiated a move to assure that all legitimate theaters have theatrical names. The Uris became the Gershwin, but the Minskoff remains unchanged.)

Meanwhile, the great old Broadway theaters languished. Approximately one hundred theaters were built between 1895 and 1929 with incomparable workmanship and materials, such as horsehair insula-

---

* The first provision of the law's general purpose states: "To preserve, protect and promote the character of the special theater district area as the location of the world's foremost concentration of legitimate theaters—an attraction which helps the City of New York achieve pre-eminent status as a cultural showcase, an office headquarters center and a cosmopolitan residential community."

tion, which produced excellent acoustics. These theaters are unreproducible. By the early 1970s, half of them had been either torn down or converted into pornographic-movie houses. American theater was at a low ebb, with many of the remaining Broadway houses dark much of the time.

Theater or Real Estate: Hard to Distinguish

The nature and economics of the Broadway theater had changed radically. Broadway was increasingly dominated by two theater-owning chains, the Shuberts and the Nederlanders.* Over time these two owner groups effectively replaced the independent "angels" as primary investors in productions. The Morosco and Helen Hayes Theatres were independently owned and, because of their high quality and desirability, provided stiff competition to the dominant multitheater owners. Had those theaters been part of the Shubert or Nederlander chain, Portman's hotel probably would have been built on another site.

Times Square was a favorite mayoral target. Announcements of new cleanup campaigns came regularly, often when not too much else was going on or coincidental with a new building scheme. "The war on the three P's—pimps, porn and pushers," a *Daily News* editorial once called it. Nothing much ever came of these empty efforts. A few tawdry places were closed, but prostitutes, pimps and pornographic outlets seemed to increase anyway. Each new building scheme was heralded as a great step in the efforts to clean up Times Square. The false notion that removing buildings removes social problems was thoroughly entrenched.

The Curtain Rises

So it was that in July 1973 Mayor John V. Lindsay and John Portman announced the Times Square Hotel Project, to be located on the west side of Broadway between Forty-fifth and Forty-sixth streets. Three

---

* The newest theater-owning force is Jujamcyn Theaters, Inc., with five theaters, but Jujamcyn was not active when this story unfolded.

theaters, the Morosco, the Helen Hayes and the Bijou, and one hotel, the Piccadilly, would be demolished. In its first version, the hotel was to have a new theater *underground,* seven floors of shopping, six floors of convention space, a street-level café and a full assortment of flamboyant amenities. The cost was $150 million, and it was to be *a completely privately financed project.*

Many observers thought this was just another one of those clean-up-Times-Square plans that would never happen. City officials, however, were taking no chances. Planning Commission Chairman John Zuccotti announced, the day following the mayor's announcement, that the Planning Commission would "expedite" the approval process by holding a public hearing two weeks later, August 1.* Portman needed a special permit to include a movie house and a legitimate theater in the hotel, and a zoning change to allow construction of an underground garage.

The local community board, which reviews development projects within its borders, dealt with the permit requests with the same head-spinning speed. One week after the City Hall announcement, the board's real-estate committee approved all requests. Six days later, July 25,† the executive committee of the community board met, voted approval and, without bringing the matter to the full community board, wrote a letter to the Planning Commission indicating the full group's approval. The Planning Commission held its public hearing August 1 and voted approval August 7, 1973, *less than one month after the project's announcement.*

This had to be one of the speediest approval processes—years later in court papers and public argument it would be referred to as "extensive public review"—ever witnessed on the New York development scene, where the common complaint is that developers are overburdened with a tedious and expensive public-review process. As "expedited" as it was, however, this project went nowhere.

---

* Summertime, when so many citizen watchdogs are vacationing, is a favorite time for expediting plans by the city.
† This chronology was reconstructed from records in the files of the community-board office.

Nothing stood in its way except the economics and content of the project. Portman could not get the financing, and by mid–December 1974 he announced that the project was dead. It took city officials a little longer to accept the project's hopelessness. Within days after Portman's announcement, Zuccotti met with him and was quoted in the press as saying that "it was not inconceivable that the planned hotel might be built on another Times Square site." Portman apparently was so convinced of the finality of the hotel's hopelessness that he let his land options lapse.

Washington, D.C., and Boston Say No to Portman

Not every city fell under the spell of John Portman. In 1978, Washington, D.C., resoundingly defeated a plan of his that included tearing down the National Theatre. The 1835 National Theatre is the oldest continuously operating legitimate theater in the country, where virtually every major theatrical star in American history has played and which every President since Andrew Jackson has attended. Not long before the Portman demolition proposal, the National underwent a $1 million refurbishing. Portman sought to replace almost an entire block of assorted structures with two 16-story atrium hotel/office/retail buildings. He argued against both the retention of the National and the building of a new theater in the new office tower, saying it would interfere with the design and economics of the new project. Instead, he offered to help the National raise the funds to relocate.

After considerable controversy, the Portman proposal was rejected in favor of a smaller complex of offices, hotel and stores surrounding the historic National. The National was restored completely and a hotel developed incorporating the theater.

Earlier, Boston also had resisted Portman, in the very same year, 1973, that New York was welcoming him. Warning against a proposal for a Portman Hotel on the Boston waterfront, Boston *Globe* columnist Ian Menzies wrote on March 22, 1973:

> What we have in Portman is in fact not only an architect
> but a bankrolled private developer, a combination as

powerful as any public renewal agency of old; perhaps more so. And with renewal agencies suffering from federal financial malnutrition, the private power potential of a Portman becomes extremely attractive to city administrations and chambers of commerce.

The trouble is that Portman is selling an architectural package that can be dropped on any city which gives encouragement. But what is forgotten is that though a Portman package may be good for Atlanta or Detroit or Dallas, it could be a disaster for Boston. There has to come a time when architects, planners and developers will distinguish between American cities, recognize their differing personalities and characteristics, and not place or superimpose the newest plasticized high-rise package in every American city as they would a box of nationally distributed cereal.

Boston doesn't need a Portman, even if Atlanta does; it needs a truly new and distinguished architect who can blend the future with the past and maintain a scale of values where buildings serve to complement man, not overwhelm him.

All this could have been said of New York as well. Yet, under pressure of the city's financial woes of the early 1970s, that view was not to be heard. Nothing was standing in Portman's way. To announce a big new construction project was to show that something was "being done." This is a common government habit.

Genuine Free Enterprise Gets Bulldozed, Too

In 1977, new investors purchased the 600-room Piccadilly Hotel on West Forty-fifth Street, adjacent to the Morosco Theatre. They bought the Piccadilly for $3 million and spent an additional $1.5 million refurbishing it. Erected in 1927, the Piccadilly was a 25-story building of modestly interesting architecture but great economic value. In 1980, when it was difficult to find a New York hotel room for less than $80–$120 per night, for example, the Piccadilly was charging $40–$50. The 1979 edition of *Fodor's New York* described the Piccadilly as "one of the best hotels in its area, with warmth, charm, and comfortable, adequate rooms." With an occupancy rate of 95 percent—extremely high for any hotel even during the hotel boom—the Piccadilly was a classic of that endangered species, the modestly priced hotel suitable for middle-class visitors without big expense accounts who yearn to enjoy New York.

In the true spirit of private enterprise, the Piccadilly was owned by an investment partnership in business to refurbish run-down Broadway hotels and operate them as high-quality tourist-class hotels. These investors receive no subsidies, but quietly they bring new life to a neighborhood. In 1980 the hotel earned an income of $1,250,000; not a bad business—the kind of enterprise that any economically hard-pressed city should encourage.

The Piccadilly's owners thought that they had made a good long-term investment. It was not meant to be. Mayor Edward I. Koch took office on January 1, 1978, and, soon after, his administration sought to renew Portman's interest in the Times Square project, which included the Piccadilly on the development site. Kenneth Halpern, head of the Office of Midtown Planning, became the city's coordinator for the project. Of the government promoters of Portman's plans, Halpern was the most unabashed fan of the nationally known architect. Halpern did his job so well that Portman hired him away from the city after the project was approved* but before the theaters were demolished and the hotel went up. Ironically, however, in 1976, before he became the city's shepherd for the Portman project, Halpern wrote an article about the special-theater-district zoning for *Urban Design* magazine in which he said: "There are still no provisions in the special zoning to save existing theaters, many of which are fine old buildings. Although not of historic architectural significance per se, these theaters are an integral part of New York's cultural life and certainly an attempt should be made to preserve them. To resolve this problem, an extremely simple zoning amendment has been proposed that would

---

* Planning Commission records show that Halpern left February 26, 1982. The theaters were demolished March 22, 1982.

encourage a developer to build around an existing theater." The developer would get the same bonus for preserving and renovating an existing theater as for building a new one, Halpern explained. Thirty percent of the existing theaters, he calculated, were adjacent to development parcels large enough to utilize this proposed provision. But this simple and splendid zoning amendment never happened.

In cities all around the country, wrote *New York Times* architectural critic Ada Louise Huxtable, there are old theaters "restored and adapted for modern cultural uses and serving as economic catalyst for the reawakening of downtown."[2] Certainly by 1978 some of the biggest developers in the country had caught onto the economic wisdom of recycling the solid remnants of the past. The 1976 tax-law changes gave old buildings new appeal by giving them tax advantages comparable to new construction. New investors everywhere were eagerly looking for old buildings to incorporate into new development plans. Portman's design formula with its massive interior atria left no room for the imaginative blending of old and new buildings.

Glen Isaacson, the man in charge of the project for Portman, said in 1979[3] that preserving the old theaters was "discussed," but preservation was found to be impossible because of the "kind of hotel Mr. Portman wants to build. The design is not compatible with preservation. Time is of the essence. It is vital to get on with it. The rest is emotional."

City officials were eager in 1978 to revive the Portman Hotel plan and to sweeten the pot with a piggyback assortment of subsidies that was estimated to be worth nearly $100 million. In March 1978, a *New York Times* story indicated that Portman was willing to revive his hotel plan with financial help from the city. Since land options had lapsed, "several sites," the story noted, "are under consideration," the original Forty-fifth Street site and another one across Broadway, the site of the old Bond's clothing store. The Bond site, which included no historic theaters or functioning hotel, was somewhat smaller than the original site and, therefore, unacceptable to Portman because it would mean a slight diminishment of the scale of the new hotel. Some community activists tried to interest Portman and the city in siting the hotel on the Broadway blockfront between Forty-eighth and Forty-ninth streets, location of assorted pornographic places.* "Taking over that site," says local-community-board member Barbara Handman, one of the earliest opponents of the Portman project, "would have done twenty different good things at once to improve the area, and not one bad thing. Portman wouldn't even consider the site even though it was the same size as the Forty-fifth Street site, which only shows how rigid he was."

The March 1978 *New York Times* news story also mentioned the city's intention to apply for federal funds on Portman's behalf—specifically a $15 million Urban Development Action Grant (UDAG), the popular federal grant program covering projects with substantial private investment. Eventually, this grant was increased to $21.5 million, at that time the largest grant of its kind in the country for a hotel. That generous subsidy, however, was only a portion of the total public subsidy that launched this project.

To calculate the full extent of subsidies is difficult because of the complicated formulas built into the more than 1,000-page, 12-inch thick Byzantine agreement between Portman and the Urban Development Corporation, the tax-exempt state agency to which the city turned over the project in order to expedite it unencumbered by normal review procedures. The obvious subsidies include the $21.5 million UDAG (a five-year loan to Portman at 6 percent interest that was renewed for another five years at 8 percent), a tax abatement calculated in 1979 as $33 million and an exemption from state sales tax on $15 million spent for construction products.† In addition, the hotel pays no rent for the first seven years (UDC legally owns the land) and then pays rent out of earnings, *if any,* after expenses, fees and debt

---

* In 1986 this site was demolished for a new office tower.
† These funds were put into a public-purpose-project fund that has not yet been spent. It started as $4 million but with accrued interest was worth $5.2 million in March 1988.

service.* In the end, this rent payment will not exceed the $900,000 (after seven free years), the amount the real-estate taxes would be if the property were not tax exempt.

In exchange for its generous financial support, why didn't the city pressure Portman to incorporate either the Helen Hayes or the Morosco or both into the design of the new hotel? Even most advocates of a new hotel agreed that if any other builder started with this project in the late 1970s—others were ready to step in if Portman stepped out—the old and the new would have been incorporated for good economic reasons.

"Implicit in the beginning was our willingness to accept the demolition of the Helen Hayes and Morosco," admitted Halpern, referring to the city's turning anew to Portman in 1978. *"We were looking to do whatever was necessary to get the hotel built."* No architectural or preservation group advocated alternatives.

The professional theater community valued those houses as theater, not real estate, and considered the Helen Hayes and the Morosco of superior, irreplaceable quality. "Any promise that the new theater replacing them will be wonderful is almost certain to be broken, as the record of recent theater-building in New York will bear out," said Richard Maltby, Jr., who conceived and directed the Tony Award winner *Ain't Misbehavin'*, then running on Broadway.[4] Portman's scheme would have been totally inappropriate and antiurban even if no historic theaters had stood on the site, because it destroyed a perfectly functioning city block integral with the district. The loss of those theaters, however, drew the most attention.

City leaders dismissed the importance of the Helen Hayes and the Morosco. In April 1978, the staff of the city's Landmarks Preservation Commission declared that "architecturally, the Helen Hayes is one of

---

* The minimum annual rent of $900,000 commenced with the signing of the lease with UDC in July 1982. For the construction period plus three years of operation, rent is payable out of net profits payable to the owner. After that, rent is 7 percent of gross annual revenues, with the minimum of $900,000. This obligation is abated over fifteen years, 75 percent the first year down to 5 percent in the fifteenth year of operation.

the finest theaters in the Times Square area." But the commissioners ignored their staff's judgment and did not even consider designating the theater a city landmark. This Landmarks Commission action was the critical first in a long line of acts of governmental abdication. The Landmarks Commission staff had not even been asked to evaluate the Morosco. Halpern argued that Broadway had plenty of other theaters that were better. And, he noted with pride, the city would help offset the loss by encouraging (through more tax and zoning incentive programs) the conversion back to "legitimate" use of eight small but architecturally distinctive theaters on Forty-second Street that had long ago been converted to movie houses; only one of the eight contained more than 1,000 seats and had a chance of operating without government subsidies.

This led to a curious and inconsistent position that was later embraced by countless public officials and promoted by the press. Portman defenders kept referring to the Morosco (1,009 seats) and the Helen Hayes (1,160 seats) as too small to be economic, with the Helen Hayes having the added disadvantage of a hard-to-sell second balcony. (A *New York Times* editorial referred to them as "two unused and probably unusable theaters.") The new 1,500-seat theater in Portman's hotel, they argued, would be much more appropriate in size and economics. Any landmark loss, they argued further, would be more than compensated by the city's encouragement of the reconversion and refurbishment of the Forty-second Street theaters, what the same *New York Times* editorial referred to as "eight equally old and interesting theaters." Only one of these theaters contained more than 1,000 seats, as already noted, and the rest were planned to be operated as either nonprofit theaters, retail space or movie houses—all requiring heavy public subsidies. In effect, hotel proponents were applauding a vague plan for the costly restoration of a series of architecturally worthy but economically troublesome theaters* in exchange for the destruction of two functioning and long-proven jewels whose retention was a much

---

* At the end of 1988 these theaters were still unrestored and nonfunctioning despite city promises.

better cultural and economic investment. The argument did not make sense, but it kept the project moving. By then the project had an unstoppable momentum. Government's objective simply was to get it done.

A Concrete Bunker or Else

Sydney H. Schanberg wrote in *The New York Times* March 13, 1982:

> Everybody's always trying to stand in the way of progress. Take the plan to put up the Portman Hotel—a modernistic concrete bunker worthy of "The Guns of Navarone."
>
> Just when our only hope is pushing New York City out of the crime-and-street-anarchy 20th century into what has to be a brighter spinach-salad 21st, up pop some soft-headed celebrities who oppose boondoggles and would rather lay down in front of bulldozers than get on with this sweetheart deal. . . .

Too often, when a large agency or a collection of government agencies get behind something and make commitments, leaders of those agencies are afraid to admit a mistake. It is not that they can't alter their commitment. In fact, when it's convenient, they do it all the time. Often, they argue that a commitment cannot be altered, because they fear either that entrenched powers prevent that change or that altering a commitment will show that the bureaucracy can't function. Government can't look as though it is floundering. Thus government leaders would rather stick with a bad decision.

When the Portman Hotel project was launched again in 1978, many elements in the design of the 55-story hotel had changed from the original 1973 design. The new underground theater was raised to the third story, and the street-level café was now a rooftop revolving restaurant. Most significant, perhaps, now there was a pedestrian plaza as part of the front of the hotel, a plaza which required that three blocks of Broadway traffic be diverted, allowing the hotel to be built out, over and partially on the Broadway sidewalk. Substantial subsidies, tax abatements, condemnation privileges and tax incentives and a federal grant were added now. City spokesmen insisted these were all "minor modifications." No further public review was necessary, they said, only approval of the city's application to the federal government for the $15 million UDAG.

Officials claimed that five years earlier the project had gone through an "extensive" review process. In fact only the executive committee of the local community board had approved the original project in 1973 before full Planning Commission approval, as we have seen. In one of the more blatant manipulations of the public process that was characteristic of this project from start to finish, Ken Halpern, head of the city's midtown planning office, convened a community-board committee meeting in his office, but he failed to alter that committee's position that enough had changed to require new public review. Eventually, the full community board *was* persuaded to reverse that position. Actually, throughout 1978 the city was ahead of Portman, applying for the federal grant before the developer had either acquired the land or secured the private financing.

Bypassing the Public

The city's only concern was to expedite the scheme. The project was transferred into the hands of the New York State Urban Development Corporation, thus bypassing all sorts of city-planning, zoning and taxing requirements. The UDC had been created by the late Governor Nelson Rockefeller as a quasi-public private corporation to sidestep voter referenda on bond issues for low-cost housing. It has obtained awesome power since its beginning in 1968. With the power to override local zoning, to condemn property and to write its own public-review procedures, UDC was now in the business of "economic development" and "commercial revitalization," which brings us back to the Piccadilly Hotel.

UDC can condemn private property for the purpose of removing "slums and blight" and sell or lease the condemned land to a private or public firm for an "improvement" project. That was a formidable weapon held over the resisting Piccadilly owners. News reports in 1979 made the project sound inevitable—despite Portman's long-standing and continuing difficulty in securing financing. Understandably, the Piccadilly's business was suffering. Reservations fell, and tourist groups which book a year or more in advance went elsewhere.

The city's stock of moderately priced hotels had been diminishing at an alarming rate in recent years, a common trend in large cities. A tax-incentive policy made it very appealing for owners of fading old hotels in need of repair to convert those hotels to lucrative apartment houses. On the Op Ed page of *The New York Times* October 3, 1979, Commissioner of Cultural Affairs Henry Geldzahler wrote:

> If New York is to fulfill its destiny as the London or Paris of the 20th century's last decades, midtown hotels that charge $60 to $120 a day simply will not fill the bill. These prices are stretching things even for the intended clients of these midtown hotels—middle-class tourists and businessmen, American and foreign. Our hotels are full now, but think of the visitors who stay away, discouraged by the expense. I'm thinking of students and young artists, for example, or less-prosperous families. These people need an alternative.

At first the Piccadilly owners sued to prevent their property from being condèmned. It was a difficult lawsuit. UDC's condemnation power was solid. Eventually, the Piccadilly settled and sold to Portman.

Herein lies the greatest irony—or tragedy, depending on one's view. Government agencies that were mandated to remove "blight" were obliterating one of the most nonblighted blocks in the hub of the Theater District. It offends common sense to call "blighted" a block that contains a thriving hotel, nine legitimate theaters, one movie house, restaurants and assorted other enterprises. Actor Barnard Hughes, writing on the Op Ed Page of *The New York Times* February 10, 1980, called Forty-fifth Street "the quintessential Broadway street, a concentrate of what the theater has to offer with musicals, comedy and straight drama thriving in proximity." Hughes noted that "building on the present site seems a needless sacrifice" and took issue with official claims that the properties being pulled down were "obsolete and underutilized" and that the new hotel would remove "blight" from the neighborhood. "After playing 549 performances of 'Da' at the Morosco, I have a right to take that last crazily expedient statement personally. For the business of those streets is my business. They do not contain a single porno shop or massage parlor."

The removal of blight, however, was the justification for the lucrative tax and zoning bonuses provided to Portman. The project otherwise would not be eligible for public funds. But blight removal was only one of many false premises on which the project rested.

In January 1982, late in this project's tortuous history, architect and critic Michael Sorkin wrote in *The Wall Street Journal* a scathing critique of the hotel plan. "Mr. Portman's buildings," Sorkin wrote, "are exciting without really being interesting. . . . Paradoxically, his buildings, which practically scream their aspirations to urbanity, are virtually without a sense of urbanism. . . . Mr. Portman's buildings are like giant spaceships, offering close encounters with the city, but not too close. The buildings are always adamant about their alien status."

To the hotel's proponents, Sorkin observed, Portman was "seen as a man with great vision, an entrepreneurial genius, frustrated by a planning process that smothers artistic freedom in pettiness and parochialism." And, Sorkin noted, the hotel had "undergone so many tribulations that it seems sometimes less an actual project than an icon for the byzantine conflicts inherent in large-scale urban development."

Indeed, both the architect and his project early became symbols of government's determination to prevail. Portman came to represent the Misunderstood and Unappreciated Developer in need of official protection. The hotel came to symbolize government's ability "to get things done." With every aspect of this project, the city, supported by state and federal agencies, acted as if every question raised, every

disagreement voiced, every alternative offered and every legal challenge and every economic doubt voiced were obstacles to be overcome or ignored.

The most common defense of the Portman plan heard from city
officials during the 1979–80 height of the controversy was that the
city could not renege on its commitment to an important developer
like Portman. If it did, said officials, the city's word would be mud
among developers, who would then, presumably, take their business
to Kansas City or Houston. That was patently ridiculous. Far-flung
developers were spending plenty of their own money at the time
planning New York City projects for which they had no guaranteed
approval.

And who was worrying about government's commitment—and
obligation—to do right by the resident public? What about its
commitment to private property owners who invest their own
money with no government help to upgrade their property, as the
owners of the Piccadilly had done? Projects that once seemed right
but now are wrong remain impossible to refashion, because they
develop their own irreversible momentum.

Through all of the controversy and the temporary detours it
caused, Portman showed remarkable endurance and political savvy.
When the federal UDAG was not approved in the final days of the
Carter Administration, at the end of 1980, Portman rearranged his
project partners to make things politically attractive to the incoming
Reagan Administration. The designated hotel operator of the project
up to that point, according to government papers, had been Trust
House Forte Ltd. Suddenly, it became the Marriott Hotel chain. J. W.
Marriott was chairman of Ronald Reagan's finance committee during
the 1980 national campaign. Within three months after Reagan's
inauguration, despite the new Administration's early intention to kill
the whole UDAG program, Portman's UDAG was approved.

Public Opposition Is Ignored

While Portman was reviving the project and trying to line up his
financing, opponents tried to mount an effort to save the theaters. A

Save the Theaters Committee was organized in 1979 by Actors Equity, initiating a long series of protest activities. Petitions were circulated, gathering more than 200,000 signatures. Ads were taken in *The New York Times*. Rallies were held, the first one in February 1980. In late 1979 and early 1980, Joan K. Davidson, a longtime sensitive urbanist willing to publicly oppose inappropriate development schemes irrespective of the power of the proponents, organized a group called Save Our Broadway (SOB) to formalize the efforts of the few preservationists and community activists willing to take this fight to court. In a short time, this effort merged with the Save the Theaters group.

Save the Theaters organized thoughtful testimony on the irreplaceable qualities of the existing theaters for every public hearing. Film and stage stars met privately with everyone possible from Koch to Portman. The list of supporting actors, playwrights, critics and scene designers read like a who's who of stage and screen, including President Reagan's close friends Charlton Heston and James Stewart. At every turn, public officials accused these artists of sentimentalism and emotionalism that had nothing to do with the real world of economic development and progress.

It took two years and two lawsuits to get city, state and federal-government officials, first, to acknowledge that the Morosco Theatre had been overlooked as a potential historic landmark eligible for listing on the National Register of Historic Places and, second, to examine the arguments and evidence for its designation and permanent protection. On November 17, 1981, the Department of the Interior designated the Morosco eligible for the National Register, noting that the theater was an excellent example of "functional theater design" and citing its noteworthy scale and sightlines and its particularly notable acoustics. And even if the architectural reasons for preservation were not sufficient grounds, wrote report author Jerry L. Rogers, the department's keeper of the National Register of Historic Places, "the Morosco's disinguished record of association with important plays is strong enough that it would be eligible."

Pressure Politics: The Bottom Line

It may have taken two years for the Interior Department to declare the Morosco a national landmark, but it took the Advisory Council on Historic Preservation, a presidentially appointed body with an underexercised mandate for independence, less than two days to approve the Morosco's demolition. The Council is supposed to seek alternatives to destroying a landmark, a process that normally takes weeks and sometimes takes months. In the record-breaking short period that it took the Council to seal the fate of the Morosco, there was no public hearing (these hearings are customary but not mandatory). Advisory Council Chairman Alexander Aldrich insisted that the Council's decision was not made under strong political pressure, despite phone calls from Lyn Nofziger, White House political chief under President Reagan, and Interior Secretary James Watt, and despite the fact that the Council was being threatened with the loss of its budget. According to sworn statements, Nofziger called Council officials on November 17, 1981—the day the Interior Department declared the Morosco a national landmark—and ordered them to approve the Morosco's demolition "by the close of business" on November 20 or else the White House would put the Advisory Council out of business. Also according to affidavits, Watt delivered the same warning but through staff intermediaries.

Ironically, the federal Advisory Council on Historic Preservation considered the Helen Hayes quite a landmark, enough so to force the developer who would destroy it to pay for architectural drawings of it. The drawings, rather than the building, would be preserved for posterity in the national Historic American Buildings Survey. For the Morosco not even the drawings were demanded.

A lawsuit also was necessary to force the city to comply with the required environmental-impact review process. Since project approval already had been given, compliance was in form, not in substance or spirit. This procedure was one of the most intellectually dishonest chapters of the entire saga. The air-quality analysis included in the Environmental Impact Statement,* for example, was based on an eight-hour average *which did not include the 7-to-8 P.M. precurtain hour, when Theater District traffic is at its height.*

The City Could Have Had It All

One of the most basic rationales for the environmental review process, for which the environmental-impact statement is supposed to be the working analytical document, is to first determine if a planned project will have a negative impact on the environment and, second, devise alternatives to avoid them. Eight months before the demolition of the theaters, but *long after* the environmental review process was over, a UDC executive confided in a private meeting with a Save the Theaters director, Lenore Loveman, that the issue of an alternative design of the hotel to save the theaters had *never* been explored. Alternatives referred to in the EIS were alternative sites, not designs. The UDC official sketched crudely the hotel built over the theaters, suggesting that if the Save the Theaters Committee had an architect explore this possibility, UDC would have to examine it. Loveman took the sketch and gave it to award-winning architect Lee Harris Pomeroy, a member of the local community board and a critic of the hotel's design. Pomeroy set to work immediately and produced a feasibility study that showed that building over the theaters was decidedly possible. The Pomeroy plan—meant only to show the build-over's feasibility, not meant to be a definitive design— eliminated the proposed new 1,500-seat theater, saved the two existing theaters, retained all the Portman features, such as atrium, exhibition halls, restaurants, lobbies and retail shops, but made access from the street easier and eliminated the need to build over and onto the Broadway sidewalk.

City and Portman spokesmen argued that the alternative was not feasible (corroborative studies were never produced, though they were asked for during litigation), would take too long, would be too

---

* This is the official environmental review document in which all the analysis appears.

costly and would destroy the entire project. Although they claimed that the Pomeroy alternative presented a structural problem by spanning the old theaters, Portman's proposal included a 120-foot span over *his* theater, while the Pomeroy redesign required only a 90-foot span over the Helen Hayes and the Morosco. Pomeroy's plan was taken no more seriously than the entire four years of thoughtful opposition.

Only two years earlier, when Rockefeller Center moved to demolish Radio City Music Hall because it was allegedly no longer profitable, another architect, Lewis Davis, showed how an office tower could be built over that theater, thus making it possible to save the Music Hall *and* build a profitable office tower, if the city were to approve such a project. The Music Hall is a sizable building to be spanned. Building over existing buildings was not an unknown feat. Clearly the theaters could have been saved *if* Portman had wanted or if either governmental agencies or funding sources had demanded that he do so.

Chapter Sixteen

THE QUESTION IS WHY

Concrete Bunker or Else

■

Everyone knows what. The question is why.

—DASHIELL HAMMETT

Not blind opposition to progress, but opposition to blind progress.

—ANONYMOUS

March 22, 1982. It is windy and bitterly cold. The gray morning sky threatens more of the sleet and snow that for the past month have steadily covered New York City streets. Despite the dismal weather, a crowd gathers early on West Forty-fifth Street, and a steady stream of people continues to arrive. By 9:30 A.M., police estimate that the swelling crowd has already reached a thousand people.

They gather around a makeshift stage that, for weeks, has been the central arena of public protests in one of the most significant urban-development battles of recent decades. The outdoor stage stands in front of the famed Morosco Theatre, where seven Pulitzer Prize–winning plays first made American theater history and where even an actor's quietest words could be heard in the balcony without electronic amplification.

Not just the Morosco Theatre makes this block unusual. This is West Forty-fifth Street between Broadway and Eighth Avenue, the core of the world's richest theater district. Here are *eight* of Broadway's greatest theaters—Booth, Plymouth, Royale, Golden, Bijou, Morosco, Imperial, Music Box and, across Eighth Avenue, the Martin Beck—more theaters clustered in one place than on any other Broadway block, and probably more marquees in one line than on any other street anywhere. It is a one-of-a-kind urban ambience. In midblock is historic Shubert Alley. West Forty-fifth Street is quiet but very much alive. Not one visible illicit use—no porno shop, no Times Square sleaze—mars this most vital of urban streets. Yet expert urban planners and government officials, in whose hands rests the fate of city life, have declared this block "blighted."

One theater on this incomparable street has already been torn down—the Bijou, one of Broadway's useful small houses—along with the world's largest billboard facing Broadway, where movies and beer proclaimed themselves to the world. The Morosco is destined to join the pile of rubble on this blustery March day, along with the equally famed Helen Hayes behind it on Forty-sixth Street. Scheduled to fall as well is the Piccadilly Hotel. In all, three legitimate theaters, the Piccadilly, two movie houses (both of which once had been legitimate theaters), several restaurants and a small assortment of retail shops and offices will disappear to create the site for the Portman Hotel.

In place of this assortment of buildings and uses will come John Portman's self-contained megastructure, one of the world's largest hotels—1,876 high-priced rooms. In deference to the glittering signage that is the hallmark of the Great White Way, a curved billboardlike sign, so out of step with Broadway's glittering signage, will be included over the hotel entrance.

The design of this hotel is an exaggeration of the forbidding, fortresslike towers rising in many American cities in the past decades, the definition of urban vitality accepted or promoted by planners, architects, government funders, financial institutions and public officials. The blank gray walls of this hotel look like corrugated metal in cement and stand in deadening contrast to the lively and colorful, even if troublesome, street below. People inside are well protected and insulated from the people outside.

The crowd gathering on this dismal March Monday clings to a different urban vision. Thousands of protestors, some of them the most familiar names of American theater, have been coming to this site during the past month in a final attempt to force a humanizing redesign of the new hotel, one that would at least preserve the irreplaceable historic theaters, if not the other elements of urbanity that characterize the block. They were not opposed to a hotel, but they wanted one that would not destroy the theaters and the Theater District in its wake. But this March day will see the final curtain fall on a drama running more than two and a half years.

Both the demonstrators and the demolition crews are gathered in anticipation of a Supreme Court decision on a legal motion to block the demolition of the theaters. After six months of legal efforts in state and federal courts, it is clear that the technicalities of the case, as distinguished from the merits, will determine the outcome. Several court decisions have delayed the end, but the courts deferred resolution of substantive issues to the administrative agencies. Courtroom deliberations never reached the stage of the merits of the argument.

In addition, the true dimensions of the issues and their significance in the post–World War II history of urban destruction have not been given well-deserved press coverage until the very end. Even now, it is the demonstration that finally draws media attention. Until then the Portman project primarily has been covered as the "long-stalled" and "rescued" project that would be the "linchpin," "centerpiece" or "key" to the revitalization of the "decaying and crime-ridden," "ramshackle" or "deteriorating" Times Square area. The landmark quality of both theaters and the early designation of the Helen Hayes as a national landmark were facts obscured in press coverage. Press stories reported the official view of what was "promised" to be gained, not what was being lost. Three days *after* demolition began, however, *The New York Times* carried a prominent article about how carefully the "artworks" of the Helen Hayes were being dismantled and preserved. There were photographs of the elaborate cupids, statues and other decorative plasterwork of the landmark theater. No mention of these artistic embellishments existed in any of the earlier pre-demolition stories about the hotel project.

Drama to the End

Producer Joseph Papp orchestrates the drama's final scene. Until now, he has done little in this fight. Papp is a short man with a large ego and a sharp tongue. He knows how to take full command of a situation and focus national attention on it. This is what he has done in the final moments of the fight to save the Morosco and the Helen Hayes. With Papp staging this effort a year earlier, the script might have had a different ending.

On this March day, Papp has been on the street since 8 A.M. During the previous weeks of constant demonstrations on West Forty-fifth Street, he and his equally energetic and determined wife, Gail Merrifield, have been headquartered in the Piccadilly Hotel next door to the Morosco. Whether on the street with a microphone or in the hotel room with a telephone, Papp is a tireless demon. He seems never to sleep. He has tried to change the mind of everyone from Mayor Edward I. Koch to President Ronald Reagan. Somehow, he expects reason and rationality to prevail. Until the final moments, he expects to win.

For the last scene, Papp's voice is hoarse. He has been on the phone arranging details with the New York Police Department for a peaceful act of civil disobedience and arrest. He has talked late into the night, explaining to the assembled theater stars all that is involved in the planned protest in which they have agreed to participate. Before the final curtain, Papp is going to make sure that the world knows what has happened on Forty-fifth Street. The American press is represented now in full force for the star-studded finale. Even Japanese television is there to carry the day's proceedings.

Word of the Supreme Court's decision is expected from Washington at 10 A.M. Colleen Dewhurst, Celeste Holm, Raul Julia, Estelle Parsons, Richard Gere, Treat Williams, Christopher Reeve, Michael Moriarity and Susan Sarandon have all gathered on stage with Papp. Three weeks earlier on that same street stage, despite a wet, driving snow, an all-star cast participated in three days of speeches and a round-the-clock marathon reading of plays that had been presented at the Morosco and the Helen Hayes, including eight Pulitzer Prize winners.* Jason Robards recited from memory from O'Neill's *Long Day's Journey into Night,* in which he had starred at the Helen Hayes. It was a performance of remarkable quality. The audience was hushed; it was "one of street theater's finest hours," noted *New York Times* reporter John Corry. Robards delivered the lengthy speech in which the father, an actor, tells his younger son how he was ruined by "the promise of an easy fortune" and how by surrendering to commercialism he had ruined his life. "I'm so heartsick, I feel at the end of everything," Robards said with a turning glance at the Morosco behind him.

Yet by D-Day—Demolition Day—and the end of the three weeks of intense street activity and press coverage, it was obvious that destroying theaters to revitalize the Theater District did not have to make sense in order for it to happen.

The crowd waited. Word came about 10:30 A.M. Papp interrupted a reading of *Strange Interlude,* solemnly took the microphone and announced, "These theaters are going to come down. The Supreme Court has lifted the stay."

---

* Eugene O'Neill's first Broadway play, *Beyond the Horizon* (1920), George Kelly's *Craig's Wife* (1926), Thornton Wilder's *Our Town* (1938), Arthur Miller's *Death of a Salesman* (1949), Tennessee Williams' *Cat on a Hot Tin Roof* (1955), Charles Gordone's *No Place to Be Somebody* (1970), Michael Cristofer's *Shadow Box* (1977)—all at the Morosco; O'Neill's last Broadway production, *Long Day's Journey into Night* (1956), at the Helen Hayes.

There was silence. No one moved. About two hundred of the assembled awaited further direction from Papp, who had worked out in detail the scenario to follow this announcement. Followed by Colleen Dewhurst, José Ferrer, Celeste Holm, Richard Gere and other stars, Papp slowly descended from the stage and quietly walked across the street to the demolition site. Drums rolled. Bagpipes skirled.

Suddenly and unexpectedly, an independent spirit grabbed the mike on the stage and yelled, "Shame on Koch!"

Those words became an angry chant as hundreds of protestors moved past police barricades with the intention of peacefully submitting to arrest. The chant was the only improvisation in the well-orchestrated act of civil disobedience. Once all those who chose to be a part of the mass arrest were assembled on the site, a police officer announced to the crowd that they would be arrested. Actress and tireless opposition leader Sandy Lundwall stood, five feet tall, still as stone, red hair blowing, in front of all the protestors, staring defiantly at the crowd of police and demolition workers. Within minutes, a score of police fanned out among the demonstrators, each instructed to tap five or six people on the shoulder and escort them to a paddy wagon. Within minutes, 170 people filled thirteen police vans. Many more protestors tried to be arrested, but once the thirteen vans were full the police wouldn't take any more. A mixed spirit of conviviality, sadness and numbness pervaded the group as they rode in the dungeon-dark vehicles to a nearby station house. Each was booked on a charge of criminal trespass and released. En masse, they returned to the site, the pink summons slips pinned to their coats with black ribbons as badges of honor.

Back on Forty-fifth Street, they sang "Give My Regards to Broadway" and "America the Beautiful." This time they stayed behind the barricades. The fight was over. Now they were there to watch the final curtain. The demonstrators waited for the bulldozers to get to work, still hoping for some last-minute miracle. The demolishers, in turn, waited for the final word that all legal impediments had been removed. Shortly before 2 P.M., the battery of lawyers for the state and for the Atlanta developer arrived at the site to watch the final moments. They had, during the past many months of court appearances, wrongly insisted that the hotel could not physically be built over and around the two historic theaters—only one of many deceptions. They had claimed that Portman's financial package was secure long before it was. (Portman claimed this for three years before it was true.) Portman had repeatedly said that if he were forced to redesign the hotel he would drop the project. His lawyers had told the courts that it would take at least eighteen months to redesign the hotel to accommodate the theaters if it could be done at all, and in that time the project would die. Yet almost eighteen months passed from the first time the lawyers made that claim until the site was actually cleared.

Shortly after 2 P.M., the operator of the giant-clawed wrecker slowly edged his machine toward the side wall of the Morosco. The wrecker's massive jaws bit at the wall again and again until the first bricks fell. The august walls of the Morosco put up their own brave resistance, but, when the dust had settled, the first gaping hole appeared. One could see the chandeliers still hanging inside. Also visible was some of the sparse ornament that graced the proscenium. Modest elegance was the word for the Morosco. It did not have the excessive embellishments of a 1920s movie palace or the elaborate ornamentation of the Helen Hayes. In fact, the Morosco was purposely designed in understated fashion in 1917 by its architect, Herbert J. Krapp, so as not to detract from what was happening on stage. The beauty, the appeal and, yes, the perfection of the Morosco were in its totality as a theater.

Actually, few people outside the theater world fully understood the true importance of the Morosco until too late. By the time government officials understood what they were helping to destroy—if they did at all, or cared—they did not want to interfere with the political process to stop the needless demolition.

The intractability of the project's promoters and the unwillingness of political bystanders to get involved was the source of the opposition's greatest frustration, as it is so often in all similar urban conflicts. Barbara Handman, vice-chair of the local community board and one of the project's earliest outspoken critics, was constantly, quietly and ever so politely alerting a variety of political and governmental leaders to the dangers of this project. Handman, a longtime political activist on local and national levels, was one of the few among the opponents with enviable access to centers of power. Her alarms, however, remained ignored. At one point, in uncharacteristically exasperated tones, she noted, "This project is like the Rock of Gibraltar. It cannot be moved. I know you can't move the Rock of Gibraltar, but this thing isn't even here yet!"

When I wrote my first article on the subject of the Portman Hotel controversy, in *New York* magazine in November 1979, it was titled "Save the Helen Hayes." That theater was the more obvious architectural treasure, with its heavily embellished exterior and interior. By the time I stood watching the giant claw rip at the 1,009-seat Morosco two and a half years later, I had learned well from theater people that the Morosco was the greater treasure, and that its incomparable acoustics and sightlines and its magical intimacy made it one of the best theaters Broadway had to offer. Besides its physical appeal, the Morosco was as historic a theater as any on Broadway. American theater began at the Morosco with the 1920 opening of O'Neill's *Beyond the Horizon,* the first play to come out of the American experience. Prior plays are considered European imitations or replications, but with *Beyond the Horizon* American theater found its own voice.

Only the final scene of this American theater tragedy was played out on the public stage. As in similar tales in too many cities, the real action had already been played out off stage and behind the scenes.

Demolition Was Priority

On March 22, 1982, the theaters went down, but three months later Portman's financing was still not secured and the final closing between Portman, the lenders, the city and UDC had still not occurred. Portman was having trouble coming up with the $18 million he needed to exercise his option to buy the Piccadilly Hotel.

As Jack Newfield reported in the *Village Voice* that June 15:

This is all curious, because during the lengthy litigation process, several top officials of the Portman Corporation testified under oath that even the slightest delay might be fatal; that delay would increase debt service and the costs of construction by $2 million each month. The Portman Company also submitted affidavits assuring all the financing was already permanently in place. This latest delay and extension of the option suggests possible perjury by Portman executives when they were trying to rush the demolition of the Helen Hayes and Morosco theaters.

Portman finally purchased the Piccadilly and closed the deal by summer, signing the lease July 2.

In the end, the hotel was redesigned anyway, not to preserve the two historic theaters but to eliminate the Broadway mall in front of the hotel. With the mall, the front portion of the hotel would have projected out to the street, the sidewalk below would have been taken up by two sizable hotel escalators, and a pedestrian mall would have been created out of three blocks of Broadway. The first hint of public disapproval with the mall had come in a *New York Times* editorial on October 1, 1981, entitled "Misguided Mall." The demolition of the theaters and the construction of the hotel were reasonably assured before this editorial objection to the mall appeared. Noting the generous federal grant that would help pay for "a private preserve out front" of the Portman Hotel, the editorial said, "At the risk of sounding ungrateful, we still think the project is a poor idea . . . all the enthusiasts ought to think again. Do they really want to enlarge the scope for Times Square's prostitutes, drug salesmen, three-card-monte dealers and derelicts? And do they want to live with the chaos that will result from choking off Broadway traffic for two crucial blocks?"

The city postponed the approval process for the Broadway mall until after demolition of the Helen Hayes and the Morosco. If that public process had preceded demolition, it would have revealed that a redesign of the hotel was inevitable. Thus a truthful analysis of the alternative to build over and preserve the Helen Hayes and the Morosco was never meant to be. Proponents of the hotel—including the newspapers, led by *The New York Times*—who had not been on the side of altering the hotel favored killing the mall. Quietly, after the old theaters were gone, the mall project was dropped.

The final insult of the long battle came with the completion of the building. The new theater in the hotel—Broadway's first new theater in a decade and the rationalization for the destruction of the Helen Hayes and the Morosco—was seriously flawed and lacking in promised provisions, because of the constraints of the building's design. Though the theater had been promised as a state-of-the-art facility, its backstage space, scenery hanging height and loading access, and dressing rooms did not even meet normal standards, let alone surpass those in the two theaters it replaced. *And the city had granted the developer a bonus of 25 percent more building space for the promise of a new state-of-the-art theater.* Every insufficiency of the new theater that allegedly caught city officials and theater-industry leaders, Portman hotel supporters all, by surprise had been flagged by project opponents even before demolition of the historic theaters. At this point, as regularly happens when builders defy the permits approving construction, city officials considered no serious penalty. The resolution, in fact, was this: in exchange for releasing the hotel from the requirements of the special permit under which it was built, the City Planning Commission required that the theater be made available for one month a year for the use of community groups, *if it is empty.* The theater's first production, a revival of *Me and My Girl,* was a smash hit, and as of the end of 1988 the theater has never been empty.*

---

* The backstage defects of the theater were so terrible and hazardous that Actors Equity threatened to close down *Me and My Girl.* Fumes from the driveway under the theater permeated dressing rooms, backstage heating was so poor that temperatures sometimes dropped to 40 degrees, causing illness in the cast, and plumbing problems brought noxious fumes backstage. Those were only some of the problems. Actors Equity demanded either correction of defects or extra pay working under dangerous conditions. The matter had to go to arbitration and by mid-1988, the problems were reportedly being corrected.

Appropriate Change Never Had a Chance

The Portman controversy reflected a dramatic confrontation between two distinct approaches to urban development.

Opponents were repelled by the bulldoze-and-replace approach that had been changing the face of American cities since the 1950s. They advocated less drastic solutions based on sound economics, the kind of creative development that had already proven to be appealing, durable, labor-intensive and profitable. They favored the kind of reasonable, nondisruptive change that ensured some degree of continuity of character, scale and heritage. It was a conservative view—one that favored conservation of energy, resources, money and quality. It was a view that broke with decades of projects that exalted the new and brassy at the expense of the old, gracious and enduring.*

Hotel proponents held a view firmly rooted in the bulldozer approach which, like urban-renewal projects of earlier days, promised jobs, increased tax revenue and improved real-estate values. It was the all-the-eggs-in-one-basket approach: Start something big, and new big things will follow.

In this game, government's role is to nourish the big project with tax incentives, zoning bonuses and funding subsidies, in the name of "encouraging" development. This is called "forging a partnership." In this partnership, government's role is to help "get things done," whether overcoming the knotty problems of assemblage, with threats of condemnation speeding the public review process, or providing direct subsidies.

---

* Even Portman was capable of appreciating old, gracious and enduring buildings, if they did not stand in the way of one of his new buildings. When, after the Times Square fight was over, the 1911 Georgian Revival Capital City Club in downtown Atlanta was threatened with demolition, Portman called for its preservation. "There are things in every community which are footprints of the history of the city," he told *The New York Times.* The club is surrounded entirely by towers of concrete and glass, some of them designed by Portman. He also opposed plans for a three-story elevated walkway from the century-old Georgia State Capitol to a legislative office building because it would destroy the architectural purity of the gold-domed landmark.

This game-playing tragically guarantees perpetuation of the urban-development trap. Bigness is promoted for its own sake. The bankrupting cycle of heavy public subsidies continues. Progress is measured by the Big Change standard. Worst of all, the benefit of modest, conservative change goes unrecognized.

In these conflicts, promoters of ill-conceived development plans inevitably argue that "time is of the essence." When time instead of substance is of the essence, the project has taken on a momentum unrelated to the quality of the content. Time is really an excuse. If something must happen at a given moment or not at all, it probably lacks any inherent justification.

The High-Stakes Poker Game That Is Real Estate

A universal theme was articulated by the Portman Hotel advocates in a September 13, 1979, *Daily News* editorial that identified the Portman project as "the greatest hope" and declared, "This soaring glass-and-chrome dazzler could become one of the city's great tourist attractions, drawing an army of visitors, inspiring other investors and developers, driving up property values, driving out the sin merchants."

The editorial acknowledged "questions" raised about the giveaway nature of the scheme and called for "city lawyers" to "check terms of the deal carefully to protect the public interest." In fact, those questions were first raised publicly by *Daily News* columnist I. D. Robbins in a stinging column that same month questioning the financial arrangements of this "sweetheart deal." The *Daily News* editorial, however, noted: "The bottom line is simply this: The Portman Hotel as a redevelopment magnet is worth a reasonable incentive." (One wonders what an unreasonable incentive would be.)

That was the key. The Theater District had become the newest pawn in the high-stakes real-estate poker game. Let the hotel proceed; other towers would follow. No one was asking what would be left of the Theater District after the kingly towers moved in. The concern was not for the Theater District, after all. "Removal of blight" was a code phrase. The true interest of the hotel's proponents was exclusively the development of real estate at the highest profit.

Kingly Towers Keep Getting Bigger

In 1984, two years after demolition began on the Morosco and Helen Hayes Theatres, a public hearing was held on another Times Square revitalization plan. To accommodate the large number of people expected to testify for and against, this hearing was held at historic Town Hall, the nearby 1922 McKim, Mead and White landmark.

The subject of the hearing was a $1.6 billion plan to rebuild Forty-second Street, to attack the grime and crime of that celebrated thoroughfare from Broadway to Eighth Avenue, which clearly has more and deeper problems than most other streets. The proposed plan provided for the building of 4.1 million square feet of office space in four towers—two of which would be twice as bulky as zoning normally allows—ranging from 29 to 56 stories, a 2.4 million-square-foot merchandise-and-apparel mart, a 500-room hotel/retail complex, and direct and indirect government subsidies of incalculable value. No one knew for sure what to do with the much-abused Times Tower, which, although sorely in need of redoing,* still anchored the physical configuration—where Broadway and Seventh Avenue intersect—that gave Times Square its name. The plan called for replacing it with open space.

Town Hall was filled with proponents and opponents of all kinds. Opponents didn't get to speak—unless they were elected officials—until after 5 P.M., when all the press were past their deadlines and gone. Among the proponents were ministers, housewives and theater producers saying that drug dealers, prostitutes and every other kind of criminal make the district unbearable and that anyone opposing this plan obviously was working on the Devil's behalf. Architects, preservationists and actors testified that the plan would sanitize Times

---

* The Times Tower was remodeled in 1966 and renamed the Allied Chemical Tower in honor of its new owner. *The AIA Guide to New York* notes that "the original Italian Renaissance terra-cotta skin was stripped off and replaced with Miami Beach marble."

Square into a "crossroads not worth coming to" and so inflate real-estate values as to price out of existence all but the remnants of the theater-related businesses in the Theater District to the north and the business of fashion in the Garment District to the south.

Governor Mario Cuomo began the hearing by proclaiming, "What we now have is the largest, best-designed, most carefully planned redevelopment project in the nation. . . . It will restore Times Square, rejuvenating its physical surroundings, redeeming its soul." There were, he said, only two choices,—one, "to do nothing, to wait, to hope, to expect that somehow, someday, the tide of the past two decades will reverse itself and Times Square will gradually become again what it once was," or the second and "only real choice," to "rebuild the entire area in its totality, massively, drawing together the resources of the city, state and private sector." All over the country and in New York City were examples of choices many degrees in between, but with one brushstroke the governor made it clear the direction was set.

Mayor Koch followed and endorsed the same two-choice vision, but added, "If you want to improve what we are doing, tell us how to improve it. Maybe you are right, maybe you are wrong. It will all be examined, but do not just knock it."

The Public Process Is Mocked

The public process, in which all opinions were invited, would allow for ample criticism, was the promise, but the public was challenged to be for or against the project, period. There would be room only for tinkering with the design of the plan, some minor changes here and there, but nothing to alter the basic overwhelming scale that unavoidably accompanies the concentration of 4.1 million square feet of office buildings. The scale and the style of the vision were set. Any change would be merely cosmetic. Only a change of heart by the developer could alter things to any substantive degree. Government clearly had made its commitment. This was another project with its own life and its own irreversible momentum.

With this announcement, the city and the state broke an earlier commitment to guidelines assiduously worked out with public involvement that would have, in some limited measure, retained the spirit and razzle-dazzle of Times Square. The commitment to the public in this case, apparently, was not binding like the commitment to the developer in the Portman case.

Under this new plan, the heavy concentration of crime-inspiring sex shops and video arcades might disappear from Forty-second Street, but so would the eye-level extravaganza of bright lights, blinking signs and ever-changing billboards that mark the colorful core of Times Square. Banks, law firms and advertising agencies would replace as tenants the theatrical agents, costume designers and rehearsal studios that are the meat on the bones of the Theater District.

There were promised trade-offs, in the form of nine restored legitimate theaters and a $70 million rebuilt subway station, but no guarantees and no questioning of whether they were even worth the price tag. These, of course, were the theaters the city had promised years earlier would compensate for the loss of the Helen Hayes and the Morosco. They remain in 1988 in their unrestored, unused and unresolved state.

The Negative Impacts Will Be the Next Decade's Albatross

Government studies predicted that traffic and air-pollution problems would be enormous. Area thoroughfares were already choked with traffic and often nearly impassable, but somehow, officials promised, these problems would be "mitigated." The 880-page draft study of the environmental impact of the plan predicted that many of the sex-related enterprises would move north on Broadway to the Forty-seventh-to-Fiftieth-Street area. There wouldn't be such a large concentration of them, however, the report noted as if to answer the rhetorical question of why spend $1.6 billion just to have them move a few blocks away. The subway stations that are now unbearable because they can't accommodate the crowds of people that use them would somehow be redesigned so that *more* people could wait less unbearably for the same subways.

As expected, there was a loud chorus of opposition at the public hearing, not to the idea of a major Forty-second Street development effort but to this particular plan that was so out of step, scale and style with a legendary place worthy of a future. Ironically, Forty-second Street is one of the few Manhattan sites legitimately worthy of a substantial development scheme, where a large catalytic development would be truly appropriate, but one that does not totally erase the sense of place. That, however, was not what this blueprint for change was about.

Yet the Forty-second Street scheme was a perfectly logical next step. After all, City Planning Commission Chairman Herbert Sturz* told *The New York Times* in January 1982, "As you get one big thing going, others follow. So I think there's a synergistic effect." The Portman project—on which many of those now opposing the new Forty-second Street plan remained silent—was exactly the breakthrough Sturz and hotel proponents said it would be. It set the stage for the future of the Theater District just as its opponents feared. The Portman Hotel *was* the "linchpin," "fulcrum," "centerpiece" or "key"—as the press always reported it—of a much larger Times Square revival project, just as all its official promoters said it would be. This was it. Why should the new twist in the sorry tale have surprised anyone?

This was exactly where the Portman Hotel left off. Nothing had been learned from the Portman controversy other than that the hotel was unstoppable. Here was another project with a momentum and life of its own. It reflected the same lack of understanding of the genuine urban-development process. History wasn't repeating itself; it was just continuing.

In a column entitled "Purging of Times Square" in *The Washington Post*, George F. Will commented, "A community is not a Tinker Toy that can be pulled apart and reassembled by acts of will. A community is a living organism, like a flower (or, in this case, a weed). It can be delicately pruned, but pulling it apart means death."

---

* Sturz left the Planning Commission in 1987 to join the editorial board of *The New York Times*.

Planning on a Grand Scale

Opponents appropriately criticized it as representative of the architecture of authority and predicted that in the end Times Square would be transformed from something unique and lively with problems to something dull and cavernous with problems. Yet that was all beside the point. Those were issues of design when architecture had become irrelevant. Overwhelming scale leaves no room for design creativity. The architecture of destruction has unavoidable built-in contradictions.

Ironically, opponents of the Forty-second Street Plan complained that the project reflected the city and the state's lack of planning. How wrong was that assumption!! This scheme tied in perfectly with large-scale planning around New York City and, according to the city's own report, was meant to encourage similar projects northward, which it did. Planning certainly was occurring in New York and elsewhere. Sensitive planning it was not, but it *was* planning. This was Planning on the Grand Scale, planning for radical surgery not revitalization. Many downtowns across the country were already examples of this futuristic nightmare. New York simply had not yet run out of areas to be transformed. Urban renewal, 1950s style but bigger, was back in vogue.

The Forty-second Street Plan followed by two years the finish of the Portman fight. Two years later, Columbus Center was put before the public, a massive development scheme to replace the closed New York Coliseum at Fifty-ninth Street and Columbus Circle. At this circular traffic intersection, Broadway diagonally cuts through the city's prevailing north–south, east–west street grid at the southwest corner of Central Park and forms the gateway to the Upper West Side; it is one of the city's major focal points.* The Coliseum was the city's primary exhibition and convention space until it was replaced by the Javits Convention Center, which opened in April 1986. Built

---

* Columbus Circle happens to be the point in New York City from which distances to other points around the country are measured.

in the 1950s by master builder Robert Moses, the Coliseum was a classic urban-renewal clearance project that included the unfortunate closing of Fifty-ninth Street*—a major crosstown thoroughfare—between Broadway and Columbus Avenue, resulting in unresolvable traffic problems. As part of this "urban-renewal" package, two 14-story apartment buildings with a garden between them were built where Fifty-ninth Street had been.

When, in the mid-1980s, the city put this property up for sale after the Coliseum was closed, and requested developer proposals, it made clear that the number-one consideration would be the amount of money offered—"the highest financial return from the sale," the request-for-proposal document made clear. Thus, this large, complicated and high-impact site was up for grabs to the highest bidder. When a city sells its assets to pump an ailing economy, disaster is unavoidable. Assets run out, but the systemic economic problems remain.

From the outset, responsible critics objected to the city's price-tag priority, but their objections were ignored. The winning proposal—two futuristic towers, 68 and 58 stories (925 feet tall), containing 2.7 million square feet of offices, condominiums, movie theaters and shopping mall—had the staggering purchase price of $455 million. Decidedly, half of those funds would have been spent on needed subway improvements,† although the "half" aspect of the deal was downplayed by city promoters. As critical a need subway improvements are for the entire city, those needs hardly justify developments that cannot justify themselves on their own merit. The project was so large that it rendered architectural design irrelevant. It

---

* In January 1988, in a column in *The New York Times,* Joyce Purnick made a good case for the re-creation of that street, an idea that is increasingly recognized as advantageous for an assortment of reasons. The street's re-creation will probably not happen, for many reasons, not the least of which Purnick dubs the Toll Factor. "Bridge tolls, originally intended to last for a limited time to pay off some government debt, have a way of never going away," Purnick wrote. "Even after the original debts are paid off, the tolls continue." In this case, the original "need" to close the street was to provide the Coliseum with plenty of exhibition space.

† The other half was going directly into the city operating budget.

was so massive that it would have cast huge shadows into Central Park, one of those sacred city treasures that one interferes with at great risk. Opponents were accused of flatly opposing change or being obsessively antidevelopment. Substantive criticism was dismissed out of hand.

The Coliseum controversy capped more than a decade of bigger and bigger development mistakes in New York City with counterparts, unfortunately, in too many American cities. But it was not to remain the biggest or most controversial for long. Donald Trump proposed an absurd, urbanistically destructive scheme on 76 acres of former railroad yards along the Hudson River at the edge of one of the densest and most vibrant urban neighborhoods in the entire country, Manhattan's Upper West Side. For Trump City, the developer planned a world-record 152-story building, eight 60-story skyscrapers and the nation's biggest regional shopping mall in any city, all guaranteed to choke Manhattan streets with new traffic, produce unbreathable air, wreak incalculable havoc on residential and commercial real-estate markets and undermine assorted retail centers around the city. The disastrous dimensions of this project were endless. Yet government officials took it seriously, set out to study it and permitted the project to wend its way through a governmental process that was thwarted only by vigorous citizen opposition (including litigation), instead of appropriate city zoning restraint.

Fron the Portman Hotel to Columbus Center and then on to Trump City (with assorted projects around the city in between), nothing changed but the size of the development projects. Lessons remained unlearned, and the path of urban destruction, occasionally interrupted, remained essentially unbroken.

The cities our parents and grandparents built cannot be sold for temporary and deceptive solutions to economic problems of the moment, offering short-term answers and new longer-term problems. Cities are constantly in danger of bigger and more destructive incursions that destroy the delicate balance of an urban fabric. We ignore the danger at our peril.

Schemes as large in proportion to their locale as the Portman was in New York prevail nationwide. Some are less mean-spirited than others, but, despite the endless numbers of modest, humane and creative successes throughout the country, big is still better, the bankable formula.

Mencken's one easy but wrong solution still prevails.

Epilogue

Manhattan's Lower East Side. So many different images are conjured up—immigrants, poverty, crowded streets, peddlers, pushcarts, laundry lines, Jacob Riis photos of crowded tenements and dangerous sweatshops. All such images, and more, are valid. Yet, more than anything else, the Lower East Side is the quintessential *urban* neighborhood. To understand how and why it works, how and why it still functions today as it did one hundred years ago, is to genuinely understand urbanism. To understand *and respect* urbanism is to know how to help neighborhoods like the Lower East Side live. The success stories related in this book reflect places where urbanism has been nurtured; the failures, those places where urbanism has been crippled, if not killed outright. No better place exists to learn the essence of urbanism than Manhattan's Lower East Side.

Unfettered Urbanism

For several years now—in fact, while writing this book—I have been working on the restoration of an historic synagogue on the Lower East Side. My almost daily trips to the synagogue have provided occasions to explore and observe the neighborhood in a way I never did in all the years I've lived in New York, even in the fifteen years I worked at *The New York Post,* not far away from the Lower East Side.

Quickly I realized I was watching a neighborhood in flux. The population occupying the diversified and rich assortment of buildings was changing. Brick tenements with their year of construction proudly imbedded below the cornice were the first homes for Irish, German, Italian and East European immigrants of the nineteenth century. The same tenements were quickly becoming the first home of Asian immigrants, primarily Chinese. Small loft buildings—sometimes embellished with terra-cotta ornament, but more often with simple and sparse detail that reflected the practical commercial nature of the building's purpose—had been the birthplace for earlier immigrant businesses. Those same loft buildings were being vacated by the vestiges of that last wave of immigrants and tenanted by the newest wave of budding entrepreneurs. Local shops, many of them two and three generations in one family, changed hands. A Jewish-owned dry-goods store was replaced by a small grocery run by proprietors who don't speak English and who sell bok choy, snow peas, live blue crabs, eels and lo mein. A Jewish bookstore of long standing, managed by the kind of knowledgeable elder who himself had become an institution, gave way to the wrecking ball only to be replaced by a 12-story apartment house tenanted by new Asian Americans. An elderly Jewish jeweler retired and was replaced by a Chinese barber. The fabled Garden Cafeteria, where Yiddish literati (or intelligentsia) and political dissidents debated the great issues of an earlier time, became a Chinese restaurant, its old New York murals lost to memory and its terrible food now only the ingredient of affectionate jokes. My favorite kosher luncheonette, where the old cook spoke only Yiddish and measured ingredients by pinches and *bisels,* where the waiter was a recent Russian refugee, where the neighborhood poor were never turned away and where the Formica tables were graced with plastic flowers, was replaced by a spiffy Thai restaurant.

The nature of some of the new businesses was sometimes hard to determine. Some storefront windows are blackened with paint or covered with signs in Chinese. That air of mystery, of course, piqued my interest. Guessing the nature of the business in a blackened storefront was a private game I played as I passed through the changing streets. I had a favorite mystery building, an eight-story, modestly ornamented loft building with the name "Witty Brothers" carved at the top of the gray stone facade. All the lower-floor windows were covered over. Witty Brothers, I learned, is a men's-suit manufacturer well known in the uptown Garment Center. The business began, as did so much of the American garment industry, in this Lower East Side neighborhood. It was here, after all, that the tailors and seamstresses of Eastern Europe merged their age-old craft with the techniques of the nineteenth century Industrial Revolution to create one of this country's great contributions to modern manufacturing history.

The following short description of Henry Witty contained in *Distinguished Jews of America,* in fact, reads like the prototypical immigrant success story:

> Henry Witty came to this country at the age of 15, from Taktin, Russian Poland, where he was born April 15, 1871. He had no particular trade and he became an operator. Later he became cutter and finally designer. An unexpected quarrel with his employer made him quit his work, and in his search for a new job, he ran across an auction sale, which for the moment opened his eyes to business possibilities. Having no available cash, he pawned his jewelry for $75, and with this sum he started his retail clothing store. Today he has one of the largest manufacturing plants on the East Side, employing over 400 "hands," housed in an eight story, up-to-date plant.

On a warm summer day a few years ago, I approached the midblock Witty Brothers building from the corner in the same manner I had done hundreds of times. From the distance, however, I could see that the doors were open and that for the first time I would have a chance to see inside. As I approached I heard a steady whirring sound that told me exactly what I was about to see. Sure enough, inside were five rows of Asian women bent over sewing machines, hard at work, adding to the piles of garments accumulating at the end of each row. It felt as though time had stopped. If I blinked, instead of Asian women I saw Europeans with black skirts, white long-sleeved blouses, upswept hair. It was a moment of wonderful realization, when everything that I had been watching in bits and pieces over time came together. One part of me was disheartened somewhat to see that labor should still be conducted so meanly. Another part was fascinated, in spite of myself, by the persistence of history and the economic productivity of an old neighborhood not replaced or redeveloped by some misguided renewal program.

Here was the garment center being reborn, just as it had begun one hundred years earlier on the Lower East Side, before it moved uptown in adulthood. Sweatshops are all over the Lower East Side in loft buildings like this one, where they had been before. Fire safety codes and modern equipment probably* mean better workplace conditions, but they are still operated like sweatshops. The garment industry still provides employment for the minimum-skilled and opportunity for the first-time entrepreneur.† Everything happening here parallels what happened more than one hundred years ago.

If Allowed, the Urban Process Continues

The parallels to the earlier immigrant experience are endless. This vital process continues so productively in part because of the enduring

---

* According to reports from some neighborhood people, however, conditions are comparably as bad in some shops with blocked and locked doors that could lead to another Triangle Shirt Waist Co. fire.

† Noting there are 500 or so garment factories in Chinatown, Peter Grant wrote ("Firms in Chinatown Facing Pressures," *New York Observer*, October 19, 1987): "The Chinatown garment industry, which produces only women's and children's apparel, emerged to dominate the 'spot market' largely because of a major overhaul of U.S. immigration law in 1965. Before the law changed, immigration from China, Taiwan and Hong Kong averaged about 4,500 people a year. Afterwards, each year more than 15,000 Chinese immigrated to the United States, with many of the new arrivals settling in Chinatown.

"Like Jewish immigrants before them, many of the Chinese were attracted to the garment industry. The business was easy to learn, did not require strong language skills and allowed small entrepreneurs to begin operations with a relatively small investment."

physical fabric with its particular mix of strengths and weaknesses. Although in some places the physical fabric has been adjusted, updated or repaired, most of the Lower East Side has been spared the grand visions and disruptive development that have erased so many urban neighborhoods. The Lower East Side evolved over time and remains the quintessential urban neighborhood, with an almost limitless mix of uses and structures.

All over the Lower East Side, the urban process continually repeats itself. Mom-and-pop stores are everywhere. A young Asian family runs the delicatessen/grocery where I buy my coffee and almond cookie across from the synagogue, the way others before me bought coffee and bagels.* A few doors down from Witty Brothers, a small Chinese printer has opened. A cabinetmaker has taken over the adjacent store. Chinese renovators are upgrading tenements for newer Asian arrivals. Investing in and renovating a single building is a classic immigrant strategy, the first step of real-estate investment taken long ago by many of today's large real-estate owners. Local real-estate offices in the Lower East Side display properties out of the neighborhood, places to which the successful immigrants consider moving when they feel secure enough to leave the first insulated ethnic enclave, the next step further into American society. Mostly the properties are in Flushing, Queens, where upwardly mobile Chinese have been moving from Chinatown and the Lower East Side in the way that Germans, Irish, Italians and Eastern European Jews moved out of the Lower East Side generations ago.

Immigrant History Is Urban History

What is urbanism if not the absorption and nurturing of the new, whether a new group or a new industry, which often comes with a new group. Immigrants constantly replenish society and the economy

---

* In October 1988 the store closed. The landlord, Asian like the proprietors Henry and Lilly, asked for a 500 percent rent increase at lease-renewal time. Henry and Lilly were not totally bereft. They were planning to move to the suburbs "one of these days," Lilly said, so they were accelerating their plans.

with new energy, new money and considerable skills. Whole neighborhoods in today's downtowns have been reborn by new immigrants from everywhere between Cambodia and Greece, and, in fact, the city of Miami is alive and well today due more to three decades of Cuban and other Latin-American immigration than any assortment of urban-renewal programs, despite what government press releases boast. This fundamental urban process has been occurring on the Lower East Side of Manhattan since it was settled in the 1830s.

Even the "micro" patterns of immigrant settlement repeat themselves. Rumanians, Hungarians, Lithuanians, Galatians and assorted other subgroups each had their own distinct territory within the larger "Jewish immigrant" community. A similar pattern is now taking shape among the Asians, I'm told by the community workers. When Yiddish was the most common language spoken on the Lower East Side, an assortment of dialects could be found, as is now reportedly the case with the Chinese.

My favorite parallel is the newspapers. At the height of Jewish immigration on the Lower East Side, approximately twelve publications in either Yiddish, Hebrew or English served the population. Similarly, twelve Chinese newspapers exist there today.

The Lower East Side is not a precisely defined area. What I refer to is the neighborhood south of Houston Street, north of Canal Street, and east of Broadway. Within this district, this gateway to American society for so many immigrants—historian Richard Rabinowitz calls the area "the most profound example of the mosaic of American immigration"—there are urban layers that can be peeled away like an onion.

In 1847 there were 13,000 Jews in New York. By 1880 there were more than 200,000, and by 1920 almost two million. For more than forty years, between 1880 and 1920, 40 percent of the Lower East Side residents were Jewish refugees from religious persecution and economic distress in Eastern Europe. The neighborhood is still filled with the vestiges of their presence, even if those remnants have been somewhat transformed for new use.

Taking the Microview

The synagogue I am working to restore is one of the untouched reminders of that era. It is on the southern end of Eldridge Street, a north–south street that starts under the shadow of the Manhattan Bridge and runs north to Houston Street. Never immortalized in fiction, film or song like Hester, Delancey, Orchard and others, Eldridge has qualities found in all of them. Tenements with ground-floor stores and fire-escape laundry lines predominate. Loft buildings are interspersed among the tenements, and even a low-rise public-housing apartment building fills one half block. The Witty Brothers building is on Eldridge, one block north of the synagogue. A 1960s public school is across the street from the Witty Brothers building. The school population seems to be primarily Asian. Within the three-block stretch of Eldridge Street, Chinese food wholesalers are the primary commercial activity. In the early-morning hours, trucks are double-parked, loading and unloading quantities of bean sprouts and tofu that are probably heading for groceries and restaurants around the city. Throughout the day at various locations, racks of clothing, coming out of tenements as well as loft buildings, get loaded onto trucks.

Although Chinese businesses predominate—most of them having opened in the four or five years I've been observing Eldridge Street—several strong vestiges of the century of Jewish dominance persist. A few doors away from each other on the north side of the Witty Brothers building, for example, are J. Levine & Company and Ziontalis. Levine's is probably the foremost national Jewish bookseller, with the aura of the Old World bookstore in which the proprietors, in this case two generations of Levines, not only know their stock intimately but seem to have read it all. Ziontalis is a treasure of a Jewish-ritual-object store proudly run by the young grandson of the founder and with the original interior cabinetry still in place. Jews from all over still seek out these stores, along with others in the neighborhood. A block south and closer to the synagogue is Pesselnick & Cohen, a wholesale jewelry store in what was a firehouse in the 1800s. Jewelers still dominate the commercial mix of the larger neighborhood—especially along Canal Street—a holdover from the days when it was the diamond and jewelry center (this industry has since shifted to Forty-seventh Street between Fifth and Sixth avenues).

The manager of the local Merchants Bank branch knows his accounts by sight and calls them when they are overdrawn. A message can be left in a store on the block where, as well, help can be found in any emergency. A sense of neighborliness, or caring, persists, and memories and continuity prevail amidst the more obvious and constant change.

Landmarks Anchor History

The Eldridge Street Synagogue* anchors the history of this segment of the Lower East Side just as historic landmarks anchor whichever neighborhood they are in. The story of recycling buildings tells the history of a place, and the recycling process ensures the continued productivity of the neighborhood. Like most historic buildings worth retaining, the Eldridge Street Synagogue contains levels of interest, all of which are interesting in themselves or instructive for current purposes.

Built in 1887, the synagogue is a melange of Gothic, Moorish and Romanesque styles and a complicated reflection of both European and American synagogue history. Moorish keyhole windows and a majestic Gothic rose window dominate the imposing yellow-brick facade. Arches, domes, stenciled and vaulted ceilings, vibrant stained-glass windows, trompe l'oeil murals, and the hand-carved Ark adorn

---

* The official name of the synagogue is K'hal Adath Jeshurun with Anshe Lubz (Community of the People of Israel with the People of Lubz). The congregation was founded in 1856 by Polish immigrants, thirty years before construction of this building. Shortly after construction in 1887, another small congregation without its own building, called Anshe Lubz, merged with the original congregation, adding its name to the title.

the main sanctuary with details drawn from the rich traditions of Judaic folklore and Talmudic learning.*

This was the first and grandest synagogue built on the Lower East Side by East European Orthodox Jews, and it belies historic impressions that all those immigrants—"your tired, your poor, your huddled masses"—were penniless. Elegant, lavishly detailed—no expense was spared in the synagogue's construction, to proclaim a deep faith in Judaic heritage. Some congregants, according to synagogue records, were paying $500 a year for membership—expensive even by today's standards, astonishingly generous one hundred years ago. The building cost $37,000 to build. East European Jews, refugees from pogroms, religious persecution and other variations of oppression, were unused to arriving in a new land where the freedom to worship was part of the social fabric. In Eastern Europe, where anti-Semitic violence was a fact of everyday life, Jews followed a tradition dating from medieval days of deliberately obscuring their houses of worship. Building synagogues to look like ordinary buildings protected them. In the radically different atmosphere of America, it did not take long for these new immigrants to assert their claim to the rich tradition of American religious freedom. At first, the immigrants pouring in from Russia and Poland worshiped in converted churches and in storefronts vacated by the Germans and Irish who preceded them. (Today, the Chinese on the Lower East Side and elsewhere convert vacated synagogues and churches into Buddhist temples.) When the opportunity came for the Eastern European immigrants to build their first synagogue, the Eldridge Street Synagogue was what they built. It is an important architectural expression of American religious freedom and symbolizes immigrant aspirations in the broadest sense.

In the earliest stages of our synagogue restoration effort, the growing Chinese character of the neighborhood was a source of

---

* Jewish religious art and décor does not permit the use of human images, in accordance with the Second Commandment, which states: "Thou shalt not make any graven images." Thus, numerical and mystical symbols take on significant importance in synagogue design.

discouragement to visitors and potential supporters. It took a while to recognize the changing environs as a source of strength and interest, as well as an educational tool, a living example of both immigrant history and urbanism.

Throughout this book, the strongest surviving urban neighborhoods described and the most hopeful reviving ones are located *only* in areas where the historic urban layering process and the physical environment that nourishes it remain. In very few places has that layering process been so continuous as it has been on the Lower East Side. In most downtowns, a period of decay, dormancy or disuse has occurred, but if the physical fabric has remained essentially intact, as it has on the Lower East Side, genuine revival has been possible. All the rebirths we have looked at in this book have happened in places where enough remained on which to build and nurture, where the rebuilding strengthened what existed, without overwhelming or replacing it. The successful new developments we have examined, like Toronto's St. Lawrence Neighborhood or Battery Park City, have succeeded by reflecting and fitting into the existing city.

The Lower East Side exhibits many of the urban lessons described in this book and is instructive for the rethinking that should go into our approach to strengthening urban neighborhoods nationwide. Even the large swath within the district that was "renewed" with publicly subsidized cooperative apartment houses in an earlier day of public-housing programs offers an important lesson. Standing tall amidst acres of green, the "co-ops," as they are lovingly referred to by proud tenants, relate not at all to the streets on either side. In the co-ops, 37,000 Jews still reside. That fact, however, always comes as a great surprise to visitors, who never sense their presence on the neighborhood streets. In fact, that separateness is a source of comfort to the residents, who fear the potential crime of adjacent streets, even though the crime rate of this neighborhood is, according to police, not high. Unfortunately, with the isolation comes a heightened tension with the surrounding but alienated neighborhood. If anything, co-op residents, in their islands of isolation, are more of a target than if they blended in with the rest of the community. They are secure only as long as they are locked in their high-rise apartments. Critics of this urban-renewal design pattern have long noted that superblocks minimize the use of streets and sidewalks, thus making more vulnerable the few remaining pedestrians. A variety of alternative ways exist to gain the same quantity of modernized housing for the neighborhood without creating residential islands.

All cities at one time had and may still have their equivalents of the Lower East Side. Such neighborhoods often are misunderstood and underappreciated, labeled as slums because the messy mixture of the proud, the profane and the unfamiliar camouflages the vibrancy of the area. Districts like these are either ignored because redevelopment interests lie elsewhere or, worse, "renewed" under the ruse of removing blight or rebuilding a slum (but more accurately because an agenda of outside interests, not of the neighborhood residents and businesses, becomes important). How readily a city permits these older neighborhoods to flourish is a measure of the city's health. The dead cities are those where these neighborhoods are only a distant memory or a pitiful remnant.

An economic and social mix exists among the residents of the immigrant neighborhoods such as the Lower East Side, although it is not readily visible to the visitor. The common impression of the outsider is that the neighborhood is only "poor." A wider cross-section of people reside, work and socialize in enduring urban neighborhoods than is fully appreciated by outsiders. This is an urban pattern. Nevertheless, the outside "experts" call such areas slums or "blighted." They fail to recognize the energy and productiveness that make these areas so successful economically. This deep and genuine diversity is the first thing destroyed by large-scale projects of any kind and the most difficult quality to rekindle in decimated neighborhoods—whether they are areas like the South Bronx where bulldozed lots and empty buildings represent lost activity or rebuilt downtowns where one self-contained megaproject stands side by side with another, preventing anything but the planned and the pristine from happening in between.

Far from being the backward outpost these neighborhoods are

thought to be, districts like the Lower East Side are so up-to-date that nostalgia boutiques are as rare here as they are common in the redone neighborhoods sprouting up everywhere. And while ownership is gradually changing throughout the Lower East Side stores, the uses are not changing as much. The Chinese are buying from the exiting Jews, and they are making adjustments (a running-shoe store opened on Grand Street not long ago, something that certainly would not have been expected to happen much sooner), but the essential nature of the retail mix remains. This is, after all, one thing that immigrant life is all about. As newcomers find their place in American society, they behave like others to some extent, making comforting modifications without clinging too strongly to patterns that might underscore their newness.

Some observers label the current change on the Lower East Side "gentrification," but it is not, certainly not if that is defined as the pushing out of local residents and businesses by wealthier occupants. Residential property owners and businessmen, while often under excessive pressure to sell, do so when they choose to and at a handsome profit. More often than not, as previously noted, the commercial establishment remains and is not replaced by an expensive boutique offering little to local customers. This is primarily healthy* change in a neighborhood of constant change.

The role of government in the Lower East Side and similar neighborhoods is a tricky one at best. Without a commitment to sensitivity and small scale, and a responsiveness to the local populace over the demands of outside speculators, damage is bound to occur. The Lower East Side and countless old urban neighborhoods around the country easily could suffer the fate of the "renewed" communities of the past unless we learn the lessons of the success stories reported in this book. It is never too late to do the right thing for what is left of our invaluable cities.

---

* Ugly incidents of threatening notes, mysterious fires and protection rackets have been reported, but I can't confirm them personally. Such happenings have long been true of ethnic neighborhoods run more by imported social and extralegal institutions than by official local government.

Notes

Introduction

1. Harry De Rienzo and Joan B. Allen, *The New York City In Rem Housing Program: A Report for the New York Urban Coalition* (New York, 1985).
2. New York: Praeger, 1971, pp. 87 and 89.
3. For a further discussion of issues relating to the urban segregation and broad disruptions caused by urban-renewal and highway programs, see, among others, Helen Leavitt, *Superhighway—Superhoax* (Garden City: Doubleday, 1970); Herbert J. Gans, *The Urban Villagers* (New York: Free Press, 1962); Robert Goodman, *After the Planners* (New York: Simon and Schuster, 1971); Jane Jacobs, *The Death and Life of Great American Cities* (New York: Random House, 1961); and Martin Anderson, *The Federal Bulldozer: A Critical Analysis of Urban Renewal, 1949–1962* (Cambridge, Mass.: MIT Press, 1964).
4. The book was coauthored with Richard Child Hill, Dennis Judd and Michael Peter Smith (White Plains, N.Y.: Longman Inc., 1986) and also covers Detroit, New Orleans, Denver and San Francisco.
5. New York: Praeger, 1969, p. 245.

PART ONE: THINKING SMALL IN A BIG WAY

Chapter One: Process Is People

1. As quoted by Robert Campbell in *Preservation News,* August 1975.
2. Donald Appleyard, ed., *The Conservation of European Cities* (Cambridge, Mass.: MIT Press, 1979), as excerpted in *The Livability Digest* (a publication of Partners for Livable Places), Fall 1981.
3. Steve Lohr, "Tourist Traffic Plummets, British Plead for U.S. Visitors," *New York Times,* May 30, 1986.

Chapter Three: Gentrification and Displacement

1. Neal R. Peirce and Carol F. Steinbach, *Corrective Capitalism: The Rise of America's Community Development Corporations,* A Report to the Ford Foundation (New York, July 1987).
2. Edward R. Carpenter, "The Mount Auburn Good Housing Foundation," *Urban Design* magazine, Fall 1977.
3. Ibid.

4. Arthur P. Ziegler, Jr., "Renewal of the Spirit and the Place: The Manchester Community Restoration Program in Pittsburgh," a publication of the Manchester Program, Feb., 1977.

Chapter Four: Winning Skirmishes, Losing Wars

1. Susan Baldwin, "The Master Plan: A Modest Proposal?" *City Limits* magazine, October 1980.
2. Lyrics by Lorenz Hart, music by Richard Rodgers, from the 1925 *Garrick Gaieties*.
3. Donald Sullivan, *Devastation/Resurrection: The South Bronx* (New York: Bronx Museum of the Arts, 1979), p. 37.
4. Robert A. Caro, *The Power Broker: Robert Moses and the Fall of New York* (New York: Knopf, 1974), p. 878.
5. David W. Dunlap, *New York Times*, May 11, 1987.
6. Donald Sullivan, op. cit., p. 40.
7. Samuel G. Freedman, "Co-op City: A Refuge in Transition," *New York Times*, June 25, 1986.
8. Jack Newfield and Paul DuBrul, *The Permanent Government* (New York: Pilgrim Press, 1981).
9 Donald Sullivan, op. cit., p. 36.
10 *Historic Preservation*, July–September 1974, p. 16.

Chapter Five: Understanding the Lessons

1. New York: Norton, 1983.
2. Neal R. Peirce and Carol F. Steinbach, *Corrective Capitalism: The Rise of America's Community Development Corporations*, A Report to the Ford Foundation (New York, July 1987).
3. E. F. Schumacher, *Small Is Beautiful* (New York: Harper and Row, 1973), p. 165.
4. "The Good News About New York City," *New York Times Magazine*, Sept. 28, 1986.
5. Peirce and Steinbach, op. cit.
6. Lydia Chavez with Richard J. Meislin, "From the Ashes, Bronx Faces Uncertain Future," *New York Times*, June 1987.

Chapter Six: Urban Husbandry: The Economy of Wisdom

1. Testimony before the New York City Board of Estimate, Feb. 6, 1987, against approval of a proposed replacement for the New York Coliseum.
2. "The Shadow Market in Housing," *Scientific American*, November 1986. Baer is associate professor of urban and regional planning at the University of Southern California.
3. Free Press, 1962.

Chapter Seven: Planned Shrinkage: The Economy of Waste

1. A cogent and thoughtful analysis of triage is contained in a paper entitled "Triage: Programming the Death of Communities," by Peter Marcuse, Peter Medoff and Andrea Pereira, prepared at Columbia University, Nov. 1, 1980, for the Working Group for Community Development Reform.
2. *The New York City In Rem Housing Program,* written with Joan B. Allen.

Chapter Eight: Urban Dispersal

1. Houghton Mifflin, 1986.
2. Jane Jacobs, "Downtown Is for People," in *The Exploding Metropolis,* ed. William H., Whyte, Jr., and the editors of *Fortune* (Garden City: Doubleday, 1958).
3. From the private papers of the late Victor Gruen, provided by his son, Michael Gruen.

PART TWO: THE CITY REDISCOVERED

Chapter Nine: Big Steps, Modestly: The Stories of Ithaca and Corning

1. "U.S. Journal: New Orleans—Making Deals."
2. Garden City: Doubleday, pp. 24.

Chapter Ten: Outside, Inside: Burlington and Pittsfield

1. "A Mall Covers the Waterfront."
2. "Regional Malls and Central City Retail Sales: An Overview," in *Shopping Centers: U.S.A.,* ed. George Sternlieb and James W. Hughes (Center for Urban Policy Research, Rutgers University, 1981).
3. In re: Pyramid Co. of Burlington, Application No. 4C0281. Decision of the District Environmental Commission, Oct. 12, 1978.
4. "Pedestrian Malls: Twenty Years Later," *Planning* magazine, December 1982.
5. Laurie M. Grossman, "City Pedestrian Malls Fail to Fulfill Promise of Revitalizing Downtown," *Wall Street Journal,* June 17, 1987.
6. Adele Chatfield-Taylor, "Recycling Reconsidered," *The Livable City* (a publication of the Municipal Art Society, New York), September 1980.

Chapter Eleven: Avoiding Wrong Lessons: The Remnant Complex vs. Small Improvements, Big Differences

1. New York: Harcourt Brace Jovanovich, 1938
2. Information on the Pastures' history is taken from a 1971 report to the National Register of Historic Places by the City of Albany.
3. In *Town and Country,* September 1978.

4. Linda S. Glisson, *Main Street: Open for Business,* A Three-Year Special Report (Washington, D.C.: National Trust for Historic Preservation, 1984).

Chapter Twelve: Culprits

1. E. F. Schumacher, *Small Is Beautiful,* New York: Harper and Row, 1973, p. 36.
2. See *Shopping Centers; U.S.A.,* ed. George Sternlieb and James W. Hughes (Center for Urban Policy Research, Rutgers University, 1981), Chap. 6, "Community Conservation Guidance: A Promising Initiative," by Marshall Kaplan, HUD planner.
3. In *Shopping Centers; U.S.A.*

Chapter Thirteen: Streets Have Value

1. "The Greatest Street Life in the World."
2. "Toward a Return of the Public Place: An American Survey,"*Architectural Record,* April 1985.
3. Peter Wolf, *The Future of the City; New Directions in Urban Planning* (New York: Watson-Guptil Publications, 1974).
4. "Why Don't We Do It in the Road?," *Planning* magazine, May 1987.
5. *Pride of Place* (Boston: Houghton Mifflin, 1986), p. 226.
6. Ibid., p. 225.
7. "Providence Trying to Join the Boom by Luring Business from Elsewhere," March 29, 1987.
8. "The Ultimate Marketplace: A Toast to the Milan Galleria," Oct. 24, 1982.
9. Peter Wolf, op. cit.
10. New York: Random House, 1961.
11. Suzanne Stephens, "Introversion and the Urban Context," *Progressive Architecture,* December 1978.
12. Victor Gruen, "New Forms of Community," in *Who Designs America? The American Civilization Conference at Princeton* (New York: Anchor Books, 1966).
13. Vincent Scully, *American Architecture and Urbanism* (New York: Holt, Rinehart and Winston, 1969) p. 154.
14. Victor Gruen, op. cit.

Chapter Fourteen: Old Areas Flourish Anew

1. "Pushcarts Belong in the City."
2. Calvin Trillin, "U.S. Journal: New Orleans—Making Deals," *The New Yorker,* July 28, 1980.
3. Jane McC. Thompson, "Boston's Faneuil Hall," *Urban Design International,* November 1979.
4. William H. Whyte, *The Social Life of Small Urban Spaces* (Washington: Conservation Foundation, 1980) p. 93.

5. Mildred F. Schmerz, "Boston's Historic Faneuil Hall Marketplace," *Architectural Record,* December 1977.

6. New York: Gondolier Press, 1984.

PART THREE: THE TROJAN HORSE: BIG PLANS, BIG MISTAKES

Chapter Fifteen: The Past Over and Over Again

1. "Reflections; Experiencing Places—II," *New Yorker,* June 29, 1987.

2. "Theaters, Recycled," *New York Times Magazine,* April 27, 1975.

3. An article of mine, "Save the Helen Hayes," appeared in *New York* magazine Nov. 19, 1979. Some of the material in this chapter first appeared in that article.

4. Interview with Paul Sachner published in *Federal Design Matters* (a publication of the Design Arts Program of the National Endowment for the Arts), Spring 1980.

Index